HISTORY OF MIDDLE EAST

HISTORY OF MIDDLE EAST

Radhey Shyam Chaurasia

ATLANTIC
PUBLISHERS & DISTRIBUTORS

Published by

ATLANTIC
PUBLISHERS & DISTRIBUTORS
B-2, Vishal Enclave, Opp. Rajouri Garden,
New Delhi-110027
Phones : 25413460, 25429987, 25466842

Sales Office
7/22, Ansari Road, Darya Ganj,
New Delhi-110002
Phones : 23273880, 23275880, 23280451
Fax : 91-11-23285873
web : www.atlanticbooks.com
e-mail : info@atlanticbooks.com

ISBN 81-269-0448-8

Printed in India
at Nice Printing Press, Delhi

Preface

Lord Bacon remarked, "History makes man wise" but historians are of the opinion that "man never learns from History" and this remark is true about Middle East, Egypt and Mesopotamia (*i.e.*, Iraq), which once considered cradle of ancient civilizations are now war-torn territories as these were many thousand years ago. Special feature of Middle East history is that war is going on due to same reasons and on the same territory. This shows that in spite of scientific progress man has not learnt to live in peace. Arab-Israeli wars remind us of the Arab-Jew and of Eygptian-Jew conflicts; Iran-Iraq wars remind us of the Shia-Sunni conflicts and Lebnan reminds us the age of crusades. As the modern history of Middle East cannot be understood without some knowledge of the past, so I have written history of Middle East from the beginning to the present day; but the syllabi prescribed in the various universities include only the events of the 18th, 19th and 20th centuries hence these periods has been dealt with in detail.

As History of Middle East is a very difficult and complicated subject, no Indian writer has written any satisfactory book on this subject.

I have made a humble attempt to bring out a book on History of Middle East in easy and understandble language and hope this book will be useful for students as well as for general readers.

I am really indebted to many foreign writers and publishers whose publications have helped me in writing this book.

I am also thankful to Dr. K.R. Gupta, Chairman of The Atlantic Publishers and Distributors, who has taken keen interest to publish this book in a short time.

Suggestions, if any, for the improvement of this book in the next edition will be thankfully received.

RADHEY SHYAM CHAURASIA

1

Introduction

A Short Introduction of Middle East

According to George Unzoushric, "the Middle East encompasses all those countries of Asia situated south of the Soviet Union and west of Pakistan and Egypt in Africa." In the mid-twentieth century the term Middle East refers to that area of the world comprising the present political states of Lebanon, Syria, Israel, Jordan, Iraq, Saudi, Arabia, Kuwait, Bahrain, Qatar, Turkisi Oman and Muscat, south and north Yemen, Egypt, Sudan, Turkey and Iran etc. In addition to this, Middle East is employed as a cultural designation for a society and civilization found not only on that region but also to a certain degree in a number of adjacent Muslim localities such as Afghanistan, Pakistan, Libya, Tunisia Algeria, Morocco and Sudan etc.

The geographical features of the Middle East have been significant in all periods of history. Its location has given it an important place due to its strategic location between Africa and Eurasia and between the Mediterranean world and between Asia and India and between the Far East Nations of China and Japan. Its tribes, traders, armies, and pilgrims etc. brought people on the move. They have traversed the Middle East in finding the land bridge convenient to bring different nations together. They discovered the wealth of this rich area and rich civilization of its people. The Middle East is considered as cradle of civilizations. Historians are of the opinion that human civilization began in Egypt and Mesopotamia.

The second important geographical feature is the relative magnitude and vastness of the Middle East. Arabia, the central land mass of the Middle East, embraces an area about of the same size as that of India. The southern shore facing the Indian Ocean from Aden to Muscat is as far as from New Orleans to Boston in U.S.A., on the west, the Red sea is as wide as the

Black sea. It is very long, and the distance from Aden to Port Said is nearly the same as from New York to Denver. Northward from Arabia proper to the Turkish frontier is about 400 miles. If Egypt, Iran, and Turkey are added to Middle East, its area becomes equivalent to that of continental United States or double to that of India.

Stretching about 2,000 miles westward in a narrow land from the mouth of the Nile river to the Atlantic Ocean lies North Africa which is a cultural part of the Middle East since the end of the seventh century. Moreover, this delimitation of the Middle East has omitted Turkestan, Afghanistan and Pakistan and historic cities of Bukhara, Samarkand, Kabul, and Lahore etc. Thus, the physical size of the Middle East becomes impressive to Europeans and Americans who are accustomed of seeing the area pictured on maps of Asia or Africa, the large continents. Pakistan is geographically part of India so it need not to be studied in Middle East. Afghanistan was also a part of India from ancient times to 1739, but now it is conflict of great powers, so it has been briefly narrated here.

Physiography. The geological characteristics of the Middle East show a wide variety of land features-great areas covered by water; low-lying land and swampy regions creating coal beds. In the last six or seven thousand years, however, there is little evidence of any important physiographical change except that the deltas of the most of the rivers have grown and extended to the land side from seaward sites. In western Turkey, for example, camels and cattle now graze on the food plain of the Meander river in front of the ancient walls of Miletus and Priene, in the exact spot where the Persian navy vanquished the Greeks almost five centuries before the Christ. The Middle East has been cradle of Zionism, Christianity, Zoorostism and of Islam etc.

Arabia, in general, is a desert and a tilted plateaus going upward from the north-east to the south-west with a sharp drop in Yemen from 1200 feet down to the Red Sea. Central Turkey and central Iran are elevated plateau, in places reaching an altitude of 8,000 feet. Rugged mountains dominate Middle Eastern geography. Iran in the neighbourhood of Mt. Ararat, mountain ranges up to 18,000 feet in altitude branch out in several mountain chains, the Elburz group running eastward south of the Caspian Sea; the zagros system, a wide series of ranges protruding in a south-easterly direction to Afghanistan and India. The famed Taurus Mountains are pushing south-west ward towards the Mediterranean sea and separating the Anatolian plateau from Arabia.

Rivers. River have played an important role in society and have deeply influenced the development of civilization in the Middle East. Two are fabled and basic in the history of the area from the time immemorial. These are the Nile and the Tigris-Euphrates rivers, flowing from central Africa and Abyssinia, the Nile passes through a relatively flat region in the Sudan until it reaches to the cataract zone north of Khartoum, where a gorge has been cut. Below Aswan, the Nile flows through a well-developed valley about six miles wide to capital Cairo from where the delta begins. In August the river Nile starts to rise in Egypt, reaching its peak in September, eighteen feet above the low level of April and May. Annually some 110-million tons of sediment, rich, in mineral substances, are carried into Egypt and more than half of this silt reaches to this delta. This made Egypt as gift of river Nile. The other great river system is of Tigris Euphrates which rises in the highlands of eastern Turkey. Winter snow fall feeds both the rivers which turn and twist through precipitous and narrow defiats emptying out upon the plateau plains of Syria and Kurdistan. Rushing south-ward, they converge upon Baghdad but meet only about 230 miles farther on where they form the shat-al-Arab which flows gently for about seventy-five miles to the Persian Gulf. The fall in the river beds between Asia Minor and Baghdad is very marked, producing a swift current with strong erosive powers. These rivers are at their lowest in the months of September and October but begin to rise appreciably in December to reach flood stage of about eighteen feet in April for the Tigris and about eleven feet in May for the Euphrates. In ancient times the Tigris and the Euphrates flowed and made the land of Mesopotamia fertile. The two Iranian tributaries of these rivers namely the Karkeh and the Karn flowed to the Persian Gulf from near the site of Baghdad to the present line. No longer a tributary, the Katkehis dissipated at the present time in the marshes of lower Mesopotamia and made it fertile. Thus, river Nile contributed a lot in making. Egypt fertile and same was done by Tigris and Euphrates for Mesopotamia. So these lands became cradle of civilization from the very beginning.

From the ancient times struggle began between Egyptians and Hebrew people which subsided during Roman rule and Arab and Turkish domination. It flared up during mandatory period of Anglo-French domination between 1919-1945. After Second World War these countries got independence but Middle Eastern countries have become cock pit of rival powers. As such wars are still going on though roots of enemity lie in ancient past. Arab powers are determined to destroy Israel while Jews are determined to preserve their hard won freedom. So continuance of war has become an accomplished fact. Now Egypt and Israel are in peace.

Similarly, germs of Iraqi-Iranian war of 1980-89 lie in old rivalry of Shias and Sunnies of Muslim religion. Now Afghanistan which was part and parcel of India since the time immemorial to 1739 has become now cockpit of super powers. Russia occupied Afghanistan by force and is determined to keep his puppet Govt. of Nazibullah in power in Afghanistan. On the other hand Pakistan, U.S.A. and Saudi Arabia and other Muslim powers with the help of Mujahidin are determined to have a Govt. in Afghanistan which may be free from Russian domination. Now new Govt. under control of NATO has been formed.

As seeds of conflict in Middle East lie in ancient past so history of the Middle East requires history of past also to be studied with recent history. As such history of the Middle East has been narrated from ancient days to present days. History of Middle East has special importance in present age so its study is necessary to gain the knowledge of contemporary world.

2

ANCIENT EGYPT

Brief Introduction of Egypt

Introduction. Egypt is considered as the oldest country of the world, so historians begin world history with Egypt. Its capital is Cairo its area is 997,677 sq. kms. and population is 7 crore. Its language is Arabic and religion is Islam and Christianity. Its currency is Pound (US $1=1.83£E.) It is also called United Arab Republic or U.A.R.

Egypt is traditionally known as the Gift of the River Nile. It occupies north-east Africa but it is included in Middle East countries.

Egypt has one of the oldest civilizations in the world, its recorded history goes back to more than 5000 B.C. In 1922, Egypt became an independent monarchy and in 1952 a republic and it is called United Arab Republic or U.A.R.

The main agricultural area is lower Egypt which covers the delta of the river Nile. The chief crops are cotton, onions, wheat, maize, millet, rice, sugarcane and fruits of various kinds. It was famous for cotton.

Principal exports are cotton, rice, mineral products, textiles, refrigerators, tyres, cement and electrical instruments etc.

President : Hosni Mubarak. Prime Minister : Atef Mohamed Naguib Sedki.

Egypt is famous for its Pyramids. It is a member of Non-Aligned countries as well as of Arab League. Egypt has concluded treaty with Israel and it is making efforts for reconciling interests of P.L.O. *i.e.*, of Palestinian Liberation Organization with Israel.

As Egypt is considered as an oldest land so we will begin history of Middle East with Egypt.

Glimpse of Egypt's Geography and Ancient History

Egypt is cradle of human civilization. Pyramids remind its glory. Egypt as the Greeks said is the Gift of the River Nile. Like a gigantic snake (720 miles from the first cataract to the sea). River Nile slithers through the desert which isolates its green valley. East-ward desert continues to the Read Sea and, beyond it, into Arabia; West-ward it passes into the Sahara. When, in about 2000, an Egyptian force marching to the Red Sea had to cross about 90 miles of the desert, donkeys carried spare sandals for the soldiers walking on the burning sand. Fertility of Egyptian land depends on river Nile. South-ward, the cataracts prevented any large invasion and until about 730 B.C. it was conquered by Arabs so ancient peoples and its civilization has been replaced by Islamic and Arabic set up. Egypt was conquered by Alexander, Romans and later on by Napoleon. In Mesopotamia mountaineers from the east and the nomads from the west of the Euphrates could enter the shown lowland at will. The enemy could invade Egypt only over the narrow isthmus of Suez canal. This happened in the eighteenth and in the seventh and also in later centuries S.C.

The Nile Valley is so narrow that from the banks of the river Nile one can sometimes see the desert sands on right and left. Thus, though Egypt is as large as nearly Pakistan together (3,86,000 square miles), but 99 per cent of the population crowds in some 13,000 square miles of the "black land" (as the Egyptians called their country). The rest is the tan desert. Fertile land is situated on the bank of river Nile which provides it with fertile soil and water so Egypt is called Gift of Nile. Villagers clustered along the margins of the cultivated land and during the annual inundation stood out of the water like islands in the sea, as the Greeks used to say. The prevailing wind facilitated navigation upstream, and the current carried the vessels north-ward. An energetic ruler could easily dominate the whole river valley. Territorial unity was normal in Egypt but exceptional in Mespotamia which is considered the oldest county of the world.

Swollen by the rains in Abyssinia, River Nile begins its rise in the middle of August in Cairo and attains its maximum height in the beginning of October. Thus, the inundation comes mostly after the harvest and moistens the earth parched by the summer heat that kills weeds and aerates the ground. (In Mesopotamia, the inundation comes in the spring; summer evaporation makes the ground saline and thus, in the end, unproductive.) This is the difference between Egypt and Mesopotamia.

The brown water of the flood leaves behind a deposit of silt rich in organic matters which renews the top soil. After inundation' the Egyptian needed no more than a wooden hoe to till the muddy ground capable of yielding two and three bumper crops in the year. Greek authors spoke with envy of the farmers who without effort collected the bounty due to river Nile and called it Gift of Nile.

Probably it was the backbreaking work of the fellah which sustained the agricultural civilization of Egypt through six millennia. The sand blown in from the desert encroached upon the cultivable land. Dikes and canals which regulated the flood and extended its benefits across a wider area had to be built to be reconstructed after each inundation. At the dawn of history, the Egyptians already marked the height of the successive rises of the river Nile. Even the Nile could default, and the seven lean years which Joseph predicted to his pharaoh could become dire reality. As soon as man's effort slackened, the population of Egypt dwindled. It totalled 8 million under the Romans in the first century A.D. It was probably 2 million at the beginning of the nineteenth century, under Turkish rule.

The crowding of population in the irrigated land of Egypt determined the nature of the evidence available to us. Since the Egyptians wrote on sheets made out of stalks of papyrus (our word "paper" comes from this Egyptian plant name). Humidity and time destroyed the Egyptian archives. The mud brick buildings also disappeared, since the Egyptian did not use baked bricks. But Pyramids and graves built at the desert's edge remained. The Egypt that we know is mainly an Egypt of the dead. The pyramids are tombs. To understand life in the ancient Egypt we have first to know the world of the dead.

The Civilization of Egypt

The Egyptian civilization was unique. Mummification was already known to Egyptians at the beginning of the third millennium. Palaces and shrines were built of sun dried mud bricks, and the first Egyptian building of limestone was pyramidal grave of a great ruler *i.e.*, of Pharaoh. For the Egyptian, as an Egyptian formula says, "the grave was the eternal home." And it is the "eternal home", its inscriptions, statues, relief, paintings, furniture, etc. tell us about the past of ancient Egypt.

Proverbial wisdom tells us that only good words are to be said about the dead. The Egypt of the dead is peopled by well-fed men, and ladies who are young and good-looking. The pharaohs are benevolent, officials efficient, the lower classes busy and satisfied. Even the slave woman who grinds grain of some time looks optimistic and bright. It shows they were contented people.

The first agricultural settlements on high ground along river Nile and the Faiyum, probably established in the fifth millennium, reveal no surprises. The villagers cultivated barley of the Mesopotamian type, emmer, and flax. They raised livestock and used pottery, flint tools, and also some copper articles. Life of the same kind continued in Nubia as late as the third millennium, but in Egypt two new powers appeared around 3000 which for the next 3,000 years determined the style of Egyptian life. These were Pharaoh and Hieroglyphs.

In predynastic times pictorial representations of hunt and battle show warriors who are equal. Then, suddenly, representations appear in which a giant bestrides his own men and his adversaries, single handedly destroying the enemy or digging a canal. He is the ruler king Pharaoh, and his name is written alongside the picture in hieroglyphs. The images of fish and of chisel, read in Egyptians Nar-mer, give the name of a Pharaoh.

The first representations of the great Pharaohs show them wearing, now the white crown of the south, now the red crown of lower Egypt. It seems that the ruler of the south conquered the Delta. The history of Egypt became the story of the Pharaohs. Its three millennia are divided among thirty dynasties, the last of which reigned between 378 and 342 B.C. Probably the first two dynasties laid the foundation of the Pharahoic civilization. The third settled in Memphis, near modern Cairo, immediately south of the delta of river Nile and here, about 2600, the king erected the pyramids. For the whole period of the "Old Kingdom," form the unification of Egypt to the last Pharaoh of Memphis (Eighth Dynasty), the Egyptian king lists about 955 years.

Storehouses where grain was laid up for the use in lean years covered the land. Barley remained the basic foods. ("Barley and bear" often meant any kind of salary.) Vegetables, particularly onions, supplemented the diet. Grapes and wine are first mentioned under the Second Dynasty (twenty-ninth to twenty-seventh centuries). Agricultural techniques in Egypt remained simple. A wooden hoe was sufficient for the muddy ground and a small plot. From the Second Dynasty on, a light lough drawn by cattle aided the farmer. The houses were built of mud bricks, those of the wealthy were quite comfortable. As early as the Second Dynasty, tombs were equipped with bathrooms for the next life of the owner.

Egypt abounded in excellent stone, form limestone, the building material of the pyramids, to porphyry and granite.

The use of copper become more and more widespread during the third millennium. Toward the end of it the payments to workers, besides food and linen, often included copper utensils. From about 2750 copper tools, hardened by skilful hammering, facilitated large exploitation of quarries and the use of stone of building. Copper points for arrows were in use by 2100.

It seems that the powerful pharaohs intentionally isolated the valley of the river Nile and endeavoured to make its economy self contained. Cultural influence of Mesopotamia and Syria-Palestine was also tangible in the predynastic times and under the first Pharaohs about 3000. The Sumerian motif of entwined monsters appears on Narmer's palette. But when Egypt become powerful, the Pharaohs preferred tribute to trade. Under military protection, the Egyptians exploited malachitee and turquoise veins and also copper mines of Sinai. About 2600, the Pharaohs conquered Nubia to the south of the first cataract; near the second cataract they established foundries for working Nubian copper.

Egypt, was perhaps the richest agricultural country of the world, so it could well dispense with foreign trade, which mostly brought in objects of luxury. In the beginning of the fifteenth century B.C. Queen Hatshpsut, the main product brought back by her five ships was incense for temple service. Probably Elizabeth I of England could not have been more mercantilistic in the sixteenth century A.D. In punt as well as in a bazar in Egypt, goods were disposed of by barter; for instance, beads were exchanged for onions or cakes. The Egyptians did not invent money, but they used copper, grain, silver, and gold as common and popular denominators of value. Yet, as later as about 1170 a sarcophagus valued at about 5 pounds of copper was purchased for about 2½ pounds of copper, I hog, 2 she-goats, and 2 sycamore trees. By contrast with Mesopotamia, the self-contained Egypt remained probably primitive.

The Pyramids of Egypt

The pyramids express the self-confidence of self-centred Egypt. The Great Pyramid, built in the middle of the twenty-sixth century, covers more than 13 acres and remains one of the largest buildings in the world. For 4,500 years it was the tallest (over 480 feet). It was erected perhaps without machinery or scaffolding by the sweat of perhaps 100,000 workers and the ingenuity of Egyptian engineers who used levers and ropes. Men and cattle probably drew sledges up brick ramps to make a pile of some 2,300,000 limestone blocks weighing about two and a half tons each. The sides of the pyramid were oriented according to the four cardinal points, and the maximum error was only one-twelfth of a degree. Each side was to be 756 feet long at the base, and the maximum error was about a few inches, Pyramids are greatest feats of Egyptian civilization.

The mobilized peasants were paid in kind, as such the building of the grand pyramids was also a kind of relief work system. Modern man may ask whether the capital and labour extended in erecting the enormous funerary complex centred on the royal pyramid could not have been better devoted to low-cost housing. The same question, can also be asked about Gothic cathedrals or the Temple of Jerusalem. The first need of any social system is to create incentives to make people do more work then that which is required by their immediate wants. (As Economist Adam Smith writes : "The desire of food is limited in every man by the narrow capacity of the stomach," but the desire for "conveniences and ornaments" is unlimited). The greater part of the rich people the chief enjoyment of wealth consisted in the parade of riches so pyramids may be considered as show of grandeour. In earlier and poorer societies religion provided the incentive for works of economic supererogation; it raised common labour perhaps to the dignity of a ritual gesture. The Sumerian king is represented carrying on his head a basket with bricks for the foundation of a temple. When men of Lagash had to repair a canal, it was the canal of their god Ningirsu. In India kings used to sometimes plough the field to show dignity of labour.

In Egypt, the Pharaoh, a "great god" himself probably linked mortal men to the eternal. He was represented on the temple walls worshipping the gods and association with them, "the servants of the god" (priests, in our terms) were his delegates, and none of his subjects were also pictured in association with a deity. The common people needed the Pharaoh for eternal salvation, as offerings without which the deceased could not exist were officially the Pharaoh's gift. He alone had the key to the afterlife. This eternal life in the pyramid, thus, was probably related to the well-being of every Egyptian. Princes and courtiers were entombed around the royal pyramid, and images of their tenants and servants appeared on the walls of these tombs, so that their names, too, were "established forever." Through this living chain of hope the humblest worker on the Great Pyramid participated with zeal in the sacrament of pharaonic immortality as men who raised the Gothic cathedrals laboured in the hope of the eternal reward for their paints. Thus pyramids came into existence. The natural path of Egyptian expansion lay through Nile river. Between 1550 and 1450 the Pharaohs of the New Kingdom, following in steps of their predecessors, colonized and Egyptianized the gold-producing land of Namibia advancing the frontier to the fourth cataract. The savages to the south of this could not endanger the pharaonic forces. Despite some setbacks, Egypt held the greater part of Nubia securely-firmly almost to the end of the second millennium, and when the southern province finally became independent its rulers remained the devoted protégés of Amon-Re of Thebes.

The story of Jews and Moses and of Hebrew Kingdom

It is said in heyday of the imperial rule, Egyptian empire included Palestine and lot of Jews began to live under Egyptian rule, Palestinian, were treated harshly by Egyptian rule, Palestinian, were treated harshly by Egyptian. A great man called Moses rescued Jews from the clutches of cruel Egyptian rule and founded a separate Hebrew kingdom and Jews religion. This Hebrew kingdom rose to its Zenith during the rule of David and Solomon who is considered as a very wise King by Jews. Israel is new Hebrew state.

With the rise of power of Hebrew kingdom and power of Assyrians, the power of Egyptian kingdom declined and during the rule of Hammurabi and Nebuccodozar Babylonian empire reached to its zenith.

With the decline of power of Egyptian and Babylonian empire, power of Persian empire reached to its zenith and city states flourished in Greece. Attack of Persian forces proved unsuccessful against Greek states. Later on Alexander the great conquered Egypt. Alexandria city of Egypt still reminds his name.

3

EGYPT'S RELATIONS WITH GREEKS AND ROMANS

Relations of Egypt with Greeks and with Roman empire

In the world famous battles Marathon Thermopyle Greek forces showed great valour and were able to give rebuff to vast hordes of Persian forces. Failure of Persian forces showed rottenness of Persian army. Later on Alexander the Great defeated Persian forces and also conquered Egypt. Probably Greeks empire of Alexander the Great was the Greatest ancient empire — honour to history but it depended only on personality of Alexander the Great and it fell to pieces after him. Port of Alexandria was founded in the name of Alexander and Greek branch of P. Tolemy rulers established Greek rule over Egypt.

During the rule of beautiful queen Cleopatra, Egypt was conquered by famous Roman conqueror Julius Ceaser, but he came under the charms of beautiful queen Cleopatra. After him, Antonio was also captivated by beautiful and charming queen Cleopatra but Octavian Caeser defeated Antonio and Cleopatra was forced to commit suicide. After this Egypt came under Roman rule like Britain. With the rise of Christian religion in Roman empires-Christianity also gained religious ascendancy in Egypt and Alexendria became an important center of Christian religion of Roman Civilization and remained as such till the decline of Roman empire.

The Conquest of Egypt by Arabia and Its Impact

With the rise of power of Muslim religion in Arabia, Islamic religion empire began to spread far wide. After Muhamad, Abu Bakr, became Khalifat Rasul Allah the successor of the Apostle of God. Abu Bakr in less than a year subjugated most of Arabia and in July, 634, in the battle of Aziradyan conquered Palestine. His successor Umar is considered as one of the greatest rulers like Constantine and Ashoka who pioneered the cause of religion. Constantines spread Christian religion, Ashoka, Buddhism and Umar, Islam.

After the conquest of North Syria in 637, and of Jerusalem in 638, Arab generals attacked Egypt in 639, and captured Pelusuimal Farma near Port Said. In 641, Arab general Omar conquered Alexendria and Egypt became Muslim possession. During the Caliphate of Umar, Iran, Iraq, Syria, Palestine and Egypt became parts of Muslim world. They together with Arabia and Afghanistan are still today the heartland of Islam.

With the establishment of Islamic rule of Arabs, old Egyptian civilization gave way to the establishment of Islamic civilization of Arab. Arabic language became language of Egyptians and Egypt began to be considered as Arabic state and new name of Egypt is United Arab Republic or U.A.R.

In the Ummayed Abasid conflict of Caliphs, Egypt favoured fugitive Ummayed Caliph and remained center of Islamic Sunni religion for a long time.

Glimpse of Rule of Ottoman Turks over Egypt

With the decline of power of Caliphs and Arabs, Turks became rulers of most of the Islamic lands, Osman a Turkish warrior was the founder of ottoman Turk state. Famous Ottoman Turk King, Selim defeated Shah Ismail of Iran and after that conquered the Mamuluk, empire of Egypt in one campaign. Mamuluk rulers of Egypt were like the slave kings of Delhi who were first governors and then became rulers. At Alappo, the puppet Abbasid Caliph-al Mutawakil, whom the Mamuluks brought along on the expeditions fell into Selims possession. Selim made Caliph a state prisoner but in 1543, Caliph was permitted to return Cairo, where he died. It was claimed that the last Caliph transferred his authority to the Ottoman Turkish ruling family. As such in later years Ottoman Sultans began to use title of Caliph and began to exercise authority of Caliph. During Selim's rule Ottoman empire became heir of medieval Ummayed and Abbasaid empire and ruler of Muslim holy lands.

Ottoman Sultan did not destroy Mamuluk lands. In fact lands in Egypt were parcelled out to Mamuluks to control and manage for the state. With the decline of power of Ottoman Turks, Sultan's authority gradually became nominal. In the 18th century, Egyptian governors and Mamuluk's groups began to defy Sultan's order to remit taxes.

Taking advantage of chaotic condition of Egypt, Napoleon conquered Egypt but had to leave Egypt in 1801 due to collaboration of British forces with Turkish forces. Ottomon Turks had to face various revolts in their empire and they had to fight with Russians. Ottoman Turks were able to check the designs of Peter the Great but notorious queen Catherine the Great was able to defeat Turks and force them to give vast territory of Turkish empire. In spite of all this, Ottoman empire in 1815, successfully whithered the wars and effect of the French revolution and of Napoleon. Beservia was lost, semi-autonomous regime was legalized in Belgrade and in 19th century, Egypt became independent; In 19th century Egypt was the creation of Albenian adventurer, Muhammad Ali.

4

MEHEMET ALI OF EGYPT

Career of Mehemet Ali of Egypt and His Achievements

The next episode in the Eastern Question was opened by the ambition of Albanian Mehemet Ali, who was the Pasha of Egypt and governor. He sought to take advantage of the weakness of Turkey which was weakened by revolts as revealed by the War of Greek independence. He had rendered valuable services to the Sultan of Turkey against the Greeks, and was rewarded with the governorship of the island of Crete. Able and ambitious, he considered this reward as quite inadequate. So, in 1831, he proceeded to tear Syria from his suzerain. His soldiers carried everything before them and even threatened to march upon Constantinople. The sultan of Turkey appealed to the European Powers, but no response came from any of them except Russia who was willing and ready to give help in order to fish in troubled waters. However, unwelcome the Russian help might be, the Sultan of Turkey like a drowning man clutching at a serpent, had to accept it. But the spectacle of Russian troops pouring into Turkish dominions made the Western European Powers uneasy and so England, France and Austria put pressure upon Turkey to buy off the hostility of Mehemet Ali by the cession of Syria, thus making Russian help unnecessary. But Russia was not to be befooled in this way. She demanded and obtained her price in the Treaty of Unkier Skelessi (1833) by which Turkey agreed to give Russian warships free passage through the Straits, and to close the Dardanelles in time of war to all ships of war except those of Russia. The Black Sea thus became a Russian lake and Russia virtually secured a protectorate over Turkey. This treaty was probably the high watermark of Russian influence at Constantinople.

The Treaty of Unkier Skelessi excited the liveliest apprehension in England. Lord Palmerston, who was Foreign Ministers of England was ever hostile to Russian influence in the East and always nervous of Russian designs, was determined to upset this treaty. His opportunity came when the Sultan of Turkey was beaten for the second time in his premature attempt to recover Syria from his Egyptian vassal Muhammad Ali. At this point the western European Powers intervened. France wanted to support Mehemet Ali and gave him secret aid in the hope of developing her interests in Egypt and Syria. She also wanted to weaken British influence in the Mediterranean sea. The British Minister Lord Palmerston saw in this situation the possibility of a French dominance in Egypt. This was as dangerous as the dominance which Russia had recently secured in Constantinople by the Treaty of Unkier Skelessi. To England either was equally undesirable and so Lord Palmerston set himself of maintain the integrity of Turkey, and to prevent the isolated interference of any single Power. Russia found herself in a very false position. She realized that replacement of a weak ruler by a strong one in Constantinople will weaken her influence and in that case she would have to give up her ambitious projects in the East. On the other hand, if she was to befriend the Sultan of Turkey against his powerful vassal, she would have to do it in co-operation with England and other European Powers. In that case she would lose the advantages which she had already secured by the Treaty of Unkier Škelessi. Dreading the designs of France and Mehemet Ali, Russia drew closer to England offering to renounce her special position and agreeing to collective and positive intervention. The result was the Convention of London by which Great Britain, Russia, Austria and Prussia agreed, without the knowledge of France, to force terms upon Mehemet Ali of Egypt. France, under King Louis Philippe was furious at the slight offered to her and threatened war with England, but eventually drew back. The successful operations of the allied fleet compelled Mehemet Ali to submit and to accept the Treaty of London (1841). By it Mehemet Ali agreed to give up his claim to Syria, but was confirmed in the hereditary pashalic *i.e.*, governorship of Egypt under the suzerainty, of the Sultan of Turkey. The strait of Dardanelles were to be closed to the warships of all nations in the time of war. This clause tore up the Treaty of Unkier Skelessi and thereby saved Turkey from dangerous dependence on Russia. This Treaty of London was a great triumph for Lord Palmerston. It administered a rebuff to France and acted as a check to Russian designs. It made it clear that England would tolerate neither the Russian protectorate over Turkey, nor the French protectorate over Egypt. It also preserved the integrity of the Turkish Ottoman Empire which was threatened with dissolution by the ambition of Mehemet Ali.

Life of Mehemet Ali. He was an Albanian adventurer who came to Egypt when that country was occupied by Napoleon. He was a man of great tact and resourcefulness. "He did well as a tax-collector, better as a tobacco merchant, best of all as a commander in the Ottoman army". He gradually made himself master of Egypt, expelling the Turks and the British, and carried his victorious army to Mecca and Khartoum. He was thus the founder of modern independent state of Egypt. According to Sydney N. Fisher, he "must be recognized as one of great rulers of his age". For 40 years, he ruled Egypt. He created a new government and cabinet and ruled like a benevolent despot. He died in 1849. When he died, he had given Egypt constructive leadership and sown the seeds for the establishment of a national state.

The Condition of Egypt upto 1919 and the Main Events of Egypt from 1849 to 1914

Muhammad Ali was succeeded by Abbas Pasha and later on by Said who granted a broad concession to his French friend Ferdinend-de-Lesseps to construct the Suez Canal Said died in 1863 and Ismael succeeded him. The cost of Suez Canal, to Said and Ismail was estimated of 11500000 for which in the beginning Egypt received no return but cotton trade was very profitable. From 1863 to 1879, during Ismail's rule, life in Egyptian Court was sumptuous and money flowed like the waters of Nile but Ismail was spendthrift and Egypt became a debtor country.

Ismail was deposed in 1878 and was succeeded by his son Tawfic and a joint Anglo-French control was established over Egypt and this was resented by Egyptian people So France withdrew but English occupied Egypt in 1882. Egyptian revolt failed against British forces and rebel leader Arabi Pasha was exiled to Ceylon, Sir Evelyn Bering became British Agent and Consul General and Lord Cromer ruled Egypt autocratically from 1892 to 1907. Sudan revolted under Mahdi who killed British General Gordon and his men in 1885 but it was conquered by lord Kitchner in 1896 Egyptian nationalism was aroused by the privileged position of foreigners, by the construction of Suez Canal, and by numerous rich Turkish families. The uprising of Arabi Pahsa in 1880 was due to outburst of these feelings. In spite of failure of Arabi's revolt nationalism in Egypt grew.

5

NATIONALISM IN EGYPT

The Development of Nationalism in Egypt and Its Consequences

When Great Britain went to war against Turkey in 1914, she freed Egypt from Ottoman suzerainty of Turkish Sultan and made Egypt a British protectorate. The prevailing ferment of nationalism was working in Egypt and so the Egyptians though welcoming the removal of Turkish overlordship, did not take kindly to the increase of British influence and power. Hence when the 1st World War of 1914-18 came to a close the Egyptian National Party called (Wafad) led by Zaghlul Pasha demanded that Egypt should be represented at the peace Conference of Paris of 1919, as an independent power. Zaghlul Pasha was preparing to lead a delegation and to embark for Paris, to put demands of Egypt's freedom and of Egyptian aspirations but the British government arrested him and his associates and deported them to Malta. This precipitated a serious insurrection and the British rulers had to employ a large army to put it down in (1919). Coercion increased but nationalist feeling Egyptians as in India and other countries. In Egypt (as also elsewhere) the British policy was one of alternate coercion and conciliation and of granting dominion status or limited freedom.

The British Policy towards Egypt from 1919 to 1936

British Government sent Lord Milner on a mission of investigation to known the cause of Egyptian dissatisfaction. His recommendations formed the basis of Anglo-Egyptian treaty which was signed by Great Britain and Sultan Fuad of Egypt in 1921. By it Egypt was granted independence like other dominions subject to a number of restrictions and to the supervisory authority of the British High Commissioner. This treaty was unhesitatingly rejected and opposed by the Nationalists and their discontent vented itself in renewed riots. The British authorities again deported Wafad leader Zaghlul Pasha and proclaimed the treaty by unilateral declaration. In the Egyptian parliament created by the new constitution the Wafdists secured an overwhelming majority. Zaghlul Pasha was recalled and he became the Premier of the new Egyptian ministry. Friction with the British continued and a serious crisis arose in 1924 when the British Governor-General of the Sudan, Sir Lee Stack, was murdered in Cairo. Zaghlul Pasha denounced this crime and promised swift prosecution of the culprits. But the British rulers issued a severe ultimatum demanding a heavy indemnity, suppression of all political demonstrations and the immediate withdrawal of all Egyptian soldiers from Sudan.

They also announced large-scale irrigation projects in Sudan, Which threatened the enough water supply of Egypt. Zaghlul Pasha was ready to accept all the terms except those relating to Sudan. The British would not modify their demands and to put pressure upon the Egyptians Britishers occupied the customs house at Alexandria. Zaghlul Pasha thereupon opposed these measure and resigned in protest. He died shortly after in 1927. He is considered as a great Egyptian-nationalist leader like Tilak in India or Sun Yat Sen in China.

Zaghlul Pasha's mantle fell upon Nahas Pasha who became the new leader of the Wafdist party. Nahas Pasha refused to accept a new treaty proposed by Great Britain as it fell far short of the nationalist Egyptian's aspirations. The people became restless and the parliament of Egypt was suspended. Thereupon Sidky Pasha, leader of a rival party known as the People's Party (Shaab), for a short time assumed dictatorial control and promulgated a new constitution of Egypt in (1930). He tried his best to suppress the Nationalists but without success. He resigned in 1933. The Waldists were brought to power by the elections held in 1936 and Nahas Pasha again became a Premier of Egypt. The same year King Fuad died and was succeeded by his son Farauk. He was inefficient ruler who was unable to rule successfully.

Meanwhile Italy's Ethopinian venture in 1935 and aggressive tactics in eastern Africa alarmed the Egyptians and also made the British uneasy. Hence British and Egyptian nations became willing to come to a settlement lest the common enemy should steel a march upon them. Nahas Pasha entered into negotiations with Britain and the result was the Anglo-Egyptian Treaty of Alliance of 1936. It also provided for reciprocal help in case of war. Great Britain agreed to recognize the Independence of

Egypt and also to an exchange of ambassadors and promised to withdraw all troops from Egypt except a small force for guarding the Suez Canal. Sudan was to be placed under joint Anglo-Egyptian control. Britain also promised to support Egypt's admission to the League of Nations and to use her influence to induce the other Powers to surrender their extra-territorial rights in Egypt'. In 1937 Egypt became a legal member of the League of Nations. Thus Egypt became an independent country conferring some rights to Britain.

According to her promise, Britain helped to arrange for and international conference at Montreux in Switzerland in 1937. Next year the conference sat and consented to the abrogation of foreign law courts and other extra-territorial rights by 1949, and to the adoption of some immediate steps in that direction. Thus the treaty of 1936 gave Egypt freedom subject to some Previlege to Britain.

New Developments in Egypt and the Condition of Egypt up to the Second World War

Egypt remained under British sovereignty up to Second World War. On the outbreak of the Second World War in 1939, Egypt joined the Allied Power against Germany and cooperated with them whole-heartedly and famous general Rommel was defeated by British forces due to Egyptian co-operation. But the Egyptians ware bitterly offended by the high-handed conduct of the Britishers who treated them not as allied but as conquered subjects. Hence after the close of the Second World War their dormant anti-British feeling flared up. They were determined to remove all traces of British supremacy from their own country. They felt bitterly aggrieved by the presence of British troops on Egyptian soil. Besides, this, the question of the future status of Sudan greatly embittered their relations with Britain. In 1947, Egypt laid the question of the removal of British troops from the Suez Canal zone before the U.N. Security Council, but nothing came out of it. Hence Nahas Pasha the Wafd leader took the matter into his hands and prevailed upon the Egyptian parliament to enact laws abrogating the Anglo-Egyptian treaty of 1936. King Farauk of Egypt took this opportunity to cancel the Anglo-Egyptian condominium agreement as to the joint control of the Sudan and proclaimed himself as ruler and "King of Egypt and the Sudan." The British Government refused to acknowledge this unilateral repudiation of Anglo-Egyptian treaties but expressed their willingness and inclination to open negotiation for their revision. At the same time they declared their firm intention to maintain their rights fully. The mounting tension on both sides led to armed conflicts in the Suez Canal area followed by a terrible outburst of mob violence in Cairo in January 1952. In this violence foreigners and pro-British Egyptians were the greatest sufferers. King Farauk who disliked the Wafadists took advantage of these disturbances to dismiss Nahas Pasha. In this way King Farauk made himself unpopular and lost support both of Britishers and Egyptian people and like Loius XVI and Czar Nicholas II of Russia which paved the way for revolt.

6

EGYPT AFTER 1945

The Condition of Egypt after the IInd World War

Crisis in Egypt and in the Arab lands, possessing most of the world's known oil resources and forming a vital artery of the east-west communication, the Middle East had proved a particularly explosive area since the World War II of 1939-45. In 1945 the former French mandates of Syria and Lebanon became independent after conflicts with the French Government while Jordan, previously under British protection, was also granted independence in 1946.

Another British mandate, Palestine, soon became the battleground for two rival nationalisms; Arab and Jewish. In 1948, after British control terminated and the new state of Israel was proclaimed war broke out between the young republic of Israel and seven Arab states. Although the U.N.O. arranged an armistice in 1949 that acknowledged the Israeli victory, peace was not restored because the Arabs refused to recognize the emergence of the new state of Israel.

The Palestine campaign, in which Egypt had participated, revealed the poor leadership and defective military supplies of the Egyptian forces, resulting from widespread governmental corruption in Egyptian government. In 1952 a clique of army officers seized the Egyptian government of Cairo and forced the dissolute king Farauk to go into exile. Corrupt politicians were convicted and large estates were broken up for distribution to the peasants. In 1953 a republic of Egypt was proclaimed. Subsequently, the strongest officer, Colonel Gamal Abdul Nasser (1918), assumed leadership and became the rallying figure for dynamic Arab nationalism not only of Egypt but of Arabs states everywhere.

President Nasser's plan was to construct a high dam at Aswan. This brought offers of American and British assistance.

But when his request for arms was refused by Washington, he turned to the Soviet Bloc, and the offer of American aid was abruptly cancelled. Nasser retaliated in July 1956 by nationalizing the Suez Canal and by imposing heavy shipping tolls on Suez Canal, and he expected to finance to Aswan dam.

Two years earlier, British troops had been withdrawn from their base in the Suez Canal zone, and an agreement which was signed at that time between London and Cairo stipulated that the Suez Canal was to continue as an international highway "that shall always be free and open, in time of peace, to every vessel of commerce or of war without distinction of flag, or race or religion. France interpreted nationalization of Suez Canal as a threat to their national interests, so a conference was held in London to determine whether some form of international control on Suez could be agreed upon. Egypt refused to denationalize the Suez Canal zone, and so this issues was taken to the Security council of U.N.O. where various proposals by France and Britain were blocked by the Soviet veto. As such no solution could be found and this led to war between Egypt and Israel, England and France.

Meanwhile, Egyptian guerillas were filtering over the border into Israeli territory and Israel bound shipping and communications were harassed as it sought use of Suez Canal. This led to the Israeli invasion of Egypt. Two days later, British and French troops also invaded the Suez Canal zone, ostensibly to clear the combatants away from this vital canal. But when the Suez adventure was condemned by the United States, the Soviet Union, and India etc. Britain and France bowed to the U.N.O. General Assembly's call for a cease-fire and the Suez Canal remained under Egyptian control. To check war, a U.N. emergency force was organized to patrol the Egyptian-Israeli border. Thus in 1956, Egypt emerged triumphant.

The Problem of Egyptian Sovereignty of Sudan

While the Arabs in the mandates had been struggling for the right of self-determination, a parallel development was taking place in Egypt. When the British diplomats refused a delegation of Egyptian nationalists of Wafad party permission to attend the Paris Peace Conference of 1919 and deported them along with the spokesman of the group and his followers. The Nile valley rose in revolt and Britishers had to face a difficult situation.

After three years of disorder the British government in London announced that Egypt was no longer a British protectorate. It was to be an independent sovereign state, subject to certain reservations agreement about British privileges. Britain was to remain responsible for the defence of the Egypt for protection of foreign interests, and for communications vital to the British empire and above all for the management of Suez Canal. Egypt grudgingly adapting itself to this British declaration made its sultan the king. As new Egyptian Constitution was in 1923, Anglo Egyptian relations remained unsatisfactory in the beginning but later on frequent negotiations between the two governments were fruitless. In Egypt from 1924 to 1936, corruption in high places, the increasing number of university graduates unable to find suitable employment and the wide gap between the very rich and the absolute poor people and the bitter feud between the king the most important political party (the wafd) helped to create unrest all over Egypt.

In spite of the long record of Anglo-Egyptian administration Acrimony came about through the threat of Italian Fascist's aggression in Africa following Italian dictator Mussolini's conquest of Ethiopia. In 1936 Britain and Egypt negotiated a treaty of alliance. In the case of war there was to be mutual assistance on a wide scale, and the status of Sudan was to continue unaltered. This treaty for the time being served useful purpose.

Sudan had been influenced by Egypt for many centuries and in 1820, it was brought under Egyptians control but it revolted and put to death General Cordon, the governor of Sudan who was the ruler and the agent of the Egyptian government. In the 1890's the British reconquered Sudan and declared it a condominium that is, a territory theoretically under the dual sovereignty of British and Egyptian government although it was really under British control. The treaty of alliance of 1936, stated that Sudan would remain technically under joint Anglo-Egyptian administration for the "Welfare of the Sudanese". Now Sudan is independent but in anarchical condition.

The Sudan is called Jumhuriyat as Sudan *i.e.* Republic of Sudan. It is largest African country in North east Africa. The white Nile flows through the middle of country and joins blue Nile at Khartoum. Its area is 2505,813 sq. km. Population is 3 crore mostly Muslim and of Christians and of tribal beliefs

The 12 northern provinces are predominantly Arab-Muslim while 3 southern provinces are predominantly by Christians and animists, so there is conflict between Arab-Muslims and

Christians who demand a separate Christian state. Due to famine and anarchical conditions millions of persons have died. Due to efforts of U.N.O. peace pact has been signed to decide question of separate state by referendum.

7

Revolution in Egypt of Col. Nasser

Revolution in Egypt and Role of Col. Nasser in it

Dismissal of Wafadist government made king Farauk unpopular and due to chaotic conditions came revolt. Events now began to move very fast in Egypt. King Farauk's regime, marked as it was by anarchy, bribery, inefficiency and corruption, was not popular. But what discredited the monarchy most was its defeat and inability to overthrow Israel. A group of young army officers headed by General Neguib engineered a military coup and forced the king Farauk to abdicate. Farauk fled to Italy and his infant son was proclaimed king. General Neguib assumed control of the Egyptian government and he negotiated an agreement with Britain whereby Sudan might become independent after three years of trial and transition. Next occurred a very dramatic change of great consequences in the political situation of Egypt. The monarchy was abolished and Egypt was proclaimed a Republic with Neguib as its President and Premier. Neguib signalized his accession to power by concluding an agreement with Britain in October, 1954, by the terms of which all British troops were to be withdrawn and to evacuate the Suez Canal zone within twenty months but were to be entitled to return in case of certain eventualities of war. This agreement marked the end of British military ascendancy not only in Egypt but in the whole Middle East. It was a great diplomatic success on general Neguib's part, but in spite of it, he was regarded by the extreme nationalists as too moderate. Hence he was relieved of his office and Gamal Abdul Nasser assumed the supreme power in the Egyptian State.

The rule of Col. Nasser over Egypt

Colonel Nasser was a man of initiative and energy and was very ambitious with a strong will and determined spirit. He presumed that he has assumed office with certain definite aims in view, such as the elimination of Western influence from the Middle East, Egyptian leadership of the Arab nations and the destruction of the new state of Israel. He opposed and condemned the Baghdad Pact of 1955, as he regarded it as a serious challenge to his leadership in the Middle East for which he was making subtle bids. He sought to offset the Baghdad Pact by a new alliance with Syria and by establishing close diplomatic contracts with Arab countries such as Saudi Arabia and Yemen etc. By 1956 Egypt, Saudi Arabia, Yemen, and Syria etc. came to an agreement providing for a unified command of their armies. Thus at Nasser's initiative was set up a new alignment of Middle East states to counter-balance the Baghdad Pact sponsored by Britain and America, Meanwhile Nasser procured the dismissal of Glubb Pasha (General Sir John Glubb), the pro-British Premier of Jordan and thus brought Jordan also within the orbit of Egypt's influence. Egypt, Saudi Arabia and Syria promised to give subsidy to Jordan in compensation for the loss of British subsidy which Gen. Glubb's dismissal entailed. Mean while Nasser negotiated an arms deal with Soviet Russia and revived an enormous supply of weapons from both Soviet Russia and Czechoslovakia. This move alarmed Isreal and seriously embarrassed Britain and the U.S.A. and France, as aim of Col. Nasser seemed to destroy Israel and western power's influence in the Middle East.

Mean while, Egypt's relations with Isreal drifted from bad to worse. Since 1949 the Egyptians along with Arab states had been carrying on a desultory and guerilla warfare with tiny state of Israel. Israel in her turn retaliated with effect. The increasing tension between the two states was producing an explosive situation in the Middle East. This situation was further complicated by the reaction which Col. Nasser's policy produced in Britain and France. In England President Nasser was looked upon by the British Premier Sir Anthony Eden as a dangerous dictator while the French had come to believe that he was the abettor of disturbances in their possessions in North Africa. Both the Powers came to think that the abetment of Nasser was essential to the security of their imperial interests. The U.S.A. also looked askance at Nasser for his recognition of the communist China. Probably the situation in the Middle East was ominous in the extreme due to over ambitiousness of Col. Nasser. He was one of the architect of non-aligned movements and relied for help both on non-aligned countries and Communist countries in case of war.

At this posture of events the United States and 'Britain in July 1956, withdrew their promised offer of financial aid to Egypt in building the Asuan High Dam, a project vital to the economic rehabilitation of Egypt. It was a blow which turned Nasser bitter and sour and stirred him to take immediate action. He staged a demonstration in Alexandria and dramatically announced the immediate nationalization of the Suez Canal Company (1956, July 20). He declared that the income accruing from the Suez Canal would finance the Assuan Dam Scheme. Nasser's decision of nationalisation of Suez Canal was hailed with enthusiasm in Asia, Africa, India, Pakistan and Russia etc. as a great snub to the imperialist powers, French and Britain etc. But these powers were not willing to accept Nasser's decision as final. A conference of twenty-two nations was duly summoned in London to discuss the future status of Suez Canal; eighteen of them agreed that there should be some form of international control. At their instance the Australian Premier, Mr. Menzies led a delegation to plead before Nasser for the acceptance the London formula, but the latter refused to accept it. Thereupon a Suez Canal Users' Association was set up and canal payments were withheld from Egypt. The result was deadlock, which led to war in which Col. Nasser emerged triumphant.

The outbreak of Hostilities and Suez Canal Crisis of 1956 and its Results.

Suez Canal was necessary for International commerce and for Israel's survival. As such when all prospects of a negotiated settlement of the Suez Canal question seemed doomed to failure, the drastic action taken by the new tiny state of Israel. This precipitated the crisis and led to war. Relations of Israel with Jordan were becoming more and more strained and at last reached a breaking-point when a joint army command was established by Egypt, Syria and Jordan all these powers aimed for destruction of Egypt in defiance of U.N.O. Apprehending imminent danger, Israel forestalled it by invading Egypt and routed the Egyptian forces by capturing huge quantities of equipment and taking thousands of Egyptians as prisoners of war. Britain and France under the pretext of separating the warring forces, also joined this fray. France-British forces captured Port Said and destroyed the Egyptian aerodromes by air attacks A very critical situation developed. The Arab League became restive and the conflict tended to develop into a large-scale warfare between the Arab nations and Israel and her supporters. Russia threatened nuclear attack and intervention to stop Anglo-French aggression. The U.N. Assembly acted quickly and promptly. It passed a resolution for immediate cease-fire and the withdrawal of troops of Anglo-French and Israel nations to the respective borders. The U.N.O. Emergency Force, composed of contingents from all over the world, quickly arrived and acted as a buffer until the withdrawal of Anglo-French Israeli troops. The Anglo-French troops withdrew from Port Said in December, 1956 and three months later Israeli troops evacuated the Gaza area. The Egyptians assumed control of all the territories recently occupied by the enemy troops. U.S.A. refused to help England and France and Israel and India all Islamic countries sided with Egypt in this conflict.

As such role of the U.N.O. in the Suez Canal crisis was prompt vigorous and very effective. The speedy dispatch of the U.N. Emergency Force had the desired effect of confining within a narrow compass the hostilities which threatened to 'develop into a large-scale warfare and forced Britain, France and Israel to withdraw their forces. Besides, it set the precedent of arming the U.N.O. with its own force to deal with critical situations likely to disturb the peace of the world. Another result of the Suez crisis was the lowering of the British and French prestige in the Arabian peninsula which caused trouble in Yeman and betokened future difficulty for the Aden Protectorate and the Hadhramant etc. Col. Nasser whom the Britishers and the French had sought to humilitate, emerged out of the conflict with the increased prestige as the champion of colonial people against. Western imperialism. Fame of Nassar reached to its zenith and he along with Jawaharlal Nehru and Tito of Yugoslavia become acknowledged leader of non-aligned movement of non-aligned countries. Impact of this war was great on England and British Prime Minister Sir Anthony Eden had to resign. It gave death blow to idea of maintaining British empire and British prestige and gradually British empire disappeared and the remaining countries which were under British control became free.

In spite of all this easy triumph, Nasser was unable to conquer Israel and Arab-Israel conflicts inspite of help of all Islamic-Arab countries. Egypt was always defeated by Israel. Constant defeat of giant Egypt inspite of help of all Islamic countries lessened the fame of President Nasser of Egypt and he died of crest fallen. In spite of all this credit of giving Islamic democratic set up to Egypt and of bringing Arab league in an organized way and as a pioneer of non-aligned movement along with Nehru and Tito goes to Nasser Truimphant emergence in Suez crisis was a great feat of Nasser. Probably he can be considered as maker of modern Egypt and a great leader of Egypt.

Result of Suez War. In the final analysis, the prestige of the U.N.O. was enhanced, Nasser's position was strengthened, and the Anglo-French prestige fell, while the Soviet Union continued to pose as a defender of Arab nationalism and this encouraged Egypt to defy U.N.O. The Suez Canal issue remained controversial, for, disregarding his pledges due to President Nasser in defiance of the U.N.O. by persisting of denying the use of Suez Canal to Israel-bound shipping and by keeping it exclusively under the control of Egypt.

Western fears of Soviet aims in the Middle East were strengthened by Moscow's massive aid to Egypt in the beginning for the construction of the Aswan Dam. In the meantime, however, Cairo had apparently become wary of the high price to be paid for continued dependence upon Moscow, so in 1959 it ended good relations with Russia. Egypt resumed diplomatic relations with Britain and later on with others.

The central factor in this unstable situation of Arab lands was Egypt and its leader, Nasser. This idol of the Arab world saw in himself as the new "Bismarck" who would unite all the states of the Middle East. There was, however, much rivalry and enmity between the Arab leaders. Syria joined Egypt to form the United Arab Republic in 1958, but retained this tie only for a scant period of three years. This was a setback for Nasser. In 1962, revolt in Arab state of Yemen against the conservative ruling. Immam brought a new government, the Yemeni Arab Republic, into power. The deposed Immam however, continued to fight; thereupon, Col. Nasser intervened on behalf of the Yemeni Republic with 28,000 Egyptian troops. The Yemen civil war exposed Arab rivalries as both Jordan and Saudi Arabia sent arms to deposed Immam. Despite several attempts to achieve a cease-fire, sporadic fighting persisted in 1966 after more than three years of civil war. Yemen is now divided between south and north Yemen. Notwithstanding the numerous revolts and coups, important economic gains are being made in Egypt in the Middle East. Encouraging progress can be noted in most areas in the discovery, utilization and control of new water resources. The Arabian desert may, bloom again. The great Aswan high dam on the upper Nile is the most ambitious and exciting water development in the Middle East costing I billion dollar. It was completed in 1970. It is a dam up a lake 395 miles long and add approximately one million precious acres to Egypt's cultivatable area. With the completion of dam Egypt gained prosperity but 1967 war with Israel brought it disgrace and defeat, so popularity of Col. Nasser declined and lot of Egyptian territory conquered by Israel which Egypt was able to get back due to mercy of America, who forced Israel to give back conquered territories and to make a treaty.

8

CONTEMPORARY EGYPT

Short Note on Contemporary Egypt

Egypt gained name and fame during President Nasser's regime though even during life time of Nasser, Israel defeated Egypt and all other Arab powers in Arab-Israeli war of 1967. Later on Arab-Israeli war took place in 1973 in which Egypt and Syrian forces attacked Israel with the help of other powers. In this war also Israel gained an upper hand.

Nasser was succeeded by President Saadat and he was not of ambitions and aggressive nature like Nasser so he tried for reconciliation with Israel. On 20 Nov., 1977, President Anwar Saadat went to Israel and established cordial relations with it. U.S.A's., foreign Secretary, Henary Kissinger and later on President Carter took pains in bringing Egypt and Israel together. At least after peace proposal at Camp David brought reconciliation between Egypt and Israel.

At last on 25 March, 1979, a treaty was concluded between Egypt and Israel at Washington which patched up differences between Egypt and Israel. By this treaty Egypt recognized Israel and established diplomatic relations. Israel also promised to return all conquered territories of Egypt. As such this treaty may be considered as a great feat of Egyptian diplomacy. By winning U.S.A's sympathy Egypt got back all territories peacefully which he failed to get by war.

This Egypt Israeli treaty annoyed other Arab powers and so Egypt was expelled from Arab league and its headquarter was shifted form Cairo to Tunisia. President Saadat was killed by a fanatic and he was succeeded by President Hosni Mubarak. He also carried policy of friendship with Israel and got back all Egyptian territory from Israel without war.

President Hosni Mubarak is a very intelligent and shrewd person, so after getting back, all Egyptian territories from Israel, he won over leading Arab states and became member of Arab League and President of African organization and a leading leader of non-aligned movement.

After gaining Egypt's, territory, membership of Arab League and Presidentship of African Organization, he changed his policy and began to support cause of Palestinian Liberation Organization *i.e.*, of P.L.O. Being encouraged by Arab powers, India and Soviet Union, P.L.O. leader Aseer Arafat began to demand establishment of Palestinian homeland by taking territory of Israel. Egypt is trying to gain territory from Israel to establish homeland for Palestinian refugees and this demand is being supported by all and is even by U.S.A. Thus due to successful diplomacy of Egypt, Israel is losing what it gained by war. If Israel agrees to give her territory to establish to P.L.O. then tiny state of Israel becomes just like a district of India and may not survive as an independent state but Egypt may emerge as a very powerful state. Thus Egypt gained by diplomacy which others failed to gain by war.

Now Israel has been forced to establish state of Palestine within her territory by giving it to new Palestinian state, so Egypt has gained prestige and peace while Israel has lost territory as well as peace.

At present Arab Republic of Egypt *i.e.*, Jumhuriyat Misral-Arabiya possesses an area of 997677 sq. km. and population of 70 millions. Language is Arabic and English as mostly Arab Muslim and few Christians live. President in 2003 is Hosni Mubarak and Prime minister Atef Obeid.

Suez Canal 173 km. provides navigation and prosperity. The Aswan high Dam 1971 provides irrigation but Islamic militancy, Jehad has created disturbances, but now situation is under control.

9

IRAQ

Introduction of Iraq. Iraq's Capital is Baghdad. Its Area is about 438446 sq. kms. and population is about 25158000. Its language is Arabic (official) and Kurdish; Religion is Islam; Currency is Iraqi Dinar equal to US$1 = 311 Dinar.

Iraq is the modern name for Mesopotamia (Meso-middle, potamia rivers) which means the land lying between the two river, Euphrates and Tigris.

Iraq is one of the most ancient countries of the world and has produced various cultures such as the Mesopotamian civilization, Sumerian and Assyrian culture which have influenced European and Asian civilizations.

Petroleum is the most important product of the Iraqi economy. Iraq occupies the fifth place among oil-producing countries of the world. A programme of industrialization is on which is depended on the oil revenues. Three quarters of the population depend on agriculture.

Iraq is the greatest producer of date. Its President is Saddam Hussain. It fought successfully with Iran from 1980 to 1989.

Short Description of Modern Iraq

The ancient land of Mesopotamia *i.e.*, land of two rivers watered by twin rivers of Tigris and Euphrates now forms part of Iraq. In ancient period Samarian and Babylonian and Assyrian empires rose and declined. These empires included Iraq, Syria, Lebinan and Israel etc. Boundaries of empires constantly changed but all empires remained in conflict either with Egyptian empire or with Persian empire. Islamic empire of Arabs and later on of Turks were firmly established in these lands but conflict continued as Islam was divided between Shia and Sunnies. Thus Shiate empire of Persia came in conflict with the Sunni Turkish empire in medieval ages. With the establishment of Israel and Sunni state of Iraq and Shiate state of Iran, this land of Middle East has again become cockpit of the world. As the seeds of conflict were sown in remote past, so ancient history of the Middle East countries have been briefly narrated.

The area of Iraq is of 438446 sq. kms. Its population is about 25 millions. Religion is Islam the language is Arabic and the Capital is Baghdad. Its coin, Iraqi dinar is equivalent to 0.311 dollar. About 75% population is of farmers but the land is famous for oil and dates.

Its President is Saddam Hussain Tahirite.

The Earliest History of Human Kind and Rise of Civilization in Mesopotamia

Historians are of the opinion that more than two million years ago, man's ancestors appeared on earth surrounded by enemies of all kinds. Man developed tools from stones and later on learnt farming, hunting and taming of animals and utilizing them for his own benefit. As such ancient period of human development has been divided into many ages by the historians.

In Mesopotamia or Iraq came development of civilization probably first. The first great period of cultural evolution is called the Paleolithic, or Old Stone Age in history. The chief instrument for all-purposes tool of this cultural stage was the human hand and axe. Late Paleolithic age which begins about 12,000 B.C. included features such as the making of blade tools and the life like depiction of animals, painted on the walls of caves. Perhaps eight thousand years ago, the Neolithic stage was initiated in Mesopotamia with the appearance of food-producing communities in Western Asia. Neolithic cultures are generally characterized by the cultivation of grains, the domestication of animals, pottery making, and the fashioning of polished stone tools. The revolutionary change from a food-gathering to a food-producing economy made possible the rise of civilization based on farming. Historians state in Ancient day wheat was found here first.

10

Ancient Iraq

Civilization rose in Mesopotamia during the course of fourth millennium B.C. and in Egypt nearer the end of the same millennium. These two civilizations were river made, one by the river Nile, the other by the rivers of Tigris and Euphrates. In each case their respective inhabitants succeeded in making the transition from a food-gathering to a food-producing economy. They constructed great dams and all irrigation ditches and thus achieved a still more sedentary ways of life in which towns developed, along with new norms of economic, political, and social organization.

While the age of most nations is no more than a few centuries, the time span of Egyptian civilization must be reckoned in thousands of years. The words monumental and timeless are best to describe Egyptian culture. The Egyptians built colossal statues and huge tombs; their burial customs were designed to outwit time itself. The state centred upon the absolute rule of the pharaohs economic life was patterned on the seasonal ebb and flow of river Nile so Egypt began to be called Gift of River Nile.

The story of ancient Mesopotamia is primarily concerned with the achievements of the Sumerians and the later on adoption of their civilization by various invaders. The most important of this new states was Babylon, created by Hammurabi. Following an era of very brilliant Babylonian civilization, the Hittites conquered Syria and Babylon. In Syria the duel between the Egyptions and the Babylonians weakened both contestants. This gave small nations for example, to Phonenicia and the Hebrew kingdoms etc., a chance to enjoy a brief period of independence. Political diversity was ended by the rise of the Assyrian empire, which lasted about three hundred years (900-600 B.C.). After the fall of Assyria, which under powerful king Nebuchadnezzar became a powerful civilization, but the expansion of Persia terminated its independence. Persia, in its turn, became one of the greatest empires which the world had seen.

In a large and complex canvas of human history, at a glance, it may seem that, like the Sphinx and the Hanging Gardens of Babylon, peoples and events depicted there belong to the long-deal past. Yet features of our own civilization can probably be traced back to cultural elements of those by-gone days, and the political strife which rocks the region now has some of its roots in this period of ancient days. Thus causes of Arab-Israel conflict lie in past.

Persians incorporated Mesopotamian territories in their empire but Persians were defeated by Alexander the Great so Greek rule dominated over these ancient lands. Greeks were replaced by Romans and Romans were replaced by Muslim Arabs Caliph Umar conquered Mesopotamia and so Ummayed dynasty of Caliphs ruled from 661 to 750 over their lands having its capitals at Damascus in Syria. Arab conquerors imposed Muslim rule and converted all nations into Islam and made Baghdad center of Islamic civilization.

11

IRAQ UNDER CALIPHS

The Rule of Abbasid Caliphs over Iraq and Adjoining Lands

Ummayad Caliphs ruled over a vast Muslim empire having its capital at Damascus in Syria but in June 747, Abu-Al-Abbas a great grandson of Al Abbas raised the standard of revolt and under his Iranian agent a band of Iranians, Khurasanians and South Arabians conquered Iraq in 749 and defeated Ummayads in 750. Abu-Al-Abbas was recognized in Kufa as Caliph Abbasid attempted to extirpate the whole Ummayad tribe but few escaped. Among those who escaped was Hisam's grandson, Alid-al Rahman, who made his way to Spain and established Ummayad Caliphate of Cardobar and later on in Egypt from whom Turks claimed Caliphate later on.

With the establishment of Abbasid Caliphate at Baghdad Persian culture and administrative set up became prominent and Baghdad became capital of Abbasid Caliphs. Abbasid's family ruled from 750 to 1258 when it was extinguished by Mughal forces of Changiz Khan and his grandson Halaku.

During the Abbasid's rule, Baghdad was the hub of universe. It was probably the wealthiest and most populated city of the whole world. The wealth and splendour of court of Haraun-Al-Rashid were world renowned and through the tales of Arabian Nights the magnificence of court and life in Baghdad has captured popular fancy everywhere and in all ages. In Islamic world lot of fairy tales and stories are still popular. Both Ummayad and Abbasid Caliphs brought Islam to height of its zenith but later on they became pale persons in petty coats and Mongols and Turks gained prominence.

The great conqueror Muhamad Ghazni and Ghori established their successful rules in India and Seljuk Turks in western countries and in Middle East. Later on Seljuk Turks were succeeded by Ottoman Turks in the middle East and in eastern European Countries. Mongols called Tattars established their rule in Russia and Mughals led by Babar in India. Àt last in 17 the century power of these dynasties declined Emergence of Russia gave death blow to Tattar rule and began to threaten rule of Ottoman Turks in 18th century. In India after the death of Aurangzeb in 1707, rule of Mughals became merely a shadow of its glorious past.

In Persia Saffavi Shia rule was established and during Saffavi rule Persia made great progress but in the beginning of 18th century, its power declined due to constant wars with Uzbegs and Ottoman rulers and anarchical conditions began to prevail in Persia.

Taking advantage of the weakness of Saffavi rule, a great conqueror who was a shepherd and later on a docoit and conqueror namely Nadir Shah rose to power. Nadir Shah conquered Iran, Turkistan, Khurasan, Afghanistan and part of Hindustan. Probably he was one of the greatest conqueror of Asia. But after his death independent rule in Afghanistan was established by his general Ahmad Shah Abdali and Persia lost its glory and splendour in 19th century and anarchical conditions began to prevail there.

The Rule of Turks over Iraq and on Adjoining Territories and a Glimpse of Condition of Iraq from Abbasid Caliph to Ottoman Turks Rule

Empire of Abbasi Caliphs was destroyed by Mongols led by Chengiz Khan and later on by Halaqu Khan in 1258. It is such that Mongols slaughtered so many persons that water of rivers of Tigris and Euphrates flew red for many days. Thus Baghdad faced destruction from the hands of Mongols and they ruled for a short time mercilessly.

Mongols were replaced as rulers of Muslim empire by Ottoman Turks who ruled a vast Muslim empire containing Egypt, Sudan, Algeria etc. in Africa, Balkan countries in Europe and whole Middle East and Arab lands in Asia Ottoman Turks became a world power and declared themselves as calipah of whole Muslim world. Gradually their power declined and after their defeat in 1st world War, Iraq and Palestine fell under British mandate. For Ottoman rule, detailed description has been given in chapters of Turkey.

Ummayad Caliphs imported Sunni religion of Islam but Abbasid caliphs imposed Shia religion and made Baghdad as its Capital.

12

Iraq under British Mandate

Iraq after 1st World War of 1914

Great Britain after assuming her mandates on behalf of League of Nations thought it politic to conciliate the Arab sentiment. She compensated Feisal for the loss of his Syrian kingdom by making him King of Iraq in 1921. Another son of Sherif Hussein named Abdullah was made king of Trans-Jordania. Feisal was an able ruler and under him Iraq grew in wealth and power. He adroitly guided the agitation for self-government, wringing one concession after another from the British High Commissioner. At last in 1932, Great Britain concluded a treaty at Baghdad by which she recognized the independence of Iraq and promised to sponsor its admission as a member to the League of Nations. Britain retained a defensive alliance and some economic privileges in Iraq. King Feisal died in 1933 and was succeeded by his son Ghazi.

In 1937 Iraq signed alongwith Turkey, Persia and Afghanistan a non-aggression pact known as the Eastern or Saadabad Pact. When the Second World War broke out in September 1939 certain elements in Iraq became pro-Nazi in their attitude. Their leader was Rasid Ali Beg Gailani who engineered a military coup in Baghdad and made himself premier of Iraq. Nazi agents now flooded the country of Iraq and began to carry on vigorous Axis propaganda in favour of Germany and Italy. British troops poured in and quickly suppressed the Pro Nazi Iraqi revolution. Rashid Ali was forced to flight. When the World War II ended in 1945, Iraq became a member of the United Nations Organisation and confirmed her friendship with Britain by signing a friendly treaty of alliance and of mutual help for twenty years in 1948. Iraq was wary of the political twists of the Arab League and drew closer to her neighbours particularly with Persia and Turkey. His alignment developed into the Baghdad

Pact. In Trans-Jordania Abdullah proved less forceful and less able than his brother Feisal. He was more dependent on the Britishers for military and financial assistance. Hence, the progress of self-government in his small kingdom made very little progress.

In 1958, a group of young army officers overthrew the ministry of Nuri-el Said who was a staunch supporter of the West and killed King Feisal and proclaimed a Republic with Addul Karim Kaseem as Prime Minister. Abdul Karim Kaseem showed sympathy with left and he gave a death blow to Baghdad pact but he was murdered in 1963.

In Iraq after some initial nationalist rioting, the British set up an Iraqi national government in which each minister had a British adviser. The Amir Feisal (who had just been driven out of Syria by the French forces) was accepted a king of Iraq. Although extreme nationalists did not approve this set-up, but it was agreed by the Anglo-Iraqi Treaty of 1972 and Feisal as a king worked well. An elected parliament was introduced in 1924 and Feisal, a man of great personal charm and of political ability, proved to be an excellent ruler. With British help, industry and agriculture were encouraged, and organized and an efficient administrative system was introduced. The Britishers won Iraqi support by successfully opposing Turkish claims to the province of Mosul with its vast oil resources. In 1932, Iraq became fully independent, though Britain was allowed to keep two air bases allowed some privileges. According to one Arab nationalist, George Antonius, the modern state of Iraq owes its existence largely to the efforts and devotion of its British officials.

The British Policy in Iraq

Great Britain's vital interest in the mandate was of Iraq's rich oil resources. Its growing importance in East-West air transportation, and its proximity to the Persian Gulf. But these interests did not prevent the British diplomats from taking steps to satisfy Iraqi nationalism after the out break of rebellion in June 1920. In march 1921, the Iraqi throne was offered to Feisal, who had lost his throne in Syria. In a plebiscite Faisal was strongly supported as ruler of Iraq, and a few months later, he was proclaimed as king of Iraq. In 1922, Britain was only to supervise the finances and military affairs of the new Government of Iraq which made the country a constitutional monarchy with a bicameral legislature like England. In 1930, an Anglo-Iraqi treaty was signed which granted Iraq full Independence, and in 1932, Iraq was admitted as a full member to the League of Nations. By these concessions Britain avoided the conflict experienced by France in Syria and Lebanon but kept their vested interests intact.

During the late 1930's, however, the skilful propaganda of Fascist Italy, combined with Arab hostility regarding the British Policy in Palestine, brought about a decline of goodwill sympathy towards Britain in Iraq. So conditions in Iraq became anarchical.

Three dominant ingredients contributed to this situation : emotional and fierce nationalism coupled with political inexperience on the part of the masses of these new Arab states and prevailing economic frustration based on universally low standards of living for the common man (often complicated by the misuse of great wealth by the Government officials and a privileged aristocracy). Finally, the driving objective of Pan-Arabism, the achievement of some form of Political unity for all the Arab world, which would increase its influence and status in world affairs created unstable conditions.

The Middle East continued to be unstable and tumultuous after 1959; revolts occurred in Iraq and Syria. General Kassem of Iraq was assassinated in 1963 and his government which was sympathetic to left was overthrown. In Syria eight governments. Had been toppled by revolts between 1950 and 1964.

British Occupation of Iraq and British Mandate over Iraq

After the defeat of Ottoman Turks in 1st World War, Britain became ruler of Iraq as mandatory power on behalf of League of Nations but the British were having their troubles in Iraq. At the end of the war the British were occupying Basrah Baghdad, and Mosul etc., and controlling much of the land in between and on the far sides of both the rivers of Tigris and the Euphrates. Many British administrators coming in at the end of war to rule as mandatory power, brought their families, evidently with the understanding that this territory was not a temporary acquisition. Sir Arnold Wilson, acting High Commissioner, made a virtue of efficient government, irrespective of sentiment, prestige or local desires of Iraqi people. Arab unrest grew from the uncertainties of an Arab state of Iraq. When the news from San Remo arrived of establishing British mandate over Iraq the rebellion came. From May to October, 1920 a ferocious war, reportedly costing the British nearly £ 40,000,000, raged in Iraq with resistance forces dominating the whole land except the three cities of Basrah, Baghdad, and Mosul.

Hurriedly, Sir Percy Z. Cox was recalled form the ambassadorship in Tehran and was sent to Iraq as High Commissioner. The affection and esteem with which he was held by Iraqis was attested by the welcome showered upon him at his arrival on October 1, 1920 and by Iraqi rebellion's termination. Having been British political agent for the Persian Gulf for a number of years and Civil Commissioner in Iraq during the war years 1914-18 and immediately thereafter, Sir Percy Z. gathered around him a star-studded galaxy of advisers and assistants such as Miss Gertude Bell, his oriental secretary, and H.St.J.B. Philby. He organized a provisional council of State in which Sayyed Abd-al-Rahman-al-Cailani, Baghdad's nagub became prime Minister. Other portfolios were also distributed among influential families and religious sects from different part of the state. Each Minister had a British adviser, and in reality the council was supervised and guided by these advisers. All were finally under the direction of the High Commissioner, who wielded power like Viceroy of India. So very few Iraqis held any illusion that they had a true national government. This British mandatory rule was established in Iraq in 1920.

The State of the Kingdom of Iraq during British Mandatory Rule

Sir Percy Cox proposed convener of a national assembly to draw up electoral laws and to establish an Iraqi constitutional Government; but none was called until 1922 and it did not meet until 1924. The difficulty was the question of a ruler, and the British were fearful least an assembly choose someone unresponsive unfavourable to their interests. Although the Damascus Congress named Abdullah as king of Iraq but British selected his brother Faisal as king of Iraq. In 1920 Churchill's, Cairo conference nominated him. There were also other candidates, but the return to Baghdad of several hundred Arab officers who had served with the British in the Hijaz and Syria gave the necessary weight to the acceptance of Amir Faisal as ruler of Iraq. As such Abdallah withdrew his name and his brother Faisal arrived at Baghdad at the end of June, 1921. The council of state of Iraq invited him to become the king. As such a referendum was held in various districts of the state; and Faysal was elected and enthroned as king of Iraq on

August 23, 1921. Sir Percy and his associates managed this affair wonderfully and smoothly without much opposition.

Until his death twelve years later Amir Faisal served as King. His charm tact and broad tolerance made him an admirable choice; and his knowledge and experience made him acceptable to desert shaykhs, Bedouins, and the traders and townsmen of Iraq. At the same time Amir Faisal recognized fully the British position of control and appreciated the fact that without British support, he would never have become the king. Through the winter and spring of 1922 a treaty was drafted by the British in conduction with Amir Faisal and al-Gailani. At the last stages the council of state was brought in, and after a serious crisis in August this treaty was ratified in October 1922. It defined the special position of Great Britain in Iraq, actually giving to the British, military and economic control and, in a veiled manner, granted English nationals many immunities and privileges in Iraq. British advisers were accepted in all offices of Iraq. Its many articles justified the objections by the nationalists that the Treaty was probably only a sugar-coated mandate which, however translated, meant "subjection and colonization." Of Iraq under British supremacy.

Anglo-Iraqi Affairs during British Mandate over Iraq

In Iraq much uncertainty and agitation accompanied the elections for a constituent assembly that was convened in March, 1924. King Faisal in his speech from the throne urged the assembly to ratify the treaty with Britain, pass upon the constitution, and enact an electoral law for a parliament etc. So all of which was done in 1924. A new treaty with Britain was signed in 1926 and yet another also in 1927. The British pledged under certain qualifications that Iraq would be supported in 1932 for membership in the League of Nations: the qualifications stated however, raise such doubt with respect to Britain's sincerity because the treaty of 1927 was never ratified.

Later loopholes as to get League of Nations' support were removed, and the momentous Anglo-Iraqi Treaty of 1930 was achieved. This Treaty which became the prototype of the Anglo-Egyptian Treaty of 1936 and the treaties of France with Syria and Lebanon in the same year, was an alliance between Iraq and Great Britain for twenty-five years. The two countries agreed to follow a foreign policy and inconsistent with this Treaty, which meant that Iraq assented to "full and frank consultation in all matters" of foreign affairs to Britain. Iraq concurred to the presence of British troops in Mosul and in other districts for five years and gave a lease to several aerial bases. In return Britain contracted to defend Iraq in case of war. Attached to this Treaty, were annextures giving Britain considerable power in matters of finance, business, and education etc. and indicating that only British advisers were to be employed in preference of other nations. The signing of this treaty by Sir Francis Humphrys, British High Commissioner, and Nuri-al-Said Pasha, the Iraqi Prime Minister cleared the way for Iraqis membership in the League of Nations, which voted admission unanimously on October 3, 1932. The high commissioner became British ambassador the mandate was terminated and Iraq stood apparently as an independent state having friendship with Britain.

The Government of Iraq during British Mandate

The constitution of Iraq placed executive and administrative power in the hands of a cabinet headed by a Prime Minister and composed of at least six other ministers. This cabinet was jointly responsible to the chamber of deputies, which could force the cabinet to resign upon a vote of no confidence like Parliamentary Government of England. The king, however, would dissolve the chamber. Parliament was bicameral. The chamber of deputies was elected indirectly by universal manhood suffrage. It had one representative for every 20,000 male inhabitants with a special provision that four Christians and four Jews were also to be elected to give them representation in Iraqi parliament. Maximum life of a chamber was four years. The first chamber was elected in 1925 and elections in 1930 were held for the ninth chamber The senate *i.e.* Ist chamber or upper house was appointed by the king and had a membership of not more than one fourth of the chamber. Senators were appointed for eight years, and half were appointed every four years. Only the chamber could initiate legislation; and in appearance the chamber, was representative of the Iraqi people and held dominating position in the Iraqi government and public.

In practical application, however, the cabinet was the most powerful body like cabinet of India and no ever fell a vote of the no confidence. The cabinet controlled elections and obtained dismissal of the chamber when it deemed necessary. Yet there were twenty cabinets from 1925, when this constitution came into force, until the outbreak of World War II in 1939. A cabinet would promise to obtain full independence from Britain, and when it failed, it invited the opposition to try its hand, Ministers moved about from post to post in succeeding cabinets. Nuri-al-Said Pasha was elected four times as Prime Minister during this period, appropriately quipped; with a small pack of cards, you must shuffle them often. As such Iraqi cabinets were dominated by influential persons.

Perhaps the political and ministerial ferris wheel would not have been so pronounced had king Faisal lived longer. In 1923 Faisal became worn with fatigue. His health broke, and he died in Switzerland where he went for rest, for healthy environment and for medical care. He was succeeded immediately and without any opposition by his twenty-one-year-old son Ghazy. Young and inexperienced, the new king followed a constitutional policy based on the western tradition. However, Iraq might have been spared some of her political confusion of those years had Ghazi been sufficiently mature and sufficiently concerned with government to play an impartial and advisory part in national affairs. Addicted to fast motor cars, he was killed in an accident in 1939. Now he was succeeded by his four-year old son, who became the boy-king Faisal II, under the regency of prince Abd al-Illah, the king's maternal uncle and son of Prince Ali, king Faisal I's oldest brother.

Problems of Kurds in Iraq

Iraq was country which had many problems. But Iraq's problems were far from solved by the adoption of constitutional government, technical independence from Britain, and its admission to the League of Nations. In the northern part of the state Kurdish tribes were preponderant, and with their fellow tribesmen in Turkey and Iran they hoped for the peace settlement by establishment of Kurdistan. The Kurdish tribes were seminomadic and roamed about the mountains and valleys of the eastern highlands, moving freely from country to country and resisting control of outside authorities. They had no desire to be taxed or organized. The Iraqi government took punitive measures repeatedly against Kurdish uprisings in the neighbourhood of Mosul and Suleiment and served in the 1920's and early 1930's. Kurds were elected to Parliament and allowed to stay in Baghdad, but settling of the Kurdish tribes was by no means complete and in 1939 as Kurds were habituated to nomadic life.

During world war I, a group of Assyrians (Nestorians living along the upper Eupharates) joined with the British and fought against the Ottoman Turks. Leaving Turkey at the end of the conflict and finding themselves a homeless minority in Iraq, many accepted services in the British army stationed there. In 1933 after Iraq was free and a member of the League of Nations' incidents occurred between Assyrian villages, and a "pacification" by Iraq forces commanded by General Bakr Sidki. British helped Iraq to obtain a generous whitewash of the affair before the League in order not to jeopardize her position in Iraq. Assyrian leadership in this incident was probably not entirely blameless, for they were working for separate recognition of their community such as was accorded under the old millet system of the Ottoman Turkish Empire. Since this was contrary to Iraqi nationalism and unity so Baghdad could not consider it.

The most serious religious problem in Iraq arose from the lasting Islamic schism between Sunnites and Shiites. The latter held a population in majority but the former dominated the government and society. As long as king Faisal I lived, little trouble developed, for many Shiites were fondly under the delusion that he secretly belonged to their Shia sect. Shiites divines easily stirred their followers; and preachers, entering Iraq from Iran, could easily retire across the frontier when asylum was needed. As such Shia-Sunni-conflicts began after Amir Faisal.

Social Problems

In addition to the problem of minorities and of varying religious sects, there was a grave social and economic cleavage between townsmen and the tribes. The government of Iraq was definitely in the hands of townsmen, yet the tribes, and particularly their Sheikhs were powerful and influential forces in Iraq. At least eighty per cent of the population in Iraq earned their livelihood from the land, much of which was irrigated from ancient times. But the science of the irrigation had so degenerated over the centuries in Iraq that soils became salty and channels silted rapidly, compelling peasants to move frequently to new fertile lands. In the middle of river Euphrates areas the tribes also engaged themselves in stock raising, moving their herds from sparse pasturage as the cover was grazed. Thus the tribes had a constant tie with desert beduins. The tribal Sheikhs were recognized, perforce, by the British in their occupation of Mesopotamia the responsible heads of the districts, thereby obtaining a quasi-title of ownership of these lands. Every assembly and Parliament in Iraq always had a large number of these Shikhs as members of Iraqi Parliament.

They were invariably conservative and friendly to the British, in whom they saw a protection from the town dwelling middle class and educated Iraqi politician. Since the tribesmen were good soldiers, the tribes of the middle Euphrates were a force with which to contend until the Iraqi army which was equipped with the strength and mobility of more mechanized weapons. General Bakr Sidki again won his spurs of acclaim in 1935 by leading an armed expedition to quell a rising of the tribes of the middle Euphrates, with support of such army.

Iraqi Oil

One of the jarring factions in Iraqi politics, domestic as well as international, has been the oil resources of the country and their exploitation. Before the World War, I oil rights were granted by the Ottoman government to the Anatolian Railway company and the Baghdad Railway company. When the D' Arcy Exploration company became interested in the Mosul fields, the Turkish petroleum company was formed in 1912 with German, Dutch, and British ownership. The San Remo Conference turned over the German interests to the French, and during the Lausanne Conference the British agreed very reluctantly that half of their holdings, which by this time were owned by the Anglopersian oil company, would be made available for purchase by the American Standard Oil Company of New Jersey and its associates.

The Mosul controversy between England and Turkey was partly over oil; and when in 1925 it appeared likely that Mosul would be awarded to Iraq, British government gave a seventy-five year concession to the Turkish Petroleum Company. The terms granted rights to twenty-four rectangles of land, each of square miles, to be selected by the company within four years, after which all remaining areas would be opened to other companies. Several months later this concession was amended, changing royalties from a profit-sharing arrangement to a tonnage basis, but substance remained same.

Oil development, however, moved very slowly. Whereas the oil production by 1930 in Iran had increased to nearly 46,000,000 barrels, in Iraq it was only 909,000 barrels. Iraqi leaders charged that the Western oil concerns were holding back hampering oil production in Iraq and exploiting their wells in other parts of the world. Although this might be good business for the companies, but to Iraq it seemed entirely negligent, for she was losing revenue when it was sorely needed for its development.

A gigantic gusher was stuck at Babu Gurgur near Kirkuk in 1937, but the company did not select all of its plots by 1929 and the Iraqi government refused to extend the time. After consideration by the League of Nations and much negotiating a new concession was made in 1931 to the Iraq Petroleum Company, the company, name having been changed in 1929. The 1921, agreement gave outright concession to lands in the Baghdad and Mosul etc. Provinces east of the Tigris, except for a few districts where the Anglo-Persian Oil company had historic rights. Furthermore, the company pledged to build before 1936 a pipeline system to Haifa and the Syrian coast and also to begin annual payments of point £ 400,000 against future royalties. Half of this sum would be non-recoverable. Royalties were fixed at four gold shillings a ton for a period of twenty years. This pipeline was built from Kirkuk across the Tigris and the Euphrates. Thus it divided, one branch going to Haifa and one to Tripoli. Both branches began delivering oil in 1934. Properly.

Other companies also showed interests in Iraqi oil and development possibilities, and in 1932 a concession was given to the British Oil Development Company to lands west of the river Tirgis and north of the 33rd parallel. Payments of £ 100,000 began in 1933 and it steadily mounted. Thus, by the time Iraq attained her independence, she was also fast becoming independent economically. The concession to the British Oil Development Company just mentioned and another for the district in the south around Basrah have, through holding companies become affiliated or controlled by the Iraq Petroleum Company. Through further concessions in 1938 the latter company came to hold the oil production of all of Iraq in her hands. Thus foreign companies dominated all business in Iraq.

While oil brought Iraq in touch with the great powers, order raids by nomads on the deserts and also in the mountains led interminable negotiations and difficulties with the smaller states upon her frontiers. Boundary settlements with varying degrees of permanence were also made with Kuwait, Saudi Arabia, Trans Jordan, Syria, Turkey, and Iran etc. As Iran due the Saadabad pact and Arabia, took further step in regulating the frontiers and relations with Turkey and Iran the Saadabad pact was signed by the foreign ministers of Iraq, Iran, Turkey, and Afghanistan etc. at the Shah's palace near Tehran on July 8, 1937. Thus Iran marched to a path of progress, peace and economic prosperity.

Politics in Iraq during Mandatory Period of Britain

British advisors and Amir Faisal tried for political stability in Iraq domestic politics from the very beginning in Iraq were heavily changed with personalities. Each dynamic figure gathered about him. A clientele, published a newspaper, and he organized a political party. Eagerness for personal power, prestige, and position, however, was sublimated in the struggle for independence from Britain. Many parties emerged and flourished, and died quickly; members and even leaders went one after another with considerable ease. In the 1920's the three most important and influential durable parties were the National Party the Progressive Party and the People's Parties. Each political party pledged to throw off the British treaty mandates subterfuge and obtain real independence for Iraq. The Progressive Party collapsed in 1929, when its leader, Abd-al-Muhsin al-Sadun, who had served as Prime Minister on three separate occasions, committed suicide. The people's party was headed by Yasin al-Hashmi, who in the 1930's led his followers into a collective party known as the National Brotherhood (Ikha al-Watani), he was Prime Minister twice and he was active in politics and held various portfolios in a number of ministries until the coup. He served different ministries and organized the National Party. Disillusioned by the acts of his political associates, he moved and leaned toward the left. In 1933, he joined the Reform Party and took an active part in the coup.

In 1930 when Nuri al-Said Pasha concluded the Anglo-Iraqi Treaty of Alliance, he revived the pre-war Covenanters Party (Al-Ahd). But its members were soon swallowed up by the political confusion of independence. Nuri Pahs, an Iraqi, who served in the Ottoman army and then joined the Hijaz force supporting the cause of Arab revolt, returned to Baghdad, where he worked for the kinship of Faisal. He held office in many cabinets as foreign minister. He was Prime Minister four times before the outbreak of World War II. In 1939 there was a strong stabilizing force for better government in Iraq.

Nuri's opponents in 1930 joined under both Yasin al-Hashimi and Rashid Ali al-Gailani to form the National Brotherhood Party. This party dominated the Iraqi government and the cabinets from 1930 and when Iraq was admitted to the League of Nations. It dominated politics until it was overthrown by the 1936 coup. Meanwhile, another political party was created. The Reform Party (Ahali) resulted from the meetings and discussions of younger Western-educated men who were liberal in their views and outlook and were desirous of a more democratic and socialistic government to be established in Iraq. They were disgusted with the shuffling corruption of the conservative governments conducted by their elders. For a few years through their party newspaper, they had wide influence, but they soon succumbed to experienced politicians like Hikmat Sulayman and Jafar Abu al-Timman etc.

Realizing that the power of the National Brotherhood Government could not be broken and that the cabinet of Yasin al-Hashimi and Rashid Ali-al-Gailani could not be removed without active assistance of the army, Hikmat Sulayman brought about a coalescence of the Ahali group with disgruntled army officers who felt that Iraq was not yet ready for full Western democracy. The Army intervened. The army "hero" who engineered coup proved to be Bakr Sidki. The plot ripened and in the autumn of 1936. So Bakr Sidki Pasha moved to Baghdad. Yasin al-Hashimi, Rashid Ali-al-Gaoamo and Miro etc. brought military coup in Iraq. Parliament was dissolved and new elections were so rigged as to return a great number of deputies who had never served in any previous chamber. The socialist predilections of the Ahali group led to quarrels with Bakr Sidki and his army officers. Other officers became jealous of Bakr Sidki and in August 1937, he was assassinated. Another army coup detat soon ended the first coup lasted until 1941 one army coup followed another coup most methodically, while politics of Iraq descended to personal vilification and vulgar invective. As such Iraq was deeply immersed in this national suffering when World War II began in September 1939. Thus British mandatory rule did not prove successful in Iraq and even after that political condition of Iraq proved unstable. As such Iraq did not feel peace, progress and prosperity between the period of two wars. Inspite of all this great progress was made in oil exploration which made Iraq rich. Education, railway and scientific inventions modernized Iraq inspite of unstable political conditions.

As such British writers claim mandatory rule of Britain over Iraq as beneficial while others claim it as failure. To be fair and impartial, it may be stated that mandatory rule of Britain over Iraq was beneficial to her in economic, education and transport spheres but in political sphere constitutional and parliamentary government provide unsuccessful.

13

Iraq Towards Independence

History of Iraq till it became Independent and Problems of Iraq during British Mandate

Iraq in ancient history was called Mesopotamia and is considered along with Egypt as cradle of human civilization. As such it is one of the important countries in today's world political map. It has drawn more world attentions after World War II, when both power blocks tried to win her cooperation. But historically the country has remained a part of the Turkish Ottoman empire. For centuries together there was close relationship between the two. The people were not political by conscious even within the empire. Therefore for a very long time politically upheavels of that country did not influence their traditional outlook and conservative approach which continued in 19th century as it was. It was only in the last years of the 19th century that same sort of national awakening came in this country due to western influence and awakening among Arabs.

First World War and Iraq. During the First World War of 1914-18 Britain and France repeatedly declared that they would give full freedom to Arabs after this 1st World War was over. It was in this hope that the Iraq extended maximum co-operation to Britain during the World War I against Turkey. She was sure that after the war was over, she would be helped in getting freedom from the Turkish empire. But as the war was over, Britain did not honour her commitment and pledge. Instead of this Britain became mandatory power over Iraq on behalf of League of Nations and a situation which was intolerable for developed Iraq who had expected full freedom and had also made sacrifices for independence. Iraqi nationalists organized themselves with the result that there was a rebellion in the country in 1920. Britain was all along hopeful that it would be in a position to control the situation but riots and disturbances made it clear that the situation was much worse than was expected and that there was a need of change in British policy. As such Britain decided that whereas mandate system should continue, relations between the two countries should be governed on the basis of treaties which may be signed between the two countries. This was an important break though in the relationship between the two countries. Relations should be governed on the basis of treaties which may be signed between the two countries inspired hope of goodwill. This was an important break also in the relationship between the two countries in the sense that a via media could be found out under which Britain's supremacy remained unchallenged keeping in the national aspirations and situations could be changed and people may be kept satisfied. It was also important in the sense that an arrangement became possible where negotiations and not force was accepted as a media for solving all problems between Britain and Iraq.

Faisal as a King of Iraq

Amir Faisal had been expelled from Syria by French forces but Britain decided to place him on the throne of Iraq. This was not acceptable to some people who demanded that there should be a Constituent Assembly in the country, which should frame constitution and should also decide the form of government for Iraq. There were riots in the country but these were crushed by Sir Percy Cox, who was British High Commissioner in that country. He also set up a Ministry under Naqib. This was obviously a situation which was not acceptable to nationalists and extremists who had been crushed simply for demanding a Constituent Assembly and a democratic form of government which probably suited them most and not an imposed monarchy. In order to solve this thorny problem at Cairo a meeting was convened. In April 1921, to solve not only the problem of Iraq but of the whole Middle East meeting took place. As a result referendum was held in Iraq to choose their monarch and Amir Faisal was the choice of Iraqi voters by referendum.

Problems of Faisal. Amir Faisal became monarch of Iraq, but his coming to the throne created many difficult problems. His first problem was that he had no real links with Iraq over which he was to rule. Then another problem was that the people of Iraq felt that he was the choice of Britain and in fact representative of that government who had been imposed her rule on them. Accordingly he could not win love and affection of some people of Iraq which was badly needed at this critical juncture. Then another difficulty was that the people of Iraq were backward and feeling of nationalism were strong only among a small minority of educated middle class people. Accordingly they needed much goading and training. Since the people of Iraq were backward therefore it was always difficult to mobilize them as and when need arose. There were different elements in Iraqi population and some of them were nomads to whom it was a difficult task for any ruler to consolidate them into a compact nationality so that the people were not in a position to win freedom from British control. Due to their backwardness it was increasingly difficult to raise their living standard and achieve progress. Though the nationalists wanted much yet they were very much handicapped because they had no mass support both due to economic backwardness and lack of feelings of nationalism and political consciousness of their rights.

Then there was another great difficulty. In Iraq there were several tribes. Britain had followed a deliberate policy of keeping them in isolation. These tribes were nomads and in constant state of backwardness. With the passage of time an impression had been given to these tribal people that Britain was their only well wisher and that they could rise and prosper only under the British patronage. Accordingly they were not keen to associate themselves or co-operate with the nationalists who according to them were creating unnecessary problems for the Britishers. Probably they were right as Britishers treated all Iraqies equally while Iraqies hated these tribal people.

Then there was another problem in Iraq. The Arabs were of course in majority but there were some important minorities. These included the Kurds and the Assyrians etc. and others. There were traditionally against the Arabs and as such Arab nationalism in Iraq had no meaning for them. In fact they wanted to check the consolidation of the movement with all power at their command. For the monarch then there was another problem. Dealing with the minorities as it was in no way less problematic, but unfortunate situation was that the Arabs who formed the majority were themselves divided. These were divided in Shias and Sunnis factions in this country. As such the Arabs were in majority, yet they were economically backward as compared with the others, so they were bitterly opposed to

British rule in the country as the rulers did not belong to their religions. But their political influence was much less as compared with those of the sunnies in Iraq. Next then comes the problem of political awakening. There was no political consciousness in that country. There was no active and enlightened political leadership in fact in the political field, as such it can be said that political consciousness was very badly missing. So there were very knotty problems and everything was in mess. Amir Faisal faced many problems. Military officers in Iraq were very much politically awakened since they had worked for a long time with Amir Faisal before he was installed as the king. They had many expectations. Amir Faisal was in horn's dilemma as how to tackle knotty problem of Iraqi people, it was no firm attitude of Britain towards Iraq. British political leadership was sharply divided on their attitude towards Iraq, there was no way out and politicians who believed that Britain should govern the country with all firmness and there should be no relaxation in that. According to them Iraq was of such a strategic importance that British control was unavoidable. Moreover, they also argued that British blood was shed so that Iraq became free from Turkish Yoke. They also felt that there was moral and political justification of British control over Iraq. On the other hand : there was another section of British society which felt that Iraq should be given considerable freedom. According to them British Government is committed for Arab statehood and that Iraq has made certain sacrifices in the World War I to win their freedom. So it would be absolutely wrong to betray Iraqi nationalist. As such this divided approach and non-firmness on the part of Britain and its flexibility created many problems and a situation of uncertainty prevailed.

Amir Faisal's Role as Monarch. Amir Faisal had been elevated as a monarch, with British help and by plebiscite but at a time which was full of difficulties. Under these circumstances many would have lost courage and tact as throne was not bed of roses. But King Faisal showed extraordinary courage, and tact etc., and got ready to face the problems which faced his country. He wanted to give a path for other Arab leaders as to how could they make progress under the mandatory rule of Britain and France. He played the role of a sober leader between the British government and Iraqi leaders through interests of both clashed. Whenever there was, a problem between the two, he would make his people realize their limitation and make the British politicians feel the strength of the people of

Iraq. In this way he would try to strike a balance between the two. The British Government already had faith in him but in the beginning the people of Iraq had no faith in him and it as felt that the King Faisal was British agent. But king, by his conduct and behaviour in soon became acceptable to Iraqi leaders as well. They also began to appreciate his views to every problem.

Iraqi leaders began to feel that the king Faisal was working for their welfare. The king also created political awakening among his Iraqi people and made them realize that unless and until there was political awakening nothing remarkable was possible. Faisal remained king of Iraq for about 12 years *i.e.* from (1921-33) and during the course of his stay he became a real bridge between the people of Iraq and the British administrators. He showed to the Arab world that with sincerity of purpose, it was possible to awaken the people and consolidate and guide them in the right direction. During rule of Faisal, many treaties took place.

British Treaties with Iraq. As there were riots so British Government arrived at an agreement with the people of Iraq that whereas mandate would continue and in fact would not be challenged but their mutual relationship would be governed with the help of certain treaties which would be concluded as and when time and need and opportunity would arise. Accordingly some important treaties were concluded between the British and Iraqi Governments. Since these played an important role between the mutual relations of both the countries so it is useful to discuss these in some detail.

Treaty of 1922. This treaty was concluded at a time when there was sufficient misunderstanding between the king Faisal and the people of Iraq. Iraqies still considered their kind as imposition of Britain and tool of British imperialism. According to his treaty, it was provided that the British Government would have the special power to appoint advisers to the Government of Iraq. It would have army in Iraq to protect the foreigners settled in that country. Another important provision of this treaty was that British Government would help Iraq both in the formulation of forming fiscal policies of Iraq. The provisions of this treaty were to remain in force for a period of ten years. In this way, this treaty completely established British supremacy over Iraq and did not relax very much he control to mandatory power over Iraq. It was, however, provided in this treaty, that as soon as possible, mandatory power would try to secure a seat for Iraq in the League of Nations. On March 27, 1924, Iraqi Constituent Assembly was convened to ratify this treaty. The extremists and nationalists very vehemently opposed this treaty and a stage came when British Government openly stated that in case this treaty was not ratified armed force would be used to get it enforced. It was under this there at that this treaty of 1922, was enforced and accepted by Iraq.

Treaty of 1926. Another treaty between Iraq and Britain was concluded in 1926. In 1925 Mosul's question came up to the front and became an apple of discord between Iraq and Turkey because both Turkey and Iraq claimed that they had heir claim over the territory of Mosul. This case was referred to League Council which decided the issue in favour of Iraq. Accordingly a meeting of representatives of Britain, Turkey and Iraq was convened to settle the boundaries between Iraq and Turkey. A treaty was concluded in which among other things, it was provided that British control in financial and military matters, would be relaxed. It was also made clear that the British Government would make every effort for the entry of Iraq in League of Nations.

Treaty of 1930. In 1930 another treaty was concluded between the two countries. According to provisions of this treaty, Britain agreed to sponsor Iraq's membership to League of Nations. There would be Anglo-Iraqi alliance which would be continued for a period of 25 years as described before. During this period of 25 years both the countries would consult each-other in all foreign affairs and would try to follow a common foreign policy. In other words Britain indirectly wanted to have control over Iraq's foreign policy. It was also provided that all such powers and responsibilities which Britain had as a mandatory power of League of Nations would be transferred to the king of Iraq; which included the defence of Iraq also. The Government of Iraq would however, allow British Government to retain its air force bases in the country. There would also be a British military mission in the country which would help Iraq in building up a strong national army on modern lines. It was also provided in this treaty that in case war broke out both Iraq and Britain would act as allies and would help each other in winning war with mutual co-operation.

It was on the basis of this treaty that Britain sponsored Iraq's case of admission to League of Nations and in 1932, Iraq became League's member and soon thereafter British mandate was terminated. She began to establish diplomatic relations with other nations and also began to improve in internal administration. Britain and Iraq secured, peace the later progressed and prospered during British rule.

The Condition of Iraq after Mandatory Rule of Britain

In 1933 British mandate over Iraq came to an end and with that there also came an era of political instability in that country primarily because Amir Faisal who was controlling the situation in Iraq died in 1933 and there was no political leader of his stature standing who could control the situation in Iraq. He was succeeded by his son Ghazi, who was quite inexperienced. Under him the ruling party got itself divided into pro-British and anti-British factions. Taking advantage of this political instability, a mily, coup was staged in this country in 1936. In 1936 Ghazi also died in an accident and was succeeded by his minor son Faisal. In order to enable him to carry on his work as a monarch a regency under Amir Abdullah was set up. Since the monarch was minor therefore real power was enjoyed by the reagent. As the Second World War broke out in 1939, Iraq-decided to finally to sever its relations with Turkey.

When world War II broke out there was absolutely no political stability in that country. Several world powers desired its support till a pro-German political leader Rashid Ali captured power in Iraq. He was not prepared to give British troops, a passage to pass through Iraq which obviously was against all treaties. So it was intolerable for the Britishers. There were some negotiations which ultimately failed and Britain decided to invade this country in 1941. Rashid Ali could not check the onslaught of British invasion and was ultimately ousted and in his place British Government managed to bring his own favorable people, to power. In 1943, Iraq also joined war against Nazi Germany under Nuri-al-Sayeed. He was Pro-British and a very powerful person and he ably guided his people during difficult war days. It was under him that Arab League was founded and an Arab-League pact was signed in 1945. This is how the situation prevailed in Iraq when World War II came to an end in 1945.

Iraq continued to be good friend of British-American Alliance even after the war. Iraq joined military pacts with these powers. As such United States of America gave massive military and economic aid to Iraq to improve and build her economy. This military alliance culminated in Baghdad Pact but it was terminated when Kasim came in power. General Kasim leaned towards left and followed anti British policy.

Condition during World War II and after it

In 1939, when World War II was declared Iraq leaned towards Germany but from the declaration of war against the Axis by Iraq in January, 1943 Iraq followed pro British policy until the Revolution of 1958. There were twenty-one changes of Prime Minister between 1943 to 1958 comprising thirteen different men. On six different occasions Nuri al-Said Pasha occupied that august position; and generally he was the most powerful political leader in Iraq. When he was not Prime Minister, he served as Minister of defence or from his seat in the senate he pulled the strings and directed his political followers to buy others in order to gain majority for himself.

Elections for the chamber of deputies were usually well managed and were probably neither four non-impartial so these elections lacked public support and coups became common feature of political life of Iraq.

In 1939 when king Ghazi was killed at the age of twenty-seven in an automobile accident, the throne passed to his four-year old son Faysal II. King Ghazi's cousin Abdul-Illah the son of Ali and dispossessed king of the Hijaz, became regent and heir to the Iraqi throne. The authority of the king was prescribed by the Iraqi throne. The authority of the king was prescribed by the Iraqi constitution; yet the regent's influence was fell in all quarters of Iraq through these most difficult years of World War II during the Palestine war, and the end of imperialism. On May 2, 1953 king Faisal II reached his eighteenth year and assumed full power.

The experience of the British with the Rashid Ali episode during the World War II opened their eyes to the necessity of revamping their attitude towards Iraq. Iraqi leaders, indirectly encouraged by growing American interest in this area of middle east pressed for a new treaty to replace the treaty of 1930. Negotiations led to the signing of an Anglo-Iraqi treaty at Portsmouth by which England on January 15, 1948, agreed to withdraw her forces from her two air bases of Iraq but retained the right to send troops in case of need. This incited the opposition parties for reasons recited in Baghdad, and the regent declared publicly that this new treaty did not realize the national aims of Iraq. The day after the Prime Minister Salih Jabri reached Baghdad from London and had to flew for safety to Transjordan. As such this treaty was never ratified, and the 1930, treaty remained in force until Britain joined the Baghdad Pact in 1955.

In 1947, Salih Jabri, who was serving as convenient screen for Senator Nuri al-Said, tried to bring about Iraq's union with Transjordan as both were ruled by Hesmite Kings. In the end, he settled for a treaty of friendship and of brotherhood by which each party must consult the other in matters of foreign affairs and announced its Intention to establish security and co-operations in the Palestine and complete mutual understanding all matters. Although it was criticized in parliament but it was ratified in June and served as the basis for joint operations in the Palestinian wars. The treaty of friendship with Turkish possession of the Sanjak of Alexandria aligned Iraq with powers opposed to the Soviet Union and her satellites. More significantly, the Egypto-Saudi camp within the Arab League, (Transjordan signed one treaty with Turkey, too).

Iraq, however, did not consider her actions as violating the letter or the spirit of the Arab aims and inspirations. Actually, the moment for the formation of the Arab league had some of its roots in Baghdad, and Iraq leaders heartily supported actions of the Arab league except in cases directed against Iraq and of establishment of Israel, so in 1947, Iraq protested against the partition of Palestine; and between 15,000 and 20,000 soldiers were at the front alongside the Arab region of Transjordan in the Arab Israeli war. These forces were probably the most successful of any Arab army; at one time they were in sight of the Mediterranean sea coast and were only eight miles from this coast when armistice negotiations began in 1949. Since Syrian and Egyptian forces had been defeated by Israel and since Iraqi troops were obviously unable to risk facing the entire Israeli army alone, the Iraqi troops withdrew. As such Iraqi leaders agreed to accept, pursuant to the Iraqi Transjordan treaty of friendship and brotherhood, whatever armistice arrangement Transjordan could make. When these were made in April, Iraq's unpaid and ragged army, sold its equipment and went home. This created bad precedent.

Although the geographical position of Iraq precluded any appreciable number of Arab Palestinian refugees locating there, sympathy in Iraq for them ran high. Responsible officials declared, they would not open any negotiations with Israel until the plight of the Palestinian refugees was relieved. Ill feeling towards Jews in Iraq mounted in proportion to the misery of the Palestinian refugees and aggravated by the general disillusionment over the Arab Israeli war's outcome. In October, Nuri-al-Said made the suggestion that Iraq Jews should be sent to Israel. Public acts against Jews in Iraq multiplied following foot steps of Nazi Germany. In March, 1950, law was passed permitting Jews to renounce their Iraqi citizenship and in the following months many thousands Jews left Iraq. In May, over 50,000 Jews were flown to Israel and before the year of war out almost all Jews were forced to leave Iraq. Most of them went to Israel but some went to U.S.A. and other western countries. Frustration and unrest mushroomed in Iraq. This was especially true about Baghdad, whose population was expanding very rapidly. Lack of full independence from Britain, the Palestine war fiasco, brought, political corruption, nationalization of oil in Iran and the new fifty-fifty profit-margin arrangement in Saudi Arabia. The high cost of living and ownership of land and the disastrous annual flooding of section of Baghdad were the concern of many Iraqis since the political structure in Iraq hardly touched the ordinary person as such "grass roots" stability in Iraqi government was absent. An explosion occurred in November 1952 over some examinations given by the dean of School of Pharmacy. Demonstrations turned into general riots, which were greatly exploited by the Communists. The regent declared martial law in Iraq called upon the army, and appointed Chief of Staff of army General Nur al-Din Mahmud as Prime Minister. The later abolished political parties, jailed rigid and left-wing party leaders, closed the schools and all but one newspaper was allowed and imposed curfew on Baghdad. Thus a kind of emergency was imposed in Iraq.

This emergency was clamped just in time, but professional politicians were frightened and realized that reform of many kinds had to be initiated. Fortunately new financial resources were at hand. Oil production, because of the close-down of oil refinery at Abdan, had been expanded; and a new 30-inch pipeline from Kirkuk to Banyas on the Mediterranean sea had just been opened.

More important was that the Iraq petroleum company's agreement in 1952, to a new schedule of royalties, increasing them to fifty per cent of the profits before taxes. This treaty was retrospectively to 1951 and as world requirement of petroleum spurted so royalties mounted until in 1955 they were estimated of more than $ 250,000,000. Thus Iraq become rich due oil exploration by a law passed in 1950 seventy per cent of all oil royalties were devoted to economic development of a permanent nature. The most outstanding achievements were flood control and irrigation projects on the rivers of Euphrates, the Tugrusm and the Diyeli rivers. Aided by a loan of $ 12,800,000 in 1950 from the International Bank, the development board began scheme of flood control and irrigation works at Samarra on the river Tigris and at Ramadi on water. As dry depression of the size of the Dead lake was created in the rather depression which made it possible to reclaim valuable land by irrigation. Another project at Musaiyb, about forty miles south of Baghdad, was completed in 1957. This land irrigated and drained by new schemes provided plots for 5,000 peasant families. Since a survey made in 1950 revealed that nearly eighty per cent of cultivable land in Iraq was state owned and unoccupied, the development board through the Musaiyb project and similar actions under the Homestead Act (Dyhatlah) of 1945 made concrete developments to improve the lot of poverty ridden sharecroppers and landless labourers and poor farmers.

Other useful development cleared vast slum areas in Baghdad and launched public-housing projects. Schools were extended to push down illiteracy rates. The state aided the Date Growers Association in processing, storing, and in marketing its products. A large government owned oil refinery was opened in Basrah in 1952; and the Baghdad Light and Power Company was nationalized in 1955, with compensation of about 56,00,000 to the owners. In Mosul in 1953, a cotton-spinning factory was opened; to supply one third of Iraq's requirements. A five year development plan was Outlined to run from 1956 to 1960 and to extend : $ 430,000,000 for flood control and irrigation etc. Thus $ 190,000,000 were spent for industry, mining and electric power; $ 180,000,000 for roads $ 90,000,000 for public buildings, including schools, $ 80,000,000 for hospitals and sanitation; $ 70,000,000 for public housing and $ 65,000,000 for bridges. In 1957, $ 40,000,000 was added for a social-development programme. Even the great reduction of oil production for several months in 1956-1957 during the Sinai was did not curtail or lessen the programme of the development board, which announced that it held over $ 280,000,000 in unspent funds. Many Political leaders looked into the future to see a great and prosperous Iraq, provided there was internal peace and no attacks from the Soviet bloc.

Others were extremely impatient and believed that the government of Nuri al-Said moved too slowly, too inefficiently, and too indifferently to achieve a batter life for the Iraqi people particularly for downtrodden masses.

Iraq because of its proximity with U.S.S.R. and because of the two Soviet States in Kurdistan and Azerbaijan, in 1946-1947 Iraqi leaders had a more discerning respects and fear of Russian power and of Russian expansion than other Arab leaders. Consequently, it was expedient to favour cordial relations with U.S.S.R. Consequently, it was natural and expedient to Arab leaders to cultivate friendship with Russia. Consequently but some favoured cordial relations with Turkey, Great Britain and the United States to check Russian expansion. Although the public attacked these three foreign states from time to time but the concerted policy of the Iraqi government was to continue friendly relationships with each. The treaty with Turkey was concluded in 1947. In 1951 Iraq requested for aid from U.S.A. and which was arranged.

In the second election of 1954 his Constitutional Union party received 94 seat, and Independents, all of whom were supporters, won 29 seats. This left 12 seats which were divided among the Umma, Istiklal and Popular Front parties, all of these were dissolved in November, 1952 and again in 1954. These moves were instigated to force political parties to reorganize or to reapply for party licence, which might be denied to some parties. The Communist party remained underground and worked assiduously through other groups and parties Istiklal, which had been fascist, collaborated with the Communists, whose leader was Yusuf Salman Yusuf, better known as Fahd. In Iraq the Communists found their following mostly among the in educated unemployed youths of the lower-middle class in Baghdad, Basrah and in other large cities and in the fascists who adhered to the Rashid Ali movement from 1935 to 1942, but influence of Communists remained negligible up to coup of Gen. Kasim.

In 1955, however, the situation changed rapidly. The U.S.S.R. entered the Middle East diplomatically, and Iraq reacted by signing on February 24 the so called Baghdad pact with western powers and Turkey. In general this pact repeated the terms of the treaty of friendship, but it added military co-operation and co-ordination between Iraq, Turkey and Britain etc. In April, Britain adhered to the treaty by signing an exceedingly important agreement with Iraq. Among other things, this agreement wiped out the treaty of 1930, provided for Britain to evacuate her troops and air force from the Habbaniya and Shuayba air fields, and gave fuller sovereignty and independence to Iraq to fulfil her desires. It was similar to those granted earlier by Britain to Egypt and to Syria by France soon Iran and Pakistan. joined the Baghdad pact making an alliance of a chain of states separating the Soviet block from the strategic areas of the Middle East. Although the United States did not join this Baghdad Pact but she sent military missions to provide military equipment for member states of Baghdad Pact and affiliated officially with the pact's military and economic committees. Iraq received twelve Centurion tanks in 1956 and twenty-eight more in 1957.

14

IRAQ AFTER BAGHDAD PACT

Condition of Iraq after Baghdad Pact of 1955

Baghdad Pact was disliked by Soviet block and Col. Nasser of Egypt viewed this Baghdad Pact as a threat to her control over the Arab League and her leadership in the Arab world. Nuri-al-Said was accused of being the tool of British imperialism and of restoring colonial status of Iraq. Syria first tried to reconcile the quarrel between Cairo and Baghdad, but in the end succumbed to Egyptian oratory and Saudi money and participated in the Damascus pact in opposition to this Baghdad Pact. But Iraqi leaders calling Nasser a dictator and declaring that the Baghdad Pact was Iraq's concern, Nuri al-Said held firm to this Baghdad Pact. He was confident that peace and security from fears of Russia, economic development and an increased standard of living, and a cultural and social renaissance would create in Iraq's life and society to parallel the modern Turkey as well as the medieval splendour and wealth of the days of Caliph Harun al-Rashid. Thus Iraq's leaders painted a rosy picture of Baghdad Pact.

Although Nasser was regarded as a genuine rival for leadership in the Arab world, Nuri al-Said always defended Arab feelings against the west and vehemently opposed that Western threats of force when Nasser nationalized the Suez Canal in 1956 and western powers violated the United Nations charter. When Israel, France, and England invaded Egypt in 1956, Iraq was in a very embarrassing position. Her army, poised on the Jordanian border because of the apprehension of Israel which military build-up of Israel had endangered, entered Jordan; and she also broke diplomatic relations with France. The claim against Great Britain was fiery in Baghdad. The Iraqi officials boycotted all meeting of Baghdad Pact from November, 1956 to March, 1957 whenever Britain was represented. Iraqi

Parliament was suspended in December; five opposition leaders were arrested; and numerous non-Iraqi Arabs were deported. When parliament was reconvened in February, Nuri received a vote of confidence of 79 to 14. Syria complained of insistently over the presence of Iraqi troops in Jordan and urged that they were to be recalled in December. World opinion having halted further military action in the Palestine-Sinai region and assured a containment of this the Suez Canal war of 1956 Any semblance of normalcy was not attained until March 1957, when, the pipelines in Syria were repaired. At this time, oil production was resumed reports indicated that Iraq's a loss $ 90,000,000 in royalties because of this break.

With the coming of spring, the return to relative peace, and the flow of oil, Nuri al-Said resigned. As such Ali Jawdat assumed the office, to be followed a few months later by Nuri's close friend, Abd-al-Wahhab Marjan. The Iraqi government faced opposition from Cairo and Damascus, so Nuri al-Said visited several European capitals and Washington to discuss and see in more support fro the Baghdad Pact and amicable solution to the Israeli problems. As the process of the United Arab Republic' formation materialised so the union between Iraq and Jordan which had been discussed for many years gained popularity. The annexing of Jordan of Palestinian territory was not liked so it began to be openly proposed in December, 1956. The Union of Syria and Egypt forced the issue in Jordan, where the government of king Husain could not endure opposition of Syria and Egypt as a solitary force. In February, 1958, King Faisal went to Jordan and Capital of Amman; and after visits there by Nuri al-Said and Crown Prince Abd-al-Illah, often called the real power in Iraq and an Arab federation of Iraq and Jordan was proclaimed. King Faisal was recognized as chief of State and King Husain as chief. Jordan as second in leadership and successor to the headship should his cousin die or be removed. Defence, foreign affairs finance, and education etc. for the whole state were consolidated but treaties and law retained their validity separately only in each state and were not binding upon the other state. In March a federal council composed of fifteen members from each state was named, and new constitution was drafted and duly proclaimed.

In Iraq Nuri-al-Said resumed the post of Prime Minister; Parliament was dissolved; and a call went out for elections for a new Parliament to ratify this new constitution based on Iraqi and Jordanian friendship.

Upon hearing this news President Nasser congratulated the two kings for completing this federation; but in a few weeks the friendly remarks turned into violent condemnations and open invitations to Arab nationalists in each state to remove the kings, by revolt and assassination, if necessary. The May elections of Iran turned out as expected. Nuri al-Said's supporters were returned in overwhelming majority. In most districts there was no contest; and in some perhaps not even a vote was taken. On May 10, 1958, Iraqi Parliament ratified this constitution of the federation of Iraq and Jordan, King Husain supposed that he had found someone who would protect him, precisely at that moment, however, rebellious disturbances in Lebanon shook the Arab world.

Impact of Federation of Iraq and Jordan and Coup of Gen. Kasim and Republic of Iraq after Federation of Iraq and Jordan

Federation of Iraq and Jordan annoyed Egypt and Saudi-Arabia to traditional unity and Soviet both its pupet Syrian Government. So all these powers largely waited for an opportunity. Iraqi troops were ordered in July to march into Jordan to be ready to safeguard the Shamun administration if needed. But their commander, General Abdul Karim Kasim, refused to fight against other Arabs and he turned upon Baghdad; and in an easy and swift coup date on July 14, 1958 over threw the king and Nuri al-Said. As they were bought unawates so both of them lost their lives in their revolution. The Baghdad mob became delirious with excitement, sacked the British Embassy, and also seized a few Europeans and Jordanians. Order, however, as quickly attained. The reverberations from this successful blow were felt all around the world, and secondary reactions to it were more pertinent else-where than in Iraq. This ended pro British regime in Iraq and gave death blow to Baghdad pact and to federation of Iraq and Jordan. Probably this coup come due to support of Soviet Union, Egypt and Saudi Arabia and Syria etc. General Kasim proclaimed the Republic of Iraq and became Prime Minister of the state. Oil production did not stop; the pipelines were undamaged; and apparently neutrality was pronounced as the policy of the state. Within less than a month this new government was recognized by Soviet block countries and by Egypt etc. and also by the United States of America. Kasim declared that the Republic would honour Iraq's international obligations and did not formally resign from the Baghdad Pact. When king Husain announced that he was assuming the position of chief of state of the Arab federation Gen. Kasim renounced this union and Jordan was forced to acknowledge the demise of the federation of Jordan and Iraq.

The completeness of this revolution and its full acceptance by the general Iraqi population throughout the state amazed only those who were not familiar with social and national conditions of Muslim Arab world, Nuri-al-Said was probably thoroughly disliked in Iraq, and perhaps the crown prince was also hated. The same government had been in power for too long and had failed to satisfy the ambitions aspiration and of the majority of extremist leaders. Land reform, poverty and the low standard of living, defeat in Israeli wars, lack of social advances for the urban masses, lack of sanitation and health, and the depressed state of the education created dissatisfaction. Its supporters were people of middle class, but a few of these problems which the people of Iraq felt pressing upon them brought revolution the belief as widespread that Nuri-al-Said and the Hashimite rulers had not tried to cope with these problems adequately. As this revolution of General Kasim gave a death blow to monarchical pro-British rule in Iraq and opened a new chapter in history of middle East so it may be dealt briefly later on.

15

Contemporary Iraq

Condition of Contemporary Iraq

Policy of Hasmite rulers of Iraq and Jordan's federation annoyed Soviet block, Egypt and Saudi Arabia etc., Rulers of Iraq and Jordan were pro-British and so these were not liked even by U.S.A. As such a plot was formed in Iraq by Brigadier Abdul Karim Kasim and Abdul Salam Aref in 1958 to overthrow rule of Hasim King and of Nuri Sayed. A coup took place in which King Faisal II, Prince Abdullah and Nuri Sayed was killed and in Iraq republican Government was established. A new constitution of Iraq was proclaimed. In this new Government Kasim became Prime Minister, Aref Deputy Prime Minister. These coup leaders sentenced to death to supporters of previous Government and terminated Federation with Jordan and Baghdad pact.

Kasim leaned towards Soviet block and got massive Soviet aid and arms. Kasim Government attacked over Kuwait but failed to conquer it. Dictatorial attitude of Kasim annoyed people of Iraq so on February 8, 1963, Brigadier Kasim's Government was overthrown and Col. Aref was appointed President. Kasim and his supporters were captured and sentenced to death.

Col. Aref remained in power from February 8, 1963 to 14th April 1966; He followed policy of friendship with Egypt. He also tried to establish common market incorporation with Egypt, Kuwait, Jordan and Syria on the lines of European common market. Aref favoured Arab unity and Arab brotherhood and supported Arab League. Aref was succeeded by Abdul Rehman Aref who ruled April 1966 to July, 1968 but his non-cooperation in Arab Israeli war of 1968 made him unpopular so he was succeeded by Ahmad Hassan Bakr. During the regime of Ahmad Hassan Bakr, relations between Iran and Iraq became strained and Iran refused to pay taxes on water and oil resources. About 20 thousand Iranians were forced to leave Iraq. This step annoyed Iran. In 1973, Arab-Israeli war, Iran sent her forces against Israel but in this war also, Arab forces were defeated by Israeli forces. In October 1978, a compromise was done between Syria and Iraq. Oil treaty between Iraq and India also took place but relations with Israel remained bitter. As such when in 26th March, 1979 Israeli and Egyptian treaty took place then Syria and Iraq took lead to expel Egypt from Arab League and to transfer Arab League's headquarters from Cairo to Tunisia, Ahmad Hassan Bakr was succeeded by Saddam-Hussein in 1979 and was ultimately defeated in 2003 by Anglo-American forces.

Contemporary Iraq and Achievements of Iraq during Rule of Saddam Hussein and a Short Note on Iran-Iraq War

Policy of Saddam Hussein was to enhance military power of Iraq and also to increase power and prestige of Iraq. On the other hand in Iran, a coup took place which forced Shah Iran to run away from the country and fanatic Shia religious leader Ayotullah Khomeni came in power. Ayotullah Khomeni was fanatic Shia religious leaders who was eager to prove himself as greatest Muslim Shia leader. In Iraq there are lot of Shia population but Sunnies are in power. As such clash of religion and of personalities and eagerness of both leaders to enhance power and prestige resulted in long Iraqi-Iranian War of 1980-89. dispute of Iran and Iraq over Shat-At-Arab and on other minor territories added fuel to fire so in September, 1980, long drawn Iraq-Iran war began.

According to Iranian version, Saddam Hussein began war over the question of Shat-al-Arab in September, 1980. Due to this war, Arab powers became divided. Syria opposed this war but Jordan and Saudi Arabia in the name of Arab unity supported Iraq because Iran is a non-Arab Shia state. Taking advantage of this situation. Israeli forces attacked Iraqi nuclear places and destroyed them. As Arabs are daggers drawn with Israel so Arab states sympathised with Iraq but Egypt remained neutral.

Iraqi-Iranian War which began in September, 1980 continued for a long time. All the efforts of Muslim powers and of Arab League and of non-aligned nations miserably failed. This Iraqi-Iranian War proved to be a long battle and continued up to 1989 *i.e.* of 9 years, a period longer than I and II World Wars.

In the end due to efforts of U.N.O. cease fire took place between Iran and Iraq in 1989. In this war superpowers generally remain silent spectator and so this war was considered by others as war between two local countries. Due to this attitude billions of dollar was lost due to destruction of oil fields and millions of persons were killed and suffered casualties. This war shattered economy of both Iran and Iraq. It was useless war which achieved nothing and this long drawn battle ended because both parties were exhausted and tired and their economies were shattered.

Dispute of Iran and Iraq is still unresolved and both sides are blaming one-another for this war and even in October, 1989, Iran requested Iraq to give back conquered territories of Iran, but Iraq kept mum. In comparison to Iran, Iraq is a small country because population of Iraq is only about 1/3 of Iran but in this war, Iraq under the leadership of Saddam Hussein gained an upper hand so it enhanced power and prestige of Iraq.

Kurd Problem of Iraq and in Adjoining State

The Kurds are in a sizable minority in Syria, Turkey, Iran and Iraq. The Turkish territory includes the headwaters of Tigers and Euphrates rivers and sites of several large dams and hydrolic projects like Jews these have suffered from the tyranny of all these above mentioned countries so they are demanding Kurdistan. In Iraq they are about 20% of its population and number more than 30 millions. These Kurds line on the borders of Turkey, Syria and Iran and may total about ten million while many Arab states are much smaller and some contain population of only 5 lakhs but Kurds have been denied any political right. P.L.O. is supported by all nations of the word but nobody is supporting the cause of Kurds. After World War I, they have been very cruelly treated by Turkey and less cruelly by Syria and Iran but in recent Iraq-Iran War Baghdad Government of Iraq launched a full scale offensive and forced tens of thousands of them to migrate to Turkey, Iran and other places as Nazi of Hitler forced Jews to migrate to other places.

Iraq Government of Saddam Hussein has forced Kurds to leave fertile boarders and plains of Tigris and Euphrates and forced them to live in desert of Basra by providing them some compensation. The policy of de-population and re-allocation of land to Kurds would impose much hardship apart from draining a huge sum from the exchequer to settle them. But Iraqi Government is certainly going to press ahead with its plan of forcing Kurds either to migrate or to settle them in desert area without caring for world opinion.

Kurd also require a homeland like P.L.O. which can be allotted to them by allotting them area where they have lived to make homeland of Kurdistan. This will bring peace to Kurds as well as to Turkey, Syria, Iran and Iraq etc.

Condition of Iraq after Iran-Iraq War of 1980-1989

The Iran -Iraq War of 1980-89 ceased on 20th August, 1939 in the make of a U.N. sponsored cease fire. It was perhaps the most turbulent part of the history of the Arab world and reminds us of Shia-Sunni conflict of medieval age. It left more than 1.5 million dead and more than 5 million de-wounded and depopulated and property worth 300 billion dollars destroyed.

Today while the Iranian are still in middle of a sand storm for ensuring a course of domestic foreign policy after the death of Ayatullah Khomeni the Iraqies are rapidly making efforts to reconstruct war torn territory of Iraq.

Iraqies consider them victorious and about 300 yards away from Presidential palace at Baghdad on the banks of Tigris, they have placed Entrance Arch of victory containing, the Arab sword, the Iraqi Palm tree and the helmets of the vanquished nation Arab sword symbolizes victory of Arabs of 637 A.D. over Persians. Helmets depict Sumerian symbol of 2740 B.C. and Palm leaves indicate Assyrian victory over its enemies. It was started under the rule of the Babylonian monarch Nebucudizar.

President Saddam Hussein is popular in Iraq and people celebrate victory with joy as Hail Saddam. Efforts are underway to re-build Baghdad and Basra and other towns. Roads, ports, buildings and bridges are being rapidly constructed. More than a million Iraqies are taking part in building Iraq. Volunteers from Egypt and Sudan and workers from India and Pakistan are helping Iraqies to reconstruct their war torn territory. Money for reconstruction is provided by Saudi Arabia and Kuwait as aid for reconstruction but reconstruction task is enormous. It may require 7 billion dollars immediately and 30 billion dollar in long process of reconstruction. Export of oil which brings lot of money has started in Iraq as well as in Iran but still full scale international business of export and import are not in full swing.

An uneasy calm prevails along 1400 miles Iran-Iraq boarder with U.N.O. observers of 20 countries to maintain cease-fire between Iraq and Iran. Iraq still holds Iranian territory and question of above Power and of Shatt-al-Arab which was bone of contention is still unsettled. As such Iran's new President Mr. Rafsanjani is trying to put a bold face on Iran's humiliation. It is feared in such a situation war may flare up again when they are strong enough to challenge each other's supremacy in this region.

Iraq has plenty of water resources and oil reserves next to Saudi Arabia. Probably Iraq is the most experienced and strongest military power of the Middle East now and it may emerge in future as Arab leader and citadel of Sunni Islam while Iran has become citadel of Shiaites Islam.

Later on Iraq conquered Kuwait, so U.N.O. forces lead by U.S.A. attached Iraq. The forces of U.S.A. defated Iraq, so Iraq had to free Kuwait and accept U.N.O. supervision. Now it is alleged that Iraq is making dangerous weapons, so Britain and U.S.A. are threatening to attach Iraq again but most of the counties of the world are not supporting them.

In Iraq there are lot of Shia but power is in the hand sunni Muslims. Baghdad was capital of Shia Abbasid caliphs, so Iran being a Shia country resents Sunni control of Iraq but differences lessened due to Iraqi conflict with about Kuwait. Iraq under Saddam Hussein occupied Kuwait after attaching, U.N.O. forces lead by U.S.A. and Britain forced Saddam Hussein to make Kuwait free and imposed sanctions on Iraq. In 1999 Iraq had to face famine but rule of Saddam Hussein remained continuous, U.S.A. and Britain opposing it and attacked it. Forces of Saddam Hussein were defeated and Anglo-American forces occupied it without the permission of U.N.O. Later on U.N.O. approved occupation of Iraq by American and allied forces and urged other states to help in maintaining law and order and peace in Iraq and to strife for its development. Occupation of Iraq was opposed by other states including India. They demanded democratic government in Iraq. Americans promised to hold election and set a council of Iraqi leaders to help in administration but people of Iraq did not like American occupations, so there are constant disturbances in Iraq. Solution lies in establishment of democratically elected govt. in Iraq.

IRAQ

Modern Iraq Upto Date in Brief

After winning war of Iran, Iraq's President Saddam Hussein

attacked Kuwait and annexed it defying U.N.O. U.S.A., defeated Saddam Hussein and forced him to give back Kuwait. An estimate puts causalities at 85,000. President Saddam Hussein, it is alleged tried to build destructive weapons but his attempt was nipped in bud as forces of Britain and America again attacked Iraq. Forces of Iraq led by Saddam Hussein were defeated and Anglo-American control was established over Iraq with local leaders' help and with the support of Italy Spain & Poland etc.

Though free from the yoke of Saddam Hussein, pressing problems loom large for Iraq and its new administrators, including the need to restore civil order and to create a new political system and to maintain law and order and development.

US-led military forces face almost-daily guerrilla-style attacks, blamed on supporters of the ousted president Saddam Hussein or on "foreign fighters". International agencies have been targeted by suicide bombers, dealing a blow to the much-needed humanitarian effort.

Saddam Hussein's regime collapsed in April 2003, three weeks after a major US-led military campaign.

American missiles hit targets in Baghdad on 20 March 2003, heralding the start of the campaign to remove the Iraqi leader, Saddam Hussein and his supporters.

U.S.A. and British ground forces entered the country from the south, with the leadership in Baghdad remaining defiant. By 9 April U.S. forces had advanced into central Baghdad and Saddam Hussein's grip on power had withered, so he was defeated.

Iraq under Saddam Hussein had engaged in two previous wars, against Iran in the 1980s and against an American-led alliance in 1991 after it invaded Kuwait.

Baghdad United Nations Iraq's interim authority has submitted a timetable for self-rule and asked the U.N. Security Council for a new resolution that would end the US-led occupation in June, 2004.

In a letter to the Security Council on Monday, Jalal Talabani, president of the Iraqi Governing Council promised to establish the "principle of civilian control over the Iraqi armed and security forces."

The US-appointed council said it would select a "provisional legislative body" not later than May 31, 2004, which would elect a provisional government by the end of June.

Then "the Coalition Provisional Authority will be dissolved and the occupation will end."

The future of their country was on the minds of Iraqis as thousands of Muslims gathered at Baghdad's Abu Hanifa mosque, one of Sunni Islam's holiest shrines, to pray and participate in the Eid-al-Fitr, the celebration that marks the end of a month of dawn-to-dusk fasting on Nov. 26, 2003. Thus, Iraq may soon emerge as independent states.

Facts

Population	:	25.1 million
Capital	:	Baghdad
Major languages	:	Arabic, Kurdish
Major religion	:	Islam
Life expectancy	:	59 years (men), 62 years (women)
Monetary unit	:	1 Iraqi dinar
Main exports	:	Crude oil

Leaders

The US-led Coalition Provisional Authority (CPA) in Iraq is headed by American career diplomat Paul Bremer.

Mr. Bremer is the top civilian official in Iraq. He is responsible for overseeing the reconstruction and the political transformation of the country. He has said that his priorities are to restore law and order and to stimulate the moribund economy.

An interim governing council held its first meeting in July 2003. Its 25 members were appointed by Mr. Bremer. They broadly reflect Iraq's ethnic make-up. The council can appoint ministers and pass the budget, but ultimate control of Iraq rests with the US administrator.

In November 2003, the council announced that the C.P.A. would transfer power to a transitional government by June 2004, and that a full sovereign Iraqi government would be formed after elections in 2005.

16

Israel

History of Israel

Israel's capital is Jerusalem. Its area is 20,872 sq. kms. and population is 6.4 million. Language is Hebrew (official) and Arabic; Religion is Judaism; Currency is Shekel which is equal to US 1-783 Shekel. Israel is a very ancient country and cradle Christian and Jew religion. Now it is A republic of the Middle East (West Asia) Israel is surrounded on the three sides by Arab countries, which are hostile to it. The republic of Israel occupies only the minor portion of ancient Palestine. On the November 29, 1947 the UNO partitioned Plaestine between the Jews and the Arab. A new zionist state called Israel was proclaimed in the Jewish area of Palestine on May 15, 1948. Now Israel has accepted to establish Palestinian state of Arabs with autonomous status.

Israel has developed both agriculture and industry in the little land allotted to it with considerable expertise and efficiency. They have literally made the deserts flourish. Kibbutzim (collective cultivation), irrigation schemes and reclamation of desert, land reforms. In diamond-cutting, Israel comes next only to Belgium. The valley of Jordan and the Dead sea yield rock salt, sulphur and potash etc.

President : Moshekatzav, P.M. : Ariel Sharon

Brief Historical Introduction. Israel is a small part of Palestine or of Hebrew lands where Jews used to reside and where mythological kings such as David and Solomon mentioned in Bible held their sway. Jews probably suffered from a long time *i.e.* from thousands of years except during the rule of Moses, David and Solomon etc.

Jews were treated harshly in Babylonia and suffered during Assyrian period. They were kept as slaves in Egypt from where Mr. Moses brought them to Egypt and a prosperous Jews kingdom was established but it was of short duration later on Roman conquered it. During Roman rule Christ was born. He was opposed by Jews Priests so Christian hate them even now though greatest Christian preacher, St. Paul was a Jew later on Muslim power such a Arabs, Ummayad Caliphs, Abasid Caliphs and Ottomon Turks ruled over them. After the fall of Ottoman Turkish empire Palestine came under Britishers as mandatory ruler. After the end of mandatory ruler, Jews established state of Israel in 1948.

State of Israel is a very tiny state and a very small part of old Palestine. Inspite of this Muslim powers particularly Arab powers were determined to destroy in direct defiance of U.N.O. resolutions, consequently Irsael had to face a fight constant wars from 1948 to 1973 and conflict is still going on. Jews have to face prosecution and humiliation from the very beginning all over the world probably except in U.S.A. Hitler was determined to exterminate them and killed and prosecuted lakhs of Jews. In Russia they used to be treated and are treated very harshly, same is case of Jews in all Muslim lands. In India where Jews used to live from time immemorial have been forced to migrate to Israel and hardly any Jew can be found in India because Indian Government sides with their staunch enemy P.L.O and its leader Asseer Arafat. Thus Jews are pariah or untouchables or whipping boy every where except in U.S.A. As such existence of Israel is question of their survival so Jews state of Israel is continuously fighting for its survival even now. Mily service is compulsory both for Jews male and female because its population is only about 50 lakhs about half of Delhi.

Jews have produced great men like Moses, David, wise Solomon, Abraham, St. Paul etc. Intellectuals like Karl Marx, Einstein and Harold Laski etc. Generals like Marshal Foch who was commander-in-chief of all allied forces during first World War and leaders like Disraeli, Trotsky of Russia and now Kissinger in U.S.A. and ex Lady Prime Minister Mrs. Golda Meir etc.

Hebrew literature particularly old testament finds a respectable place in Christian religion and according to some historian Hebrew law and traditions influenced Islamic law and traditions also but inspite of all this, Jews have suffered a lot and are still fighting for the survival of their tiny state of Israel which is hardly as big district of India China, America, Russia or of Egypt or Iraq having lesser population than big city of India such as Delhi.

Whether Jews or their tiny state of Israel possesses the right to survive or not? Whether Jews state of Israel will survive or not in future are the questions which are beyond. The purview of historian but how Jews have survived inspite of long prosecutions and have succeeded in establishing Jewish tiny state of Israel has been narrated here in brief. Geographically Israel is part of Middle East and Jews belong to same sematic race as Arabs but religion is different and this has created rift and brought constant wars so Israel inspite of the fact that it is a very tiny state has been stated and dealt separately along with new autonomous state of Palestine.

Israel is now a very powerful and progressive state having an important role in world affairs.

The Ancient History of Israel and Their Religion etc.

Israel is an ancient land where Judism and Christian religion took birth. Christ was born here when it was under Roman rule. The Hebrew kingdoms, in war, diplomacy, inventions, and art, the made Chart of progress Moses and Christ preached here and old and new testaments reflect its culture but Hebrews made little impact in the stream of history. In ethics and religion, however, their contribution to world civilization was tremendous, even though they were few in number and weak in political power. Form the Hebrew people we have received Judaism, and Christianity-the two faiths that after two thousand years remains dominant in the western world. The great Judaic-Christian tradition of ethics and morality, still hold great sway.

The earliest Hebrews dwelt for a time at Ur in Sumer before moving up the river Euphrates, led by the patriarch Abraham, in search of a homeland. Eventually, they filtered into the land of Canaan, later on to be called Palestine, Tucked between the desert and the sea, this small region was only 150 miles long and very narrow, about the size of the sate of Punjab. According to tradition, some of the Hebrews were enslaved by the Egyptians, but they were led out of bondage by prophet Moses, who gave his people the Ten Commandments and a new conception of a single tribal deity, Yahweh. His teachings form part of Jewish religion and of old Testament

The Hebrews had to contend for Palestine against the Canaamites (a mixed semitic and Hittite people). Who were defeated, and later on the Philistines, a war like people from whom the word Palestine originated. Under famous King. David (1005-965 B.C.) the Hebrews subjugated the Philistines and established a promising kingdom, David's son, wise Solomon (965-925 B.C.) created a bureaucratic state and became famous as a great oriental potentate, king Solomon has been highly praised for his wisdom and justice.

Great king Solomon reigned over all kingdoms from the river (Euphrates) unto the land of the Philistines, and unto the border of Egypt.... And Judah and Israel dwelt safely...all the days of king Solomon......(His) Wisdom excelled the wisdom of all the children of the east country, and all the wisdom of Egyt...and his fame was in all nations round about...Now the weight of gold that came to king Solomon in one year was six hundred three score and six talents...(He) made a great throne of ivory, and overlaid it with the best gold.... So king Solomon exceeded all the kings of the earth for riches and also for wisdom. As such Solomon began to be considered wisest king and English proverb as wise as Solomon became common.

Despite his proverbial wisdom, however, king Solomon levied such heavy taxes and married many wives, that when he died discontent split the realm into two kingdoms Israel and Judah. The divided and weakened Hebrews were vulnerable to attack and invasion. In 722 B.C. the Assyrians conquered Israel; In 586 B.C. Judah fell to famous conqueror Nebuchandnezzar, a Chaldean king, who captured Jerusalem and carried all Jews but the poorest inhabitants into exile. After the and of Chaldeans rule who had been defeated by the Persians later in the fifth century, the Jews (term derived from "Judeans") were permitted to return to Judea and they rebuilt the Jerusalem temple destroyed by king Nebuchadnezzar, who built hanging garden and who is considered as one of the greatest king of ancient age.

Persian rule was followed by that of the Greeks and later on by the Romans. In the first century A.D., the Jews rebelled against the rule of Roman emperors. Jerusalem was totally destroyed by Romans and the Jews are driven to all parts of the earth, and this Diaspora, this "Scattering" brought sufferings to the Jews for many centuries to come.

The years since the scattering have been filled with sorrow and tragedy for the Jewish people all over the world. To the miseries of the medieval ghetto (the city quarter to which Jews were restricted was added the horror of the pogrom (organized massacre) in early modern times. Recent years witnessed brutal persecution in many lands, especially in Nazi Germany by Hitler. It is against this background that we should examine the passionate struggle of the

Zionist to re-establish a Jewish-homeland in Palestine and the pride of present-day Israel.

Monotheism Among the Hebrews. Originally the Hebrew religion was a primitive polytheism which consisted the worship of many gods. Gradually the concept of one tribal god, Yahweh (Jehovah), a stern, warlike deity, developed. After their entrance into Palestine, however, many of the Hebrews adopted not only the more sophisticated and luxurious manner of living of the Canaanites but probably also their religious customs. This was especially true of the northern Hebrews.

About 750 B.C. a succession of great spiritual leaders, called Prophets, such as Moses etc. before purged Hebrew thought and religion of all corrupting influence. In doing so, they elevated and dignified the concept of Yahweh to the exclusion of other gods, thus, establishing a monotheistic religion based on one all powerful God. Such prophets as Amos, Isaiah, and Ezekiel etc. taught that God was a loving Father, that He alone was the true God of the universe. In the words of Micah; often cited as containing the essence of higher religion of Jems.

He hath showed thee, O man, what is good; and what doth the LORD require of thee, but to do justly, and to love mercy, and to walk humbly with they God?

When the Jews returned to Jerusalem to rebuild the sacred temple, the writings of the Law, the prophets, and the Psalms etc. were collected. Not until Christian times, however, were these and other writings put into one book, called the Old Testament. Jews and Christians are familiar with the power and beauty of some of its great passages. As a work of literature Jews believed it remains unsurpassed; but it is more than that. "It is Israel's life story — a story that cannot be told adequately apart from the conviction that God had called this people in his grace, separated them from the nations for a special responsibility, and (also) commissioned them with the task of being his servant in the accomplishment his purpose. Thus Jews believe themselves specially favored son of God so other people hate them and for this belief, they have to suffer later on. Jewish state survived for a very short time and when Alexander the Great conquered Persians Jews came under Greeks rule and later on under Romans dominations.

Rise of Jewish Nationalism

Jews a are stubborn people whose spirit remained subdued inspite of ups and downs due to rise of Jewish nationalism. At the very time when the participate of Roman emperor Augustus was laying the foundations of Rome's imperial greatness, events were taking place in a distant Roman province that would one day alter the course of western history. In order to study these events in the proper perspective, let us examine the story in Hellenistic Palestine.

Following the conquests of Alexander the Great in the Near East, Palestine was ruled at different times by his successors *i.e.*, by the Ptolemies and the Seleucids with their fervid adherence to monotheism, the Jewish people had already created a theocratic community, based upon the Torah, God's Law-originally revealed to prophet Moses and contained in the Pentateuch (the first five books of the Old Testament), and later this was supplemented by the teachings of the Prophets and the writings of scholars. Religious life of Jews centerd on the great temple at Jerusalem. The most powerful figure was the High Priest office that seems to have emerged during the Persian period. Assisted by the Sanhedrin, it was the high court of Jews for the enforcement of the Law. Since there was no distinction between civil and religious law, so the jurisdiction of the Sanhedrin covered all aspects of Jewish life. The Hebrews, who considered themselves as the chosen "People of God" were a tightly knit clan; even the Jews of the Diaspora, who were "scattering" throughout the civilized world, and were more numerous than those residing in Palestine, were linked by the spiritual bonds to this temple of Jerusalem and to law which they believed to be divinely inspired and they began to feel that they are divinely favoured people.

At the same time Hellenic influences were constantly at work among the Jews. Many learned to speak Greek, a valuable asset to merchants etc. trading in the Near East. Jerusalem itself acquired gymnasiums, temple worship and Greek amusements. The translation at Alexandria in Egypt in the third or second centuries B.C. of the Hebrew scriptures into Greek-called the Septuagint (Latin for "seventy") from the tradition that it was the work of seventy scholars whose independent translations miraculously were identical. This not only stimulated the use of Greek language among Jewish intellectuals but also broadened Jewish thought. Thus Hebrews were effected by Greeks culture, language and thought.

Greek influence might have become stronger had it not stirred up factionalism within the Jewish community in

Jerusalem. Eventually, one puritanical group came to blow with the aristocratic. Sadducees, as they began to be favoured by the Seleucid rules of Palestine. This conflict gave the Seleucid an opportunity to intervene, and in about 168 B.C., he ordered the Jew temple to be dedicated to the worship of Zeus. Viewing this decree as a blasphemous defilement, the Jews rebelled. Under their leader, Judas Maccabaeus, the Jews won military success and secured religious freedom, and they rededicated the Jew temple of Jerusalem to Yahweh. In 142 B.C., the Seleucid king was forced to recognize Jewish Independence.

A Maccabean dynasty was created which reigned over most of Palestine. Later on, these rulers became cowardly and corrupt, and factionalism again flared up. It was in the midst of a civil war that the Roman legions appeared on the scene and conquered Israel.

The Rule of Roman Empire over Israel

Roman occupation of Palestine. Adopting the practice habitually followed by eastern Mediterranean states, one Jewish faction appealed to Rome for aid. Pompey, who was then completing his pacification of Asia Minor and Syria etc. and the civil war of Palestine by annexing Palestine in 63 B.C. The Jews, however remained the one people to whom the Romans were never able to pacify. Israel got name and fame as Jesus Christ was a Jews born in Israel and preached here.

Eventually, Herod, a leader from a tribe that had long been enemies of the Jews, rose to power as a tool of the Roman rulers. Appointed by the Roman Senate, he served of a puppet king of Judea from 37 to 4 B.C. Of exceptional ability, Herod fortified Jerusalem with great walls and towers and rebuilt the temple of Yahweh on a lavish scale. To the Jews, however, he remained an usurper, who professed Judaism as a matter of expediency. Soon after Herod's death, Judea was made a minor Roman province ruled by Roman governors called procurators, the best known of whom is Pontius Pilate (26-36 A.D.), under whom Jesus was crucified. It is alleged Jews took leading part in accusing Christ so Christians began to hate and torment Jews. During Roman Rule, the Jews themselves were unhappy and divided. During centuries of tribulation, the Jew Prophets had taught that God would one day create a new Israel under a God-anointed leader, the Messiah. In time the Jews, with the notable exception of the Sadducees, conceived of the Messiash as a divine being sent by God to lead the righteous and resurrected dead to a spiritual kingdom. But a group of Jewish nationalist, who were called zealots, favouring the use of force to drive the hated foreigners, out of God's land, precipitated a fatal revolt against Rome.

Destruction of Jerusalem. In 66 A.D. violence erupted. The Roman garrison at Jerusalem was massacred, and the revolt of Jews spread beyond the walls of the city of Jerusalem. The wholesale destruction of Jerusalem in 70 A.D. by Titus, son of Vespasian spelled the end of the Hebrew state. After that the Jewish dream of an independent political state was to remain unrealized for almost about nineteen centuries, until, as a result of United Nations action the republic of Israel was proclaimed in 1948, Jerusalem the birth place of Christ become part of Israel.

The Development of Jewish Religious Thought

The destruction of Jerusalem did not destroy the most important single aspect of Jewish culture *i.e.,* their religion. Through centuries of suffering, captivity, and subjugation, the Jews had been taught by a succession of Prophets to cleave to their covenant with God Yahweh and to safeguard and preserve their religious inheritance.

In the centuries just preceding and following the birth of Christ, Judaism exhibited great vigour and strength. Advocating unswerving fidelity to the traditional beliefs probably the Pharisees made up the strongest and most learned of the religions factions. From their ranks came the rabbis, *i.e.* Jew scholars who expounded the Hebrew Law and applied it to existing conditions. In the Gospels of many Pharisees are severely criticized for their arrogance and for concerning themselves with the later rather than with the spirit of the Law. But from the second century B.C. to the second century A.D., it was the case with its greatest intellectual leaders. Moreover, by reestablishing rabbinical schools *i.e.,* Jew following the fall of Jerusalem, the Pharisees did much to ensure that Judaism would endure as a religion.

The Dead Sea Scrolls. Contemporary with the Pharisees was another sect of Jews called the Essenes. In recent years the discovery of the Dead Sea Scrolls has added greatly to our knowledge of the Essenes and has enhanced their importance. It is not known what became of this ascetic group after the destruction of Jerusalem, but prior to their death or dispersal they managed to hide their manuscripts.

Some scrolls are portions of the Old Testament and are many centuries older than the earliest text previously known. The analysis of the scripts used on the scrolls and radioactive carbon dating of fragments would place their composition in the first century B.C. Jewish and Christian scholars alike have been thrilled to read the Book of Isaiah in such ancient manuscript and to discover that the version, which has been used, although based on much later sources, has been generally accurate except in some details. After Romans Jews came under the rule of Arabian Caliphs who propagated Islamic religion. Later on Turks ruled over it and crusades took place but Turks were able to rule Palestine till first World War of 1914-18.

The Position of Jews in the Arab World

Jews suffered during rule of Assyrians and Romans and later on came under Muslim rule. The renowned toleration that the Jews enjoyed under Muslim rule was probably not the product of native Muslim liberality. No less than Christians, the peoples of Islam claimed exclusive possession of the truth and exhibited unconcealed contempt for other religions particularly for Jews. Muslim theologians and demagogues produced an anti Jewish literature that was formed by hatred of the Jews and Judaism that in no way falls short of its Christian counter part.

The Jewish experience under Islam was bitter and it began with massacre and expulsion from the northern half of the Arabian peninsula. The "Pact of Umar", although historically questionable, nevertheless reflected the prevailing attitude of Muslim ruler and jurists. Infidels deserved protection only at the price of displaying marked subservience to Muslims and their faith. The Persecution and humiliation endured by the Jews of Almohade in North Africa and Zaydi Yeman were unmatched in their brutality by any Christian sate prior to the anti-semitic excesses of nineteenth-century Czarist Russia and of Nazi Germany under Hitler.

Nevertheless, it remains true that in Babylonia, Spain, North Africa. Egypt, and also in Ottoman Turkey, Jews enjoyed centuries of uninterrupted tranquility. In these countries, where felicitous conditions deprived them of much of a political or economic history, the story of the Jews is perhaps the record of Jewish activity within the framework of their own autonomy of their internal tensions and also due to adjustments to new political cultural contexts. Men of distinction reflect and individuality reflect and frequently and originality, that were all but unknown in the Jewish communities of Christian Europe.

The crucial factor probably favouring the Jews was that in every land conquered by the Muslims, the Jews were generally one of the several non-Arab groups. In states where political alignments often corresponded to ethnic loyalties, the presence of the Jews was not felt much as in areas peopled predominantly by one ethnic stock. Secondly in many areas the Muslims found the Jews concentrated in considerable numbers and possessed tradition of communal organization. In such cases it was far less costly, and often quite advantageous, to mobilize the services of cooperative Jewish leader whose interests in maintaining a quiescent and disciplined Jewish community coincided with those of the alien conquerors. As such probably during Arab and Turkish rule Jews were treated probably in a better way than Egyptians, Romans and Christians.

When the armies of Umer-ibn al-Khattab over ran Mesopotamia and Iran (636-640), they found Jews living alongside several other Aramaic-speaking people Eager for a swift return to normality. The Muslims confirmed the relationship to Jews etc. that had prevailed under the Persian empire between the central government and subject peoples. They also appointed native personnel to administer the internal and local affairs of the various groups. As a tolerated people of Holy Koran the Jews of Babylonia, like their Christian neighbours, were classified as a protected minority to be governed directly by leader from their own ranks. Besides keeping the peace in the Jewish community, this prince was to be accountable for the regular collection of the poll tax and other special tributes imposed by the Muslim rulers on all conquered peoples. In this way Arab conquerors left Jews alone in their religious, local and community affairs.

The great majority of about million-odd Jews in the new Arab-empire were mostly concentrated in one area. Many cultivated their own fields and others worked as artisans or merchants in towns frequently peopled overwhelmingly by Jews. All aspects of their civil, social and religious life etc. were administered by their own Jewish officials in accordance with their own laws codified in the Babylonian Talmud and by the institutions financed by taxes collected from all Jews living in these territories from Persia to Byzantium. The powers of legislation and adjudication reposed with rabbinic academies, or high courts, patterned largely after those of the Palestinian robbinate and headed by presidents known as Geonim, Highly developed communal machinery of Jews was run with a tight discipline by an officialdom largely recruited from a limited circle of leading and learned Jewish families which made the Jewish settlement in Mesopotamia a kind of oligarchical tiny Jews state — within a Muslim state of vast empire.

By 725, the burdensome taxation and the heavy hand of the Jews oligarchy aroused the same kind of organized opposition among disaffected Jews that the Ummayad Caliphs had generated among Persian and Arab Muslims particularly in the outlying area of Persia. Later on political and economic resentment of Jews erupted in a armed revolt coupled with programmes of legal and religious reforms and as small group responded to the appeals of charismatic chieftains to establish independent Jewish societies. Although there revolts were quickly crushed but discontent continued in many quarters of Ummayad caliphs' empire.

Perhaps the most impressive coup of these missionaries was the conversion of the ruling families of the Khazar tribes north of the Caucasus mountain to a syncretist form of Judaism. However, this lone tiny Jewish kingdom survived until about 1000 and remained isolated like Israel from Jewish society at large, although it became a byword for Jews dreaming of the resurgence of Jewish political power. But in the Near East itself, these sects quickly receded into obscurity and failed to present any sustained challenge to rabbinic control among Jews who ever scattered everywhere.

The internal policies of the Abbasid Caliphs following their seizure of power in 750 A.D. from Ummayeds provided further opportunities for the extension of Jews influence but influence of religion and community structure among Jews retained a basic uniformity.

The great social changes that overtook Arab society in the wake of the Abbasid rule economic, social and cultural programmes in the eighth and ninth centuries inevitably had probably profound effects on Jewish society. This increased premium placed on ability rather than on ethnic or even religious origins opened new avenues to Jews. By 900 A.D. Some Jews had gained employment as civil servants and right to practice medicine. In 908 A.D., Jews were empowered to function as state bankers also. Thanks to their connections with the Caliph's court, the new Jewish rich played an ever increasing role in the affairs of their Jews community and especially in the highest echelons with the admission of foreigners of talent and of scholarly members of the bankings families to Position of influence in the academies of Abbasid Caliph's empire.

However, the most pervasive effect of the new luxurious atmosphere in Baghdad was in the cultural and religious affairs that could also be discerned in all quarters of Arab society. The adoption of Arabic as the language of the Muslim empire coupled with the Abbasid sponsorship of a huge programmes of translation of works of many subjects from Greek Syriac and Persian etc. converted Baghdad into the cultural emporium comparable to that of Alexandria of Hellenistic times. Muslims Christians and Jews exchanged ideas freely in Abbasid Caliphs empire Philosophical circles abounded and with them skepticism and religious deviation of every sort.

The splintering of the Abbasid empire by the Fatimids of North Africa and Ummayads of Spain in the tenth century enabled the Jewish communities of Iraq, Egypt, Palestine and Spain kept them bound to one another due to religious unity.

Jews as friendly dhimmis or zimmies in an area where all-Christians were openly hostile, the Jews were accorded, the full measure of Muslim rulers' toleration and, also employment as petty officials. Active in commerce, in vine and silk cultivation, in textile manufacture, and in the state-supported slaves trade, many Jews amassed considerable wealth in Spain under Muslim rule. While educational facilities to Jews in Spain by 800 A.D. to 1000 A.D. and was a major benefactor of the Babylonian academics. The first Jewish prayer book was complied by a Gaon of Sura (c. 860) in response to a request by a Spanish community, perhaps of city of Barcelona.

The decisive turn in the Jews fate came in the wake of the campaign of Abd al-Rahman III (912-961) and al Hakam II (961-976) they tried to make Spanish Cordova the capital of Ummayads as the Baghdad of the west which was capital of Abbasid Caliphs. After achieving military and naval mastery over their neighbours, these Ummayads launched an extensive building programme and attracted man of science and letters to their Spanish capital at Cardova. Libraries and universities sprang up alongside royal palaces and gardens, gaining of Cardova renowned as 'the jewel of the Maghreb.' Thus Ummayads who made Cardova as their capital tried to make it magnificent like Baghdad with the support of Jews. The temper of the age inspired the head of the Jewish community to undertake a similar programme of development for his own group, on a smaller scale. Hasdai ibn Shaprut, a Physician who had served the special court with distinction in several diplomatic missions. He lavished considerable sums to draw men of Jewish law and intellect of letters to Cardova and tried to provide them with libraries. But he made no contact with Jewish king of the Khazars.

Although civil wars of Caliphs empire in the beginning of the eleventh century dismembered the Ummayad kingdom into many petty states, so the period of the petty Muslim kings from (1020-1086) and of their successors from (1086-1148) became "the golden age" of Spanish Jewish culture

The courtier tradition among Jews prized as its outspoken goal the creation of a type who integrated and synthesizes the wisdom. Of Greece in Arabic grasp with Israel During the period Jews became poets, philosophers, mathematicians, astronomers and being influenced by Arabic verse, they strove to revive the vitality of the Hebrew language, which they set to verse in Arabic meter; so that the philosophic Treatises of Ibn Gabirol, Moses ibn Ezra, and the philosophic treatises of Ibn (Avicebron), Ibn Hiyya and Abraham Ibn Ezra etc. were the works genuine intellects sensitive to every ripple of Arabic culture and depicting beauty and knowledge of Arabic literature. In much smaller measure, Jewish culture flourished simultaneously in Egypt, and in Palestine etc. for a brief period of persecution (1009-1021) under the insane Fatimid al-Hakim, generally the Jews prospered as merchants, artisans, and civil servants etc.

Later on when Jews began to be harassed in 12th century, the majority of Jews either fled to Egypt or to Christian Spain. Later on they migrated to Latin Europe with a rich legacy that influenced the course of European scholarship and philosophy as a whole and in Jewish culture in particular.

The works of Moses Ma Imonides (1135-1204) issued in Egypt, the Jewish laws are probably the most incisive synthesis of Jewish faith. With Aristotelian philosophy. However, all of his monumental works betray the underlying despair of reflective men of Arab society — epitomized in sociological terms after two centuries later on by Ibn Khaldun who was great historian were of lasting satisfaction in public service. Maimonides was not the first philosopher to suggest that freedom could be attained only through contemplative withdrawal in a society rigorously controlled by law and reason. However, he was the first scholar to lay out a detailed Jewish blueprint for such a pattern of life, and to show the exiles of Andalus. In Ayyubid Egypt, where he found political freedom and financial security, he established a dynasty of communal heads which persisted until the end of the fourteenth century. However the society envisioned by this Jewish philosopher-king was probably never to become a reality. Long entrenched Jewish patterns of life coupled with the upheavals in the Middle East beginning with the thirteenth century, probably left the work of Maimonides a solitary epitaph to a glorious culture.

Jewish community life in the lands of Islam persisted down to modern times as rule of Ottoman Turks over Palestine remained upto first world war of 1914-18. However, the decay the weakened Arab society and culture and affected the Levantine Jews as well. The renaissance that Ottoman Jewary enjoyed in the sixteenth and seventeenth centuries was basically a resurgence of shephardic culture that had become totally Hispanicized and, in any case, probably never an integral part of Ottoman society and culture. It remained for Jews enflamed by the European Enlightenment to rediscover the glories of Babylonis lands and of Andalus and to recapture the treasures of the Judeo-Arabic experience after 1st World War.

The Condition of Israel under the Rule of Turkish Empire

Abassid Caliphs ruled over all lands including Palestine (Israel) and after the fall of Abassid Caliphs, after many ups and downs Palestine and Arab land came under the rule of Ottoman Turks who as a Caliph of Islam ruled harshly over non-Muslims consequently Jews scattered all over Europe but plight of Jews was better in Ottoman empire than in Christian Europe. In Europe Jews were prosecuted and hated so many of them migrated to America and became rich and very influential there. In Ottoman empire of Turks, Jews were very few but they were treated with tolerance like Christians and Parsies etc. Jews were harassed all over but in Czarist Russia their plight was most miserable. As Jews continued to suffer from time immemorial so many Jews began to plead for downtrodden people and Karl Marx urged exploited class to rise against exploiters and brought communist Manifesto and Das Capital which made profound influence over all humanity and changed the course of history. Jews produced intellectual and great men.

The Condition of Jews and of Palestine under Muslim Rule during the Regime of Ottoman Empire. Glimpse of Plight of Jews upto Ist World War

Jews suffered during the rules of Bylonians, Egyptians, Assyrians, Greeks and Romans but during the regime of Ummayad Caliphs and Abbasid Caliphs, they were treated in a better manner and made progress which has been already described.

Ottoman Turk leaders also treated Jews in a better way than they were treated by Christian in Europe. Jews were harassed and cruelly treated everywhere in Christian Europe so they became scattered everywhere and migrated to America where they gained position of some influence. Plight of Jews was most miserable in Czarist Russia and in Germany.

As Jews suffered most miserably since time immemorial so many Jew scholars began to plead the cause of downtrodden huminity. As such Karl Marx gave a slogan that all workers should unite against exploiters. He wrote Communist Manifesto and Das-Capital etc. whose influence changed the course of historical thought. Being influenced by Karl Marx, leftist societies came into existence every where and in Czarist Russia where Jews were most cruelly treated, a revolution came in 1917, in which Jews particularly Trotsky took prominent part.

Under Ottoman empire, Jews were treated in Much better way than anywhere except in U.S.A. Expansion of Russian empire gave a death blow to Ottoman empire. Russian imperial expansion was opposed by British people and by France so Ottoman empire survived upto First World War of 1914-18.

In the First World War Russian, Britain and France fought against Germany, Austria and Turkey. In this War Ottoman Turks were defeated so Palestine and Iraq came under British rule and Syria and Lebnan under French rule. England ruled over these lands on behalf of League of Nations as mandatory powers.

The Condition of Palestine under British Rule and the Condition of Palestine and Arab-Jew Problem under British Mandate

After First World War of 1914-18 in Palestine which had been assigned by Paris Treaty to Great Britain as a mandated province to the British Government it had to face a very difficult complex and delicate task. It had long been an Arab country but it also contained a sprinkling of Jews who in ancient days established a Hebrew state under David and Solomon etc., During a critical stage of the First World War 1914-18, Arthur Balfour, the British Foreign Minister, under Zionist pressure, made a declaration in 1917, promising to establish in Palestine "a national home for the Jewish people."

This is in history is called as Balfour Declaration of 1917. In this declaration, there was, of course, a parallel promise that nothing should be done which might prejudice the civil and religious rights of existing non Jewish communities. In Palestine as Muslim Arabs and a few Christians also used to reside there but Jews get inspiration. Hence as soon as a British administration was set up in Palestine after the war a wave of Jewish immigration set in, so that in the course of a few years the number of Jews was almost doubled in Palestine. This turn of events highly irritated and annoyed the Arabs who opposed Jews and complained, that the Balfour Declaration of 1917 conflicted with Britain's War time promise of Arab independence and also with American President Wilson's theory of self-determination. The Arabs were not in a mood to tolerate the large influx of Jews and so Palestine soon became a cockpit for Zionism and Arab nationalism. As Balfour declaration is very controversial so it is given here.

The Balfour Declaration of 1917 and Its Importance

British Government during the War years of 1914-18 became gradually committed to the idea of the establishment of a Jewish home in Palestine. After the discussion on cabinet level and consultations with Jewish leaders, the decision of British Government was made known in the form of a letter by British Foreign Minister Arthur James Lord Balfour (1843-1930) to a great leader Lord Rothschild. As such here true copy of letter is given :

Foreign Office (Britain)
November 2nd, 1917

Dear Lord Rothschild,

I have much pleasure on conveying to you, on behalf of His Majesty's Government, the following declaration of sympathy with Jewish Zionist aspirations which has-been submitted to, and approved by, the cabinet. It stated

"His Majesty's Government view with favour the establishment in Palestine of a national home for the Jewish people, and will use their best endeavours to facilitate the achievement of this object, it being clearly understood that nothing shall be done which may prejudice the civil and religious rights of existing non-Jewish communities in Palestine, or the rights and political status enjoyed by Jews in any other country." In the end it stated

I should be grateful if you would bring this declaration to the knowledge of the Zionist Federation.

Yours Sincerely,
Arthur James Balfour.

This declaration is very important because Jews were allowed to settle in Palestine and later on Jews succeeded in establishing their state of Israel as decided by U.N.O. later on.

The Agreement between Jew Leaders Weizmann and Emir Feisal, the Arab Leader

During the peace conference in Paris held after First World War Emir Feisal (1855-1933), the son of Hussain, who was the sherif of Mecca, met with various Jewish leaders and signed an agreement with Dr. Chaim Weizmann (1877) who was leader of the Jews, Feisal, who in 1921, became King of Iraq, had announced publicly ten years later that "His Majesty does not remember having written anything of that kind with his knowledge."

This agreement is not accepted by Arabs but others consider it true. True copy of some clauses of agreement between Emir Feisal and Dr. Weizmann of January 3, 1919 as follows :

His Royal Highness the Emir Feisal, representing and acting on behalf of the Arab Kingdom of Hedjaz, and Dr. Chaim Weizmann, representing and acting on behalf of the Zionist Organisation, mindful of the racial kinship and ancient bonds existing between the Arabs and the Jewish people, and realizing that the surest means of working out the consummation of their national aspirations in the development of the Arab state and Palestine, and being desirous further of confirming the good understanding which exists between them, agreed upon the following Articles :

ARTICLE I

The Arab state and Palestine on all their relations and undertakings shall be controlled by the most cordial good will and understanding, and to this end Arab and Jewish duly accredited agents shall be established. It further stated that agents shall be established and maintained in the respective territories.

ARTICLE II

Staes that immediately following the completion of the deliberations of the Peace Conference, the definite boundaries between the Arab state and Palestine shall be determined by a Commission to be a greed upon by the parties hereto.

ARTICLE III

In the establishment of the Constitution and Administration of Palestine all such measures shall be adopted as will afford the fullest guarantees for carrying into effect the British Government's Declaration of the 2nd November 1917. Thus Arabs agreed through Feisal to make Palestine as home land of Arabs and later on determination of Muslim powers to destroy Israel cannot be justified.

ARTICLE IV

All necessary measures shall be taken to encourage and stimulate immigration of Jews into Palestine on a large scale, and as quickly as possible to settle Jewish immigrants upon the land through closer settlement and intensive cultivation of the soil. In taking such measures the Arab peasant and tenant farmers shall be protected in their rights, and shall be assisted in forwarding their economic development.

Feisal and Jew Leader Frankfurter. Feisal declared that Arab and Jews are cousins in race, having suffered similar oppressions at the hands of stronger powers than themselves, and by a happy coincidence have been able to take the first step towards the attainment of their national ideals together. It was further stated "we regard proposal of Jews placed in Paris Peace conference as moderate and proper."

Jews leader Frankfurter reciprocated, "It is no easy task to build two great civilizations that have been suffering oppression and misrule for centuries.......we shall work as friends......seeking a free and full development........we cannot but live as friends side by side."

Causes of Arab-Jew Conflict in Mandatory Rule of Britain

As shown before, Arab and Jew leaders tried for good relation but conflict came because Arabs felt aggrieved and the grievances of the Arabs were not merely political. They complained that they were hard hit by the land legislation which threatened the existence of thousands of Arabs. These laws enabled the Jews due to their being rich to buy up large portions of the arable soil which was none too plentiful in

Palestine. Besides this Jewish who were new-comers were subsidized by the Zionist organizations of U.S.A. by the Western countries and so had every advantage that capital, science and organisation and intelligence could give them. Consequently result was that the Arabs were being gradually deprived of their lands ousted from most of the gainful occupations. This economic danger gave an impetus to Arab nationalistic agitation. The discontent of the Arabs found vent in violent anti Jewish out breaks and riots in 1929 and 1933 in which many Jews were killed. The British Government had to take strông military measures to restore peace and order, but failed to bring peace or reconciliation between Jews and Arabs.

The British Government tried her best to soften the conflict between Arabs and Jews and to hold the balance even between the two communities. But it was a very difficult and complicated task as the conflicting interests were many. There was Zionism, there was Arab nationalism resentment of Muslim, Arab powers and lastly there were British imperial interests. Palestine was important to Britain as an air and military base and as containing the terminus of an oil pipeline from oil city of Mosul. The Jews demanded the whole of Palestine on the basis of its being king Soloman's territory in remote past and the removal of all restrictions on Jewish immigration. The Arabs were equally determined to keep Palestine theirs being successors of Arab conquerors and to stop immigration altogether. In these circumstances the British Government in 1936 appointed a Peel Commission headed by Earl Peel to investigate the whole situation in Palestine and to make recommendations. In the report the Peel Commission submitted its recommendations in 1937 which stated that there is no possibility of compromise. In the report the Peel commission which was approved by the British Cabinet and published in 1937, it was declared that the claims of the Jews and of the Arabs were irreconcilable and the only solution of the problem lay in the partition of Palestine. Thereupon the British Government proposed to terminate the mandate of League of Nations and decided to divide the country into three parts — an Arab section, a Jewish section and a neutral area under British control. This plan aroused bitter protests from both the Jews and the Arabs. A section of the Arabs were encouraged by the Italians of Fascist Government of Italy to make violent and murderous demonstrations against British Government so a British District Commissioner was killed and Britishers were attacked. A scores of Arabian leaders were jailed or deported and for months Palestine was the scene of bomb outrages and of guerilla warfare between Jews and Arabs which British army failed to control.

The leader of the Palestinian Arabs was Amin El Hussein, Grand Mufti of Jerusalem and President of the Arab Higher Committee. He demanded that the Jewish immigration should immediately cease and that Palestine should be bound to Britain by treaty relationship similar to that enjoyed by Iraq and Egypt etc. He fled to Syria during the disturbances but his followers continued to attack and kill the Jews, the British diplomats and even moderate Arabs sought a compromise solution acceptable to both Jews and Arabs. In 1939, the British Government made another attempt to solve this difficult problem by inviting the representatives of the Arabs and Jews to a conference held in London, but to no avail. The outbreak of the Second World War in 1939, prevented further attempts in this direction of a final settlement between Arabs and Jews. During War Grand Mufti of Jerusalem met with Hitler on November 28, 1941, who was determined to wipe out Jews from the face of earth so Arab-Jew relations became bitter.

When the London Conference was being held in 1939, the so-called Hussein McMahon correspondence was published in order to quiet certain Arab claims. The Arabs said that Henry McMahon had promised Hussein the independence of the whole Arab race in return for help against the Ottoman Turks. The British Government on the other hand maintained that Palestine had not been included in the promised Arab state and was outside the scope of the agreement entered into with Hussein. The evidence on the point is obscure and it seems concocted cock and bull story as Feisal accepted Palestine as homeland of Jews.

Palestine under British Mandate

Palestine proved to be the most troublesome mandate because of the growing hostility between Jews and Arabs. The problem originated about two thousand years earlier in 71 AD when most of the Jews were driven out of Palestine *i.e.* from their home land, by the Romans due to revolt against Roman rule. In fact small communities of Jews remained behind in Palestine and over the following seventeen hundred years there was a gradual trickle of Jews returning from exile. But until the end of the nineteenth century there were never enough to cause the Palestinian Arabs to feel threatened, However, in 1897, some European Jews founded the World Zionist Organisation at Basle in Switzerland. This was an event which was to be of profound importance for the Middle East. Greatly disturbed by the recent persecutions of Jews, in Russia, Germany and France, the Zionists demanded a Jewish national home in Palestine. Even before they received the mandate over Palestine the British had become involved in this controversy and must take much of the blame for the anarchy and chaos that followed, especially after 1945. However Jews have no alternative as they were killed in thousand and harassed in millions by Nazi Government of Hitler so homeland became necessary for Jews.

British Mandate over Palestine upto the eve of II World War

During the First World War the British had made three contradictory and ambiguous promises, which were bound to lead to frustration and hostility. They promised independent states for the Arabs and the partition of the Arab territories between Britain and France. The third promise was made by the Balfour Declaration of November 1917, in which the British Foreign Minister Balfour pledged British support for a Jewish, 'national home' in Palestine. The British motive, apart from genuine sympathy with the Zionists, was probably due to a belief that the Jews would held to safeguard the Suez Canal and provide a buffer between the canal zone and the French rule in Syria.

Faced with bitter Arab protest both against the British failure to grant independence and against the arrival of increasing numbers of Jews, the British government stated in (1922) that there was no intention of British Government that the Jews should occupy the whole of Palestine and that there would be no interference with the rights of the Arabs in Palestine. The British hoped to persuade Jews and Arabs to live together peacefully in the same state but they failed to understand the deep religious gulf and difference of social and cultural set up between the two.

.Duch Jews continued to arrive complete with Zionist money, so they bought land from Arabs who were at first willing to sell, Jews started industries and reclaimed land. It was soon clear that they intended to develop not just a national home for Jews but a Jewish national state, so by 1928 there were about 150,000 of them. The Arabs rioted and began attacking and murdering Jews and consequently in 1930, the British Labour Government of MacDonald decided that Jewish immigration must cease for the time being. Now it was the turn of the Zionists to rage against the British rule and it was to such a large extent that MacDonald felt obliged to allow Jew immigration to continue.

This situation took a turn for the worse after Hitler leader of Nazi Party came to power in Germany in (1933): Nazi persecution by Hitler caused a flood of Jew refugees until by 1953 about a quarter of the total population of Palestine was Jewish. Arabs again began to attack Jews while British troops struggled to keep law and order but failed to curb Arab-Jews violence.

In 1937, the British Peel Commission suggested dividing Palestine into two separate states *i.e.* one Jewish and one Arab, but the Arabs rejected this idea of dividing Palestine.

As II World War loomed large in 1939, the British felt the need to win Arab support, and in a white paper they agreed to limit Jewish immigration only to 10,000 a year; thus guaranteeing an Arab majority in the new state. As such, nothing was resolved but the British Government hoped to shelve the problem until after the II World War.

The Condition of Palestine under British Rule from 1944 to 1948

During Second World War of 1939-45 an uneasy calm prevailed in Palestine. After the close of the Second World War in 1945 the situation in Palestine became acute owing to the increased aggressive national spirit of the Arabs and the desperate plight of thousands of Jews due to their harassment by Nazi Government of Hitler so Jews were left stranded in post-war Central Europe, In 1945 a joint Anglo-American Committee of Enquiry was appointed to investigate the Palestine situation and it recommended among other things the immediate admission of 1,00,000 Jewish who were victims of Nazi persecution of Hitler's Government. The Arabs bitterly denounced this whole report and threatened a national struggle if efforts were made to give effect to this recommendations. The Jews began to enter Palestine clandestinely and organized terrorist groups to meet the Arab menace of Arab terrorists so strife and terror became epidemic in all Palestine. At last in 1947 the General Assembly of the U.N.O. appointed a Special Committee on Palestine at the request of Great Britain who expressed her wish to leave Palestine. Seven members of this Committee *i.e.,* majority of U.N.O. proposed a partition of Palestine into three parts — An Arab state, a Jewish state and the city of the Jerusalem, which was to be governed under the Trusteeship Council of U.N.O. The General assembly of U.N.O.

next promptly appointed a Commission to assume responsibility for the administration of Palestine during the transition period between the relinquishment of the mandate by Britain and the establishment of the two independent states of Jews and Arabs. The Jewish Agency welcomed the prospect of the creation of a Jewish state but the Arabs were bitterly opposed to any plan of partition of Palestine. Hence bitter strife flared up and the terroristic activities of the Jews and the Arabs increased to a very alarming proportions in 1948. Realising the gravity of the situation, the security Council of U.N.O. began to consider the advisability of sending an international force to Palestine, but before this may be achieved on May, 15, 1948, the British Government terminated their mandate over Palestine. To the surprise of all, the Jews anticipated the U.N.O. decision and immediately proclaimed the establishment of a new independent state of Israel in the area which they had already occupied, with Tel Aviv as its capital. America and the U.S.S.R recognized this Jew's new state at once. The Jews chose as President of their state the veteran Zionist leader, Dr. Chaim Weitzmann, whose scientific services to the British nation had occasioned the Balfour declaration and agreement with Feisel. The neighbouring Arab states invaded this new tiny state of Israel and thus ensued the fierce struggle between the Jews and the Arabs. Which is still prevailing in continuous skirmishes.

Israel's Declaration of Independence along with the State of Israel's Proclamation of Independence of 1948 and its Importance

The proclamation of Independence was published by the provisional State Council of Israel in its capital of Tel Aviv on May 14, 1948. The provisional State Council of Jews was the forerunner of the Knesset, the Israeli Parliament. The British mandate was terminated on the following day and regular armed forces of Trans Jordan, Egypt, Syria and of other Arab countries attacked Palestine to wipe out the new tiny state of Israel.

The Land of Israel was the birthplace of the Jewish people. Here their spiritual, religious and national identity etc. was formed. Here they achieved independence and created a culture and Hebrew religion of national and universal significance. Here they wrote and gave the bible to the world.

Impelled by this historic association, Jewish people remained faithful to it, in all the countries of their dispension, never ceasing to pray and hope for their return and the restoration of their national freedom. After stating all this, it further stated.

Impelled by this historic association, Jews strove throughout the centuries to go back to this land and regain their statehood. In recent decades, they returned in their masses. They reclaimed the wilderness, revived their language, built cities and villages, and established a vigorous and ever-growing community, with its own economic and cultural life. It stated that they sought peace yet were prepared to defend themselves. They brought the blessings of progress to all inhabitants of the country and looked forward to sovereign independence. They gave glimpse of Zionist movement and stated that in the year 1897, the First Zionist congress, inspired by Theodor Herzl's vision of the Jewish state, proclaimed the right of Jewish people to national revival in their own country.

This right was acknowledged by the (British Government through Balfour Declaration of November 2, 1917, and was reaffirmed by the Mandate of the League of Nations, which gave explicit international recognition to the historic connection of the Jewish people with Palestine and their right to reconstitute their National home. It stated further that.

The recent holocaust, which engulfed millions of Jews in Europe, proved anew the need to solve the problem of the homelessness and lack of independence of the Jewish people by means of the re-establishment of the Jewish State, which would open the doors to all Jews and endow the Jewish people with equality of status among the family of nations. Reflecting on miserable plight of Jews in Europe, it stated.

The survivors of the disastrous slaughter in Europe, and also Jews from other lands, have not desisted from their efforts to reach Eretz-Yistael, in face of difficulties, obstacles and perils; and have not ceased to urge their right to a life of dignity, freedom and honest toil in their ancestral land. This declaration continued.

In the second world war the Jewish people in Palestine made their full contribution to the struggle of the freedom loving nations against the Nazi evil. The sacrifices of their soldiers and their war effort gained them the right to rank with the nations which founded the United Nations. Jews proved their claim on U.N.O. resolution. Declaration of Independence gave reference to U.N.O. resolution.

On November 29, 1947, the General Assembly of the United Nations adopted a resolution requiring the establishment of a

Jewish state in Palestine. The General Assembly called upon the inhabitants of the country to take all the necessary steps on their part to put the right of the Jewish people to establish their independent state is unassailable.

It is the natural right of the Jewish people to lead, as do all other nations, an independent existence in its sovereign state.

Jews on the basis of U.N.O. decision decided and stated accordingly we, the members of the National Council, representing the Jewish people in Palestine and world zionist movement, however met together in solemn assembly to-day, the day of termination of the British Mandats for Palestine; and by virtue of the natural and virtue of the natural and historic right of the Jewish people and of the Resolution of the General Assembly of the United Nations. As such jews declared established of Jews national state of Israel by declaring as below. We hereby proclaim the establishment of the Jewish state in Palestine, to be called Mainath Yisrael (The State of Israel).

We hereby declare, as from the termination of the mandate at midnight, the 14th May, 1948, and pending the setting up of the duly elected bodies of the state in accordance with a constitution, to be drawn up by the constituent Assembly not later than the 1st October, 1948, the National Council shall act as the provisional state council, and that the National Administration shall constitute the provisional government of the Jewish state, which shall be known as Israel. Thus, new state came into existence.

The state of Israel will be opened to the immigration of Jews from all countries of their dispersion; will promote the development of the country for the benefit of all its inhabitants; will be based on the principles of liberty, Justice and peace as conceived by the prophets of Israel; will uphold the full social and political equality of all its citizens, without distinction of religion, race, or sex; will guarantee freedom of religion, conscience, education and culture; will safeguard the Holy places of all religions; and will loyally uphold the principles of the United Nations Charter. Thus it becomes clear by the above statement that Jews state of Israel was established with noble ideas.

The state of Israel will be ready to co-operate with the organs and representatives of the United Nations in the implementation of the Resolution of the Assembly of November 29, 1947, and will take steps to bring about the economic union over the whole of Palestine.

Founder of Israel appealed Arabs to maintain peace and it conferred equal, rights to Arabs. We appeal to the United Nations to assist the Jewish people in the building of its state and to admit Israel into the family of nations.

In the midst of wanton aggression, we yet call upon the Arab inhabitants of the state of Israel to preserve the ways of peace and play their part in the development of the state, on the basis of full and equal citizenship and one representation in all its bodies and institutions provisional and permanent.

We extend our hand in peace and neighborliness to all the neighbouring states and their peoples, and invite them to co-operate with the independent Jewish nation for the common good of all. The state of Israel is prepared to make its contribution to the progress of the Middle East as a whole.

Thus declaration of founders of Israel wanted to leave it in peace and to work for the uplift and welfare of middle East but Arab nations were determined to wipe out Jews from the face of earth and attacked the new tiny state of Israel, so war between Israel and Arab states became inevitable.

The Attitude of U.N.O. and of Others non-Muslim Powers towards Israel on Nov. 29, 1947, U.N.O. Partitioned Palestine and Israel came into Existence.

As soon as existence of state of Israel was declared, Arab — Jews war began. So confronted with a settled fact all that the U.N.O. could now do, was to nip the war between Jews and Arabs in the bud and to restore peace in Palestine. The Security Council of U.N.O. appointed Count F. Bernadotte of Sweden as the U.N. mediator for Palestine. Meanwhile the war between the Arabs and the Jews was going on and an Egyptian Army penetrated well into Palestine and captured Gaza. Etc. but the Jews held to their position with desperate will and tenacity and refused all attacks of Arab powers to dislodge them. Count, F Bernadotte arranged a cease-fire, and on 16th September, 1948, recommended to the U.N. Assembly a modification of the proposed partition boundary in favour of the Arabs but next day he was assassinated in Jerusalem by the Jewish terrorists. Dr. Bunche, an American, succeeded Count F Bernadotte as mediator. After months of negotiation, deadlock and compromise, armistice agreements were signed between Israel and her Arab neighbours, Egypt, Lebanon, Jordan and Syria etc. in (1949). In the result, the territorial disposition which had already resulted from this war, was maintained. Due to this war about three fourth of Palestine passed under the control of Israel. In 1949

Israel became a member of the United Nations as an independent State. Thus by bringing war Arabs lost a part of territory which was given to them by U.N.O.

In 1950 Britain, France and the United States of America in an effort to prevent the possibility of a renewal of war. They undertook in a tripartite agreement not to supply arms to either side concerned in the Palestine problem. There was, however, no peace in Palestine. Frontier disputes were frequent but they never led to a renewal of war until 1956 when Israel invaded Egypt in collaboration with Britain and France and had to withdraw forces due to intervention of U.N.O.

The Arab-Jewish Conflict in Palestine, Between the Two Great Wars of 1914-18 and 1939-45

Palestine was the most tempestuous area probably in all the Middle East, as Britain sought to protect its imperial interests and at the same time tried to reconcile them with Zionism and Arab nationalism. Nevertheless, from 1922 to 1929 some peace and progress were possible chiefly because Jewish immigration was not large. But soon the Zionists reclaimed land, set up collective farms, harnessed the river Jordan's power, and established many new factories so a veritable economic revolution took place. Tel Aviv where Jews concentrated, grew into a thriving modern city and an excellent university was founded at Jerusalem. Thus Palestine became the center of a Hebrew renaissance.

This era of peace ended in 1929, when, serious disorders broke out, mainly due to Arab attacks on Jews. Violence continued to erupt in the early 1930's as the Hitler's Nazi persecution in Germany of the Jews, brought about a steep rise in immigration to Palestine and threatened the predominant position of the Arabs in the war. In 1937, a British commission of inquiry recommended a tripartite division. It was proposed that Palestine would be divided into two independent states, one controlled by the Arabs and one by the Jews, with Britain holding a third portion, having a small mandated area containing holy places of Jerusalem and Bethelhem etc. This recommendation satisfied no one and so it was not accepted. Although the outbreak of World War II, in 1939, temporarily shelved the Zionist-Arab quarrel in Palestine, later on after the II World War, the Arab-Israel controversy and war broke out again with still greater ferocity.

Due to these conflicts British withdrew from Palestine and U.N.O. accepted Jewish demand of an state to be established as a national state of Jews. The Middle East also contains the

Jewish state of Israel set up in 1948. Which is a tiny but powerful and progressive.

The Creation of Israel and the Arab/Israeli War of 1948-49 and the Causes of Arab-Israel War of 1948

The trouble in Palestine began soon after the First World War when large number of Jews began to settle in Palestine due to disappearance of Ottoman rule and due to British mandate Jews hope to set up a Jewish 'national home'. The Arabs in Palestine were implacably hostile to the idea of a separate Jewish state in what they considered to be their exclusive homeland. In order to retain Arab friendship and their own oil supplies, the British Government limited Jewish immigration only to 10,000 a year upto (1939).

The Second World War of 1939-45 intensified the problem with hundreds of thousands of Jewish refugees from Hitler's Europe left their homes looking for some where to go. In 1945, the USA Government pressed Britain to admit 100,000 of them into Palestine. This demand was echoed by Devid Ben Gurion, one of the Jewish, leaders, but the British refused because they disliked to offend the Arabs.

The Jews, after all that their race had suffered at the hands of the Nazis due to Hilter's aim of wiping them out were determined to fight for their 'National Home'. They began a terrorist campaign against both Arabs and British. The most spectacular incident of which was the blowing up of the King David Hotel, which was the British headquarter in Jerusalem with the loss of more than 91 lives in 1946. The British responded by arresting Jewish leaders and by turning back their ships such as the exodus etc. with intending Jew immigrants.

After War. The British, weakened by the II World War, were unable to cope with this problem. Ernest Bevin, the British Foreign Secretary. Invited the United Nations to deal with this problems, and in November 1947, the UNO voted for the partition of Palestine, setting aside roughly less than half of it to form an independent Jewish state.

Early in 1948, the British Government abandoned the mandate entrusted to it by Leagues and withdrew their troops, though fighting was already taking place between Jews and Arabs, who bitterly resented the loss of half of Palestine. In May 1948 Jews leader Ben Gurion declared the new Jewish State of Israel with independent status. It was immediately attacked by Egypt, Syria, Jordan, Iraq and Lebanon etc.

Main cause of war was determination of Arab states to wipe out Israel from the face of the earth.

Arab-Israel War of 1948 and Its Result

Against apparently overwhelming odds, the Israelis managed to survive against Arabs and even were able to capture more territory of Palestine including the port of Eilat on the Red Sea which was seized from Egypt. The UNO played an important part in bringing the fighting to an end. Israeli success was due partly to their own desperate resistance and to the fact that the Arabs were divided amongst themselves and poorly lead and poorly equipped; King Abdullah of Jordan was less than enthusiastic about the war because the partition gave him the chance to seize a section of Palestine situated at west of the River Jordan (known as the West Bank). The most tragic result of this war was the plight of the Palestinian Arabs who found themselves under the new state of Israel. After Jewish terrorists had slaughtered the lot of population of an Arab village, nearly a million Arabs fled into Arab states of Egypt, Lebanon, Jordan and Syria etc. where they lived in miserable refugee camps. Jerusalem was divided between Israel and Jordan, and although the USA, Britain and France etc. guaranteed Israel's frontiers, the Arabs states did not regard the cease-fire imposed by U.N.O. as permanent, so wars continued and this was only the first round in the struggle to destroy Israel and liberate Palestine.

The Suez War of 1956 and Its Consequences

(a) The causes of the Suez war were complex. This Suez war was partly due to the Arab/Israeli conflict, and partly it was the result of the struggle between Arab nationalism and the British and French interests who wanted to prolong their influence in the Middle East, and it was also an episode in the Cold War between the USA and the USSR.

(i) Colonel Gamal Abbel Nasser, the new ruler of Egypt (who came to power in 1954 soon after the overthrow of the unpopular Egyptian King Farouk), was aggressively in favour of Arab unity and aggression and independence including the liberation of Palestine from the rule of Jews.

(ii) He organized guerilla bands (fedayeen : self-sacrificers) to sabotage and murder inside Israel and block the Gulf of Aqaba leading to the Israeli port of Eilate. Thus, Naseer took steps to create chaos in Israel.

(iii) He insisted that Britain must evacuate her base at Suez Canal (as the agreement signed in 1936 allowing her to keep the base for 20 year expired in 1956). He sent aid to the Algerian Arabs in their struggle against France. He also prodded the other Arab states into opposing the British-sponsored Baghdad pact and forced King Hussein of Jordan to dismiss his British chief of staff. Thus, Naseer was determined to create chaos everywhere.

(iv) In September 1955, Nasser signed an arms deal with Czechoslovakia for Russian fighters, bombers and tanks, and Soviet experts went to train the Egyptian army. This encouraged Nasser to take aggressive steps against Britain, France and Israel.

(v) The Americans saw this as a Russian attempt to 'move into' the Middle East and so they cancelled, a promised grant of 56 million dollars towards the building of a dam at Aswan (July 1956). The intention of U.S.A. was to force Naseer to abandon his new links with the communists.

(vi) Naseer immediately retaliated by nationalizing the Suez Canal, intending to use its revenues to finance the Aswan dam; share-owners, a majority of whom were British and French, were promised in sufficient compensation. However, British Prime Minister Anthony Eden believed that Nasser was on the way to forming a united Arabia under Egyptian control and Communist influence with Russian support to cut off Europe's oil supplies at will. As such he decided that this must be prevented at all costs.

(vii) Secret negotiations took place between British, France and Israel who agreed to teach a lesson to Egypt. The British and French hoped to come down on Nasser while the Israelis wanted to stop 'Arab terrorists' raids and open the Gulf of Aquba. As such they attacked Egypt jointly.

(b) Thus, war began with an Israeli invasion of Egypt on (29 October) 1956 which within a week had captured the entire Sinal peninsula. Meanwhile the British and French air forces bombed Egyptian airfields of Egypt and landed their troops at Port Said at the northern end of the Suez Canal. These attacks caused an outcry from the rest of the world, and the Americans, who were afraid of annoying the Arabs and forcing them into closer ties with the USSR. As such the American refused to support British although they had earlier hinted that support would be forthcoming. At the United Nations Organisation's meetings, Americans and Russians joined in demanding a cease-fire. As such with the pressure of world opinion against them, British, France and Israel agreed to withdraw their forces while UN troops moved in to police the frontier between Egypt and Israel. Thus Suez war ended with humiliation to Britain, France and Israel and Nasser's prestige rose.

(c) The results of the war were important. It was a complete humiliation for British and France who achieved none of their aims and were shown to be very weak. They had failed to topple President Nasser whose prestige as leader of Arab nationalism against European interference was greatly increased. The Egyptians blocked the Suez Canal, and the Arabs reduced oil exports to western Europe, where petrol rationing had to be introduced for a short time. Russian influenced replaced American for influence. British action seriously embarrassed Premier Nuri-es-Said of Iraq who now came under increasing attack from other Arabs for this pro-British attitude, so he was murdered in 1958. The Algerians were encouraged in their struggle for independence from France, which they achieved in 1952. From Israel's point of view, the Suez war was something of a success: although she had been compelled to hand back all the captured Egyptian places which took Egyptians several years to make good. For the time being fedayeen raids ceased and Israel had a breathing space, in which it found time to consolidate.

The Conditions of Arab's State and of Israel after Suez War of 1956

After 1956, British Prime Minister, Anthony Eden had to resign and Britain followed policy of giving freedom to African states. French territories also gained freedom but relations between Arab states and Israel became bitter and both sides prepared themselves for war. All efforts of U.N.O. and of Israeli diplomats failed to appease Arab states so uneasy calm prevailed. Main cause of continuous conflict was and is problem of Arab refugees who were forced to leave Israel and formed P.L.O. that is Palestian Libration Organisation. These P.L.O. terrorists' committed acts of terror all over the world to get support for Arab lands but their cry fell into dumb ears and so they continued acts of terrorism Jews pleaded for peace but did not care for the fate of refugees. To present Israeli view point appeal of Mrs. Golda Meir is given in next question.

Israel's Point of View for Ending Arab Israel Conflict

Foreign Minister's Mrs. Golda Meir's call for disarmament, later on Mrs. Golda Meir became lady P.M.

From an address by the then Israeli Foreign Minister before the U.N. General Assembly on October 9, 1962. Mrs. Golda Meir-remained Prime Minister of Israel from 1969-74. She forcefully pleaded for peace stating, "The small and new countries, emerging into a world of armed camps, suffer two fold, our immediate aim is rapid development, but since the danger of war still looms over every dispute, we are constantly burdened with defence expenditures to the detriment of our development needs. We too quickly learn the bitter lesson that those who threaten others must be deterred by some equilibrium, and let not those whose declared policy is to attack their neighbour cry out mock indignation when the latter seeks some means of defence." On behalf of Israeli government, she stated :

My government rejects war as a means of settling disputes. From the day that the state of Israel was established, my government has called for settling all outstanding differences by direct negotiations. Mrs. Golda Meir urged Arab nations to settle dispute peacefully.

We do not rest content with calling upon the Great Powers to find a way to disarmament, and to settle outstanding problems by negotiation and conciliation between them. We are prepared to put this into practice, in the dispute in which we are involved with our neighbours. As we have done in the past, we call again upon the Arab States to agree to complete disarmament with mutual intersection, covering all types of weapons, and to accept that method of direct negotiations as the only means for solving all differences between them and Israel.

She told that in middle East not only Arab but others also reside there. There are many that are misled by two fallacies regarding the Middle East. The first is that it is an Arab region. In fact there are in it more non-Arabs than Arabs — Moslems, Christians and Jews etc. This composite pattern of various faiths and cultures has always been the pattern of the Middle East, each people with its historic continuity, past, present and future.

It was further stated by Her

The second fallacy is that all would be well in that region if it were not for the tension between the Arab states and Israel. I would be the last to undertake difficulties and dangers which arise from that conflict. But this is only one source of tension in a part of the world which is unhappily, the scene of so much political in stability, economic and social backwardness, rivalry and friction between different countries and regions and the pressure of the cold war (etc.) Anyone who follows the affairs of the middle East, knows that during this; last year the focus of trouble in the area has been the bitter struggles within Arab world which have made the Arab League no longer even a facade of unity.

Israel longs for the day when the political independence and territorial integrity of every single state in the area *i.e.* of Arab and non-Arab will be assured and when we can all concentrate on the welfare of our people. When I refer to the turmoil in the Arab world, it is because we are a middle Eastern country and therefore affected by all threats which affects the peace of our area.

As far as the Israel-Arab dispute itself is concerned, it is well to see clearly what is the basic problem. It is the denial by the Arab states of Israel's right to exist. If this attitude were to change, and if Arab states and Israel were to discuss their differences at the conference table in a frank and open manner, I am positive that solutions could be found on all the specific issues.

"Year after year Israel, has come on this rostrum with one demand — peace between it and its Arab neighbours. May I say here that we were greatful to the distinguished Deputy Foreign Minister of Ghana when he drew our attention again to the important statement of (Ghana's) president Nkrumah, during the 15th General Assembly, in which he called for recognition of the political realities in the Middle East and for insurance against non-aggression. We are entirely in agreement with that view."

"The Arab denial of Israel's existence has a direct bearing on the distressing refugee problem. We are willing, to discuss with the Arab governments what can best be done to secure the future of the refugees in the light of the political and economic realities in the region. But a natural solution to the problem is frustrated by the Arab dream of destroying Israel and openly proclaimed Arab intention of using the refugees for this purpose."

"This design has been openly propagated even from the rostrum of this Assembly. This small spot of land, in which the Jewish people have revived their ancient home and nationhood, must again be wrested from them and they again be scattered to the four corners of the earth. Our neighbours have tried to achieve this by various means, open or guerilla warfars, economic boycott, propaganda and threats."

"Negotiations and conciliation are proclaimed from this rostrum, as the method to solve all other problems in the world except this one, which must, according to these spokes men, be resolved by force. For every other nation, they claim existence, practised in peace. For Israel, Non-existence, to be achieved by war. This doctrine not only runs counter the basic principles of the United Nations Charter : its acceptance strikes at the very roots of our organization."

"The world of today is overwhelmed by ideological disputes, international conflicts and economic controversies. In face of this situation, the basic concepts of the Charter, on the eschewing of force, on the unremitting search for peace, on international cooperation, on negotiation as the means to solve problems, have gained a new depth and significance. As long as negotiation is sought, there is hope. Those who rule out negotiation in the middle East, those who year after year engage in sterile and stereotyped attacks of hostility, should know that their attitude is irrelevant to the basic theme of the international community and can have no echo in an organization which has proclaimed peace to be synonymous with human survival: that they are assaulting the foundations of human progress."

She clearly stated about the policy of Israeli government. "The policy of the Israeli government has been and continues to be peace. It is peace not only for the world, but also between us and neighbours, the day must come when we shall live in amity and co-operation. Then will the entire Middle East become a region where the tens of millions of people will dwell in peace and then will its economic potentialities and rich cultural heritage achieve fulfillment. This Israel believes towards this end and we shall devote all our efforts to get it."

Speech of Golda Meir, who was Foreign Ministers and later on became Prime Minister fell to dumb ears of Arab powers who were determined to wipe out existence of Israel by making Arab refugee problem as an apple of discord. But Israel made progress and became strong and powerful. It is strange that

UNO whose aim is to maintain peace is constantly tolerating plea of Arab powers to destroy Israel.

Progress of Israel

Israel. The progress of tiny state of Israel has confounded its foes. In this country of desert wasteland and of limited natural resources, irrigation projects were built, agriculture was extended, and new industries were established. In the councils of the nations, Israel earned respect as a stable and democratic state having progressive regime. But its future was uncertain despite its energy due to Arab determination to finish it and dedication of its people. The antipathy between this small population of less than two million people in 1967 and its more than forty million Arab neighbours continued. Boarder clashes were frequent. The presence of nearly one million Arab refugees, who once lived in this area new occupied by the Israelis, was a constant irritant to Arab nationalists. In 1965, in order to obtain more water for their parched lands, the Israelis began to channel a supply from the Sea of Galille. In response, to an underground terrorist organization from neighbouring Arab states engaged in sabotage along the Israeli border. Throughout 1966 Arab Israeli relations remained explosive. Which later on brought war between Israel and Arab States in 1967.

P.L.O. and Its Aim and Organization

The Charter of Palestine Libration Organisation *i.e.* P.L.O. was prepared in 1963 under Egyptian auspices by a Palestinian lawyer who became its President but later on he was forced to resign in 1967 due to defeat of Arab powers. Now Aseer Arafat is leader of P.L.O. due to India's support.

According to section 2, all Palestinians were to become its members. Aim of this P.L.O. is to liberate their homeland from Jews with help of other Arab states. P.L.O. constituted executive committee and many other committees to carry on its terrorists activities against Israel and other Christian countries to whom they considered sympathetic to Jews cause.

P.L.O. created civil war and havoc in Lebanan and continued its terrorist activities of disturbing sports, abducting people, kidnapping children and hijacking aeroplanes but achieved very little success against Israel.

P.L.O. has now became less militant under Aseer Arafat and demands only a part of Palestine as its homeland but difficulty lies that it demands its share only from Israel and not from Arab states who have occupied its homeland allotted to it by U.N.O. Efforts are being made to find out a peaceful solution and new Palestine state has been established in 1984 housing population of 3.3 million.

The Background to the War of Arab, Israel War of 1967

(i) Arab terrorists killed their mild leader Nuri-es-Said. After the murder of Nuri-es-Said, they had an aggressive nationalist government which was prepared to co-operate with Egypt. President Aref announced in June 1967; Our goal is clear and it is to wipe Israel off the map.

(ii) Political upheavals in Syria brought to power the left wing of Ba'ath Party in (1966) which supported E1 fatah, the Palestine Liberation Movement, which is more effective guerilla force than the fedayeen. The Syrians air force also bombarded Jewish settlements from the Golan Heights overlooking the frontier. Thus Syria attacked and started Arab Israeli war of 1967.

(iii) President Nasser of Egypt was now immensely popular in Egypt because of his leadership of the Arab world and his achievements over Suez Canal and his attempts to improve conditions inside the country with his socialist policies, which included limiting the size of farms to 100 acres and redistributing the surplus land to peasants. Attempts were made to industrialise the Egyptian country and more than two thousand new factories were built which were almost all under government control. The Aswan Dam project was vitally important, providing electricity, and water and irrigating an extra million acres of Egyptian land. After initial delays at the time of the Suez Crisis in 1956 work on the Aswan Dam eventually got under way and this project was completed in 1971. With all going well at home and the prospect of effective help from Iraq and Syria President Nasser seems to have decided that the time was ripe for another attack on Israel. He began to move troops up to the frontier in Sinai desert and asked in May 1967, the U.N.O. to remove its troops policing the narrow strip of land along the coast connecting Gaza with the rest of Egypt and closed the Gulf of Aqaba.

(iv) Syria, Jordan and Lebanon also massed troops along their frontier with Israel while contingents from Iraq, Saudi Arabia and Algeria joined them. Israel's situation seemed impossible and very critical. It seemed Israel will be wiped out of existence.

(v) Moshe Dayan, the new Israeli Minister of Defence, decided that the best policy was to attack first rather than to sit about waiting to be destroyed. He realized and attack is best defence. It has been suggested that Israel wanted a war to unite the country and to solve the unemployment problem and to attract American dollars. As such seizing the opportunity provided by the ponderous Arab troops build-up the Israelis launched a series of devastating air strikes which destroyed most of the Egyptian air force on the ground on (5 June) 1967 and this crippled Egypt's airforce.

Israeli troops moved with remarkable speed, capturing the Gaza Strip and the whole of Sinai desert from Egypt, the rest part of Jerusalem and the West bank from Jordan and the Golan Heights from Syria. The Arabs had no choice but to accept a U.N.O. cease-fire order on 10 June, 1967. Reasons for the brilliant Israeli success were their better arms and better training and superiority in the air and inadequate Arab preparation and communications and differences among Arab powers.

(b) Results of the Arab-Israeli War of 1967

The time the Israelis ignored a U.N.O. order to return captured territory of Arab powers. This meant that defence would be easier but it left them with the problem of how to deal with an extra million Arabs who now found themselves under Israeli rule; many of these were living in the refugee camps on the West Bank of Jordan and in the Gaza strip set up in 1948. The Arab states, though humiliated, were no less determined on the ultimate destruction of Israel so again a war took place in 1967.

The Israeli view point about the war of 1967 and Israeli policy about the six days war as stated by Israeli representative Abba Eban's speech in the special Assembly of the United Nations on June 19, 1967.

Israeli representative began his speech by stating "our watchword is forward to peace".

"The subject of our discussion is the Middle East, its past agony and its further hope. We speak of a region whose destiny has profoundly affected the entire human experience. In the heart of that region at the very center of its geography and history, lies a very small nation called Israel. This nation gave birth to the currents of thought which have fashioned the life of the mediterranean world and of vast regions beyond. It has now been reestablished as the home and sanctuary of a people which has seen six million of its sons exterminated in the greatest catastrophe ever endured by a family of the human race. Thus, after Jews tragedy due to Nazi atrocities, he stated."

In recent weeks the middle East has passed through a crisis whose shadows darken the world. This crisis has many consequences but only one cause. Israels, rights to peace, security sovereignty, economic development and maritime freedom — indeed its very right to exist — has been forcibly denied and aggressively attacked. This is the true origin of the tension which torments the Middle East. All the other elements of the conflict are the consequences of this single cause. There has been danger, there is still peril in the Middle East because of Israel's existence, sovereignty and vital interests have been and are violently assailed.

Israeli representative accused Russia for bringing this war and threat to Israel's existence, its peace, security, sovereignty and development has been directed against her in the first instance by the neighbouring Arab states. But all the conditions of tension, all the impulses of aggression in the Middle East, have been aggravated by the policy of one of the Great powers which under our charter bears primary responsibilities for the maintenance of international peace and security. "I shall show how the Soviet Union has been unfaithful to that trust. The burden of responsibility lies heavy upon her.

I come to this rostrum to speak for a united people who having faced danger to the national survival, is unshakably resolved to resist any course which would renew the perils from which it has emerged.

The general Assembly is chiefly preoccupied by the situation against which Israel defended itself of the morning of June 5. I shall invite every peace loving state represented here to as ask itself how it would have acted on that day if it faced similar dangers. But if our discussion is to have any weight or depth, we must understand that great events are not born in a single instant of time. It is beyond all honest doubt that between may 14 and June 5, Arab governments led and directed by President Nasser, methodically prepared and mounted an aggressive assault designed to bring about Israel's immediate and total destruction.

Thus according to Israeli evidence, Arab powers encouraged by Soviet Union and lead by President Nasser attacked Israel to destroy it. How far it is correct is difficult to say but it contains some truth.

The Background of Arab-Israeli war

The Arab-Israeli war is most controversial. Arab powers lead by President Nasser of Egypt were determined to destroy Israel. It was stated before General Assembly of U.N.O. by Abba Eban, the Israel's representative stated Middle East has affected the entire human experience. Israel is a tiny nation but it has given thought and culture to vast regions. Six million Jews were destroyed by Nazi Government of Hitler in the greatest catastrophic ever endured by on family of human race so now Israeli nation has been established whose motto is peace but its very right to exist has been forcefully denced and aggressively attacked.

On May 25, 1967, Cairo radio announced. The Arab people are firmly resolved to wipe Israeli off the map. On May 28, 1967 President Nasser said "We will not accept any possibility of existence with Israel. Thus Arab powers were determined to completely destroy Israel and wipe out existence of Israel. In this task Arab states were encouraged by Russia. Soviet Union supplied Arabs 2 thousand tanks, 100 aircraft and bombers, 176 rocket bomber, 14 submarines, 7 destroyers and numerous other weapons. Not only this Soviet Union assisted. Arabs in their desire to wipe out Israel. Thus origin of 1967, Arab-Israel was determination of Arabs powers to destroy Israel with the help of Soviet Union's same can be said of 1973 war.

The Six Days War of 1967 between Israel and Egypt and Israeli's View Point as Presented by Abba Eban on June 19, 1967.

Our watchward is "Forward to Peace" he stated on May 18, Egypt called for the total removal of the United Nations Emergency Force. The Secretary-General of the United Nations acceded to this request and moved to carry out, without reference to the Security Council of the General Assembly, without carrying out the procedures indicated by Secretary-General Hammerskjold in the event of a request for a withdrawal being made, without heeding the protesting voices of some of the permanent members of the Security Council and of the government at whose initiative the force had been established, without consulting Israel on the consequent prejudice to her military security and her vital maritime freedom, and without seeking such delay as would enable alternative measures to be concerted for preventing belligerent that sea and a dangerous confrontation of forces by land. He stated.

It is often said that United Nations procedures are painfully slow. This decision was disastrously swift. Its effect was to make Sinai safe for belligerency from north to south, to create a sudden disruption of the local security balance, and to leave an international maritime interest exposed to almost certain threat. I have already said that Israel, attitude to the peace-keeping functions of the United Nations has been traumatically affected by its experience. What is the use of a fire brigade which vanishes from the scene as soon as the first smoke and flame had appeared? I state that we are firmly resolved never again to allow a vital Israel interest and our very security to rest on such a fragile foundation?

The clouds now gathered thick and fast. Between May 14 and May 23, Egyptian concentrations in Sinai increased day by day. It was stated that Israel was forced to retaliate.

As such Israel took corresponding measures. In the absence of an agreement to the contrary it is, of course, legal for any state to place its armies wherever it chooses in its territory. It is equally true that nothing could be more uncongenial to the prospect of peace than to have large armies facing each other across a narrow space, with one of them clearly bent on an early assault. For the purpose of the concentration was not in doubt. On May 18, at 24 hours, the Cairo radio Saut-el-Arab, published the following order of the day by Abdul Mushin Murtagi, the General, then commanding Sinai:

The Egyptian forces have taken up positions in accordance with a definite plan because Egyptian rulers declared. Our forces are definitely ready to carry the battle beyond the borders of Egypt.

Morale is very high among the members of our armed forces because this is the day for which they have been waiting to make a holy war in order to return the plundered land to its owners.

In many meetings with army personnel they asked when the holy war would begin, the time has come to give them their wish:

On may 21, General Amer gave the order to mobilize reserves. Now came the decisive step. All doubt that Egypt had declared upon immediate or early war was now dispelled. Appearing at an Air force base at 6 O'clock in the morning, President Nasser announced that he would block the Gulf of Alnahar to Israeli ships. On May 25, 1967, Cairo radio announced. The Arab people is firmly resolved to wipe Israel off. As such Arab powers attacked Israel to destroy it.

To quote Abba Eban as reported in the Jerusalem post and lackquer's Arab Israel Reader, he stated the vast mass of the Egyptian armies in Sinai with seven infantry and two armoured divisions, the greatest force over assembled in that peninsula in all its history. Here there were 40,000 regular Syrian troops poised to strike at the Jordan valley from advantageous positions in the hills. Israel had to face the mobilized forces of Jordan, with their artillery and mortars trained on Israel's population centers in Jerusalem and along the vulnerable narrow coastal plain. Troops from Iraq, Kuwait and Algeria converge towards the battle front at Egypt's behest 900 tanks face Israel on the Sinai border, while 200 more were poised to strike the isolated town of Eilat at Israel's southern tip. These military dispositions tell their own story. The Northern Nigev was to be invaded by armour and bombarded from the Gaza Strip. From May 27 onward, Egyptian air squadrons in Sinai were equipped with operation orders instructing them in detail on the manner in which Israeli air field, pathetically few in number, were to be bombarded, thus exposing Israel's crowded cities to easy and merciless assault.

Egyptian air sorties came in and out of Israel's southern desert to reconnoisre, inspect and prepare for the assault. An illicit blockade had cut Israel from all her commerce with the eastern half of the world.

Thus, in Arab Israeli war of 1967, Arab states attacked Israel from all sides Israel is a tiny country while her adversaries possessed large armies, arms, equipments and above all support of Soviet Union but due to better organisation and better arms and equipments and due to more powerful air force, Israel emerged victorious against Arab powers in this war.

The main Arab concerns since 1945 included attempts to achieve some political and economic unity and problems caused by the fact that outside powers were constantly interfering in the Middle East because of its importance as a strategic crossroads and a source of oil. However the domination issue which united all the Arab states was the desire to destroy Israel, the Jews within their Muslim powers. This desire caused four short Arab Israeli wars and these wars were from the Arab point of view, unsuccessful wars of 1948- 1956, 1967 and 1973 in which Israel survived and is making progress.

Israels Viewpoint in U.N.O. after 1967 War as stated by Israeli Representative in U.N.O.

"Israeli representative began for the first time in history, no mediterranean nation is in subjection. All are endowed with sovereign freedom. The challenge now is to use this freedom for creative growth. There is only one road to that end. It is the road of recognition, of direct contact of true co-operation. It is the road of peaceful co-existence. This road, as the ancient prophets of Israel foretold, leads to Jerusalem. Israeli representative stated."

"Jerusalem, now united after her tragic division, is no longer an arena for gun emollacements and barbed wire. In our nation's long history there have been few hours more intensely moving than the hour of our reunion with the western wall. A people had come back to the citadel of its birth. It has renewed its link with the memories which that reunion evokes. For 20 years, there has not been free access by men of all faiths to the shrines which they hold in unique reverence. This access now exists. Israel is resolved to give effective expression, in co-operation with the world's great religions, to the immunity and sanctity of all the Holy places. The prospect of negotiated peace is less remote than it may seem. Israel waged her defensive struggle in pursuit of two objectives security and peace. Peace and security economic and demographic implications, can only be built by the free negotiation which is the true essence of sovereign responsibility. A call to the recent combatants to negotiate the conditions of their future co-existence is the only constructive course which this Assembly could take."

"Israeli representative asked the great powers to remove from this tormented region from the scope of global rivalries, to summon its governments to build their common future themselves, to assist, it if they will, to develop social and cultural levels worthy of its past, he requested the developing countries to support a dynamic and forward looking policy and not to drag the future back into the out worn past."

To the small nations, which form the bulk of the international family, we offer the experience which teaches us that small communities can best secure their interests by maximum self reliance. Nobody will help those who will not help themselves; we ask the small nations in the solidarity of our smallness, to help us stand firm against intimidation and threat such as those by which rallied to us in our plight to accompany us faithfully in our new opportunity. We ask the United Nations, which was prevented from offering us security in our recent peril, to respect our independent quest for the peace and security which are the charter's higher-ends, we shall do what the Security Council decided should be done and reject the course which the Security Council emphatically and wisely rejected. It may seem that if Israel stands along against numerous and powerful adversaries. But we have faith in the undying forces in our nation's history which have so often given the final victory to spirit over matter, to inner truth over mere quantity. We believe in the vigilance of history which has guarded our steps. The Guardian of Israel neither slumbers nor sleeps. It was urged.

"The Middle East, tired of wars, is ripe for a new emergence of human vitality. Let the opportunity not fall again from our hands."

In spite of all this U.N.O. did nothing to chastize Arab powers and they again attacked Israel in 1973 but like previous wars Arab Muslim powers were defeated and Jews and their national state Israel emerged victorious as is shown briefly in next question.

Arab Israel War of 1973

Two elements mainly combined to produce a joint Egyptian/ Syrian attack on Israel in October 1973 and brought Arab Israeli war of 1973.

(i) Pressure was brought on the Arab states by the Palestine Liberation organisation.

Organisation (PLO) under its leader Yasser Arafat urged for some action. The PLO tried by committing acts of terrorism, on Christian western states to draw world attention to what it considered to be grave injustice done to the dispossessed Arabs: PLO resorted to hijacking of aircrafts, shooting down passengers waiting in airport lounges, and killing members of the Israeli sports team at the 1972 in Munich Olympics in

Germany. However, such outrages only alienated world sympathy and failed to gain its objective.

(ii) Egypt (ruled since 1970 by President Sad at after Nasser and Syria re-equipped their armies with Russian help. Then they felt themselves strong, they felt justified in attacking Israel to regain territories lost in 1967 war. They were probably incited by the Russians who informed them, incorrectly, that Israel was about to attack them. Thus, like previous wars, it also began due to Russian support.

Egyptian and Syrian forces attacked early on the feast of Yom Kippur which was a Jewish religious festival, hoping to catch the Israelis off guard. After initial Arab successes, the Israels, using mainly American weapons, were able to turn the tables in this war managing to keep all territories which they captured in 1967 and even more after crossing the Suez Canal into Egypt. Thus in war of 1973, Arab forces were again defeated and Israel survived.

Describe the Result of Arab-Israel War of 1973

The USA was committed to support Israel against the Arab states, and this was another reason for the Russians to work for an Arab alliance and encourage them to attack Israel.

During the 1970 both east and west became much more cautious in their attitudes towards the Middle East. The western powers particularly Britain and France etc. took care not to offend the Arab states lest oil supplies may be cut off.

This time in 1973, the fighting was tough and was more evenly balanced and both sides were glad to accept a cease-fire organized by the USA and the USSR with UNO co-operation. At the end of this war of 1973, came a glimmer of hope for some sort of permanent settlement when Egyptian and Israeli leaders came together (though not in the same room) at Geneva. The Israelis agreed to move back from the Suez Canal (which was fully closed since the 1987 war). This move of Israel enabled the Egyptians to clear and open the Suez Canal to all in 1975 (but not to Israel).

An important development during the war of 1973 was that the Arab oil producing states tried to bring pressure to bear on the USA and western European states friendly to Israel by reducing oil supplies.

This caused serious oil shortages in many countries especially in Europe. At the same time producers, well aware that oil supplies were not unlimited, saw their action as a way of preserving oil resources. With this view in mind, the Organisation of petroleum Exporting Countries (OPEC began to raise oil prices substantially, contributing to inflation and causing an energy crisis in the world's industrial nations which forced them to oppose Israel and support Arab nations.

Camp David Agreement and the Egyptian/Israeli Peace of 1978-79 and Its Consequences

Being tired of continuous wars Egypt and Israel showed a readiness to continue negotiations and President Sadat of Israel took the courageous step of becoming the first Arab leader to talk peace to Israel, even to talk with Israeli leader was meant a recognition of the lawful existence of the state of Israel, and this would be resented by the PLO and the more aggressive Arab states such as Iraq and Syria etc. However, President was becoming increasingly convinced of the foolishness of squandering Egyptian resources on fruitless wars. At the same time Israel, in spite of her success in farming, industry and commerce, was facing acute economic problems partly caused by her enormous defence expenditure, and partly by loses of men and money in wars and by the world recession. The U.S.A. apparently growing impatient with the Middle East situation, pressed Israel to settle her differences with at least some of the Arabs Amers, President Sadat of Egypt visited Jerusalem in November 1977 and Menachem Begain, the Israel Prime Minister, visited Egypt on the following month *i.e.* in December 1977. President Carter of the USA played a vital role in bringing about opening of negotiations between the two leaders who were daggers drawn to one another at Camp David (near Washington) in September 1978. With President Carter of U.S.A. acting as intermediary these talks resulted in a peace treaty being signed in Washington in March 1979 which ended the state of war that had existed between Egypt and Israel since 1948. Israel promised to make a phased withdrawal from Sinai, while Egypt undertook not to attack Israel again and guaranteed to supply her with oil from the recently opened wells in southern Sinai. Thus a compromise between Israel and Egypt brought reconciliation.

This treaty was condemned by the PLO and by the most Arab states (except Sudan and Morocco). As such there was clearly a long way to go before similar treaties could be signed by Israel with Syria and Jordan etc. World opinion began to move against Israel and began to accept that the PLO had a case, but when the USA tried to bring Israel and the PLO together in an international conference, the Israelis declined to co-operate. In November, 1980 Israeli Prime Minister Begin announced that Israel would never return the Golen Heights to Syria even in exchange for a peace treaty, and would not allow the west Bank to become part of a Muslim Arab Palestinian state, which would be a permanent and mortal threat to Israel's existence. At the same time resentment among West Bank Arabs mounted at the Israeli policy of establishing Jewish settlements on lands owned by Arahs. Many observers feared fresh violence unless Prime Ministers Begin's government adopted a more moderate approach but no war took place. Efforts to bring reconciliation succeeded.

Efforts succeeded in favour of P.L.O. led by Yassar Arafat by Arab powers and India to force Israel to give land to P.L.O., to establish an independent state of Palestinian people. U.S.A. and western powers favouring P.L.O. and so Israel was forced to give its territory to Palestinian Arabs to establish an independent Palestinian state in near future. Strange thing is that P.L.O. is demanding territory from Israel and not from any Muslim Arab state?

From the time immemorial Jews have suffered innumerable hard-ships and ups and downs. Moses gave them freedom from Egyptian slavery. Romans Christians and Muslim rulers harassed them. Recently Nazi rulers lead by Hitler tried to exterminate Jews and Russians harassed them, so Jews came to conclusion that Jews homeland is necessary for their survival but now Arab powers supported by Soviet Union and India are determined to destroy Israel by forcing Israel to give her territory and if Israel accepts this demand, it may not survive at all. P.L.O. deserves homeland but it can be given in territories of Palestine annexed by Jordan or in the territories received by Egypt from Israel but every body is after Israel to give territory to P.L.O., so territory has been given to P.L.O. and autonomous state of Palestine has been established.

In the opinion of author Jews as well as Israel possess the right to exist and to have their own homeland and own state but problem can be solved by allowing Israel to exist as it is and to give P.L.O. lands which were given to it and have been annexed by Jordan and other powers. Israel is acid taste for U.N.O. as Abyssinia was to League of Nations. It is hoped humanity will gain an upper hand and home land for P.L.O. and Israel may be allowed and both may live peacefully as now P.L.O has got land.

17

PALESTINE

Jesus of Israel forced Arabs of Israel of Israel to leave Israel. They formed Palestine Liberation Organisation *i.e.* P.L.O. in 1964 under the leadership of Yasser Arafat. In 1974, the U.N.O. granted it permanent observer status and in 1976, it became member of Arab league. On Nov. 15, 1988 its headquarter was in Juris of Algeria and in 1994, Jericho became its headquarter. About 80 nations including India recognized new state of Palestine. In August 1993 Israel approved limited Palestinian autonomy, withdrew Israeli forces and gave Ghaza district. On May 13, 1994, Israel handed over Jericho to Palestinian police and on July 5, 1994 Palestinian self govt. was established. On Feb. 12, 1996 Yasser Arafat became president of Palestine. In Palestinian council there are 82 members. Palestinian police is of 15 thousand men and population is about 20 lakhs.

Arabs have got autonomous state of Palestine but they are demanding more territory and Jerusalem which is very ancient city and capital of Israel and are creating disturbances, so agitation is going on. Thus Arabs have got autonomous state of Palestine but Arab Israel conflict is continuous because India and Arab countries are supporting Palestinian and America is supporting Israel. It is hoped with U.N.O. efforts will be soon solved and peace may prevail between New state of Palestine and Israel.

Israel is supported by U.S.A. Now relations of Israel with other countries including India are satisfactory and with Muslim countries are also better as Israel has allowed existence of Mulsim Arab state of Palestine having population of about 3.5 million.

On November 29, 1947, U.N.O. partitioned Palestine between Jews and Arabs in which Israel got very little portion of ancient Palestine but Jews accepted it and proclaimed new Zionist State of Israel on May 15, 1948.

Forces of Muslim Arab countries led by Egypt attacked Israel to wipe out its existence in 1948, but were defeated, so Israel emerged as a powerful nation and Arabs residing in Palestine became refugee as they have to leave Palestine.

They formed PLO *i.e.*, Palestine Libertarian Organization under Yasser Arafat in 1964, and committed terrorist attacks against Jews but remained fugitives as in wars of 1967, and of 1973, Arab countries' forces were defeated by Israel in all wars.

Due to defeat, Egypt agreed to make peace on gaining back territories lost in war with Israel. Similarly other muslim Arab states become reconciled with the existence of Jewish State of Israel, but PLO under the leadership of Yasser Arafat continued its strive for independent state of Palestine form its head quarters in Algeiers.

Palestinian Liberation Organization (PLO)

Palestine Liberation Organization (PLO), political body representing Palestinian Arabs in their attempt to reclaim their homeland from Israel continued agitation and terrorist acts.

Structure and Organs

The PLO was founded at a congress in the Jordanian sector of Jerusalem in May 1964.

Dedicated to mobilizing the Palestinian people to recover their usurped homes, the organization, seeks the replacement of Israel with a non-sectarian democratic state and has sponsored numerous terrorist acts both inside that country and internationally.

The functions of the PLO are carried out by three main organs: the Executive Committee, a decision making body in which the major fedayeen groups are represented; the Central Committee, an advisory body; and the Palestine National Council, which is considered as an assembly of the Palestinian people.

Since February 1969, the PLO has been headed by Yasser Arafat, leader of Al Fatah. At an Arab summit meeting in Rabat, Morocco, in 1974, the organization was recognized as the sole legitimate representative of the Palestinian people, and Arafat subsequently addressed the United Nations, where the organization has an observer status.

In 1970, the PLO fought a short, bloody war with the army of Jordan, where most of the fedayeen were then stationed.

Expelled, they settled in Lebanon. Israel's invasion of Lebanon in 1982, greatly weakened the PLO presence there, intensified the organization's factional splits, and forced the dispersion of some 12,000 PLO members to Syria and to other Arab countries. PLO members loyal to Arafat made their headquarters in Tunis; an Israeli bombing raid in October 1985, severely damaged the main buildings. In July 1988, King Hussein of Jordan ceded to the PLO all territorial claims to the Israeli held West Bank.

In November 1988, at a meeting of the Palestine National Council in Algiers, Arafat declared the establishment of an independent Palestinian state with Jerusalem as its capital. The council also voted to accept UNO resolutions 242 (1967) and 338 (1973), recognizing the sovereignty of all states in the Middle East, and also the Palestinian right to self determination.

The United States agreed in December 1988 to initiate direct diplomatic dialogue with the PLO. Relations with the U.S.A. and the pro-western Arab states deteriorated in 1991, however, as Arafat publicly supported Iraq during the Persian Gulf War. In July 1992, the Lebanese army, with Syrian backing, forced the PLO to abandon its strongholds in Lebanon.

In January 1993, Israel repealed its ban on PLO and entered in negotiations. In September 1993, Arafat and Israeli prime minister Yitzhak Rabin signed peace accord that paved the way for limited Palestinian self-rule in Israeli occupied territories.

In a major breakthrough in Aug. 1993, Israel approved limited Palestinian autonomy. Israel would withdraw from Gaza Stip (Preferred Palestinian term, Gaza district) and Jericho. In early September, PLO and Israel announced mutual recognition. On 13th the historic accord was signed in Washington. On May 13, 1994, Israel handed over Jericho to Palestinian police, and on July 5, Arafat established Palestinian self-government there. In January, 1996, he became the first elected Palestinian President with a massive 88.1% of the vote, and took the oath of office as President of the Palestinian Authority on Feb 12. The electorate was 1,013,200. The Palestinian Council is an 82 member body.

Israeli currency is in use. There is a Palestinian police of about 15,000 men.

President Clinton of U.S.A. hosted a summit meeting between PM Netanyahu and Arafat in Oct. And peace talks were resumed. Israel halted talks in July '97 following the suicide bombing in a Jerusalem market which killed about 20 and injured

150. Israel yielded more West Bank territory to Palestinians, under an interim accord signed by Netanyahu and Arafat in Oct. '98. Palestinians gave new security guarantees in return. Inspite of all this Palestinian Arabs are committing terrorist attacks therefore Israel has not allowed establishment of full sovereign state but it is hoped that soon full sovereign state may be established and peace may prevail. U.N.O. and U.S.A. are striving for peaceful relations between Israel and Palestine and Arab-Jew conflict may end.

Israel Facts

Population	: 6.4 million
Seat of government	: Jerusalem, though most foreign embassies are in Tel Aviv
Major language	: Hebrew, Arabic
Major religions	: Judaism, Islam
Life expectancy	: 77 years (men), 81 years (women)
Monetary unit	: 1 new Israeli shekel (NIS)
Main exports	: Computer software, military equipment, chemicals and agricultural products
Average annual income	: US $ 16,750
Israel President	: Moshe Qatzal
Prime Minister	: Ariel Sharon

Palestinian Facts

Population	: 3.5 million
Intended seat of government	: East Jerusalem now Jericho
Major language	: Arabic
Major religion	: Islam
Life expectancy	: 71 years (men), 74 years (women)
Monetary unit	: 1 Jordan dinar = 1,000 fils
Main exports	: citrus
Average annual income	: US $1,350
Palestinian Leader	: Yasser Arafat

18

STATES AND ARABIAN PENINSULA

Saudi Arabia and Its Geographical Importance

Its capital is Riyadh (Royal) but Jeddah is Administrative Capital, Area is about 225090 sq. kms. Its population: 22 million; Language is Arabic; Religion is Islam. Its currency is Rial which is equal to US $1 = 3.60 Rials.

Greatest Arab state is now Saudi Arabia. It occupies nearly four fifths of the Arabian peninsula. It is now one of the richest states of the world. Saudi Arabia contains Mecca, the birth place of Mohammad and Medina where he preached.

In the province of Hejaz are Medina where Mohammad the Prophet was buried on June 7, 632. Mecca the birthplace of the Prophet is famous pilgrimage of the Muslims and center of Muslim civilization. There is a great mosque in Mecca which shelters the sacred Kaaba. On one side of the Kaaba is the black stone believed to, have been given to Abraham by Archangel, Gabril. This shrine is the place of holy pilgrimage for Muslims of whole world. According to Muslim religion pilgrimage to holy Mecca *i.e.*, Haj is holy Act.

Saudi Arabia is an absolute monarchy, with no parliament. Its administration is based on Muslim set up and Shariat of Islam.

Saudi Arabia has great oil wealth and is the foremost exporter of petroleum products today. The income from oil is the major source of public revenue. Inspite of all this Saudi Arabia remains mainly an agricultural country whose main produces are dates, wheat, barley, fruits hides and wool etc. Now industry and means of communication are also being developed.

Different States of Arabian Peninsula of Middle Eastern Countries

Saudi Arabia is the greatest state of Arabian Peninsula. Other states are Jordan, United Arab Emirates, United Yemen

Kuwait, Oman, Qatar and Bahrein etc. Syria, Lebnon, and Iraq and Israel deserve separate treatment. Egypt, Israel and Iran and Iraq are ancient lands and being cradle of civilization deserve separate treatment in detail.

Turkey on account of its importance and due to Eastern problem also requires separate treatment in detail.

Short Note on United Arab Emirates

Area of U.A.E. is 82,80 sq. kmd. Its population is 28 lakh and capital is Abu Dhabi; language is Arabic, religion is Islam and its currency is Dirham but it is equivalent to 368 per American dollar.

It is federation of seven Sheikhdoms of Persian Gulf. Its economy is entirely dependent on oil. Dubai is the main port and is the largest harbour of middle east.

Short Note on United Yemen (North and South) now United Yemen

South Yemen's area is 19500 sq.km. Its population is 12 lakh. Its capital is Senai, religion is Islam and language is Arabic, currency is Rial, one U.S.A. dollar is equal to 6.45 rials. This state was established on September 27, 1962 and is situated in western part of Arabian peninsula. Now it is United with South Yemen. Winter capital is Aden.

The main agricultural products are coffee, dates, herbs, fruits, millets, maize and cotton.

Its main exports are coffee, hides and skin.

Head of state and President is Ali Abdullah Saleh and Prime Minister is Abdul Aziz Abdul Ghani.

Yemen South's area is 63,576 sq. kms. and population is only 2066000. Its capital is As Saahah (Aden) Religion like other Arab States is Islam and language is Arabic. Its currency is Dinar equivalent to .343 dollar. Now both Yemen are United in 1990.

The people's republic of Yemen is mainly desert on southern part. It became free on November 30, 1967 as it was formerly Aden protectorate of British empire. Its main crops are sorghum, sesame, millets, wheat and barley etc. and economy is mainly agricultural. It had Communist benigns and Russian type of Government. As such Chairman and Presidium is Haider Abubaker Al-Attas and P.M. is Yassem Said Noman. Now Yemen has become one state.

A Short Note on Arab State of Kuwait

Area of Kuwait is 17818 sq.km. and population is Its capital is Kuwait city and religion is Islam and language is Arabia. Its dinar is equivalent .307 of a dollar. It is situated between Iraq and South Arabia on western coast of Persian Gulf. This tiny Arab state is fourth largest producer of petroleum so it is one of the richest countries of the world. It was founded by All Sahan dynasty in 1756. It became independent in 1961.

Its Amir is Sheikh Jabir Al Ahmad-al. Jabir al Salah and Prime Minister is Sheikh Al Abdullah al Salem al Salah. Iraq conquered it but U.S.A. and British forces on behalf of U.N.O. forced Iraq to give it back.

A Short Note on Oman

Area of Oman is 3,00,000 sq. kms. and population is about 25 lakhs. Religion like other Arabian State is Islam and language is Arabic and currency is Rial Omani.

The Sultanate of Oman formerly known as Muscat and Oman was formed in 1970. It is famous for dates, fruits and grains but economy is dependent on oil. Head of State and Government is Sultan Oalursbin Said.

Thus Arabian Peninsula consists Saudi Arabia, Jordan, Yemen united, Kuwait and Oman. Iraq, Syria and Lebnan can also be said Arabian. States but due to their importance, these may be dealt separately like Israel.

A Short Note on Qatar and Bahrein

Qatar is a tiny state having an area of about 11,000 sq. kms. Its population is only 8 lakh. Religion is Islam and language is Arabic and currency is Rial. Its capital is Doha.

It is a 100 mile tongue of land jetting into Persian Gulf. Main source of income is oil. It is full of immigrants from Pakistan, Iran and Oman. It became free in 1971 and opted for monarchy. Name of Amir is Sheikh Khalifa bin Abad Al Thani.

Bahrein : It contain 33 Islands of which Bahrein is largest. Its area is 669 sq.km., population is about 7 lakhs, capital is Manama, religion is Islam and language is Arabic.

It became independent in 1971 and is ruled by monarch Shekh Isa bin sulehman Al Khaliter.

Arabs and the Rise of Islam

Arabian Peninsula used to be inhabited by tribes. Beyond this fact that Islam originated in the Arabian Peninsula, the earliest history of the Arabs is not well established. Indigenous sources exist in the form of myths and legends, although aside from a few inscriptions, nothing in writing has been found. However, the Arabs are mentioned in ancient chronicles or the Persians. Romans, Greeks, Hebrews, and other peoples of the pre-Christian and early Christian era, and important ruins and small architects, which are still being recovered confirm these early contacts with other people. But it was only with Muhammad's coming and the foundation of Islam in the seventh century A.D. that the Arabs gained importance and began to be recorded.

The Arabs of pre-Islamic times represented two major ethnic groups : those of the south and those of the north. The difference between the two groups reflects the duality of pre-Islamic history and culture as well as Arabian geography, for the vast desert of central Arabia created a natural boundary between them. The northerners were primarily nomads; the southerners possessed a more settled, urban civilization and may be considered settled people of tribes.

Whatever their exact geographic origin, the Arabs of the south possessed; by the end of the second millennium B.C., an advanced culture similar to that of Egypt and Mesopotamia etc. They had a tradition of urban living a highly developed social organization, a unique system of irrigation and a relatively advanced technology and agriculture.

During the 1,700-odd years before the advent of Islam, several petty kingdoms flourished in this region. The most important of them. Probably was the Minaean-Sabean-Himyarite succession of states.

Sometimes one state was dominant; at other times several Arab kingdoms co-existed simultaneously. The remains of their dams, fortified cities, temples, and castles, some of which still exist indicate the sophistication and advanced level of their civilization. This Arab civilization was based primarily on agriculture and trade, but much of its wealth came from the production of frankincense and myrth. In the ancient world these substances were as precious as gold and could be compared in importance to oil in the economy of the Middle East today. Both are gum resins extracted from trees that mostly grow only in southern Arabia and Somalia. A complex organization was developed for producing and distributing and selling these precious commodity, which not only enriched the Arabs but also brought them into contact with the peoples living in the nearby lands bordering the Mediterranean Sea and the Indian Ocean.

Surviving inscriptions, show intellectual life did not match commercial and agricultural and artistic achievements. It seems to have concentrated almost exclusively on formulating a legal code for the regulation of property relationships etc.

One of the important South Arabian tribes were, the Minaeans who flourished in fertile northern Yemen between the eighth and third centuries B.C., had camel caravans, that travelled in Egypt and as far west as the Atlantic coastline of Africa. They also engaged themselves in trade with Delos, in Greece.

The Sabeans also absorbed the Minaeans and other principalities and created a kingdom based on a feudal system of aristocratic families that prevented the rise of any powerful, strong centralized system of government. In "eastern culture the Sabeans are commonly regarded as the symbol of ancient Arab culture civilization. The Old Testament narrative of Bilkis, the Queen of Sheba (Sabea), and her journey from Marib the capital of Sabea – to visit king Solmon is one of the best-known stories of the Bible and an oft-repeated theme in western mythology.

The Sabeans in turn were taken over by the neighbouring Himyarites. During the Hellenistic era, the Himyarites lost their chief source of prosperity when part of the Indian trade was diverted to Egypt, but in 24 B.C. they still had the strength to escape Roman domination by resulting Aelius Gallus, the general sent by Roman Emperor Augustus Caesar to conquer this area. Thus Arabian Peninsula never formed part of Roman Empire except Palestine and other minor parts.

In the first few centuries A.D., Christianity came to Arabia. Judaism already had a foothold, and by A.D. 525, Judaism had gained such an influence in the Himyarite kingdom that the rulers themselves were converted to Judaism and began to persecute the Christian population. This persecution of Christian together with prodding from Byzantium-which wanted to strike a blow at its ancient adversary, Persia-led to Christian Abyssinia's invasion of south Arabia in A.D. 530. The infamous Abyssinian governor, Abraha, conquered south Arabia, then tried to move northward, but he failed to advance beyond Mecca. Forty years later (575), his son and second successor lost south Arabia to Chosroes, 1, a Persian king of the Sassanid dynasty, and south Arabia remained a Persian province until the rise of Islam, invasion of the Muslims. Probably because of their pivotal geographic location between the Far East and India on the one hand and the Mediterranean sea and western Europe on the other, the Himyarites had been able to maintain their separate existence, independent status and prosperity.

Between the third and sixth centuries of the Christian era, the power of Rome remained in the north, as did the prosperity of the urbanized Yemenite states in the south. During this period, the relations between these sedentary settlements of this old Arab world and its nomads underwent a profound change. The civilized settlements of the south fell in decay, and the pastoral nomad once more replaced the peasant and the townsman.

The reasons for the resurgence of the nomads are cloudy, but they swallowed up whole settled communities and spread out not only over the entire Arabian peninsula but even beyond it to the boarders of Byzantium *i.e.* upto the boarders of Eastern Roman empire which included modern Turkey also.

The life of the desert can be roughly reconstructed from Arabic sources. Although these are of a much later date but probably they reflect a reality which has remained unaltered for centuries against an unchanging, inscrutable landscape. Although there were a few stable settlements in the interior of the Arabian peninsula, such as Mecca and Medina etc. and some Jewish agricultural colonies in the northern Hijaz. There were tiny islands in a sea of steppe, rock, and shifting sand, and the majority of the people were Bedouins roaming over the Arabian desert in a monotonous seasonal pattern in search of pasturage. The Bedouins with their camels, their tents, and their fierce tribal independence, was of ancient Semitic stock. They worshipped idols and spirits dwelling in trees, streams, and stones etc. and their Social organization pivoted around the tribe. The foundation of Bedouin life was unswerving tribal loyalty which was based on collective responsibility, the protection of the individual and the guest against outside threats, and enforced when necessary with implacable vengeance and rigour.

Tribal Conditions and Management in Arabia

Structure of Arabian was tribal. The Sheikh, or Sayyid, was the elected head of the tribe, chosen by the elders. His authority and prestige were mainly of a moral character. He was first among equals-primus inter pares. Usually he led the tribe in battle, acted as head when peace was restored and mediated in tribal blood feuds. Leaving the tribe without assurance of alternative allegiance was to invite death, for to survive in the desert alone was nearly impossible. Nevertheless the Bedouin turned away from every social organization that went beyond the orbit of his own tribal group.

The raid was a recognized outlet for aggressions and material gain and an almost everyday occurrence in the relations between various tribes. The long blooby, seemingly endless wars of pre-Islamic pagan Arabia sprang out of either raids of personal blood feuds which, because of the code of tribal solidarity and collective responsibility generally involved whole tribes. Occasional truces were declared for religious holidays and fairs etc.

Both Byzantium and Persia tried to protect themselves against the barbaric tide of these tribes by supporting new Arab Buffer states on their frontiers. On the Byzantine border of Roman Empire these were the seminomadic Ghassanids, Vassals of Byzantium, while the Lakhimids serve as stateliness of the Persian Sasanids rulers. These buffer states represent the transition from the civilized, settled life of Syria and Mesopotamia to the pure nomadism of the Syro-Arab desert and of central Arabia. Through them, foreign customs and rules and ideas filtered into the world of the nomads, breaking up its monotony and softening its austerity. Inspite of all this little change was possible.

The Ghassanids and the Lakhmids were enemies and, like their patrons, constantly hoped to exterminate each other. Their wars and the personalities and careers of their rulers live on in the colourful songs of the Bedouin poets and lords etc.

19

Arabia and Rise of Islam

The Pre-Islamic Arabia and Impact of Muhammad and His Faith on Arabian Peninsula.

Pre-Islamic Arabic in the history of the Byzantine empire, change came due to swift rise of a rival religious culture, of Islam, imbued with expansionist aims. In 1453, adherents of that faith succeeded in conquering the eastern citadel of Christianity. The genesis and meteoric expansion of Islam, together with the splendid civilization which it fostered is very fascinating and important.

The term Islam, meaning "submission to God" is derived from the Muslim holy book, the Koran. The followers of Muhammad, the founder of the faith, are known as Muslims. (This faith is often referred to as Muhammdanism, but Muslims frown on this term, which implies the worship and deification of Muhammad.) As such term Muslim is considered more popular.

The story of Rise of Islam begins in Arabian a quadrangular peninsula with an area of about 1,200,000 square miles. Much of it is desert, and rainfall is scarce in the remainder of the peninsula. Thus, vegetation is scant and very little land is suitable for agriculture and for other things.

Although the racial origin of the Arabs is obscure but it is well known that they belong to the Semitic language group. During the first millennium B.C. some Arab kingdom developed a high state of civilization, but the fourth to sixth centuries A.D. Witnessed a decline of settled life in Arabia and particularly of the interior consequently nomadism was the only way of life. Driven from place to place by the barren environment in their nomads, or Bedouins, led a precarious existence. The Bedouine lived according to a tribal pattern. At the head of the tribe was the Sayyed or Sheikh, elected and advised by the heads of the related families comprising the tribe. Aside from their flocks, the Bedouins relied for survival on booty from raids on settlements and on passing caravans etc.

The Bedouins worshipped a large number of gods and spirits, many of whom were believed to inhabit trees, wells, and stones etc. Each tribe had its own god, symbolized generally by a sacred stone which served as an alter where communal sacrifices were offered and holy occasions were celebrated.

Although the Bedouins led a primitive and largely isolated existence, they were influenced by contacts with other groups. By the later half of the sixth century, Christian and Jewish groups were living in cities situated chiefly on the caravan routes of Arabia. Their higher moral religious teachings had a strong effect on the natives, and western historians say their monotheistic beliefs were later incorporated into Islamic doctrine.

Mecca. Many of the more advanced Arab cities were in Hejaz, among them was Mecca, destined to be the key city in the Islamic religion. Fifty miles inland from the port of Jeddah, Mecca was favourably located for trade. Its merchants carried on business with southern Arabia, with Abysinia across the Red Sea, and with the Eastern Roman and Persian empires. Mecca was controlled by the Quraysh an Arabian tribe whose members formed trading companies that co-operated in dispatching large caravans towards north and south. The government of the city was in the hands of a syndicate of Quraysh merchants.

These same businessmen, were also concerned with protecting a source of income derived form the annual pilgrimage of tribes to a famous religious sanctuary at holy Mecca. Known as the Kaaba (cube). This square temple contained the sacred Black Stone, by legend brought to Abraham and his son Ismael by angel Gabriel. According to tradition, this stone was originally white but had been blackened by the sins of those touching it. The Kaaba housed the images of some 360 local deities and fetishes, etc. which were worshipped.

Muhammad, Founder of Islam. Into this environment at Mecca was born, a man destined to transform completely the religious, political, and social organization of people all over the world. Muhammad (570-632) came from a family belonging to the Quraysh tribe. Left as an orphan in early life, he was brought up by his uncle later on he was engaged in the caravan trade. Little is known of Muhammad's early years, but his first biographer relates that he was influenced by a monotheist named Zayd; who may have been either a Jewish or a Christian covert. Muhammad was a great visionary and a very intelligent man. Name of his father was Abdullah and of mother was Amina.

When he was about twenty years old, Muhammad entered in the service of a wealthy widow named Khadija, whose caravans traded with Syria. In his twenty-fifth year he married his employer Khadija, who was some fifteen years his senior. Despite the difference in their ages, the marriage was very happy one; and they had four daughter who Survived to maturity but no son. In history his only one daughter Fatima who was married to fourth Caliph Ali and famous Muhammad was apparently in the habit of retiring to a small cave in the nearby hills to meditate and pray. On one occasion he is supposed to have heard a dreadful voice saying : 'Muhammad, thou are Allah's messenger.' This was the first of a series of revelations and visions of Prophet Muhammad.

Muhammad regarded himself from the outset as a prophet. During his periods of doubt and anguish, Muhammad was comforted by Khadija, and finally he become convinced that Allah had commanded him to preach of men' duty to their Creator and repentance of their sins, for the judgment of God was at hand. These doctrines to some extent resemble the Christian and Jewish monotheistic concepts which were becoming increasingly prevalent in the Arabian peninsula.

He was brought up by his uncle Abu Talib so first Muhammad had little success in attracting followers. His first converts were his wife, his cousin Ali, and Abu Bakr, a leading merchant of the Quraysh tribe, who was highly respected for his honesty and integrity. Ali, Bakr remained the constant companion of prophet Muhammad during his persecution and exile, so later on he became the first Caliph of Islam. Most of the other early converts were slaves and members of oppressed groups but, opposition came from the leading citizens of Mecca who either ridiculed Muhammad's doctrine of resurrection (Pre-Islamic Arabs had only the vaguest notions on the subject of existence after death) or feared that his monotheistic teaching might harm the city's lucrative pilgrimage trade to the Kaaba and adversely affect social prestige and economic gain.

The Hegra and Triumphal Return of Muhammad to Mecca

The first encouraging development occurred when a group of Pilgrims from Medina, a prosperous town supported by agriculture and handicrafts, accepted the prophet's Muhammad teachings. Meanwhile, the increased persecution of the followers of Muhammad in Mecca encouraged the prophet Muhammad to migrate with his followers to Medina.

Carried out in secrecy, this migration took place in 622 and it is known as the Hegira from the word hijra which means "the breaking of formed ties." The Hegira was such a turning point in Muhammad's career that the first year in the Muslim calendar begins with this date. In Mecca, Muhammad's own kinsmen had persecuted him, but in Medina, he was acknowledged as a leader with divine authority in spiritual and temporal matters. He commanded the Muslims to turn towards Mecca when praying, This practice served to recognize the city of Mecca as the spiritual capital of Islam and at the same time emphasized the need for its conquest from the pagan trading oligarchy, that governed it and opposed followers of Muhammad. Battles took place in which followers of Muhammad were victorious. It was in the year 630, Muhammad marched on Mecca with an army. His old enemies were forced to surrender to the Prophet, Muhammad, who acted with magnanimity towards them. His first act was to cast out of the Kaaba its multitude of idols and fetishes etc.; but the temple itself, together with the Black Stone, was preserved as the supreme center of Islam, the "Mecca" became most sacred place of Islam to which each devout Muslim should make pilgrimage during his life time. It is called Haj and person who does pilgrimage is called Haji which is a respectable title.

With Mecca and Medina both under his control, Muhammad became the undisputed master of the Hejaz. Tribe after tribe of Bedouins throughout Arabia was conquered and so offered him their loyalty. In the two remaining years of his life, he consolidated Islam's position. Upon his death in 632, the Prophet left behind him a faith which had united Arabia and which was to astound the world with its militant expansion and new ideology.

The Koran. Muslims believe that the Koran contains the actual Word of God as revealed to Muhammad. These revelations occurred to Prophet Muhammad over a period of more than twenty years, and before his death many of the messages had been written down. Abu Bakr, Muhammad's successor, ordered the compilation of all these materials including the passages, which had only been committed to memory by his followers. Twenty years after the death of the Prophet, Muhammad an authorized version of Koran compiled which is the official text to the present day and Muslims all over the world adhere to it.

As the Koran should never be used in translation for worship, the spread of Islam created a great deal of linguistic unity, and ideological unity which still remains today. Arabic supplanted many local languages are used as the language of daily use. The Muslim world which stretches from Morocco to Iraq is still Arabic speaking. Further more this book of the seventh century remains the last word on Muslim theology, law, and of social institutions and culture and is therefore still the most important text book in Muslim universities. As a result of all this the use of Korans made the followers of Islam well versed in Arabic language and they have little difficulty in reading Arabic even though their speech may differ widely.

The Main Ideas of Islamic Religion

The Islamic faith. Within the Koran one may find the central tenets of Islam monotheism. There is only one God, Allah; this is proclaimed five times daily from the minaret of the mosque as the faithful are called to prayer:

God is most great. I testify that there is no-God but Allah. I testify that Muhammad is God's Apostle. Come to prayer, come to security. God is most great. In Arabic it is called "La-Il-Illah-Muhammad Rasul-Illah". God is one and Muhammad is his prophet.

Teachings. While Allah is the only God, many other supernatural figures are also acknowledged, as in Christianity. Islamic angles such Gabriel for example, are similar to those described in the Bible. In addition to this there exist jinn, who are spirits midway between angels and men. Some jinn are good, while others are evil; the most powerful of the latter group is Satan. Islam also recognizes the existence of prophet who preceded Last Prophet Muhammad. The Koran mentions twenty-eight, of whom four are Arabian eighteen are found in the Old Testament, three in the New Testament (including Moses and Jesus), and one of the remainder has probably been identified as Alexander the Great. But to Muslims the greatest prophet is, of course, Mohammad. No superhuman status or miraculous power is ascribed to him, but he was chosen to proclaim God's message of salvation.

Probably geography played an important role in the Prophet Muhammed's concepts of heaven and hell, even as it did in Hebrew in heaven and hell literature. Both heaven and hell are described in terms that incite as immediate reaction in people who live in the desert. Those who have submitted to Allah rule-the charitable, humble, and forgiving, and those who have fought for His faith-shall dwell in a Garden of Paradise, reposing in the cool shade, eating delicious foods, attended by "fair ones with wide, lovely eyes like unto hidden perels", and hearing no vain speech or recrimination, but only "Peace Peace". This veritable oasis is far different from the agonies of a desert hell, which awaits the erring. Cast into hell with its "scorching wind and shadow of black smoke", they will drink of boiling water. Thus followers of Prophet Muhammad will be rewarded with luxuries of Paradise and those who oppose Islam will suffer in hell.

Islam imposes on all Muslims four important obligations, known as the "Pillars of Faith" I-prayer, II-almasgiving III-fasting, and fourth a pilgrimage to Mecca. Prayers are said five times a day, and each occasion involves a number of recitations. They are to be repeated either alone or, preferably, in a mosque. The Muslim is required to give alms called *Khairat.* This practice is regarded as an expression piety and contributing the one's as salvation. During the month of Ramzan, the ninth month of the lunar year, Muslims fast whole month of Ramzan. Since food and drink are prohibited between sunrise and sunset, this is a very strenuous observance, although sick persons and travellers etc. are exempted, provided they fast for an equal length of time later on. The second chapter of the Koran commands Muslims to make a pilgrimage to Mecca, where they go through traditional ceremonies, such as kissing the Black stone in the Kaaba. Each Muslim should make the pilgrimage to Mecca at least once during his life time if he has the means to take pilgrimage.

The Koran also provides the Muslims with a body of ethical teachings. Idolatory, infanticide, usury, gambling, the drinking of wine, and the eating of pork etc. are all strictly prohibited. Similarly, Islam encouraged the human treatment of slaves and regulated such matters as the guardianship of orphans and divorce etc.

Muslim men were allowed four legal wives (and an unspecified number of concubines), but if he could not treat them all with equal kindness and impartiality, a husband should retain but one. Probably Islam was the first religion to give property rights to women.

Prevailing Islam was the principle of equality. There was no priesthood. There were leaders for worship in the mosques and there were the ulema, who interpreted the sacred law, but they were all laymen. Muhammad stressed the essential unity of all true believers and thus prevented dangerous class distinctions and ensured equality of all Muslims before the Islam and law. In this way Islam was spared the priestly tyranny which arose in India and in Europe where the Brahmanas considered themselves superior to all other classes in the rigid caste system and Pope began to be considered infallible by Roman Catholic.

Islamic Law. In addition to being a religion Islam offered a system of government, law, and society and of administration and social behaviour. The Islamic community was an excellent example of a theocratic state, one in which religious rulers hold all power political social and religious.

In the period of expansion after the Prophet Muhammad's death the Islamic state required detailed rules covering a variety of new situations. The Islamic code that was developed was based partly on pre-Islamic legal customs. Before Muhammad's time, each tribe had its own Sunna, or body of custom, which served as a law code. By compiling the recollections of the prophet's companions, his followers prepared a Sunna based on his conduct, life and teachings.

Using the Koran and the Sunna as their sources, Islamic jurists developed a body of canon law which regulated all aspects of Muslim life.

The Islamic law was held to be as divinely inspired as the sources on which it was based. Its development and interpretation were in the hands of doctors of law who are called as the ulema. Agreement among the ulema set the seal of orthodoxy on question of text and doctrine, with the result that Islamic law became progressively authoritarian and static and conservative

The Early Life of Prophet Muhammad and His Achievements

It is said "Prophet Muhammad was one of the greatest

religious leaders which the world has ever produced", so Islam's teachings and its extension over other lands is essential.

Muhammad, the man designed to be the Prophet of a new religion of Islam as well as the spiritual and temporal leader of his peoples, was born in Mecca between A.D. 570 and 580. Generally A.D. 570 is accepted as date of birth.

(Information about his early life and religious training is meagre.) He came from a respectable but from minor branch of the powerful Quraysh tribe. His father Abdullah died before his birth, his mother died when he was only six. The orphan was raised first by his grandfather, Abd-al-Muttalib, and then by his uncle, Abu Talib. During this period the family lived in poverty, but Muhammad achieved wealth and position at the age of twenty-five by an advantageous marriage to the wealthy widow, Khadija, who was fifteen years his senior. Her money provided him with the ease comfort and independence needed to investigate and appraise the religious situation in Arabia.

The story monotheism, theory of revelation, and the Biblical element in the Koran all suggest that Muhammad was probably influenced both by Christian and Jewish ideologies. However, versions of Biblical stories indicate that they were indirectly acquired-most likely form Jewish and Christian traders and travellers whose religious knowledge was sketchy and apocryphal. Probably he was also influenced by the hanifs, native holy men, dissatisfied with Arabian paganism, is also possible.

What prompted Muhammad to undertake his world-shaking career will always remain shrouded in mystery. What is clear, is that he was disturbed and disgusted by the idolatry of his contemporaries and their lack of devotion to Allah, the true God. He was painfully aware that the disciplined religious life of the Jews and Christians about him contrasted sharply with the materialistic paganism of his compatriots. Time and again he withdrew to a cave under Mount Hira, near Mecca, for meditation and prayer. Here many insights came to him "like the breaking of dawn." Muslims believe he was given knowledge by God, through angel Gabrael.

According to tradition, Muhammad's Call, the legendary revelation of Allah, came suddenly and dramatically in 611, when he was about forty years old. Descriptions in the Koran, as well as number of traditional stories, suggest that the Call was flash of divine insight delivered by the angel Gabriel. Muhammad formed idea then of founding a new religion. His ambitions were great and he hoped to bring all people a unified in Arab revelation similar to that of the Christians and Jews. The early chapters of the Koran are brief and evangelistic, dealing mainly with the unity of God, the wickedness of idolatory and materialism, and the imminence of divine judgment. Muhammad desired all people to follow his religion.

But at first, few answered the all, and those who did were mostly of humble position. Muhammad's few influential supporters in addition to his wife Khadija were his powerful friends Abu Bakr and Umar, and slave Zeid and his sons-in-law Uthman and Ali, who succeeded him as the four "rightly guided" caliphs. Apart from this intimate circle, few were interested in his message of divinely revelation (Ilham). However, as Muhammad was confident in the importance of his mission so he openly attacked the prevailing paganism and its leaders. Naturally this antagonized the powerful merchants who controlled Meccan society. They feared that his reforms would deprive Mecca of its unique and profitable position as a center of both pilgrimage and trade. Their opposition gradually turned to persecution, and some of his followers fled to Copite Christian Abyssinia where they found asylum under the ruling King Negus. The support of his powerful relatives enabled Muhammad to maintain a foothold in Mecca, but he experienced one setback after another. First his wife died; then the sympathetic patriarch of his clan, died and successor was hostile to him, Muhammad's lack of success in Mecca, coupled with his abortive attempt to spread his message in Tarif, led him to search for a new and more promising horizon. He found it at Yathrib (or Medina), a city 250 miles northeast of Mecca that had originally been settled by Jewish tribes so he migrated to Medina in 622 A.D.

Medina was a sophisticated city; attracted many pagan Arabs who eventually outnumbered its Jewish founders. It had no stable government but was constantly torn by feuds between the rival Arab tribes of the Aus and Khazraj, with the Jews often controlling the balance of power. After prolonged negotiations Muhammad finally agreed to his famous Hijra (immigration) to Medina in 622, a date which marks the beginning of the Islamic calendar. The Medinese saw in him a man of power, discipline, zeal, vision and of high spirits who could serve as an arbitrator and conciliator as well as a religious leader. Unlike the Meccans, they had few strong religious convictions. Muhammad had some followers in Mecca, but the majority of Medina soon embraced Islam.

This move of Muhammad and his followers to Medina in 622 A.D. to be a pivotal one for the whole development of Islam. Once in Medina, Muhammad's revelations changed in character; they became prophetic and religious and regulatory and a state, with Muhammad as the lawgiver, the supreme judge, the commander in chief, and the ruler having both spiritual and temporal powers.

Once Islamic power as thus centralized, Muhammad concentrated on conquest of his native city, Mecca, his abilities as a leader and conqueror came to the fore. His forces brilliantly defeated the Meccans in the Battle of Badr (624), and gained control of the vital caravan routes to the north. Badr was Islam's first ordeal by battle and its cause was greatly strengthened by the overwhelming triumph. This victory of Badr was considered prophetic Muslims believed the Meccan infindels had been defeated by Allah himself in the person of Muhammad and his followers. In 630, Muhammad entered Mecca as a conqueror — the victory was achieved by conciliation as well as by force. Thus Muhammad's success was complete. The Kaaba and other holy places were now in Islamic hands and purified of paganism. Religious faith replaced old tribal blood ties. Opposition was practically wiped out By 632, when Muhammad died, almost the whole of Arabian Peninsula had embraced Islam.

The Expansion of Rule and Religion of Islam after Prophet Muhammad.

Muhammad's sudden death threatened the dissolution of the Islamic community, he had struggled to create. First there was the problem of selecting his successor, or caliph. This task threatened to disrupt political and religious unity of Arabs and precipitated some of the bloodiest battles in Islam. Muhammad had left no heir or clearly designated successor. Probably he had undermined the traditional tribal system of government by taking temporal as well as spiritual power into his own hands. Since he had proclaimed himself the last of the Prophets and said that his unique mission would terminate with his death so there was no need for a spiritual successor, but someone had to fill his role as head of state, commander in chief, lawgiver, and chief justice so selection of successor *i.e.* of Caliph was necessary. During the confusion that followed his death, several rival parties arose, each claiming privilege and priority in the appointment of caliph.

The original Meccan converts, those who had emigrated with him to Medina based their right and claim on belonging to the Prophet's tribe of Quraysh and being the first to embrace Islam. His Medinese supporters, on the other hand, claimed priority because they had supported him from 622 A.D. following the Hijra. Both groups, comprising the most influential among the companions of the prophet, leaned towards the traditional tribal method of selecting a new chief from among the best qualified of their number.

A third group, the legitimists, advocating the idea of hereditary right and of divine designation as opposed to the traditional elective principle, supported Ali, a paternal cousin of Muhammad and the husband of Fatima only surviving daughter of Prophet Mohammad Lastly, there were the influential Umayyads; the aristocrats of Mecca although the most recent converts to Islam, they claimed that their traditional position of leadership, based on power and position and privilege entitled them to name the caliph.

An open breach between these diverse elements was shrewdly avoided by the swift action of a small group of senior Companions who nominated Abu Bakr as Muhammad's successor. Abu Bakr, an unprepossessing, but kindly man, slightly stooped by his sixty years, was revered for his gentleness, humility, and piety, wisdom etc. His selection seemed most appropriate, for he had been chosen by the dying Prophet to lead the faithful in prayer.

Prophet Muhammad's death created other problems. It acted as a signal for revolt to many of the outlying tribes in central and eastern Arabia whose conversion to Islam had been at best lukewarm. The disciplined yoke of Islam threatened their nomadic independence, and they were searching for the opportunity to revolt.

Caliph Abu Bakr's awesome task was not only to be an effective religious leader, but also to solidify the shaky unity of the Islamic community. He was remarkably successful. In his short reign of two years, this pious man consolidated the diverse components of Islam and launched the Arabs on their path of conquest. Before his death in 634, Syria, Iraq, the southern provinces of Persia and the Byzantine empire had all fallen to the Arab conquerors. This was marvelous achievement of Islam during Abu Bakr's rule.

Caliph Umar's Caliphat

To avoid difficulties, Abu Bakr had wisely appointed Umar to succeed him, and the nomination Umar as Caliph was unanimously accepted. The reign of Umar (634-644) saw the expansion of the Arab empire to far off places. What began as typical Arab raids for booty into Iraq and Syria developed into campaigns of permanent conquest. The small Arab detachments, were led by able commanders (Khaid ibn al-Walid being one of the best known) and struck with lightning swiftness deep into the surrounding countries. They met little effective resistance. One battle after another was won by the seemingly unconquerable Arab armies, brilliantly using the desert was their ally. In the north the Arabs entered Syria and conquered Damascus in 635. Then after the great decisive battle of Yarmuk (636) the Byzantine emperor Heraclius abandoned kingdom Syria. Holy City Jerusalem fell in 637. In the east the Arabs won even more spectacular victories against the Persian empire. After the famous battle of Qudisiya (637), they conquered the whole of Iraq. The battles at Nihaw (641) and Isfahan (643) finally broke Persian power, and the empire fell into Arab hands. In Egypt the pattern was the same : an Arab army under Amr Ibn al-Ass entered Egypt in 639 and by 642 all of Egypt was under Arab domination. Thus during caliph Umar's rule Islamic empire of Arabs spread far and wide Caliph Umar is compared with Asoka and Constantine.

Thus in a single decade a host of highly organized, sophisticated and settled societies found themselves conquered by the Islamic forces of Arab tribesmen. The Persian empire which had existed for centuries was no more and mighty Eastern. Roman Empire was forced back to the Taurus Mountains in Asia Minor. During Umar's rule, Islamic forces of Arabs became powerful most.

Causes of Muslim Success

What contributed to these spectacular Arab conquests. The inspiration of Islam was of primary importance. It provided the Arabs, for the first time, with a cohesive centralizing force and the zeal and reality of a new and vital religion. The Muslims believed that divine intercession enabled them to scatter that vast armies of the infidels. The wars on conquests, moreover, gave empire provided opportunities for heroism and booty which the Arabs traditionally relished, and which they now pursued in the name of Islam with missionary zeal. These triumph soon became religious and spiritual crusade-a holy war (jihad). Everywhere the Islamic conquerors gained converts as well as territory and booty.

For the conquered peoples, the task of shifting form old to new rulers was not difficult. Most of them had long been alienated by cruel and corrupt and inefficient Persian and Byzantine bureaucratic administrations. Moreover, in Egypt and Syria the Christian population was strongly opposed to the centralizing and Hellenizing tendencies of the Byzantine bureaucracy and of the Greek the Orthodox Church. In Palestine Jews ground under the cruel yoke of Byzantine rule who treated Jews mercilessly. Umar's organizational abilities also contributed greatly to the Arabs' success. He regularized the legal position of the millions of non-Muslim subjects in his domain and set up an able and efficient administrative system for the Islamic empire of Arabs. Muhammad had established the precedent of "tolerance" for the "people of the Book," *i.e.* the Jewish and Christian communities in the northern Hijaz. Caliph Umar left these communities undisturbed except for the payment of an annual tribute in the form of poli tax (jizya), indeed, he extended the principle of toleration to cover not only all Christians and Jews of his empire, but also to Zoroastrians of Persia. Non-Muslim groups formed their own self-administered communities, lived under their own civil codes, and were also lead and governed by their own religious leaders. This system prevailed throughout Islam until the end of the Ottoman Turkish period and still exists in a restricted way in parts of the Middle East that have not yet been thoroughly secularized. European Christians Claimed that the Muslims gave unbelievers, such as Christian, Parsis and Jews etc. the Muslims gave unbelievers, such as Christian, Parsis and Jews etc. the choice of conversion to Islam or of death by the sword, from a practical point of view, mass conversions to Islam would have meant abandoning the jizya, a considerable source of revenue. So non believers were allowed to retain their original on payment of jizya.

The Muslim conquerors, however, sought to maintain their identity as a separate ruling class. Overall authority in the conquered provinces was established by the appointment of Arab military commanders or governors. Arab garrisons maintained order throughout the Islamic empire of Arabs. Individual Arabs in newly won territories were forbidden to acquire land outside Arabia proper and were discouraged from mixing with the local population. Yet while the Arabs held the ultimate power, they wisely left control of local affairs in the hands of their non-Muslim subjects — the Hellenized Christians and Persians having experienced of local government and local customs. Caliph Umar, whose piety, sense of justice, and puritanical simplicity are proverbial, was responsible for laying the solid foundations of the Islamic empire. In 644, he was assassinated by a discontented Persian slave as he was praying in a mosque in Medina. Uthman, a son-in-law of Muhammad, and a member of the influential Umayyad family of the Meccan tribe of Quraysh, was then elected Caliph. Although noted for his wild manner, piety, and closeness to the Prophet Caliph Uthman turned out to be a somewhat irresolute ruler and was accused of appointing his kinsmen to leading positions in the vast empire. Some, however were able generals and governors who carried the banner, message of Islam north into Asia Minor and in Byzantium empire and on the eastern front, into Bactria, Kabul, and Ghazni. etc.

The problem of Islamic society at this time was the impact of the Empire upon it. The earliest Muslims were now wealthy nobles. A second urban generation was in the making, raised amid the luxury and amusements and the comforts of Alexandria, Damascus etc. and the camp cities of Basra and Kufa. Also, pomps, politics, power, and prestige had become ends in themselves. And Caliph Uthman was too weak to halt this trend. The legitimists in Kufa, being pietists and theocrats, raised the banner of revolt first. Then in 656, a party of regicides from the army in Egypt came to Medina to present Uthman with grievances concerning his corrupt misrule. Caliph Uthman, though conciliatory on the surface, was basically adamant. Revolt in his quarters ensued, in which attempts to persuade him to abdicate were made. Upon discovering that Caliph Uthman was stalling only to allow the arrival troops he had secretly sought form Muyyawiya, the Umayyad governor of Syria, to arrive in Medina to defend him, the regicides stormed his place. They murdered him as he sat, resigned to his fate, reading the Koran. The first below was dealt by Abdalla the son of Abu Bakr, the first caliph. This murder of a caliph by a fellow Muslim was the first direct challenge to the moral and religious and administrative authority of the caliphate which was a bond of unity in Islam.

Caliphat of Ali

Ali, the son in law of Prophet Muhammad was immediately elected as Uthman's successor. An esteemed and pious Muslim, a tragic-noble hero, Ali, the cousin and son-in-law of Muhammad and his male next of kin, had many virtues as warrior, counsellor, and friend. But he lacked the talents necessary to govern a divided and restive state, being both indecisive and inflexible, as well as lacking in ruthlessness energy and foresight.

Opposition to Ali began in Mecca headed by Aisha, the widow of the Prophet Muhammad who hated him, and by Talha and Zubair, who had been the Prophet's companions and who had their own eyes and ambition of the caliphate. They had previously been enemies of Caliph Uthman and had formed the real center of opposition to him in Medina even prior to the advent of the Egyptian regicides. Now, with complete disregard of their previous role in the events leading to the murder, they defiantly withdrew to Mecca, withheld their recognition of Ali, and demanded the punishment of the guilty. Ali bore no direct responsibility for the murder of Uthman, but the opposition insisted that by failing to use his prestige and standing more effectively to protect Uthman or Usman and by failing to punish the regicide after his accession, he had implicated himself in the murder. Soon afterward, a pro-Uthman party developed around the opposition crying for war and revenge. After gathering their forces in Mecca, Aisha, and Zubair moved to Basra in search of local support.

In October, 656, Ali moved against them and left Medina at the head of his army never to return there again. From that day to the present, Medina ceased to be the capital of the Islamic empire. The encounter which followed became known as the "Battle of the Camel" after the camel Aisha rode as she urged her supporters to fight on. This first battle of Muslim against Muslim ended in victory for Ali, but not before many illustrious companions including Talha the Zubair had lost their lives in this battle. Aisha, "the Mother of the Faithful," was captured but in reality she was permitted to return to Medina, where she lived in obscurity during the rest of her life.

Caliph Ali, realizing his unpopularity in Basra made near by Kufa his capital, his position as caliph appeared secure, but in reality his authority was constantly being challenged, both by tribal in subordination and by conflicting councils of priests and theorists in his own camp. Thus Caliphate to Ali did not seem to a bed of roses but a bed of thorn.

As for the rest of empire, Ali was generally recognized as the new lawful Caliph. The new governors, he had appointed, were accepted everywhere but in Syria, where Mu'awiya, the able Umayyad governor, forcibly refuse to resign. Mu'awiya, held him guilty and accused Ali of conniving with regicides. Ali led an army and met the Syrian forces at Siffin by to Euphrates in 567.

When the battle went against them, the Syrians dramatically raised copies of the Koran on the point of their-lances and appealed for arbitration. The arbitration which followed in 659 was unsuccessful, for it ended in a stalemate-Mu'awiya refused to recognize Ali as caliph, Ali neither agreed for abdication nor accepted Mu'awiya as governor of Syria. But the arbitration was, in effect, a clever victory for Mu'awiya, reducing Ali's status as sole caliph to that of a pretender. Moreover, the arbitration brought forth other difficulties for Ali. After this "Battle of the Camel", where many Meccan and Medinese supporters had perished, Ali was left at the mercy of his soldier the anarchic and undisciplined nomadic Arabs. An important group among them, known as the Kharijites (seceders), revolted in protest against his willingness to arbitrate and reconciliation. The Kharijites, the oldest religious sect of Islam, were subdued by Ali in 659, but they continued to reappear as puritanical, militant movements through out the later history of Islam.

Caliph Ali, probably weakened by the Kharijite revolt and declining morale among his supporters, was assassinated in 661 in Kufa by a Kharijite Hasan, his eldest son, was proclaimed Caliph in Kufa while Mu'awiya was recognized in Damisk. A few months later, Hasan reached an agreement with Mu'awiya. He retired on a royal pension to the pleasures of his harem in Medina, and Mu'awiya was then proclaimed the sole Caliph of the Islamic empire at Jerusalem in 661, with Damascus as his capital. As the center of state shifted from Medina, to Kufa and to Damascus, and leadership of community changed from the companions of the Prophet to the Umayyads, a new era was born in which Umayyad Caliphs ruled Islamic empire from Damasik which became the capital of Islamic empire of Umayyad Caliphs till their Khilafat lasted. Islam made great progress during rule of these Caliphs and became a religion whose followers went all over the world to make this religion popular.

20

Rise and Extension of Islam

The Rise of Islamic Arab Power and Its Impact and Arab Conquest of Middle East and Its Consequences. Conquest and Extension of Islamic Empire

Arab was a land of mystery, doing a little trade with Syria and Egypt and it also contributing some mercenaries to the Persian and Byzantine armies, but otherwise Arabian lands were as remote and inhospitable as the frozen north. Nothing likely to be reported from this scorching wilderness would be calculated to disturb the bazaars of Damascus of Alexandria. Arabian Society was still in the tribal stage during sixth century A.D. and the Hawkeyed Bedouin tribe might be confidently expected to rob and massacre each other till the crack of doom. Nowhere was there a vestige of an Arabian state, or of a regular state army, or of a common political establishment as they were not politicians. Nor had they found in religion a polytheism, so low that finer minds among them, touched perhaps by vague influences from Christianity or Judaism had begun quietly to challenge it. At Mecca, their great highway of the Red Sea, they appeared to worship at the impressions likely to prevail about the population of Arabia in the year in which Heraclius, the Byzantine emperor, concluded his Persian wars. Thus in sixth century A.D. Arabia was in an undeveloped state and society.

A hundred years later these obsecure savaged had achieve for themselves a great world power. They had conquered Syria and Egypt, they had overwhelmed and converted Persia, mastered Western Turkestan and also part of the Sindh. They had wrested Africa from the Christian Byzantines emperors and the Berbers, Spain from the Visgoths. In the west they threatened France, and the Syrian ports. They sailed over the waters of the Mediteran sea and pillaged the Greek islands and challenged the naval power of the Eastern Roman Empire. Their successes had been won so easily against the Persians and the Berbers of the Atlas mountains. The Mediterranean sea had, ceased to be a Roman lake. From one end of Europe to the other the Christian states of Europe found themselves confronted with the challenge of a new oriental civilization founded on a new oriental Islamic faith propounded in Arabia by Muhammad.

Causes of Rise of Arabia. To what causes are *i.e.* to be attributed this sudden and extra ordinary outpouring of this Arab race ? Probably the Arbas were propelled into the uttermost parts of the earth by the ferment within them of their new Islamic religion, and that they rode, battled, and conquered to extend their Islamic faith. But during the early years of the Arab expansion, the conquerors. Were at no particular pains to make new converts to the contrary, their success in government largely consisted their Islamic religion in the wise policy of toleration in the beginning which they practised towards Jews and Christians, presenting in this respect the happiest contrast to the persecuting practices of their successors. But if religion was not the primary motive which underlay this extraordinary movement, still less can it be ascribed to consistent design. The Bedouin horsemen did not ride out of Arabia with a clear-cut scheme for the conquest of the world and the establishment of new states. They made their empire as other states have made empires after them, blindly probability without set purpose and perhaps with no near and immediate project other than plunder. They began by making plundering raids into Palestine and Iraq at a time when the defences of those provinces were at their lowest point of efficiency, and finding victory easy and booty rich, they extended their operations due to their greed for plunder and zeal for Islam, success, beyond their outmost dreams of ambition, attended their attacks. In 636, they beat the last army of Heraclius at the Yarmak and conquered Syria. In 637, they entered Caspian sea and mastered Mesopotamia. In 639, they invaded Egypt, and three years later entered Alexandria. Having discovered the weakness of the middle Eastern states, they were resolved to exploit it and to hold, administer, and extend their conquests. Not otherwise did the Elizabethan buccaneers throw themselves upon the wealth of the western hemisphere. Yet if religion was not the sole originating force in the expansion of Islamic Arabis it gave to it a degree of animation and permanence which it would otherwise have lacked. Without the bond of a common religion the Arab horsemen would have lacked the cohesion failing which victories can seldom be now and never secured. Without some inspiration higher than mere appetite they could never have commended their rule to Syrians and Egyptians, Persians Hebrews and Berbers etc. No small part of their success was due to the fact that there had been evolved in the heart of Arabia Islamic religion which satisfied then, as it continues to satisfy now, the souls of men and women living under the burning skies of Asia and Africa, and that of this Islamic religion the Arabs were the armed and exultant missionaries.

Thus, religion as well a greed for plunder and zeal for empire were motive forces of Arab expansion. The Hedjaz was that part of Arabia most exposed, by reason of its trade to foreign influences. Here Jews and Christians might sometimes be found, more especially in Mecca and Medina which was the commercial center of the district and a town of pilgrimage or at Yathrib *i.e.* Medina two hundred miles north, one of the few areas in that waterless land where the arts of agriculture were practised by a settled population.

Rise of Islam in Arabia

Prophet Muhammad (570-632) was born at Mecca of a family which was neither rich nor distinguished, but of the Kuraishite tribe which controlled the local sanctuary. As a young man he entered the commercial house of Kadija, a wealthy widow whom who was about 15 years older than Muhammad to whom he subsequently married, nor perhaps is it irrelevant to his spiritual development that the pursuit of his calling involved caravan journeys across the desert and he has opportunities of converse with Christians and Jews Muhammad was one of those men of whom religious history offers many examples, in whom a passionate animal nature is combined with the temper of a spiritual thinking of a visionary.

He had the ardour of the mystic, the zeal of the ethical reformer, and also that absorbing preoccupation with the things of the soul which comes most easily to man in the solitary places of the world. By degrees the mind of this Arab merchant became went possessed of certain large religious and ethical ideas. He went into trances and meditations and in these trances, visions appeared to him. He had a vision of the one God, of a future life, of the sensual delights of paradise, of the material torments of hell, and of an impending day of retribution in which sinners would be punished. These visions, were vigorous, and worth pursing so he began to recite (Koran), first of all privately to a circle of intimates, then more widely. Mecca was sharply critical and opposed his teaching. Nevertheless he had firm faith which he persevered, winning adherents by the flow and vehemence of his zeal tact and saintly behaviour and by the large and attractive appeal of the monotheistic faith and the practice of brotherly love. It is said that he was influenced probably by Judaism and Christianity but his information with regard to these two religions, being derived form oral sources only, was dim, fragmentary, and unreliable. As such probably he was original thinker who propagated his own religious ideas. He regarded Christ as a Prophet, born of a virgin mother, but probably story of the crucifixion of christ did not reached him, probably he was also not fully aware of the differences between the Jewish and Christian creeds. The Koran is a collection of utterances of learned and original Prophet preaching the message of God to the Arab race.

Due to the opposition in his native town of Mecca, Muhammad escaped in 622 to Yathrib henceforth known as Medinat-en-Nabi, the city of the Prophet. This is the famous Hegira, or flight, which is taken to mark the beginning of the Moslem era which began from 622 A.D.

In Medina, which was tormented by rival factions, the prophet Muhammad continued his pious labours, preaching the welcome doctrine of concord, of submission (Islam) to the will of God (Allah) and developing many of those practical precepts which govern the conduct of the Moslem world to this day; the five daily prayers, thc fasting in the month of Ramjan, the yearly, pilgrimage *i.e.* Haj the abstention from wine and 1/40 income as alms etc. In all this side of the teaching the Prophet showed pragmatic insight into Arab nature as well as in human nature. He had the idea of propagating universalist religion. With that strong, practical sense which was in him so strongly combined with religious exaltation and zeal that, he aimed both at reform and revolution. He did not attempt to change everything, but tolerated polygamy and slavery, institutions too secure to be assailed with success and even temporized with the symbols of polytheism, Returning to Mecca in 631, after a long struggle marked complete victory of his faith, he adopted the black stone, and declared that the Caba was the temple of Abraham. He had founded a little state of Islamic faith of his Universal God and Mecca was his Holy city. He was able to establish his Muslim religion in whole Arabia during his life time in 632.

Islamic Religion. The new religion had from the first a great political value, into the wild, lawless, infinity divided Arab world it brought unity of belief, submission to authority, daily ritual of prayer and absence from strong drinks and religious zeal which has given so Moslem armies throughout history a mission and a special advantages. Moreover, the monotheism of Islam was not so far removed from the monophysite forms of Christianity and Jews which were popular in Syria and Egypt and Palestine as to interpose an obstacle in the way of the Arab conquest of those lands of middle East.

Impact. So the Moslem civilization spread in Middle East. Under the Umayyads Caliphs its political centre was Damascus, under the Abbasids Caliphs it was Bagdad. Under the Fatimite Caliphs it was Cairo. Syrians and Persians, Egyptians, Turks, Berbers, and Spainards contributed to bring about this great age of Moslem literature and art and culture which, for four centuries. During this period, the European mind was deep sunk in ignorance and feudalism and in sloth. It gave to the peoples of Islam the intellectual religious leadership of the world. The memory of that great Islamic epoch still survives.

Still the Palestinian Arab proudly contrasts the literature of his golden age with the scriptures of the Jews and strives to destroy their state of Israel. Muslims go the pilgrimage to Mecca, and dreams of the day when all the world will acknowledge the true faith. Still from the Atlantic Ocean to the Himalayas the muezzin calls the faithful to prayer at sunrise and sunset, the mosques fill with shoeless worshippers for prayers and the little children learn the Koran by heart, and in the shaded alcoves of the great Cairene University of Al Azhar groups of white-robed students, seated on the floor, swing back and for him a mood of fanatical ecstasy, as they intone the secured words of pious Prophet to whom all wisdom and all modern science were known miraculously revealed by divine power.

Some Features of Islam Both of Shia and Sunnies

Islam. Islam is a religion of warriors and shepherds, which, albiet without a clergy or a regular liturgy has persisted for more than 1,300 years and now is thought to number more than 400,000,000 adherents of Islam. Asceticsm after the early Christian manner was not much encouraged by the Prophet Muhammad who is reputed to have said that "two prostrations of a married Moslem are worth more than severity of a celibate." Nevertheless Islam, like Christianity, reckons its fraternities of ascetics, its enraptued mystics, its nonconformist sectaries. The hearts creed of the Arabian Islam has taken colour and content from the richer civilizations of Syria and Egypt, of Persia, India, and Spain etc. from which, at different times, it has drawn its votaries. The pious out-pourings of the holy Koran do not exhaust its message. There is in Islam a body of mystical literature, which, in the purity of its religious emotion, varies with the spiritual masterpieces of Jewish or Christian faith. Later on Sufies propagated Islam and made it popular.

Shia and Sunnies. The period which succeeds the death of the Prophet Muhammad while distinguished for many dazzling achievements in war and science and policy, is also memorable for the emergence of that deep and irreconsiderable rift within the Moslem world which still envenoms the relations of the Shite and the Sunnite sects. Iran under orthodox Shiate leader Khomeni is still daggers drawn with other Sunni states of Islam. Caliph Omar, the second of the Caliphs of Vicars and the true founder of the Arab state, the voice of discontent was silenced by the victories of the Arab generals. But his successor, Othman, was less fortunate, less able, less industrious. As such some critics say that his government was blamed for its extortions and was probably less well served. A campaign was set on foot in favour of Ali, the son-in-law of Prophet Muhammad which resulted in the assassination of Othman: and in the elevation of Ali to the caliphate in his place. From that moment the Moslem world was sharply divided into two irreconcilable factions of Shias and Sunnies. The title of Ali was disputed by the experienced governor of Syria Moawya. He was the cousin of the murdered Caliph Osman and a member of the Ummayyad house, who, having ruled Syria for seventeen years, was in no mood to surrender the throne of power to the nominee of Medina *i.e.* to Ali who is considered rightful heir by Shias.

The Shites or partisans of Ali were strong in Arabia and Iraq but the Sunnites adhered to Moawya in Syria and Egypt etc. The sinful murder of Ali and later of his family and of son's family. Hosein, left scars in the hearts of their votaries a long memory of passionates regret such as has coloured the annals of Ireland and Serbia in Europe. The strength lay with the caliphs of the Ummayyad house and so they ruled at Damascus and Islamic countries vigorously. At the cost of two civil wars they established in (692) their supremacy over the Arab world and in the countries of Middle East.

The divisions between the Shites and the Sunnites, while temporarily arresting the Moslem offensive, brought no permanent relief to other countries including Byzantine Empire. Position of Roman empire was challenged in Asia Minor and in other lands, capital of Egyptian empire was exposed to the risk of capture. The defection of those of its Christian subjects who exalted the divine as opposed to the human side of Christ was always to be apprehended. Meanwhile no great figure appeared in the Byzantine empire between the death of Heraclius in 641 and the accession of emperor Leo the Isaurian in 717. Emperor succeeded emperor in Roman empire but Assassination followed assassination. But rule of the Roman state was shaken by palace revolutions and civil wars and its annals stained by fratricidal intrigues still Asia Minor and Constantinople were held against Muslim invasions. The subdivision of the Empire into military districts of themes, garrisoned by army divisions and under entire subjection to military officers, probably helped to this end. This Roman empire was in decaying state when Islamic empire of Caliphs was extending its sway all over the world.

Battles of Poitiers and Battle of 717 and Their Impact

The Saracen expansion in Europe was ultimately checked by the victory won by the Frankish sovereign, Charles Martel, over the great army of the Muslim Viceroy Abdur Rahman on the field of Poitiers in 732. The numbers engaged on either side in that famous battle were very high the conflict between the huge Frankish footmen and the fiery cavalry of Spain and Africa was fierce and long, the victory of the Christian army was complete and decisive. But in the scale of importance probability the victory of Poitiers does not rank with the successful repulse by Eastern Roman emperor Leo, the Isaurian of the formidable Saracen attacks on Constantinople in 717 and 718, not only because Constantinople was closer to the centre of Muslim power and therefore more likely, if taken, to be retained, but also because the Saracens once established in the Byzantine capital at Roman empire would have found among the rude and imperfect Christians of eastern Europe a free field for Moslem propaganda. If the Turkish conquest of Constantinople in 1453, spread the Muslim creed for and wide through the Balkan peninsula, it may be imagined if the success which would have attended a Saraced conquest 700 years earlier, at a time when the peoples of Russia and the Balkans had received but a faint initial tincture of Christianity, and were still in a rude disorder of institutions and beliefs. Thus probably defeat of Islamic forces in 717-718 was as important as defeat of Islamic forces against Charles Martel of France in 732.

In the West the Saracens were confronted by an organized Christian society inheriting something of the strength of the western Roman Empire, and even had they won the day at Poitiers in 732, the western Europe would still have been far removed from the conquest and conversion of France. In eastern Europe probably it was otherwise. Here in eastern Europe and in Russia and Hungary, or among the Bulgarians and other Slaves states of the Balkan peninsula, there was no center of moral and physical resistance comparable to the Gallo-Roman Church or the strong Frankish culture and monarchy. Had eastern Roman emperor Leo the Isaurian had failed to beat off the imposing armada of Moslem forces, the Moslem faith might have spread like a prairie fire though the Balkans and the plains of Poland and Humgary and northwards and eastwards to the Urals. From this danger the great defence of Constantinople in 718, conducted by a young and capable Roman Emperor, with the aid of stout fortifications a superior navy, Greek fire, and the timely assistance of a Bulgar army, delivered European civilization from onslaught of Islamic forces. The name of Leo should be remembered. That the Russian Church is Greek and not Moslem due to defeat of Islamic forces in 717-718. Thus battles of 717-718 and of Poitiers in 732 checked the progress of Islam. It is remarked that a battles of 717-718 and of 732 were decisive battles of the world and by defeat in these battles dream of world conquest by Islamic forces was shattered on the sharp rocks of reality and Islam became confined to Middle Eastern countries and to those Iands in which Islam is still dominating religion. Moreover Arabs were replaced by Turks and Persians and Mongols as torch bearers and propagator of Islamic faith and conquest, who established their empires in eastern Europe, Africa and India and Indonesia etc.

21

UMAYYAD KHILAFAT

The Achievements of Umayyad Caliphs and The Disruption and Decline of the Arab Empire of Umayyad Caliphs

Mu'awiya's problem during his nineteen-year's reign was to reunite the demoralized and decentralized Arab empire in order to ensure its continuity and cohesion. His policy was not to rejuvenate the ideal Islamic theocracy of Medina, but to create a strong centralized Arab kingdom, based on Arab dominance in the empire. In Syria, Mu'awiya ruled as an Arab Sheikh, the first among equals, his authority as Caliph being more on a moral than a religious basis, depending on the consent and loyalty of the dominant Arab element in the Islamic empire. Arab participation in government was made effective through two loosely organized consultative bodies of notables, and the shura and the council of Sheiks with important executive powers, and the wufud, representing the tribes Mu'awiya rarely resorted to force. He still-fully managed the Islamic empire on a purely personal basis. He relied on his power of persuasion to "make friends and influence people".

Elsewhere Mu'awiya ruled through energetic, capable efficient and forceful provincial governors such as Ziyad, the governor of Iraq, who maintained strong discipline over that fertile but turbulent and rebellious provice. But while Mu'awiya himself ruled as an Arab Sheikh, his successors became increasingly autocratic, relying on the Syrian army to control this vast empire. Mu'awiya also established a tradition of excellence in administration which was probably more Byzantine than Arab in character. The governing procedures of the East Roman empire current in Syria were followed like predecessors. The old administrative system, together with its local Christian personnel, was also employed. The troublesome problem of the succession, which had been decided in the past either by controversial election or by civil war, was regulated by Mu'awiya five years before his death Simple hereditary succession was too alien to the Arab mind to be readily acceptable unmodified, so Mu'awiya, with characteristic diplomacy, found a compromise. He made succession hereditary but subject to the consent of the tribal parliamentary system which he had previously devised. Together with the shura of Damascus, he nominated Yazid, his son, and the nomination was confirmed by the wufud speaking for the various tribes. The compromise, though declared a heretical innovation by the Muslim Ulemas and aristocracy in Medina, tended to make the position of caliph hereditary. This procedure overly established the Umayyad empire which lasted until 750 A.D. During rule of Umayyads Islamic empire made conquests of far off lands and become mightiest empire.

The Umayyads produced able rulers who departed from the path set up by their pious predecessors. They emphasized the political and economic aspects of the government and ruled more like kings than religious leaders. Historians writing about the succeeding dynasties depicted them as his luxurious and pleasure-loving, worldly usurpers who, except for Umar II (717-720), were not fit to be called princes Caliphs following Islamic traditions. It is true that most of the Umayyads relegated religion to a secondary place and in their private lives enjoyed the material comforts and benefits of their empire. Nevertheless, despite their worldliness, they always posed themselves as the true champions of Islam. Military expansions were energetically resumed and conquests were carried forward into new far off lands. Within a hundred years the Islamic empire reached to its geographic limits. In the East, they conquered Taransoxanism, Baluchistan, and Sind in India through Muhammad Bin Kasim and Muslim rule became permanent along the river Indus in India. In the West, they swept over North Africa, and crossed the Straits of Gibraltar into Spain, where an Arab Berber (Moorish) culture was developed over eight centuries, leaving a lasting mark on both Spain and Islam. The wave of conquest in the west carried into the lands of the Frances, but was checked by Charles Martel, at the famous decisive Battle to Tours (732) only a hundred miles form Paris. In Asia Minor Arab armies conducted repeated campaigns against the Byzantine empire. In one assault, during the reign of Suleiman (715-717), Arab armies attacked and laid siege to the city of Constantinople for fourteen months. But the fortifications of the Byzantine capital proved impenetrable so in 716 Islamic expansion was checked. Only seven centuries later, with the aid of gunpowder in 1453, were the Muslims under the Ottoman Turks were able to capture the city of Constantinople and gave a death blow to Christian Eastern Roman empire of Byzantine emperors.

While vastly increasing the territory of the empire of Islam this second era of expansion caused acute economic and fiscal and administrative problems. The treasury depended on the state's share of the booty, the poll tax and a land tax (kharaj) etc. The Arabs were in a more advantageous position. They paid no taxes (except for a small religious tax, zakat, to support the needy), but were enrolled in the imperial registry (diwan), each receiving a regular payment from the state treasury. Umayyad fiscal difficulties started when their subjects adopted Islam in increasing numbers and stopped paying jeziya and other taxes. To treat all the faithful equality, Umar II (717-720) freed all Muslims, irrespective of their origin, form the poll and land tax called jeziya. This, together with the loss of booty from conquests, upset the fiscal system of Umayyad empire. The disastrous effects of the ducimelling of income forced the caliph Hisham (725-743) to stress that: "Although poll taxes fell off upon conversion to Islam, land taxes did not." This measure later on became the model for taxation policy in Islam. It was opposed by non-Arabs, who considered it unfair to non-Muslim landowners. Discontent with the land tax led to widespread alienation, even active opposition and ultimately lead to revolt and fall of Umayyads.

As rulers and subjects coalesced to form a civilization, so four social classes emerged. At the top were the ruling Arabs, who lived in garrison cities. Beneath them were the non-Arab Muslims, whose conversion to Islam was so rapid that by the eighth century they far outnumbered their rulers. Although better educated, they were rarely accepted socially, and had to attach themselves to an Arab family or tribe as clients (mawati). In the West, these mawati became Arabicized. But in the East the Arabs were ultimately absorbed by their subjects, and while Islam remained the dominant religion but Iranian, Turkish. Berber, and Indian characteristics prevailed. The non-Muslim subjects, "the people of the Bood" (dhimmis) Christians, Jews, and later on Zoroastrains, pagan, Buddhists, Buddhists Berbers, Hindus, and others-were classified as second-class subjects. They enjoyed freedom of worship and lived according to their own customs and own laws, with limited right, in civil matters.

At the bottom of the social ladder were the slaves, Greeks, Turks, Armenians, Kurds, Spaniards, Berbers, and Negroes etc. Islams, while declaring "manumission as pleasing in the sight of God," accepted slavery as an established institution. This institution left its mark on Islamic society more than in the West-economically. Through the profitable slave trade, socially through the institution of concubinage and the harem, and politically as individual slaves gained power as favourites, bodyguards and even as rulers. These slaves established their rule in India. Quttub-Uddin, Iltutamish and Balban etc. all were slaves. In Egypt Memuluks rulers etc.

The Umayyads were also responsible for the Arabization of the state and the development of a distinctive Arab culture. Trained Arab government personnel were lacking in the early period, so the Umayyads relied on local talent. These kept records in Greek or in Persian as officials of their respective lands. By the end of the Umayyad period, government records were being kept in Arabic, and Arabic had become the official language of the empire. When the Umayyads rose to power in Byzantine empire Sassanid currency were in wide circulation. The Umayyads adopted this currency as media of exchange, sometimes after stamping the old coins with a Koranic inscription. But Abd-al-Malik (685-705) introduced Arab Muslim coins with the same value as the old.

Anxious to maintain the dominance in their vast empire, and to preserve their ancient heritage, the Arabs remained proud of their culture, of their past, their language and lineage etc. in the period of four Caliphs. But during the Umayyad period, they became exposed to the influences of more sophisticated civilizations such as of Romans and Persians. And despite the political instability of mid-and late-Umayyad times, the beginning of a great intellectual awakening, which came into full bloom in the Abbasid period of Caliphs was in the making.

Internal weakness and dissension, sharpened also by the economic and social injustices perpetrated under their, rule, finally led to the downfall of the Umayyads groups among the Mawati and Arabs. Disenchanted with Umayyad policies and jealous of Umayyad dominance opponents joined anti Umayyad parties, such as the puritanical, militant Kharijites etc. who flourished in Iraq, Iran, and Khurasan etc. The Shi'ite, formerly the legitimists, who condemned the Umayyads as usurpers and considered Ali and his desendants as the only legitimate heirs to the caliphate.

The Shi'ite opposition to the Umayyads started when Ali was murdered and his younger son, Husain, became the head of the Ali's house. While Mu'awiya reigned, Husain did not oppose him strongly. But when Mu'awiya died in (680), he set out for Kufa at the head of a small band of his supporters, primarily from the families of companions of Ali in expectation of local support for his bid to the caliphate. On the way, he was surrounded at Karbala by the troops of Mu'awiya's son Yazid, who had been proclaimed caliph in Damascus and when Husain and his followers refused to return to Medina, he was mercilessly massacred together with his followers and his head was sent to Yazid in Damascus. Although the slaying of the Prophet's grandson passed without much opposition at that time, it gained significance later on as the shi'ite movement crystallized and Muslims became divided on long religious and theological lines into two major camps Sunnites (orthodox) and Shiites. To Shiites, the massacre symbolized the sufferings and maltreatment they endured at the hands of the orthodox Sunni majority. As a result, Karbala has become to them a most holy place, and Umayyad suppression of his support in Kufa, Medina, and Mecca weakened Ali's opposition. But the resentment harboured the Umayyads remained. Muharram is still celebrated to commemorate the memory of sacrifice Hussains and his followers.

Perhaps another factor contributing to the downfall of the Umayyads was the tribal wars among the nomadic Arabs, whose spirit of independence and resentment of any form of centralizing authority had not diminished much but while in pre Islamic times, they also thought among themselves in small isolated units, under the Umayyads they organized into two large feuding factions. The main division, the south Arabian party, had moved northward from Yemen about two centuries before Islam after the breaking of the Ma'rib dam and the ensuing disintegration of economic and political life in southern Arabia. They had settled in the area east of the Jordan River and the Dead sea, claiming ancestry from ancient Qahtan (Joktan of the Book of Genesis). The rival North Arabian party, which moved northward from to central and northern parts of the Arabian Peninsula, claiming ancestry from Adam (Ishmael), was probably much more nomadic in character. Rivalry between these two parties persisted throughout Islamic history, reaching its height under the Umayyads, when it affected every aspect of political, life, so revolt led by Abbasids took place which ended Umayyad rule.

Rule of Abbasid Caliphs and Their Achievement

Finally, in 750, the rule of the Umayyads was supplanted by that of the Abbasids. The center of the Islamic empire shifted eastward from Syria to Iraq, from Damascus to Baghdad. To their restive contemporaries, the Abbasids must have represented a new revolutionary force. Claiming descent from Abbas, and uncle of the Prophet Muhammad and posing themselves as the true champions of Islam in the tradition of the "right guide" Abbasid caliphs, Abbasids had conducted an intensive propaganda campaign against the rule of Umayyads about their monopolization of power, the haughty manner, and their worldly estracances etc. The fact that the campaign focused on turbulent Iraq and Persia was perhaps not merely accident. Persia, especially, because of its remoteness, its strong Shi'ite sentiment, and the awareness, rather certitude, of its populace of their cultural superiority over the conquering Arabs became an easy target for Abbasid propaganda. The black Abbasid banner of revolt that became the emblem of the new dynasty was raised in 747. In 740, Abbas, the founder of the new dynasty, was proclaimed caliph. Marwan II the last of the Umayyads, still reigned in the Syria, but the following year, his army was routed by Abbasids. The systematic liquidation of the Umayyad clan followed.

The revolt movement which had brought the Abbasids to power was based on a widespread revulsion against the impiety of the Umayyads. This impiety affected the whole organisation of Islamic society, material and moral. The new dynasty of Abbasid caliphs radically changed the existing state of things. First came the destruction of the political unity of the Islamic state under the caliph. The one important Umayyad who escaped from the wrath of the Addasids, Abdul Rahman, fled to Spain and founded a new Islamic state with a separate claim for Khilafat. He and his successors challenged the authority and caliphate of the Abbasids for three centuries, claiming for themselves the right or caliph. The caliphal dualism, which became a salient feature of Islamic political history was departure from the pattern previously established and followed. It was the beginning of a long and dangerous process of political and territorial fragmentation of authority as well as of empire. By the tenth century, as Abbasid glory of the state waned, the established pattern lost ground to such an extent that even illustrious political theorists, such as Mawardi etc. of (1059), were unable to bridge the gap between the theory and practice. It was not until much later long after the fall of the Abbasid empire and the shifting and division of the ruling power, that Islamic political thinking to came to grips with the facts. Ibn Taumiyya (d. 1328) was realistic enough to recognize that the traditional caliphate was one, once and for all. By insisting that any state in the Islamic empire administered by and accordance with the Divine Law was Islamic, regardless of whether or not it was ruled by a caliph. In this way, the legitimized the Political disunity which had become the dominent rule in practice of Islamic empire and it become divided and fragmented.

Other aspects of caliphal unity were also changed fundamentally. The immediate caliphal family, whose composition reflected the social and political tolerance prevalent at that time, underwent a gradual evolution. The Abbasids, like the Umayyads regarded the caliphal family as superior to all others, but with a difference — they had no scrupulous against marrying non Arabs. In fact nearly all the Abbasids were the sons of non-Arab begums. As such Ethnic purity counted for little and had no relevance in the Arab ruling class. He became a personal autocrat, surrounded by pomp and show, imposing his will through a skilled bureaucracy and a professional army, very much in the Byzantine and Sassanid Persian style.

Moreover, the problem that the mawatl posed for the previous regime dissipated as they were allowed to assimilate. In the name of equality, the new converts aspired to a position corresponding to the frowning effective influence. The outspoken element among them was the Persian as the principal supporters of the new regime of Abbasid caliphs. They were the chief beneficiaries of the change, but other grounds also won equal status with the Arabs. By the eighth century the term mawati had ceased to exist. This did not mean that regional antagonism had come to an end but rather that evolving into an international society wherein all Muslims were considered theoretically equal, irrespective of their national or racial origin. Hostility towards the Arabs continued, but in a modified form. For now it stemmed form a sense of equality, a healthy competitive spirits, in society open for all Muslims began. It expressed national pride, the superiority of the Persians, because Persian influence in the capital Baghdad dominated the influence of the Arabs lessened.

There was also some Persian influence in the capital Bagdad early in the Abbasid period, and it became considerable by the beginning of the ninth century. Afterward, Abbasid caliphs control in Persia began to disintegrate. Ex-caliphal officials, general and scions of local noble families founded their own petty dynasties in different parts of Persia and in central Asia. Some of these little states either coexisted or were supplanted by the more considerable states of the Samanids (874-999) of eastern Persia and Turkestan and by the Buwaihids (932-1035) of Western Persia. Abbasid control over the Islamic empire was further underminded when, in 945, a branch of the Buwaihid dynasty captured most of Iraq and even moved into the capital city of Baghdad; this deprived the caliph of all real power but his prestige. The caliph's power was eroded not only in the Persian East but also in the Western countries. In Syria, Arabia and Egypt and even in Iraq itself, a succession of short-lived, virtually independent dynasties emerged, such as the Hamdanids (929-1003) of Aleppo, and Marwanids (990-1096) etc. In Egypt and in most of Syria, where Abbasid control had never been popular, caliphal officials asserted their power and established two independent dynasties the Tulunids (865-905) and the Ikhshidis (935-969). They were succeeded by the Fatimids, who moved into Egypt from Tunisia in 969 and founded Cairo, which became the capital of the powerful and prosperous state of Egypt, noted for cultural and artistic achievements and for extensive trade relations with Europe. Even in remote Arabia, the caliph's authority was underminded. The most serious challenge was posed by Carmathian sectarians, a heretical Shi'ite sect that controlled Mecca, until the Fatimids destroyed it and brought the Hijaz with the holy cities of Mecca and Medina under their control. Thus gradually caliphs authority deteriorated everywhere.

Abbasid power was further weakened by the rise of a succession of theocratic city-dynasties, such as the Sharifs of Mecca, and the heretical Shi'ite Ibadis in Oman. Before the rise of the Fatimids, the Aghlabids (801-909) had succeeded in establishing themselves in North Africa, as well as in gaining a firm foothold in Sicily and in the parts of southern Italy. Farther west in Morocco, another independent Shi'ite dynasty of the Idrisids, came to power. In Spain, the westernmost portion of the Islamic empire the process of disintegration set in much earlier when in 756 the Umayyad Add al-Rahman, after escaping the persecution of the Abbasids, was recognized as ruler by both Arab and Berber and claimed himself as Calipha. His Umayyad successors went a step further by having themselves recognized as independent caliphs. After the collapse of Umayyad power in Spain, although the Islamic element was strengthened by the advent from North Africa of the puritanical, Almoravids in the eleventh and twelfth centuries, Spain remained politically independent having no connection with Abbasid empire. During this isolation from the rest of the Islamic world, a period of eight centuries, a remarkable Spanish-Muslim culture evolved that left a lasting imprint of the arts and sciences of both medieval Islam and over Christian Europe also.

By the end of the tenth century, the great Arab empire of the Abbasids had thus become politically fragmented among several states of varying strength, size, durability, and independence Both the capital, the wealthy and cultured city of Baghdad, and the caliphate fell under the control of secular and non-Arab rulers. The Abbasid caliph legitimized the usurpation of his power by a new princely ruler by investing them with the right to rule, in his name but that was a mere formality designed to close gap between the ideal caliphate and political practice. He had lost all but his spiritual prerogatives prestige as the head of the Islamic community. However the rise and fall of these now forgotten medieval Islamic states constitutes an important chapter in the development of Islamic civilization. In spite of their precarious existence, subject to the constant challenge form within and without of new and jealous usurpers aspirants, these states, for several countries, provided large sectors of the Islamic empire with government that were generally formal and orderly with a strong devotion to Islam and a remarkable appreciation of learning, culture, and the art and science etc.

22

Spread of Islam

The Spread of Islam during First Four Caliphs and Its Impact

Muhammad left no son to succeed him and, even if he had, either his unique position as the Prophet nor Arab custom permitted any such automatic succession. Acting swiftly, Muhammad's associates selected the prophet's most trusted friend and adviser, Abu Bakr, as his official successor, the caliph. The title of caliph (from Khalifa, meaning "deputy") carried with it the controlling power in both religious and political affairs. Thus caliph enjoyed powers of both Pope and King.

During the reigns of the first four caliphs (632–661) Islam spread rapidly. It was one of the beliefs of the Prophet Muhammad that any Muslim dying in battle for the faith was assured entrance into paradise. This sanctification of war are gave fighting people a fanatical courage that proved well-high irresistible. Moreover, the prospect of rich and fertile territory, and plunder if they are victorious proved a strong incentive to a people who had been eking out a bare existence from the desert.

The Islamic cause was also aided by political upheavals occurring outside of Arabia. The Muslim triumphs in the Near East can be partly accounted for by the long series of wars between the Eastern Roman and Persian empire. The Byzantine victory in 628, had left both sides weak exhausted and open to conquest. In the year 638, Arab forces conquered Syria, the Muslims then wrested Iraq from the Persians and, within ten years after Muhammad's death, they conquered Persia itself, Arabs conquered greater part of Egypt, where Byzantine rule was harsh and corrupt. It fell with little resistance in 640 A.D. and the rest parts of Egypt shortly afterwards. Thus, by the end of the reigns of the first four caliphs, Islam had vastly increased its territory.

The imposition of a poll tax *i.e.*, Jezia on all non-Muslims fostered a great number of conversions to Islam. Contrary to exaggerated accounts in the west of the forceful imposition of Islam upon conquered peoples, the Jews and the Christians outside of Arabia enjoyed some protection. This was because they belonged to tolerated religions having books *i.e.*, kitabias.

Islam is among the most tolerant religious in minimizing and demolishing the obstacles of a race colour and nationality. The new religion was based on Muslim brotherhood. In Africa, for example, "…..Islam recognized no race discrimination. The converted Negro was readily admitted into Islamic society, and to him the Moslem was a brother not only in name but throughout the sphere of social life". This equalitarian feature of Islam certainly aided its expansion.

Arab Domination under the Umayyads. The reign of the first four caliphs were followed by the Umayyad dynasty (661-750) which established its capital at Damascus in Syria. Henceforth, the caliphate was to be a hereditary office, not, as previously, a position filled by election or selection.

Pushing through Asia Minor, the Umayyad armies attacked Constantinople in 670, but the Byzantine capital withstood all Muslim sieges until 1453. In the West, the Muslims enjoyed great success. They subdued the whole of North Africa, even though the Berbers, a desert tribal people, resisted stubbornly. The next logical jump was across the strait of Gibraltar into the weak kingdom of the Visigoths in Spain. The governor of Muslims in North Africa sent his general, Tarik and an army across this strait into Spain in 711; seven years later this weak Kingdom of the Visigoths which ruled had completely crumbled. The Muslims swept across what is now south and central France and were only turned back by Charles Martel in the decisive battle of Tours in 732 exactly a century after Muhammad, death. Meanwhile, the Muslims had been expanding eastward into central Asia. By the eighth century, they could claim for the caliph, lands as far off as Turkistan and the Indus valley in India. It is said in battle of fours Muslims lost world empire because if they would have won, they would have conquered Europe. The source of Umayyad power were the Arabs, who formed a privileged ruling aristocracy greatly outnumbered by the non-Arab converts to Islam-Egyptians, Syrians, Persians, Berbers, and many others. Many of these such as Persians possessed cultures much more advanced than that of the Arabs themselves, and the economic and cultural life of the Arab empire depended on these people. But not being Arab by birth, they were treated as second class Muslims. Though they fought in Islamic armies but they received less pay and booty than the Arabs and at the same time were subjected to high taxation. Dissatisfaction grew among the non-Arabic Muslims and eventually helped bring about the downfall of the Arab Kingdom of the Umayyads.

The Rule of Abbasid Caliphs and Its Impact

The Abbasids, high tide of Islam. In 750, the Umayyad dynasty was crushed by rebels, and a new dynasty, the Abbasid Caliphs ruled Islam from 750 to 1258. The city of Baghdad was built in 762 as the capital of the new Abbasid situated on the banks of Tigris-Euphrates rivers.

The fall of the Umayyad dynasty marked the end of Arab predominance; henceforth, Persians and other non-Arabs were to create a new political order. The Arab aristocracy had led the forces of conquest during the great period of Islamic expansion, but with the advent of more stable political conditions, the important status thus far held by the Arab soldier was given to the merchant and administrator and Ulemas. In the social and economic spheres, changes of dynasties tooks place and it was reflected and also encouraged by new forces. The traditional Arabic patterns of nomadism and tribal warfare gave way before economic prosperity and the growth of town life. The Abbasid caliph who built Baghdad forecasted that it would become the "most flourishing city in the world"; and indeed it rivalled Constantinople in splendour, pomp and show situated as it was fertile land on the trade routes linking West and East. At the same time, such peacetime pursuits as the arts and scholarship were encouraged.

The location of the new capital at Baghdad resulted in a shift of Islam's center of gravity to the province of Iraq whose soil, watered by the rivers Tigris and Euphrates, had cradled man's earliest civilizations. In this ancient center of many brilliant and despotic empires, the Abbasid caliphs set themselves up as Oriental Potentates, surrounded by a lavish court life that would have distressed the simple-living Prophet. Baghdad was sufficiently removed from Mediterranean contacts to evolve a near Eastern cultures in which Persian influence dominated.

The Abbasid dynasty marked the high tide of Islamic Power and civilization. In the early years of the caliphate, the Abbasid empire was greater in size than the domain of the Roman Caesar. It was the product of an expansion during which the Muslims had assimilated to their creed, speech, and even physical type, more aliens there any stock before or since, not excepting the Hellenic, the Roman, the Anglo Saxon or the Russians etc. The assimilation process was not limited to Peoples; this Islamic state drew on the entire known world for customs, culture and inventions and literature etc.

The Trade, Industry, Agriculture and Lot of Peasant and Workers in Muslim Empire

Trade, industry, and agriculture. From the eighth to the twelfth centuries, the Muslim world enjoyed a prosperity such as post Roman Europe did not experience until early modern times. In contact with three continents, the Muslims could shuttle goods back and forth from China to western Europe and from Russia to central Africa. Muslims monopolized trader became rich. Another reason for Islam's economic well being lay in the tolerance of its public who allowed non Muslim merchants and craftsmen to reside in their territories and carry on trade and commerce with their home countries. The presence of such important urban centers such as Baghdad, Cairo, and Cordova etc. stimulated trade and industry throughout the Muslim world. It was trade disputes which lead Muslims to attack King Dahir of Sindh. Muslims alleged robbing of their traders by Pirates and when Raja Dahir of Sindh denied responsibility for acts of Pirates, Sindh was attacked by Muhammad Bin Kasseim. This shows how much Arabs cared for trade. The cosmopolitan nature of Baghdad was evident in its bazaars which contained variety of goods from all over the known world. There were spices, minerals, and dyes from India; gems and fabrics from central Asia; honey and wax from Scandinavia and Russia and ivory gold dust from Africa and Chinese pots and goods from China, including silks musk, and porcelain etc. Thus Arabs monopolized trade till the Arabs were defeated by Philips of Spain in 1580.

The textile industries of the Muslims, which were particularly prosperous, produced silk, cotton, muslin, and linen goods etc. leather, enamel, pottery, and luxury goods similar to Roman Empire manufactures were also produced in abundance. As in the Byzantine empire, the workers in the large Islamic cities were organized into guilds and crafts supervised by the government. Muslims encouraged artisans and looked after cared for their welfare.

Under the rule of the Abbasids, agriculture was both extensive and profitable. Vast irrigation projects in Iraq resulted in an increase of cultivable land which yielded large crops of variety fruits and cereals. Wheat came from Iraq and the Nile valley, cotton from North Africa, olives and wine from Spain, wool from eastern Asia Minor, and horses from Arbia and Persia. As in medieval Europe, the land was worked by serfs and by free peasants, whose lot was for the most part miserable. Large land-owners also used slaves on their estates.

A Short Note on the Rule of Famous Caliph Harun-al-Rashid

The opulent reign of Harun-al-Rashid. Just as the Abbasid rule was the most brilliant of Muslim dynasties, so the rule of Harun-al-Rashid (786-809) was the most spectacular of the Abbasid reigns. He was the contemporary of the great Holy Roman emperor Charlemagne, and there can be no doubt that Harun-al-Rashid was the more powerful ruler of the two and the symbol of the more highly advanced culture. The two great monarchs were on most friendly terms, even though their friendship arose out of self-interest, Holy Roman emperor Charlemagne wanted to exert pressure on Eastern Roman Emperor to recognize his new imperial title. Harun-al-Rashid saw Charlemagne as an ally against the Umayyads in Spain, who had broken away from Abbasid and ruled in Spain. Several embassies and various gifts were exchanged. The Muslim sent the Holy Roman Christian emperor rich fabrics. Caliph aromatics, and all elephant named Abu-Lababah, meaning "the father of intelligence." An intricate water clock from Baghdad seems to have been looked upon as a miracle in the primitive Western Europe. Holy Roman emperor who was supposed to champion the causes of Christianity made friendship with Muslim Caliph to crush fellow Christian Byzantine emperor, who was head of orthodox Christian-church and Abbasid Caliph Harun-Al-Rashid to crush fellow Muslim Sunni Umayed ruler because he claimed rival Caliph title inspite of all this Charlemagne is considered greatest Holy Roman emperor and Harun-al-Rashid as most famous and greatest Caliph. Relations between the Abbasid caliphate and the Byzantine empire were never cordial, and conflicts often broke out along the constantly shifting border that separated Christian and Muslim empire and their territories.

Caliph Harun-al-Rashid once replied to a communiqué from the Byzantine emperor in the following terms:

In the name of God, the Merciful, the Compassionate from Harun. Commander of the Faithful, to Nicephorus, the dog of the Greeks. I have read your letter, you son of a she-infidel and you shall see the answer before you hear it.

Whereupon the irate Caliph sent forth expeditions to ravage Asia Minor which was part of Byzantine empire at the time.

In the days of Harun-al-Rashid, wealth and splendour of Baghdad was more than that of Constantinople, and its chief glory was the royal harem and its palace. With its annexes for eunauchs, officials, and harem, the caliph's residence occupied about a third of Baghdad. Gorgeously furnished with the richest rugs, cushions, and curtains which the Orient world could create, the Caliph's audience chamber must have been breath, taking in its effect. Inspite of all this Caliph maintained justice. It is said ugly cottage of old woman remained intact because old woman refused to sell it.

The Disintegration of the Abbasid Empire

Despite the unprecedented prosperity of the far-flung Islamic world, the political unity of Islam and empire of Abbasid Caliphs began to disappear almost immediately after the Arab empire reached to its full extent. With the accession of the Abbasid dynasty, the Caliphs in the Near East, at Baghdad which became the center of Islam. It began to lose their hold on the Muslim states in the West. The first sign of political disintegration appeared as early as in 756 when a member of the deposed Umayyad family set up his own dynasty at Cordova in Spain. In the tenth century its ruler assumed the title of Caliph, as did also the governor of Egypt later on they began to claim themselves as Sunni Caliphs.

In the latter part of the tenth century, Turkish nomads called Seljuks, migrated from Asia into the Abbasid lands, where they readily accepted Islam. The Seljuk Turks than began to seize land from the Abbasid rule and after annexing most of Persian Turks gained control of Baghdad in 1055, and absorbed Iraq. Later on the Seljuks conquered Syria and Palestine and then proceeded to annex; part of Asia Minor form the Byzantine emperor. It was the great advance by the Seljuk Turks that prompted the Abbasids to retain the normal rule of Caliphs but a new and terrible enemy was early in the thirteenth century, the redoubtable and great Mongol conqueror Genghis Khan succeeded in uniting the nomads of Mongolia he and his successors conquered eastern and central Asia and swept into Persia and Iraq. In 1258, Halaqu Khan a grandson of Genghis Khan captured Baghdad and slew the Abbasid. Not only had the Abbasid dynasty come to collapse, but so did much of the vast irrigation system that had supported this fertile land since ancient time. Iraq fell into a state of collapse from which it did not recover until 20th century. The Mongol ruling class was eventually absorbed into the Muslim culture of Persia and Iraq, and the dynasty established by the Mongols survived there for only a short time and became fragmented and part of Muslim culture.

Rule of the Ottoman Turks

Following the Mongol destruction of the Seljuk Turks' sultanate in Asia Minor, this region has attracted-other Turks from central Asia, among them were Ottoman Turks. The newcomers adopted Islam fanatically and began to gain control of the former Abbasid Caliph's dominions. The Ottoman. Turks also pitted themselves against the Eastern Roman Byzantine emperors and in 1453 Constantinople fell to them. The formidable Turks pressed on into southeastern Europe, driving as far as Vienna, where they were turned back with difficulty in 1529 and again in 1683 there attacks were repulsed. Meanwhile, they had conquered Iraq including Palestine now called Israeli much of Arabia and all of North African as for as Morocco etc. This Turkish empire lived on and continued upto twentieth century, though with progressive weakness. Ottoman Turkish empire got a death blow in world war of 1914-18 and independent states emerged later on. As short review and the evolution of Islam in western Asia and in the lands around the Mediterranean sea has been given Islam's expansion as a missionary faith and as a civilization into south and southeast Asia, prevails even now.

A Short Note on Muslim Culture

Borrowing the best from other cultures. The high attainment of the Muslims in the intellectual and artistic fields cannot be attributed only to the Arabs, who as a group remained unprogressive, but rather to those peoples within the far-flung Muslim empire who had embraced Islam. Although the Muslim made some important contributions in science, the brilliance of Muslim learning probably was due not to native genius but in other cultures. Under Harun-al-Rashid and his successors, Indian and Persian works were preserved and the works of Aristotle, Euclid, Ptolemy, Aryabhatta and Charak etc. Archimedese were translated into Arabic. This knowledge formed the basis of Muslim learning, which in turn was later transmitted to scholars in western Europe. Al-Beruini and Abesieyna etc, were great scholars.

Advances in Medicine. The two hundred years between 900 and 1100 perhaps can be called the golden age of Muslim learning. This period was particularly significant for advances made in medicine.

The first and perhaps greatest Muslim physician was AL-Razi better known to the West as Rhazes wrote more than two hundred works, of which one of the most famous is on smallpox and measles the first clear description of the symptoms and treatment of these fatal diseases. His most monumental writing was the comprehensive Book, a huge medical encyclopaedia. In it he cited for each disease all Greek, Syrian, Arabian, Persian and Indian authorities and includes his own personal experiences and opinions as well. Translations of this famous encyclopaedia were later used by many European physicians.

The most familiar name in Muslim medicine is that of Avicenna, great physicist, philosopher, and physician. Into his vast Canon of Medicine, he packed all the legacy of Greek knowledge together with Arabic medical learning. In the 12th century this book was translated into Latin and was so much in demand that it was issued sixteen times in the last half of the fifteenth century and more than twenty times in the sixteenth century. It is still read and used in the orient today and is popular in Muslim medical treatment of Hakims.

Medical theory was augmented by practical application. Hospitals were operating throughout the Muslim empire. They were divided into sections for men and women. The qualifications of physicians and druggists were subject to state inspection. In spite of a ban against the study of anatomy and a few other limitations imposed on the Muslims Hakims, religious scruples, their medical men were in many ways superior to their European contemporaries upto 10th century.

Progress in Other Sciences

Although other branches of science did not keep pace with medicine, they did make considerable progress. Physics continued along the paths of inquiry laid down by Hellenistic thinkers, but, meanwhile, Muslim scientists arose who were no mere copyists. Alhazen developed optics to a remarkable degree and challenged the view of Ptolemy and Euclid that eye sends out visual rays to its object. His work was the chief source of all medieval western writers on optics. He interested himself on optic reflections and illusions and examined the refraction of light rays through air and water etc.

Significant advance were also made in the field of mathematics. In this field, the Muslims were particularly indebted to the Greeks and Hindus, from whom they learned most of their arithmetic, geometry, and algebra etc. From the Greeks came the geometry of Euclid and fundamentals of trigonometry which Ptolemy had transmitted. From the Hindu mathematicians came the nine signs now known as the Arabic numerals. It may be that the Muslims invented the all-important zero, although some scholars would assign this honour to the Indians. Two names deserve special mention when we speak of Muslim algebra: AL-Khwarizme wrote treatises on astronomy the Hindu method of calculation, algebra, and arithmetic while the poet. Omar Khayyam advanced even beyond AL-Khwarizme in equations. Where AL-Khwarizme dealt only with quadratics, Omar Khayyam devoted much of his treatise on algebra to cubic equations. In Arabic numbers are called Hindusa depicting Hindustani origin of Arabic number or mathematics. The flourishing trade and widespread administration of the Muslim lands stimulated the science of geology, geography. Greek treatises were translated, and tables of latitudes and longitudes were set up. Although the first world maps made by the Muslims showed Mecca in the center (medieval Christians honoured Jerusalem similarly), all in all, during the middle ages, the geographical knowledge of the Muslims was perhaps far superior to that of any people in Christendom. Probably in medieval age, Muslims exceeded in geographical knowledge than any other people.

Islamic Literature and Scholarship. In the western world, a knowledge of Islamic literature tends to be limited to "Alaf Laila — Hazar Dastan" over. A Thousand and one Nights and to the hedonistic poetry of Omar Khayyam. The former is a collection of tales often erotic and told with a wealth of local colour, culture tradition. The fame of the latter is partly due to the musical (though not ever accurate) translation of the Rubaiyat of Omar Khayyam by Edward Fitz Gerald. Here are some stanzas from the poem Omar Khayyam which will indicate its beautiful imagenary and gentle pessimism:

We are no other than a moving row of Magic Shadow-shapes that come and go Round with the Sun-illumines Lantern held in Midnight by the Master of the Show;

But helpless Pieces of the Game He plays Upon this Checker-borad of Nights and Days; Hither and thither moves, and checks, and slays.

And one by one back in the closet lays....

He beautifully depicts:

The moving Finger writes, and having writ, Moves on not all year piety nor Wit Shall lure it have to cancel half a Line, Nor all your Tears wash out a World of it. And that inverted Bowl they call the sky, where under crawling cool'd we live and die, die, Life not your hands to it for help for it As impotently moves as you all.

The lavish use of imagery and rhythmical phrasing characterizes much of Islamic prose literature

As the first important prose work in Islamic literature was the holy Koran. It set the stylistic pattern for Muslim writers even down to modern times. The holy Koran was designed particularly to be recited aloud. Anyone who has listened to the chanting of the Koran can testify to its credence, melody, and power and greatness.

Philosophy was also a favourite Muslim subject developed as a result of contacts with other culture. Thus Muslim philosophy is mostly Greek in origin and structure, though it also contains some Indian elements. Avicenna, the physician with many talents, wrote commentaries on Aristotle as well as some on famous Muslim philosophers. These studies were translated into Latin and had a fare aching effect on European thought and culture. Like the medieval Christian Philosophers Muslim thinkers were largely concerned with applying Aristotilian principles to religious problems as a means of bolstering orthodox creeds. Many prominent philosophers attempted to reconcile reason with faith. For example, Averroes attempted to harmonize faith and reason for Islam, project which St. Thomas Aquinas undertook for Christianity in the next century in Europe.

Islamic historiography also found its finest expression in the work of Ibn-Khaldun who has been judged the first writer to treat history as the proper object of a special science. Despite his busy life in public affairs among Velema and statesmen, he found time to write a large general history, dealing particularly with the history of the Arabs in Spain and Africa etc. This book maintains that history should analyze man's social development, which Ibn-Khaldun held to be the result of the interaction of society and physical environment. He defined the historian's function as given below.

"Know that the true purpose of history is to make us acquainted with human society *i.e.*, with the civilization of the world, and with its natural phenomena, such as savage life, the softening of manners, attachment to the family and the tribe, the various kinds of superiority which one people gains over another, the kingdoms and diverse dynasties which arise in this way, the different trades and occupations which we devote themselves in order to their livestock, the sciences and arts; in fine all the manifold conditions which naturally occur in the development of civilization."

Whereas Christian historians of the Middle Ages believed in a state concept of events, Ibn-Khaldun conceived of history as an evolutionary process, in which societies and institutions change continually. Ibn-Khaldun may be considered as Herodotus or Gibbon of Islamic history and perhaps greatest historian of Arabic Islamic culture.

Art and Architecture

Religious attitudes played an important part in Muslim art and architecture. As the prophet Muhammad inveighed strongly against idols and idol worship, there was a prejudice against pictorial representation of human and animal figures. The general, effect of this prejudice was to encourage the development of stylized and geometrical design and bring this to fore.

Like Muslim learning, Muslims are also from many sources. Islamic artists and craftsman copied Byzantine, Persian, Indian and Chinese models and learned into a distinctive and original style.

The Muslims mostly excelled in two fields — Architecture and the decorative art. As such Islamic architecture can boast of many large and imposing structures, is not surprising, because it drew much of its inspiration from the Byzantines and Persians etc., who were monumental builders. In time, an original style of building evolved; the great mosques embody such typical features as domes, arcades, and minarets, the slender towers from which the faithful and familiar feature of Muslim architecture evolved.

On the walls and ceilings of their monuments buildings, the Muslims gave full reign to their love of ornamentation and beauty of detail. This quality is shown to advantage in the Al-hambra palace at Granda, the walls of which are carved into beautiful patterns. The Spanish interpretation of the Muslim tradition was particularly delicate and charming and elegant. Other outstanding example of Islamic architecture are to be found in India; Red Fort, Jama Masjid, the Taj Mahal and Gol Gumbud and Char Minar etc. are based largely on Persian motifs, and are finest examples of Muslim architecture.

Being restricted in their subject matter. Muslim artisans and craftsmen conceived beautiful patterns from flowers and geometric figures etc. Even the graceful script made a delicate ornamentation on walls and the sides of urns. Tilos and mosaica were employed effectively to produce the lavish and conventionalized patterns. Muslim decorative skill also found expression in such fields as carpet and rugweaving, brass work, and the making of steel products inlaid with precious metals etc.

Thus Muslim religion established dynamic Islam kingdoms and of the spiritual allegiance of populations stretching from Gibraltar to Java. With the conquest of Constantinople in 1453, this Muslim civilization overwhelmed rival Christian civilization.

When Christian emperor, Constantine chose the site for New Rome, he picked a location that was geographically excellent from the point of view of protection and also for trade and commerce. Constantinople's traditions as the eastern capital of the Roman empirê encouraged emperor Justinian to attempt to recover the lost western territory which had been under Roman rule; but these efforts failed and in the long run Byzantine had to fight continually against invasion of Muslim forces and after continuous fights between Muslims and Christians, in the end, The Ottoman Turks conquered "The City" and the empire of a thousand years called Byzentine empire was destroyed and in 1453 Constantinople became part and parcel of Turkish kingdom. For a millennium this Byzantine empire had acted as a buffer state, repulsing attacks while the weak, divided Western Europe grew in strength. And, while learning was all lost in medieval western Europe, the Byzantine workes remained, the custodian of classical knowledge and ideals until a resurgent West was able to assimilate its classical heritage and scientific advancement.

City of Constantinople which was capital of Byzentine empire did much more than all this. Roman, Greek, and other Oriental elements were fused into a distinct and original culture; Slavic people were converted to Christianity; and the benefits of civilization were brought to Russia and neighboring lands and to eastern Europe.

The Norsemen who founded a Russian state by joining Kiev and Novgorod also set up trade with Constantinople which continued to flourish for centuries. Through this medium, cultural and religion were imported into Russia from the eastern Roman empire. While Constantinople itself fell in 1453, its heritage was in many ways maintained in the new Christian Slavic state, many ways maintained in the new Christian Slavic State, Spreading across the vast Russian, plain and in various countries of eastern Europe such as Bulgaria and Romania and Yugoslavia etc.

Into a desert area populated by nomadic Bediuins of Arabian desert and a few scattered groups of townsmen, was born Prophet Muhammad. After Muhammad's death, his monotheisting teachings were complied in the Holy Koran, the Muslim Bible which lead to new religious faith and holy to new inspiration to new idealogy.

During the reigns of the first four caliphs and the century of the Ummayyad dynasty rules, between (661-750), great strides were made in annexing new territories and peoples. But the Umayyad dynasty was mainly based on a ruling hierarchy of Arabs, and the resentment of the non-Arabs produced a revolution which set the Abbasid dynasty which ruled from (750-1258) on a new throne having Baghdad as its capital.

During the early Abbasid period, Islam reached to the high point of its geographical expansion and cultural achievements, and rule of Muslims extended from Spain across three continents: Africa, Europe and Asia to the Far East including Indonesia and Malaya etc. Unparalleled prosperity evolved from a combination of successful trade, Art and Craft and industry, and agriculture etc. But the Muslims were not able to maintain an integrated centralized empire; and despite a religious unity which still exists in middle East and in Muslim countries politically this Muslim empire broke up into smaller Muslim states.

The Muslims were especially gifted in science, literature, and art and architecture and part of philosophy etc. Some historians are of opinion that Muslim intellectual life was in good part the product of a genius for synthesizing varying cultures rather than probably creating original contributions. The Muslims great diffusion of Greek and Arabic and Persian and Indian knowledge was a tremendous factor in the revival of classical learning and the coming of the Renaissance in Europe.

The Islamic civilization in modern times has probably failed to retain its cultural supremacy, probably due to influx of semibar-barous people into Islamic lands during the middle ages. Another reason probably was the stagnation, resulting from a too rigid interpretation of the Holy Koran. Still another reason perhaps was the corrupt and despotic rule of such Muslim dynasties as of Selfish men and of the Ottomans in Turkey, who destroyed all progressive movements of Islam and failed to keep pace with scientific advancement in modern age.

But a new day is at hand for Modern Islam. The Muslims have amply proved that they have the intellectual and administrative gifts to make themselves a great people, and the rejuvenation of Turkey and Muslim states after the First World War under the able guidance of the late Mustafa Komal Ataturk has indicated a possible road for the modern followers of Muhammad, the Prophet. In addition to the Turks, all other Muslim people such as Iran, Iraq, Egypt and Syria and Saudi Arabia and Pakistan etc., have been on the march in recent times. The Arab people of North East-Tunisians, Morocco, Egyptians, and Syrians etc, and Indonesians, have experienced a remarkable progress and dynamic awakening. This Muslim revival constitutes one of the major themes of the twentieth century world but in middle, these Muslims are divided and fighting with one another. Arab countries are fighting with Israel, Iran and Iraq fought a long war and are daggers drawn to one another and in Afghanistan After communist rule and rule of Taliban new Govt. Has been Established with American Support. But inspite of all this Muslim countries are making tremendous progress and Arabs are richest people now inspite of rivalry between Iraq and other states.

The Rise of Seljuk Turks

With the caliphate thus dismembered and weakened, and orthodox Islam challenged by varying interpretations and even heterodoxies etc., so the time was ripe for change. This change was brought first by Ghaznavis such as Mahmud Ghaznavi and later on, it was provided by the Seljuk Turks, who had entered Persia at the beginning of the eleventh century and wrested control and rule of the whole country from Gaznicity of Afganistan and north India, and from the rising local dynasties such as Ghori, Slave, Khilji and Tughlak dynasties of India.

Origin. The Seljuks belong to a linguistically inter-connected group of Turk peoples, generally known as Turks, who emerged from the stopes of central Asia of nomadic tribes in the early Middle Ages. They over several centuries moved into Persia and western Asia in successive waves, and became converted to Islam. Turks, no doubt, existed in the Islamic Arab empire earlier as slaves and bodyguards and these were Turks slaves like Iltutamish, Quttubuddin and Balban etc. who established Muslim rule in India but it was with the rise of the Seljuks to power that the Turks element in the Islamic empire gained ascendancy. In 1055, after establishing his control in Persia, the Seljuk Tughril Beg (in 1063) entered Baghdad, deposed the last Shi'ite Buwaihid ruler and re-established rule of Sunnite orthodoxy under the titular leadership of the caliph.

Seljuk. The Seljuk empire stretched over Persia, Kurdistan, Iraq and lasted until the mid-twelfth century, but it was always loosely united and, in the twelfth century, was split up among maker but related dynasties ruled by various Seljuk princes. Simultaneously, lasting until the mid-thirteenth century. Another succession of Turkish dynasties, founded by former slaves and officers of Seljuk princes, arose in Iraq, Kurdistan and Persia etc. Despite the violence and cruelty characterizing their reign, the Seljuk Turks provided the territories they occupied with relative stability, an orthodox Islamic government, and some able rulers, such as Alp-Arslan (1063 — 1072) and Malik Shah (1072 — 1092) etc. However, their epoch represents the superiority of Persian culture over Turkish culture. The Seljuk Turks in almost all fields appreciated the administrative and artistic genius of their Persian subjects and utilized Persian talent and experience in the administration of their empire. The first three Seljuk sultans relied on Persian viziers, such as the able Nizam al-Mulk, and also on Persian bureaucracy and

Persian manners. Their restoration of Sunnite orthodoxy and their posing as the protectors of the Caliphate and as patrons of orthodox Islamic learning and scholarship were perhaps welcome changes in those troubled times. But the orthodoxy they re-established, because of the Shi'ite and Murtazilite challenge, had become reactionary as well as restrictive. It had an adverse effect on future progressive thought and development in Islam. Seljuk rule also gave impetus to the large scale westward influx and settlement of other warlike nomadic Turkish tribes from central Asia, whose language and character thus became permanently impressed on large areas of the Middle East, especially Azerbaijan, Kurdistan, and Anatolia etc.

Seljuks were replaced by Ottomons and Ottomon Turks were defeated by British and French and in conquered territories mandates were established. In Iraq, Palestine, Israel, Gordon, Syria and Lebnan, etc.

23

Arabian Countries under Mandate

The Rise of Arab Nationalism and the Condition of Arab States during Mandatory Rule of Britain.

In 1916 the Arabs in the Turkish Empire rose in revolt, and helped by the British colonel T.E. Lawrence (Lawrence of Arabia) and later on by British troops under General Allenby, they played an important part in liberating the Arab territories from Turkish rule. As a bribe to win Arab support against Turkey, the British had made vague promises that when the First World War may be over, the Arabs would be allowed to set up their own independent states. But on the other hand diplomats about the same time in (1916) due to the pressures of First World War of 1914, the British had also made the contradictory Sykes-Picot agreement with France, by which it was promised that Turkey's Arab lands would be divided between England and France. In 1919, therefore, to their utter disappointment, the Arabs found their territories handed over as mandates (to be 'looked after' and prepared for self-government); to Britain territories of Iraq, Transjordan and Palestine etc. and to France Syria and Lebanon etc. Again Britain was reluctant to sever all connections with her mandates because of the Middle East oil resources particularly in Iraq. Britain wanted to be allowed to station troops there to guarantee a sure source of Iraqien oil. On the other hand, the British dared not to offend and annoy the Arabs too deeply, for oil supplies might be threatened. Consequently steady progress towards independence was made in Iraq and Transjordan, though with strings attached to safeguard British interest however the situation in Palestine was complicated by the Jewish/Arab problem and baffled solution.

Asia Minor

Nowhere was the impact of the Seljuk Turks more probably

decisive then in Anatolia. The border which had separated Islam and Christian Byzantine Empire for more than four centuries. It was permanently breached from Christians and the Islamic-Byzantine balance of power was altered in Asia Minor. After defeating the Christian Byzantine emperor's forces and capturing the Christian emperor in the decisive battle of Manzikert (1071), the Seljuk Turks penetrated in central and western Asia Minor and established firmly, the Seljuk Sultanate of Rum with Nicaesia (Iznik) not far from Constantinople, as their Turkish capital. Other nomadic Turkish Tribes, recently converted to Islam, poured into this area. Thus, began the permanent—"Turkification" of Asia Minor.

Crusades

Meanwhile, two parallel developments appeared. One was the rise of the Ayyubid dynasty in Egypt and Syria as the defender or Sunnite orthodoxy in Islam and the other was the crusades of Christian powers. The crusades, with all their noble and not so noble episodes, meant more to the Christian West than to the Islamic East. Their effect of contemporary Arab-Muslim society was nominal; except for the ruins of Crusaders and fortifications along the Syrian coast and the memory, still lingering in the Arab-Muslim mind, of Saladin's brilliant achievement as the champion of Islam, against Christian aggression but nothing remains now except memory. Even as a medium for the transmission of Arab-Islamic culture to the West, the Crusades perhaps played no more than a secondary role. The main areas of East-West communication were effective only in Sicily and Spain etc.

Saladin

Saladin, a Kurdish-born officer of the Zanigid dynasty of Syria, rose to power in Egypt in 1169 after two centuries of Shi'ite Fatimid rule. Before him, the main military opposition was the first crusade (1097-1100) and the Second crusade (1147-1149) came from the Zangids of Syria. But it was his personal achievement to unite the Islamic opposition under his powerful leadership and effectively check the aggression of crusaders. In 1187 the Latin kingdom of Jerusalem, set up by first crusaders in 1099, was reconquered by Muslims. Saladin died in 1193, but his dynasty the Ayyubids, continued to rule in Egypt, Syria and western Arabia etc. until 1250.

Mongol Invasions and Their Impact

An invasion for more devastating and disruptive than the Saljuk Turks incursion of two centuries earlier was in the making, it was that of the Mongols, who fell upon the Islamic empire in successive waves spreading unprecedented havoc, massacre and destruction everywhere. One of the last Abbasid Caliphs, Nasir (1180-1225) had made an unsuccessful attempt to restore the original powers of his office by instigating one of the shahs of Khawarizm against Seljuk domination in Iraq and Kurdistan. By the early part of the thirteenth century, the shahs of Khawarizm were in most of Persia and in a battle in 1194 they defeated the Seljuk Turks and replaced them as masters of Iraq.

The ascendancy of the Khawarizm shahs, however, was very short-lived. Earlier in the twelfth century, again Mongolian tribes moved into central Asia and established an extensive empire under the leadership of the redoubtable Mongol Conqueror Chinggis Khan. By the time he died (1228), Chinggis Khan and his hordes had shaken to their foundations many states from China to eastern Europe. Parts of Russia and Khawarizm were left in ruins, Transcaucasia and Azerbaijan were likewise overrun, although Baghdad, situated farther south, was spared for the time being. Its vast empire lasted for three centuries. Its administration was a curious combination, partly centralized and partly a mélange of federated vassal states united under the supreme ruler, the Great Khan, who resided in remote China. Chinggis Khan was one of the greatest conqueror which world has ever produced.

Hulaqu's Conquest

In 1253, the Mongols rode westward again and this time under the leadership of Hulaqu Khan who was a grandson of Chinggis Khan. Mongol hordes swept over Persia, reaching almost in the north Persia mountains in 1256, where they put an end to the dreaded order of the assassins, whose grand master had conducted a campaign of terrorism in the Middle East. The Mongols then poured into Iraq and, as they drove toward Baghdad. They plundered and destroyed everything in their path, including the elaborate canal system, on which much of the agriculture of the land depended from ancient times. In 1258, after a brief siege, the wealthy and cultured capital of Abbasid Caliphs fell before the Mongol hordes. Lot of persons were slaughtered and the city of Baghdad was sacked and given over to flames. The sickly Abbasid Caliph Musta'in, along with hundreds of his officials, was also slain in cold blood and with the passing of the last reigning Abbasid, rulers, the caliphate came to an end except for an insignificant claimant whom the court in Cairo retained on pension for religious and political ends. Hulaqu Khan then advanced against the Seljuks Turks and conquered Asia Minor. After destroying the power of Seljuks, he moved on to Syria and came face to face with a new rising force of the Mamluks. It was a new dynasty of Turkish and Caucassian ex-slaves, bodyguards, and fief-holding officers etc. under the Ayyubids, who had risen to power in Egypt and Syria and had seized control in 1250 of a vast empire.

But Hulaqu Khan had succeeded in making changes in the political map of the Middle East. Before his death in 1256, he was the undisputed ruler of a vast empire, that stretched from India to Syria with only formal feudal homage paid to the Great Khan. After his death, Iraq and Persia passed on to his successors, the II-Khans who made Tabriz their capital. The II-Khanid's (1265-1345), at first alien and undistinguished, gradually guided the pagan Mongols to embrace Islam. Mongols learnt to appreciate and put to use Persian administrative and artistic genius. They were succeeded by a series of lesser dynasties, most of which were overrun by the armies of Taimur the Lane. He attacked India in 1398 and at the close of the fourteenth century, Taimur Lane became greatest ruler of Islamic empire as his empire extended from Samarkund to India.

Taimur Lane's Conquests

Taimur Lane, a Turk and related to a descendant of Chinggis Khan, began his destructive conquests from his base in central Asia. After overrunning Persia and sacking Baghdad in 1393, he moved on into Asia Minor and Syria etc. His extensive empire collapsed shortly after his death in 1405; but two Timurid dynasties arose as successors, one line in Persia lasting for almost a century, and the other in India becoming the Moghul empire which was established by Babar and lasted vigorously upto Aurangzeb's death in 1707 and lingered on upto 1857. Taimur Lane was a great conqueror.

At the time of Taimur Lane's invasion, Asia Minor was under the Mamluk Sultans. Mamluk rule, with its two successive dynasties, the Bahri (1250-1390) and the Burji (1382-1517) provided Egypt and most of Syria with an effective government.

In 1517, after a reign of over 250 years, Mamluk rule gave way to that of the Ottoman Turks. [For Ottoman Rule see Turkey].

Islamic Civilization and Islamic Culture

To attempt a summary appraisal of a major civilization like Islam that evolved over a period of several centuries in a large and heterogeneous part of the world is no simple task. Although the civilization that flourished during the period of its greatness of four caliphs and of Arab invaders who were able to establish Islamic empires had a relatively uniform characters. It was complex and variegated, a product of the interaction of many peoples with widely diverse religious and cultural background and traditions. The unsophisticated Arab invaders were able to impose not only themselves as rulers but were also able to impose their language religion on the more populous and more civilized conquered territories. Naturally, the Islamic culture which developed was neither purely Arab nor purely Islamic. It drew heavily upon various sources. But the new culture was not just a mixture; it was a new and original creation, whose various elements were fused together into a recognizable system. Nevertheless, in its unique assimilative power, it comparative tolerance. Its consciousness was of its own superiority and self-sufficiency, and toleration and atomistic view of life and of the universe. It was genuinely Arab-Islamic culture and Arabic was the chief instrument of culture, Islam was the unifying and dominating factor of this system.

The Arab-Muslim conquerors were like their pre-Islamic predecessors, a primitive people with a nomadic, culture particularly deficient in the materialistic and artistic fields. But they had special gifts which served them well initially racial and religious solidarity, devotion to triumphant faith, expectations of reward worldly and an openers to knowledge and development and improvement in all areas. But above all, they had a language and a religion and zeal to offer to the word.

Influence of Arabic Language

Arabic the youngest semitic tongue, had in those early times a highly developed oral, but virtually no written, tradition. Its most sophisticated expression was in the form of poetry vividly depicting the life of the producer, defiant intractable Bedouin and of brave Arabs. In a concrete and highly individualistic manner, it described the passions of the Bedouin people and tribulations and joys. The merciless Arabian desert's environment, the futility of life, but from occasional, amazingly perceptive hints, there emerges a vague hope of latter things to come. This poetry, because of the purity of its direction and form, its excellent rhyme the poetic model for later Islamic poets of Persians Jurki and Urdu languages.

Since Arabic was the language of the Prophet Mohammad and of the Holy Koran, it became the sole and divine key to knowledge and doctrine of with the Arabinization of the Islamic empire. The flowering or learning and of scholarship. Arabic became the chief instrument of everyday speech, as well as of culture, replacing Aramaic, Coptic, Greek, and Latin etc. in Islamic empire Arabic also exerted an enormous influence on other Muslim languages like Persian and Turkish Urdu etc. These languages such as Turkish Persian and Urdu etc. adopted not only the Arabic script and much Arabic vocabulary but also Arab literary tastes and traditions and culture etc. Storism of Arabian night and of Laila-Majnu gained prominence everywhere.

Islamic Culture

Besides their language, the Arabs contributed religion of Islam to the civilization of the Middle East. The Islamic religion as it evolved in the Holy Koran and the Traditions of the Prophet Muhammad had a universal appeal, despite its distinctively Arab orientation and colouring etc. Islam is a monotheistic faith whose essential core of belief is the unity of Allah, the wholly transcendent God. According to Islam, Muhammad, the Messenger of Allah and the last and the greatest of an ascending series of prophets, is wholly human, having greatness but no claim to divinity. While offering attractive concessions and promises to the believer, Islam rigidly stresses a set of fundamental dogmas and practices. It requires on the one hand belief in the uniqueness of God, the truthfulness of the Prophet's Mission, the divine origin of the Koran, a hierarchy of angels, and the Last Day of Judgment. It prescribes, on the other hand, the obligation to profess the faith, perform the five daily prayers *i.e.* Namaj to give alms (Zakat), fast during the month of Ramzan, and — if possible to make a holy pilgrimage (Hajj) to Mecca once in lifetime. To this foundation of dogmas and duties, prohibitions were added against drinking wine, idol worships, eating of pork, usury, gambling, and image representations etc. Believers were also enjoined by Islam to join holy war called

(Jihad). The new Islamic faith also accepted the pre-Islamic institutions of slavery and polygamy, but required greater restraint and more humane treatment. From this simple set of basic dogmas and regulations that claimed universal application and validity, Islam gradually developed into an elaborate political, social, intellectual and legal system with the Shari' at the divinely revealed law, its all-pervasive and universal code of Islam.

The Arab Muslim civilization represents also of the great creative achievements of human history. From the ninth century onward after the initial period of borrowing and absorption, a remarkable, stable and distinct civilization flourished, not only in and around the capital city of Baghdad, but throughout the Middle Eastern countries in Persia, Central Asia, India, North Africa, Sicily, and Spain etc. The efflorescence of the Islamic civilization was facilitated by the pressure of certain favorable conditions such as rich and diversified cultural heritage, ample wealth and leisure, a common religion, and the support by Muslim princes and their courts of arts, learning, and literature and education. Great part in development of this civilization was played by Ulemas, Sufi saints and religious preachers.

The artistic contribution of this civilization was immense. In architecture, gracious orderly and magnificent cities were built and adorned with mosques, palaces, gardens, fountains, libraries, bridges, and public baths and monuments and forts and fountains etc. The structural beauty and meticulous decoration of surviving Islamic monuments display not only the sophistication and versatility of Islamic art and architecture but also both the eclecticism and the originality of the Islamic civilization that produced them. As such Islamic decorative and industrial arts, such as pottery, titlework, metalwork, woodwork, glassware, jewelry, textiles, brocades carpets, leatherwork, papermaking, book-binding, and illumination etc. made great progress. After a period of limitation Islamic craftsmen evolved new techniques and styles producing exquisite artistic and beautiful and charming creations in all these forms.

Literary and Other Achievements of Islamic Arab Civilization

The literary achievements of Islamic civilization were abundant and diversified, reflecting Arab, Persian, Hellenistic, and other cultural and religious backgrounds. It made rich contributions in many fields of science and learning such as literature, religion and law, in music, history, geography, philosophy, medicine, mathematics, and astronomy etc. The earliest contribution was in prose and poetry. The rhymed prose of the holy Koran was the first major literary document in Arabic. It influenced the early development of the Arabic prose excelled in belles letters and the essay etc. and it achieved sophistication and grace at the hands of noted men of letters, some of whom were non-Arabs, such as Jaiz (899). Poetry, the most esteemed literary genius among the Arabs was also developed along with new lines. Pre-Islamic poetry, which had been transmitted orally, was standardized and written down during the rule of Umayyad Caliphs but a new kind of poetry, with new forms and themes, evolved during the period of Abbasid Caliphs as a result of Persian influences. The ease, pomp and luxury of life in a metropolis, and the patronage of caliphal or princely courts give it new colour. The new poetry, however, was short-lived and was superseded by neoclassical poetry, as seen in the work of the popular author Mutanabbi (*d.* 965) etc.

The intellectual awakening that began under the Umayyad caliphs as the Arabs became exposed to more advanced civilizations came into full bloom in the Abbasid period. In Mecca and Medina, certain theologians and pietists rejected Umayyad worldliness. They isolated themselves in these two holy cities to devote themselves to religious study and theology and scholarship. Interest in Islamic religious and legal sciences and learning spread to other important centers of the Islamic empire, where religious scholars formed circles in time identified as distinct "legal" and theological schools of thought. Religious, legal, and theological studies were in principle based upon the two main sources of all Islamic knowledge, the Koran Hadis *i.e.* Tradition, a collection of reports of the acts and saying of the Prophet Muhammad and his companions. The Holy Koran, which had been compiled and standardized during the reign of Caliphs Uthman or Usman was universally accepted as the basic source. But the need to interpret its symbolism and ambiguities and to explain and apply its prescriptions to new situations gave rise to the development of grammar, lexicography, thinking, exegesis, jurisprudence, and scholastic theology. As for the body of Tradition, it was in a state of flux during the first two centuries of the Islamic empire. Thus it became necessary to compile and standardize it. This gave rise to another distinctively Islamic science, which ultimately produced six standard compilations of Tradition which is most universally recognized. They are works of Bukhari (*d.* 870) and Muslim (*d.* 875) etc.

Jurisprudence

Muslim jurisprudence was also cultivated. It gave Islam its religio-legal system, of the Shari'a. The Shari'a governed all aspects of life, including belief, ritual, civil, criminal, constitutional, and international law etc. It was both a code of law and a pattern of conduct and political and social ideal with the double purpose of ensuring man's happiness in this world and in heaven or hell in the world to come. It defined man's relation both to Allah, and to the community and to its Prophet, and later on to the Islamic empire and to the reigning Caliph and monarch. This comprehensive code was developed and systemitized by the Islamic jurists in accordance with the teachings of Holy Koran and Ideal Traditions etc. which formed in the beginning an ideal Islamic system. The legal material in the holy Koran and Hadisme Tradition was limited. While adequate for the early Muslims of Mecca and Medina, it could not meet the increasing needs of a vast Islamic community expanding both geographically and culturally. As a result lawyers and judges took local custom and legal practices prevalent in the conquered territories, Islamicized them, and incorporated them into the Shari'a system. Further, the use of principles such as analogy and the consensus of Islamic scholars enabled jurists to expand the prescriptions of the Koran and Tradition to deal with unprecedented cases. The importance which prominent jurists attached to these principles and to Tradition as sources of law gave rise to different schools of legal Islamic thought. These finally crystallized, around four orthodox rites, the Malikite (after Anas ibn Malik, d. 795), the Hanafite (after Alu Hanifa, d. 767), the Shafi'ite (after Shafi'i, d. 820), and the Hanbalite (after Ahmad ibn Hanba, d. 855) In India, Hanifa school was followed. As the Shari'a become a closed system. The ascendancy of a conservative and restrictive attitude toward the development of the Shari'a was in part a reassertion of Islam's original claim, that the law emanated from God, the true and only lawgiver, even before the Shari'a ceased to be in tune with political and social realities, a secular law was being developed alongside with it. It was based on executive decrees and the decision of secular courts of Islamic rulers. In modern times the Shari'a, as a code of law, had been superseded in some countries by secular codes of law patterned on Western ones. In some countries such as Turkey and Indonesia etc. in all branches of the law except the limited area of personal law statute such as marriage, divorce, and inheritance etc. western law is followed but in Saudi Arabia, Iran and Pakistan etc. Islamic law is still followed. Now tendency of Muslim countries is to declare themselves as Islamic Republic.

Important contributions were also made in history, politics, biography, geography, and the social sciences etc. under the Umayyad, Caliphs, the writing of history acquired a new importance — that of preserving the distinctly Arab character of the Islamic empire from the inroads of the conquered civilizations. It began with biographical literature about the Prophet Muhammad but soon it developed to include monumental works covering a wide area including universal and local histories, and histories of various tribes, dynasties, and institutions etc. Major advances were also made in the methods of writing of history which culminated in the development of the more narrative and interpretative types of histories, best exemplified and written in the work of Ibn Khaldun (1332-1406) who is considered as the greatest Arab philosopher of Islamic history. Similarly, the study of geography received much attention in Islam. The extent of Islamic conquests, the institution of the holy pilgrimage, and the penetration of Muslim traders into distant lands encouraged the study of geography and it resulted in many encyclopaedic works, such as that of Yaqut etc. in (1179-1229).

Religious Literature

Islamic religious literature drew perhaps heavily on Christian and Greek and Jewish sources. Both the Koran and Tradition contain a great deal of material that according to some western historians indicates a strong Talmudic and Apocalyptic influence. The independentce of the legal system itself to these sources, along with the Roman — Byzantine legal system, seems obvious. However, Islamic theological literature, which was only initially influenced by Syriac Christianity, together with Islamic philosophy and the science, including medicine, mathematics, chemistry, physics, and astronomy, also bear some influence of the Greek thought. The intellectual awakening which began under the Umayyad Caliphs and bore fruits under the Abbasid Caliphs came partly form the translation into Arabic of Greek (as well as Persian, Sanskrit, and Syriac) books and treaties. The translation movement started under the rule of Umayyads Caliphs. The translators were mainly Syrians, Nestorians,

Christians, and Jews etc. Greek manuscripts were translated either directly from the original or indirectly from Syriac versions. Under the rule of Abbasids Caliphs this movement became well organized, reaching to its height under the reign of Caliph Ma'mun (813-833), who founded a library academy and sent scholars as far as to Byzantine city of Constantinople in search of material. The most prominent translator perhaps was Hunayn ibn Ishaq (809-877), a Nestorian Christian physician and superintendent of Caliph Ma'mun's academicians translated many important and famous works including those of Galem and Hippocrates in medicine and Dioscorides etc. in botany, as well as Plato's Republic and Aristotle's Categories Politics and Physics etc. other Syrians, the "pseudo-Sabians" of Harran, were also active in this translation movement. Thabit ibn Qurrah (836-911), the leading translator of this school, and his disciples are credited with the translation of Greek mathematical and astronomical works, including those of Greek scholars such as Archimedes and Euclid etc.

The translation movement, which lasted until the end of the ninth century, was followed by a period of original Islamic contributions. In theology, jurisprudence, philology, linguistics, and literature, creativity came earlier than it came in philosophy and in the other sciences. Muslim scholars, of Persian origin, adapted their borrowings to their needs and built up their own scientific and philosophical systems. One of the most original thinkers and physicians of medieval times was Razi (Rhazes, 865-925), whose famous encyclopaedic work on medicine was translated into Latin in Sicily as early as 1279 and widely used in Europe as a medical textbook. Ibn Sina (Avicenna, 980-1037) was perhaps best known as a philosopher physician, codified Greco-Arabic scholar of medical thought. His work was translated into Latin in Spain and soon superseded other medical textbooks. But the Arab interest in medicine was primarily clinical and surgical, rather than theoretical. They also made important contributions in alchemy and botany etc. which were closely allied to medicine, and in astronomy etc. Technical terms of Arabic of the disciplines abound in Western languages — for example, azimuth, nadir and zenith in astronomy; alcohol alembic, alkali, antimony, and tutty etc. in chemistry; Julep, sona, and syrup etc, in medicine. These indications left the permanent mark of Arab culture and of its penetration in Europe. The Arabic numeralism, together with the vital zero (sifr, cypher), were transmitted to Europe *via* Spain. Modern trigonometry as well as Algebra and geometry are the considerable measure of Arab creations.

Philosopher

In its initial stage of development, Philosophical thought in Islam was controlled and conditioned by Islamic religion, and was mainly the product of theological speculations. The Introduction of Greek philosophy and logic in the ninth century, however, gave rise to a distinct Islamic philosophy — (falsafa O) which had a far — reaching impact on the rationalistic and theological outlook of Islams Farabi (pharanius; d. 950) and Ibn Sina continued Kindi's work. They built a philosophical and political system inspired by Greek and Islamic ideas. The greatest political system was inspired by Greek and Islamic ideas. The greatest Aristotelian philosopher in Islam was Spanish Arab Ibn Rushd (Aver-roes, d. 1198) whose commentaries on the Arabic translation of Aristotle's works were rendered into Hebrew and Latin giving rise to a new Avervoism which was an important school of philosophical thought in medieval Europe. Thus Islamic literature influenced European thought also.

Different Sects of Islam

With the passage of time Islam itself as a religion and as a way of life underwent profound changes affecting its unity. As the Islamic empire expanded it became increasingly exposed to Hellenic Jewish, Christian, Aoroastrind and animistick and Buddhistic and Hindu. Sufi saints were probably influenced by Buddhist and Hindu thinkers. Some of these elements were assimilated and became incorporated in the Islamic system; others too alien to Islamicize were generally rejected but gave rise at times to certain hertical sects. The major schisms in Islam however arose earlier before alien beliefs and ideas and had a noticeable effect on belief and ritual of Islam on the one hand purely Arab and purely political arguments such as the right of succession to the caliphate led to different religious interpretations that split the Islamic community into two major branches of the Sunnites and of the Shi'ites including such extreme subdivisions and Isma'ilism with its Assassins, Carmathians Nusaryris Duruzes and other heterodoxies. The extremism of the latter movements represents the dissatisfaction of certain oppressed elements among the less privileged classes of Islam with the existing political, social and religious order and their attempt to force a change. On the other hand, contact with Greek Christianity in Syria, early in the period of Umayyad Caliphs stimulated critical thinking regarding certain established beliefs and against certain doctrines. This gave rise to new religio-Philosophical school of thought, one of the earliest of which was the Qadarte, which preached a doctrine of free will as against to the strict predestinarianism of traditional Islam, and its emphasis on the Transcendence and Almightiness of God. The qadarite thinking and Islam's initial acceptance of Greek philosophy and Greek logic led to the development of a more rationalistic theology by the Mu'tazilites based on the Unity and justice of the God-head. For a brief period, during the reign of Caliph Ma'mun (813-833). The rationalist and scientific spirit in Islam was prevalent, so the Mu'tazilite doctrine was espoused by the Islamic state and was made even the official theology. The dominance of the Mu'tazilite however did not long endure. Their extremism and intolerance triggered a violent reaction among orthodox thinkers and traditionalists, which led ultimately to the acceptance in Islam of Ash'airism (after Ashari'd). This was a determinatic and authoritarian system of theology, based on the rejection of all causalities and the stricts adherence to the literal meaning of the Holy Koran. The triumph of this static, formalist theology was perhaps a major factor in the decline of critical and rational thinking and staticness of Islam.

Impact of Sufism over Islam

Finally, Islam witnessed the rise and spread of Sufism, the Islamic counterpart of mysticism, which had far-reaching effects upon Islamic society and its faith. As a reaction against both the intellectualism of the Mu'tazilites and the other philosophers and the formalism of traditional orthodoxy, Sufism grew rapidly among both Sunnites and Shi'ites not as a separate religious sect, but rather as a more meaningful, more personal and humane approach to piety. From rudimentary beginnings exemplifying the best in Islamic piety, it became increasingly ascetic as it absorbed Christian, Ghostic, Neoplatobic, Hindu and Buddhist elements. In the process, it developed a variety of norms, including pantheistic sufism, the excess of certain devotees and their pantheistic tendencies, such as the Persian Hallaj (d. 922) and Mansur etc. who was executed for heresy. This resulted in the condemnation to Sufism by orthodoxy as condemnation of Pope to Protestants and others. But the yearning for a more personal religion made the mystic way irresistible to many devout Muslims, including Ghazali who is considered as the greatest of Muslim theologians. By reconciling the new scholasticism with the intuitive, mystical religion of the Sufis, Ghazali assured for Sufism a permanent position in Islam. By the twelfth century, as Sufism attracted more and more people from all starata of Islamic society, numerous sufi orders, each with its own monasteries, ritual and doctrine were organized and spread from one end of the empire to the other. Main were Chisti and Suhrawardi etc. Khawaja Muinuddin Chisti resided in Ajmer and his Dargah is considered next greatest pilgrimage by Indian Muslims. Nizamuddin Auliya resided in Delhi and Sheikh Salim Chisti even succeeded in making Akbar as his disciple. Thus Sufism did a great service to Islam and brought humanism and liberal outlook in it. Sufi saints made Islam popular even among non muslims. As such, Ajmer, Delhi and Fatehpur Sikri etc. are still pilgrim places which were established Khwaja Mohinudhin Chisti, Nizamuddin Auliya and Sheikh Salim etc. Followers of these sufi saints still celebrate them as pilgrimage places.

Seljuk Turks were replaced by Ottoman Turks who established a vast empire and declared themselves as Caliphs of Islam, so their description is given separately.

24

Arab World

Condition of Arabs in Early 20th Century and Arab World's Special Characteristics and Its Cultural Links between Asia and Africa and Special Features of Islam

The heart of the Arab world was and is the Middle East, a difficult region to define. The term is generally used most of the time in reference to the lands connecting Asia with Africa, the chief boundary markers being Egyptian capital. Cairo, Turkish capital of Istanbul and Iranian capital of Teheran, and the Islamic states of the Arabian peninsula. Nearly all the peoples of the Middle East except Israel and Lebnon, are united in a common faith (Islam) and share a common language and culture (Arabic). Because of the unifying force of this heritage, Muslims, North Africa (Morocco) Algeria, Tunisia, Libya and Sudan etc. are treated as a part of the Arab world.

With the exception of Morocco, in North Africa at the beginning of the nineteenth century these were nominally under the sovereignty of the Ottoman Turks, whose capital city was Constantinople. In practice, however, the various states in this area were self-governing. During the nineteenth century, all of North Africa from Casablanca in Morocco to Cairo in Egypt came under European imperialistic rule, while the Arab lands in the Middle East continued under the despotic rule of the sultans.

The Arab Revolt. In 1913, an Arab congress, meeting in Paris demanded home rule and equality with the Turks in the Ottoman Turkish empire. Because the Middle East was strategically important to Britain, so the British government followed the rise of Arab discontent with great interest. During the war years of 1915 and 1916, extensive correspondence was carried on between the British high commissioner in Cairo and Sherif Husein of Mecca (Husein ibn-Ali, 1856-1931), guardian of the holy places of Mecca and Medina in the Hejaz. In the event of an Arab revolt, Great Britain undertook to recognize Arab independence except in those region of coastal Syria which were not fully Arab and in those lands which might be claimed by France. But British commitment were purposely vague, and the correspondence has been called "a monument of ambiguity".

In addition to the British alliance with the Arab nationalist movement, the indomitable desert warriors Abdul-Aziz Ibn-Saud (1880-1953), Sultan of Nejd in south-central Arabia, was induced to adopt a policy of benevolent neutrality towards Britain and France etc. The wooing of the Arabs thwarted the Turkish attempt to rouse the whole Muslims of Middle East by preaching a jihad, or holy war, against the British and French alliance, as Turks sided with German emperor Kaiser William.

Arab Revolt

Late in 1916, the Arab revolt began. Husein raised the standard of revolt in the Hejaz and proclaimed independence of Arabs from the Turkish rule. He captured Mecca for his cause. In the fighting that followed, the Arab forces were commanded by the third son of the Sherif Husein, Emir Faisal (1885-1933), who was assisted by a remarkable English Officer, Colonel T.E. Lawrence (1888-1935), later known as Lawrence of Arabia.

Under T.E. Lawrence, the Arabs took a decisive part in the last battle against the main Turkish forces in September 1918. When the World War I ended, Syria was occupied by the victorious Allied forces and a small French force was located along the coast of Lebanon; Emir Faisal and his Arab forces were in the interior, grouped around Damascus; and the British forces controlled whole Palestine including holy city of Jerusalem.

During the First World War years of 1914-1918 a number of important commitments and treaties had been made. In 1916 in the Sykes Picot Agreement, the Fertile Crescent (Syria and Iraq) had been divided into four zones, with Britain and France each controlling two. Palestine was to be placed under an international administration. With the Balfour Declaration of (1917), the British government gave its support to the establishment of a national home for the Jewish people in Palestine, (see Israel for full declaration). In 1918, an Anglo French pronouncement pledged the establishment of national government "deriving their authority from the initiative and free choice of the indigenous populations". Thus fate of middle eastern countries depended on secret agreements and this created complicated problems in peace conference.

The Peace Settlement. At the peace conference Faisal, aided by T.E. Lawrence, pleaded in vain for Arab independence. Faisal was still ruler of Syria in Damascus. In March 1920, while the British, French and American statesmen in Paris argued, a congress of Syrian leaders met and resolved that Faisal should be the king of a united Syria, including Palestine and Lebanon. But in April, 1920, the San Remo conference of the allied powers decided that all Arab territories which were formerly in the Ottoman empire are to be administered as mandates of League of Nations. Syria and Lebanon were mandated to France; Iraq and Palestine, to Great Britain.

From the Arab's point of view, the peace settlement of Paris in the Middle East was a shabby piece of statesmanship compounded of ignorance, deception, and of conflicting aims and ideas and interests of great powers. Apologists for Britain and France point out that Britain made promise to France during the World War I, because the British could hardly deny the requests of their most important ally. Britain in 1916, made its ambiguous pledge to Husein because of its desperate need for Arab friendship. Again, in the Balfour Declaration of 1917, Britain acted according to her short-range of self interests; In order to gain the support of the world's Jews to the Allied cause and to maintain communications in the Middle East, Britain promised to make available to Jewish settlement in the Arab region of Palestine. The plain fact remains, however, that the Allied statesmen at Paris were profoundly ignorant of the intensity of Arab nationalism and awakening.

As such the events between World Wars I and II in the mandated areas (Syria, Lebanon, Iraq, and Palestine etc.) are to be studied carefully to trace the growth of tensions in Iran, Egypt, Iraq, Israel, North Africa and in all middle eastern countries.

The Condition of Saudi Arabia after World War I

The destiny of Hussein, King of Hedjaz was rather strange. He was the person who led the Arab revolt of Arabs against the Turks and was recognised by the Allied Powers as king of the holy city of Mecca, where his ancestors had once ruled. One of his sons ruled in Iraq and another son Abdullah in Trans-Jordania. Then he became Caliph of Islam for six months. He thus became temporarily the most outstanding personality in the Arab world. But his good fortune proved to be short-lived. His subservience to Great Britain aroused patriotic opposition of Muslims while his pretensions to the Caliphate displeased many of the Arabs and Muslim states. Ibn Saud, the leader of the Wahabis, took advantage of the growing unpopularity of Hussein, to oppose him and mature his plans for his own aggrandisement. He had greatly increased his power by subduing the fierce tribes of the interior Arabian Peninsula and now decided to advance on holy city of Mecca. At his back, he had an army of devout fanatic and fearless Muslim soldiers whom it was very difficult to resist. Finding resistance hopeless, Hussein fled in despair. He found a refuge in Jerusalem, where he died, crestfallen and his ambitions shattered on sharp rocks of reality.

Glimpse of Ibn Saud's Achievements

Wahabi Ibn Saud entered Mecca in 1925 and proclaimed himself king. Next he subdued almost all the semi-independent Arabian tribes and chieftains of the Arabian peninsula. He gave to the enlarged kingdom of Hedjaz, the new name of Saudi Arabia. Ibn Saud proved himself to be an able and efficient ruler. For the first time after many centuries, he unified Arabia under one rule and gave the country respite from inter-tribal feuds. He promoted motor transportation throughout the Arabian country. He annulled foreign concessions and concluded treaties of alliance with King Faisal of Iraq and Emir Abdullah of Trans-Jordania. In a word, he did much to promote the solidarity and safety and stability of Arabia.

Arabia and the Rivalry for Arab Leadership

The collapse of Ottoman Turkish rule in 1918 due to defeat of Turkey left several important Arab independent states such as Yemen, Hejaz, and Nejd etc. to adjust their relations, plus a few British protectorates on the Arabian Sea and the Persian Gulf.

The first contender for leadership of the Arabian peninsula, was religious leader Sherif Husein. In alliance with Great Britain, his sons had already been favoured by the gift of Kingdoms and Faisal was installed in Iraq and Abdullah in Trans-Jordan, this was a territory carved out from the eastern portion of Palestine. At the close of World War in 1914, it appeared that the Hashemite family of Husein would become the greatest single political force in Arbia and in the Fertile Crescent lands.

The rival of the Hashemites was Wahabi Ibn-Saud, whose family had ruled Nejd since the eighteenth century and had become identified with a reformist, puritanical Muslim Sect known as the Wahabis. Husein regarded Ibn Saud, the ruler of Nejd with contempt. But, fortunately for Ibn-Saud, Husain made a series of blunders: He alienated many Arabs by proclaiming himself Caliph and king of the Arabs. He quarrelled with Britain, which ceased to render him substantial support; and he underestimated the capacity of his rival Ibn-Saud who was king of Nejd and a warrior.

In 1919 one of Husein's sons was defeated by the Wahabi warriors of Ibn-Saud. Full war of Ibn-Saud against Husein began in 1924, and by the following year, Ibn-Saud was victorious and his troops occupied Mecca, Jiddah, Taif, and Medina etc. A treaty with Britain in 1927, brought Ibn-Saud recognition, as king of both Hejaz and Nejd. In 1932, all his holding were renamed as kingdom of Saudi-Arabia. In 1934, he defeated the last of his rivals—the king of Yeman. But king of Yemen was allowed to retain his independence. Two years earlier, vast oil reserves had been discovered in eastern Arabia. Important concessions were given to an American oil company and Ibn-Saud now commanded the vast oil wealth essential for a powerful state. All the tribal groups in Arabia were welded into a strong political entity, with enormous economic resources.

Arab Unity and Outside Interference

Since they all share the Arabic language and mostly follow the muslim religion (though about half of the Lebanon is Christian) many Arabs want some sort of union among the Arab states. As early as in 1931, an Islamic conference in Jerusalem announced : 'the Arab lands are a complete and indivisible whole...... all efforts are to be directed towards their complete independence, in their entirety and unified'. Several attempts were made to promote Arab unity. The Arab League founded in 1945 included Egypt, Syria, Jordan, Iraq, Lebanon, Saudi Arabia and Yemen etc. and its membership expanded later to include 20 Muslim states, in 1980. However, it achieved very little success politically and was constantly hampered by internal bickerings and squabbles. In the mid-1950s, Pan-Arabism seemed to receive a boost with the energetic leadership of President Nasser in Egypt who gained enormous prestige in the Arab world after the 1956 Suez crisis, in which he humbled Britain, France and Israel. In 1958, Syria joined Egypt to form the United Arab Republic with Nasser as president. However, this effort lasted only until 1961, when Syria withdrew because of resentment at Nasser's attempts to dominate this union. After Nasser's death in 1970, his successor President Sadat organized a loose union between Egypt, Libya and Syria and it was called as the Federation of Arab Republics, but it never amounted much, and there seemed little chance of success of any more progress being made towards full Arab unity. There were too many points at issue between the various Arab states, for example Jordan and Saudi Arabia are still ruled by fairly conservative royal families, who were often criticised for being too pro-British by the governments of Egypt and Syria etc. Posing themselves as pro-Arab nationalist as well as socialist. The whole Arab state world was thrown into disarry in 1972, when Egypt, the leading Arab state, reached a separate peace agreement with Israel at Camp David due to efforts of U.S.A. Due to agreement of Egypt with Israel in 1972, Egypt was expelled from the Arab League, but in 1988, it was again made member of Arab League and Egyptian President Hosni Mubarak became leading member of Arab League. Palestine Liberation Organisation *i.e.* P.L.O. lead by Yaseer Arafat Arab League to destroy Israel. As such outside interference in the Middle East was probably inevitable, given the fact that this area produces over a third of the world's oil supplies and Arab states were determined to destroy tiny Israel but Arab states stands at the cross-roads between the communist states and Africa. Disunity among the Arab states invited interference which in turn often bred more disunity and even wars such as of Iran and Iraq. Conquest of Kuwait by Iraq created disunity among Arabs and interference of western powers through U.N.O. in 1990 and it has increased as some states are supporting U.S.A. and some are supporting Iraq. Later on Britain and U.S.A. accused Saddam Hussein, the President of Iraq of making destructive weapons, attacked Iraq without the approval of U.N.O., defeated Iraq in 2003 and established puppet govt. under their control, promissing elected govt. to rule over Iraq.

25

MINOR ARAB STATES

The Arab State of Bahrein

Bahrein is a sheikhdom composed of several Islands totalling 200 sq. miles and standing off about 20 miles from the coast of Saudi Arabia and the Qatar Peninsula in Persian Gulf. Inhabited largely by Arabs and ruled by Iran for more than a century, Bahrein was taken by Arabs from Quatar and it became a British colony by manual victory of Britain in 1820. Upto 1920, it was considered unimportant, though it was famous for Pearl fishing, smuggling, slave trade and breeding of white donkeys etc. Bahrein became important due to oil discovery and for transporting barrels coming from Saudi Arabia though an underwater pipeline. It has become rich due to oil royalties, customs and taxes etc.

Bahrein has been ruled by the Al-Khalifa family for more than a century but British influence remained prominent here, which declined when Britain came in conflict with Egypt over Suez canal in 1956. Arab nationalism made here a great progress inspite of the fact that hospitals, schools, water supply, streets and sewers etc. came here in existence due to British interests, Bahrein is still developing itself in modern technology, industry and science but it has made great progress in transport, trade and in administrative set up etc.

The History of Kuwait and Its Progress and Tension in 1990

North of Bahrein, near mainland of Arabia near the head of the Persian Gulf lies the Sheikhdom of Kuwait. Lord Curzon, when he was Viceroy of India, in 1899, brought it under British control to check German infiltration and to thwart scheme of Berlin-Baghdad railway. Britishers formed an oil company to utilize its oil products but in 1958 two American companies began here but like other Arab states, here Arab nationalism made a great progress and in 1956 when Anglo-Egyptian war took place, Kuwait showed hostility to western powers and non Arab nationalism has made a great progress here.

Due to abundance in oil it has become a very rich country and city of Kuwait possesses highest per capita income in the world. Its wealth attracted people from all parts of world particularly from Egypt, Palestine, Pakistan and India etc. The influx of foreigners sensitized most Kuwait to the virtue of Arab Nationalism; now it is developing modern technology, industry and trade etc. and is making progress in all direction but on 2nd August, 1990, Iraq conquered it which created world crisis. U.N.O. took immediate action and U.N.O. forced led by U.S.A. and Britain defeated Iraq and forced Sadam Husain to withdraw from Kuwait. U.N.O. imposed sanctions to control aggression of Iraq under Sadam Husain. It is said that Sadam Husain was making dangerous weapons so U.S.A. attacked Iraq. Kuwait is now making all round progress and is moving towards democratic ideals, while Iraq lost glory as it was conquered by U.S.A. and pupet govt. is ruling under control of U.S.A.

North and South Yemen

Yemen is famous in Muslim myths and legends in stories of Arabian nights but in modern age, it came into prominence after World War I, Yemen was ruled by Imam Yahya. A British Yemen treaty of friendship was signed in Sanar in 1934, largely to establish the boundary between Yemen and Aden which was a British protectorate but Italy during Mussolini dictatorship tried to run over towards Fascist Gouts. In 1926-27, a treaty of friendship with fascist Mussolini was formed which was renewed in 1937 for 25 years, but during World War II, Yemen remained neutral. In 1946, treaty of friendship was formed with U.S.A. So Russia also began to intervene. Revolt took place in 1955 in Yemen and Soviet arms arrived in 1957. Like other Arabian states, Arab nationalists made a great progress here but civil war took place here which was supported on one side by Egypt and on the other side by Saudi Arabia etc. so country became divided as North and South Yemen whose geographical features have been already described but again united in 1990. Now its area is 53100 km population is about 2 Million.

The Condition of States of Arab Peninsula

Now Arab Peninsula is divided into many states. Most important state is Saudi Arabia, which was founded by Wahabi leader Ibn Saud. Wahabi religion was founded by Mohatmamad Ibn Abdul Wahabi 1703-1792. He was born at Aysrah. He opposed idolatery, drinking and luxurious life and spearheaded Islamic reform movement in Arabia. His followers began to be called Wahabi. They opposed Ottoman Turk's domination over Arabs. Muslim rulers tried to crush this Wahabi movement. But after the fall of Ottoman empire in Arab Peninsula Abdul Aziz Ibn Saud ruler of Dariya took Wahabi's causes and established his rule.

In 1919, Ottoman Turk rule disappeared from Arabian Peninsula, so in Hejaz, Sheriff Hussein, at Nejd Ibn Saud, at Yemen, Imam Yehva, at Asseer Indresi Mohammad and at Sammar Ibn Rashid became rulers. Sherif Hussein's son Abdulla was made ruler of Jordan and Faisal of Iraq but Sheriff Hussein himself was defeated by Wahabi leader Ibn Saud and in 1926, Ibn Saud became ruler of Nejd, Hejaz and of other lands of Arabia by conquering other rulers. Ibn Saud declared himself king of Saudi Arabia in 1934 and he became ruler of a great part of Arabian Peninsula including Mecca and Medina etc.

He organized his state efficiently and during his regime Saudi Arabia became a very strong and rich state. Ibn Saud made notable achievements and followed policy which strengthened his power and made his country strong and prosperous. He was born in 1880, in a family of petty feudal lord but died in 1953 as a ruler of Saudi Arabia which became greatest, strongest and richest state of Arabian Peninsula and modernized his country. As such he ranks with Kamal Pasha, Raza Shah Pahelvi and Col. Nasser as maker of his country's greatness.

Successors

Ibn Saud was succeeded by Amir Saud Ibn Abdul Aziz, who ruled Saudi Arabia from 1953 to 1964 but did not prove competent to govern properly, so in 1963, a revolt occurred in Yemen and an independent rule was established there. In 1963, a revolt took place and in 1964, he was replaced by Amir Faisal Ibn Aziz. During his rule, a constitution was proclaimed and a representative elective Assembly was established, 1/3rd of its members were nominated. Saudi Arabia was declared as a Islamic state and Arabic was declared its language. He followed pro American policy like Ibn Saud. Amir Faisal Ibn Aziz ruled from 1964 to 1975. He entered in military alliance with Jordan and took part in Arab Israeli war of 1967, but achieved nothing, so he stopped supply of oil to western countries. He also sent arms and army to take part in Arab Israeli war of 1973, to show his solidarity with Arab states but Arabs were again defeated. He also helped north Yemen but was unable to check its division in North and South Yemen, like his predecessors, he also followed Pro-American and pro-western policy and championed the cause of Arab and Islamic unity. He called Islamic conference at his capital Jeddah in 1975, but on March 25, 1975, he was killed by an extremist and was succeeded by Khalid Ibn Aziz. During his rule, oil production, increased. In 1976, American oil company A.R.A.M.C. was nationalized and due to oil production, Saudi Arabia became richest country of the world. Saudi Arabia is largest, most powerful and richest state of middle East. It has followed Pro-west, Pro-American, Pro-Arab and fanatic Islamic policy. Saudi Arabia has championed the cause of Sunni Arabs but kept herself aloof from Iraq-Iran war but staunchly opposed rape of Afghanistan by Soviet Union. As such Saudi Arabia is championing the cause of Afghan rebels against Pro Soviet puppet Govt. of Najibullah along with Iran, Pakistan and U.S.A. Saudi Arabia is staunch supporter of Islamic conference and of Arab League but in 1990, Iraq conquered Kuwait and threatened it but U.N.O. and western powers helped it and Kuwait was taken from Iraq and restored to original position.

A Short Sketch of Petty States of Arabian Peninsula

Arabian Peninsula contains petty states of Kuwait, United Arab Republic, Yemen South and North, Bahrein, Oman and Qatar etc. Description and brief introduction of all these states, has already been given in the beginning of this chapter. All these states are of strategic importance and are rich oil producing states. All these states follow Muslim religion, champion cause of Islam and are members of Arab League. These states are dominated by rulers who may consult or form representative assembly. Social structure is based on Islamic feudal and tribal set up but now all these states are making economic progress and are developing industry, transport and scientific set up and arms manufacture. But these states are neither politically important nor possess any quality or special feature to be described separately. Lot of Indians go to these states to get employment and livelihood there. Most of these states are pro-west and are following policy of development in all spheres but emergence of Iraq under Saddam Hussein has threatened them, but defeat of Iraq in 2003 saved them and now they are prosperous.

Arab Nationalism and Its Impact on Contemporary History

Arabia, Iraq, Syria and Jordan had always been the home of the Arabs except Israel where Jews flourished from ancient times. These regions had long been under Turkish domination but the Arabs had never taken kindly to the Turkish rule. On the contrary the Arabs despised the Turk and each Arab Tribe, had a tradition of hatred of the Turks or of victory over them. The Arabs also questioned the right of the Sultan of Turkey to be Caliph or successor of the Prophet Muhammad and his successors and many of them held that Hussein, the Grand Sheriff of Mecca and of the purest Arab descent, had a better title to that exalted position of Caliph of Islam. Hence on the outbreak of the First World War in 1914, when the British repulsed the Turks from the Suez Canal, Arab nationalism was stirred and the Arabs thought of overthrowing the unpopular Turkish rule. The lead was taken by Hussein, who dreamed of setting up an independent Arab empire stretching from the Mediterranean Sea to the Persian Gulf. He was encouraged in this ambition by the Britishers, who sought to utilise the Arab hatered of the Turk to safeguard their interests in the Near East. A group of British officers, specially Colonel T.E. Lawrence, usually known as Lawrence of Arabia, devoted themselves to the task of stirring up the Arabs to revolt, against the Turkish rule. Lawrence of Arabia succeeded marvellously. He became the friend of Faisal, who was son of Hussein, and idol of the Arab Sheiks of the Arabian desert. Urged on by Faisal, Hussien entered into correspondence with the British Govt. at Cairo. He offered to head a revolt against the Turks, to free the whole Arab race and for this, he asked for British help. The British gladly promised him, money, arms and all kind of help and supplies. In 1916, Hussein rose in revolt in the Hedjaz, and announced himself as the true Caliph of Islam and declared the freedom of the whole Arab race from Turkish rule. A wave of Pan-Arab nationalism swept all over the Middle East. Arab contingents raised and drilled by the British forces did good work against the Turks in the Palestine-Syrian area. After the capture of holy city of Jerusalem by the British troops under General Allenby, Arab forces under Faisal and Lawrence galloped into Damascus, the capital of Syria, and captured this city in 1918. In this way whole Syria was conquered and as per agreement French rule was established in Syria, and Lebanon and British rule in Iraq, Jordan and Palestine.

But Arab nationalism received a check at the Paris peace settlement of 1919-20. The Allied Powers divided the predominantly Arab areas into four parts under separate governments. France received a mandate over Syria and Lebanon and Great Britain over Palestine, Jordan and Mesopotamia (Iraq) etc. Only Hedjaz was allowed to remain under Hussein as an independent Arab Kingdom. Arab nationalism was thus sacrificed at the altar of British and French interests. The French drove out Faisal from Syrian capital of Damascus and overthrew the Arab government which Lawrence had labouriously helped to set up. The partition of Arab areas highly irritated the Arabs and agitation, always vocal and sometimes violent, portended troubles to the British and the French rulers and discontent prevailed in Middle East.

French Rule over Morocco and Algeria etc.

Morocco and Algeria etc. has been included by some writers in Near East and Middle East particularly because of Muslim religion and Arab population. Moreover these states supported Muslim Arab states in their bid to destroy tiny Zoinist state of Israel and joined Arab League. If this view point is accepted, then Libya also comes in the above country but Author is of the opinion that Morocco, Libya, Tunisia and Sudan etc. does not come under Near East or Middle East, as those are part and parcel of African continent. However to avoid controversy very brief description of these African states is given here. Morocco is an African state which was ruled by a Muslim Sultan. It became bone of contention between France and Germany, but war was avoided due to British and American intervention and French rule over Morocco with Spanish collaboration was accepted.

Morocco and Tunisia

Morocco possesses, Area of about 458730 kms. and its population is 30.5 million and capital is Rabat. Religion is Islam and language is Arabic, like Tunisia and Algeria Tunisia possess area of 164150 sq. kms. having population of 90 lakhs.

Algeria. Algeria has an area of 2381741 sq. kms. and population of 31 millions having lot of French, who from upper strata of society. Aggressive nationalism in North Africa. Long before the out break of World War I, Algeria had become politically integrated with France; Tunisia had prospered under French rule and had maintained its native ruler, the French rule was established in Morocco but Thebey; and the native sultan had also been retained in the protectorate which France established in Morocco in 1911. Nevertheless, the storm signals of bitter nationalism had appeared, particularly in Morocco.

In Morocco shortly after the First World War, rebellion broke out in Spanish Morocco under the leadership of the Riff chieftain Abed-el Krim. When this revolt spread to French Morocco, the French joined the Spanish in a vigorous campaign which brought the defeat of Krim and his Riffs in 1926. But though defeated, Abed-el Krim's exploits, had caused a sensation in the Arab world. As such again in 1930, an organized nationalist movement, fanned by the world economic depression began in Morocco. Though some administrative posts were made available to Moroccans and some other demands were also met in the late 1930's, no further steps were taken by French rulers to implement self-rule.

The year 1934, marked a major change in the concept of nationalism in Morocco. In this year a group of young Moroccans presented their Plan of Moroccan Reforms. While the efforts of Abed-el Krim had represented tribal opposition to foreign rule, the formation of a nationalist party heralded the birth of a modern Moroccan nationalistic movement. As such in 1937, there was an unsuccessful nationalist revolts. On the eve of World War II, Arab nationalism was growing but it was still relatively weak and in the main, it was driven underground by French repressive measures as revolutionary movement of India but after Second World War, Morocco gained freedom and became member of Arab League. It added Spanish Sahara in 1976 to its area. In Morocco, there is constitutional monarchy.

Tunisia

Tunisia, was the most westernized area in French North Africa and in 1919 a nationalist party called the Destour (meaning "constitution" in Arabic) was formed to secure more democratic reforms for government here. In 1934, after this party was suppressed, another, nationalist group, the Neo-Destour, was formed. Four years later this group was banned also, and the nationalist movement went underground. But after World War II, it became free like other nations in 1957. Bourcuiba Halub remained President till 1987, in 2001 general Zine-el-Akidine Ali is president. It is the ancient Carthage.

A Short Note on Algeria

In Algeria, organized political agitation against the French began in 1926, but incidents were relatively few because French were here in large numbers. As such the natives demanded an easier means of acquiring French citizenship and, with citizenship, the additional rights and economic advantages which this status implied. French citizenship had been extended after the First World War to a large number of Muslims, who qualified on the basis of war service, literacy, and other tests prescribed for it, but due to opposition, mainly from French settlers in Algeria, largely prevented further reforms during the 1930's. But after World War II Algerians revolted and French conferred freedom to Algeria also, after great reluctance in 1962.

Probably French deserved much credit for its colonial rule. Administration on the whole was just and efficient, the economy prospered and living standards advanced. Nevertheless, a fundamental split existed between the privileged Christian minority and the overwhelming Muslim majority. Until 1939, the nationalist movement in North Africa was largely a monopoly of the relatively small intellectual groups and of educated middle class, with the sympathy and support of liberals-and leftists in France. The mass of peasants, however, remained quite apathetic but great progress was achieved in cultural aspect and economic and oil development. Civil war took place in 1992 but now it is peaceful since 1999.

A Short Note on Libya

In the opinion of writer, Libya forms the part of Africa and does not come either in middle East or in near East but now Libya has become notorious due to terrorist activities of its ruler, Col. Gaddafi. It is also a member of Arab League and takes an active part against Israel and United States of America. Area of Libya is 1759540 sq. kms. and its population is only about 35 millions. Like other states of middle East its religion is Islam and language is Arabic and it is also a member of Arab League and of Islamic organization.

Italian Fascist rule in Libya. West of Egypt lies Libya, the desert land seized in 1912 from Turkey by land-hungry in Italy. The fierce nomadic tribes put fierce resistance but in time Italian authority became fully established as Italian dictator Mussolini was a strong ruler. In the 1930's an ambitious programme of development and colonization was put into effect which was of great benefit to the Italian immigrants but not to the natives.

By Sept. 1939. When World War II began, Libya had been politically integrated with the kingdom of Italy, the Libyan colonial administrative or units having been converted into Italian provinces and Fascist rule was imposed there by Mussolini. But after defeat of Italy it become free in 1949 and independent state in 1952 and deposed king in 1969.

Oil was discovered in 1957 and it became one of the leading oil producing countries. Libya changed her name like Russian as the Socialist People's Libyan Arab Jamhuria in 1977. Jamhuria means state of masses. As Col. Gaddafi became its dictator, it became notorious for terrorism and challenged even U.S.A. and U.K. and other western powers. In 1987, it changed her capital from. Its population is only 51 lakhs but it created terror among western power so in 1992 U.N.O. imposed some sanctions.

Like other Arab states Libya is determined to wipe out existence of Israel. Not only this, under Col. Gaddafi, it has became menace to western powers. U.S.A. tried to check its terror but due to opposition of other states was unable to check it so Col. Gaddafi's terror remains unabated. He keeps female body guards and rules sternly and is sympathetic to Iraq, against other states. Today Libya is one of the leading producer of oil. Col. Gaddafi is a powerful man. Now Libya is one of the leading producer of oil.

Geographical Features of Jordan and Its Characteristics

Jordan's Capital is Amman, Area is 89287 sq. kms. Its Population is 5 million and language is Arabic; Its Religion is Islam; Currency : Dinar. US $1 = JD 0.360. King: Abdulla Bin Hussein; P.M. Ali Abu-al-Ragheb

Jordan has a constitutional monarchy in south-west Asia, and so it was popularly known as Trans-Jordan till 1949, when the popular name was changed to the Hashemite kingdom of Jordan. Its population is chiefly of Arabs, of whom the majority are Muslims. In 1946, Jordan became an independent state like other countries Britain conferred independence to this state also.

Jordan is largely a desert area, but the western portion is fertile and produces citrus, wheat, barley, lentile, and watermelons. Phosphates are the country's most important export item, but tourism remains its main foreign exchange earner. Jordan was unable to make progress as it had to fight constant wars with Israel. In Iraq-Arab conflict, it has sided with Iraq in 1990 but American and British forces defeated Iraq and Jordan could do nothing. It has taken large part of Palestine called Trans Jordan.

Head of the state is king Hussein Ibn Talal, P.M., Zaid Ritai. It has taken large part of Palestine.

Trans Jordan

Trans Jordan or Jordan is an Arab state brought into existence by Britishers. In Trans Jordan the British set up Faisal's brother Abdullah as king, and allowed him to manage the country's internal affairs, which he did competently. However, Trans Jordan was a poor state, lacking in resources and with no oil, so it was dependent on Britain for subsidies and for defence etc. In 1946, it was also given complete independence, though Amir Abdullah kept on the British officers who led his army but later on British officers were expelled and it came under Arab influence and fought with Israel and sided with Iraq in 1990, but on July 25, 1994 it ended 46 years hostility with Israel and did not help Iraq in 2003.

The History of Jordan

Jordan is a part of Arabian peninsula both geographically and culturally, so its history and details have been included in history of Arab, so when Arabs nationalism was very rapidly making strides and the Arab were quite determined to win their freedom and not to change their masters. They wanted to live as independent nation. When the League mandates were created, mandate over Trans-Jordan passed on to Britain who was quite keen that there should be two Hashemite rulers, one each in Syria and Iraq. This proposal was however strongly rejected by France, with the result that England found herself in a difficult situation. Finding an opportunity one such Hashemite state was created in Jordan by Britishers. Territories of Trans-Jordan included Amman to Gulf of Aqaba. This was legally possible because under the League mandate England had been empowered to divide Trans-Jordan territories. Son of Hussein namely Prince Abdullah was elevated as the ruler of Trans-Jordan territories. Thus a separate Amirite of Trans-Jordan, came into being on April 1, 1921, due to British support. In 1994, it ended hostility with Israel but has sympthy with Iraq. King Abdulla his ruler.

Attack on Trans-Jordan. The birth of a new Amirite did not please many Arab rulers particularly Ibn Saud of Hejaz, who had the reputation of defeating Sheriff Hussein, the father of Amir Abdullah of the Amirite of Trans-Jordan. He accordingly attacked Trans-Jordan in the hope of annexing newly born territory of Jordan. But Britain did not tolerate this action and on behalf of new Amirite so British Air Force attacked armies of Ibn Saud. The armies of Ibn Saud were bombarded and a situation was created by which invader was compelled to conclude a treaty with the Amir Abdullah, which is known as Treaty of Jiddah.

This Treaty of Jiddah was important in the sense that Ibn Saud, who had all along been staking some territorial claims on Trans-Jordan territories agreed to withdraw all his claims and thus Trans-Jordan became free. After this invasion, Amman was made as the capital of Trans-Jordan. A British Resident was also posted at Amman to enable Amir Abdullah to take such necessary advice as he deemed fit. This Resident kept ruler under British influence like Residents of native states of India.

British Attitude Towards Trans-Jordan. The Britishers had created this Amirite of Trans-Jordan and wanted it to grow as well. They adopted quite rational and reasonable attitude towards the Amirite of Jordan. In order to develop it, necessary financial aid was provided. Not only this but in order to assists Amir Abdullah an Executive as well as Legislative Council was also created so that affairs of Amirite could be run in a better way. British, however continued to control foreign affairs, defence and finance of this Amirite. Not only this but matters relating to important affairs in the Amirite were also controlled by Britain. A Trans-Jordanian Frontier force was created which controlled the affairs of Amirite of Trans Jordan. In fact, in this Amirite, there was political stability. In 1928, a treaty was concluded between Britain and Trans Jordan by which the former agreed to give the independence to the later. In this treaty a provision was however made for the control of Britain over its financial and foreign policies. Thus even after independence, Trans Jordan remained under British control.

Istiqlal Party. In the Trans-Jordan state there was political stability and economic prosperity. In the political field, Istiqlal Party became powerful in Jordan and it wanted full freedom for the country. As a result of their struggle and liberal attitude of Britain, British mandate came to an end on 22nd May 1946, but emergence of state of Israel in 1948, made matters complicated as there were wars later on.

The Hasmite Kingdom of Jordan after Emergence of Israel

In 1946, Amir Abdullah was recognized as King of Jordan and he was also given independence. As constitution was promulgated which became effective in 1947. It provided a chamber of deputies of 20 members, to be elected for five years, having 12 Muslims, four Christians, 2 Bodomus and to represent the Circassians add Shisan communities. The other House like House of Lords had 10 members nominated by King.

With the emergence of Israel, Jordan had to face difficulties. It tried to wipe out Israel but Arab forces were defeated and so they were unable to wipe out existence of Israel, Abdullah took advantage of Arab-Israeli conflict and incorporated a large part of Palestine, so it became a big state and it was named as the Hasmite Kingdom of Trans Jordan. As such this tiny kingdom of 4 lakh people became kingdom of 1350000 people but Palestinians become a wandering tribe of terrorists.

King Abdullah was shrewd, moderate and realistic ruler but his policy annoyed fanatic Muslims and refugees of Palestine, so he was murdered in July 20, 1952 at Jerusalem. He was succeeded by his eldest son Jalal and on May 2, 1953, by his grand son Hussein. Attempts were made to develop Jordan with foreign aid. But signing of Baghdad pact in 1955 and rival Damascus pact created Arab rivalries in middle east and it made Jordan's position critical and Jordan had to face revolts, opposition of Arab states and financial difficulties. On 14 Feb., 1958. Hussein formed Arab Federation with Iraq but in July, 1958, King Faisal, the Hasmite King of Iraq was murdered and General Kassim captured power in Iraq. He abrogated Union and followed leftist policies but Kassim was also killed in revolt and Jordan remained intact, but due to emergences of Kassim as ruler in Iraq, Arab federation did not survive and Jordan felt disturbances but Jordan was saved due to British and American help but many ministries were changed and conditions remained unstable.

Condition of Contemporary Jordan

After achievement of independence, Jordan had to fight with Israel and rivalry of other Arab powers. Jordan had to face unstable cabinets and constant disturbances of Palestinian refugees.

In 1967, Arab-Israel war took place in which Jordan and all Arab state were defeated. Jordan suffered a disastrous defeat.

It lost lot of Palestinian territory and western bank of river Jordan and lakhs of Palestinian refugees entered in Jordan which created law and order problem, but Jordan survived due to British, American and support of other Arab powers. In 1971, Palestinian guerillas killed Jordan's Prime Minister Wasfi Tell and Ahmad Souzie was made Prime Minister of Jordan but disturbances of Palestinian guerillas continued. Border clashes of Jordan also took place with Syria.

In 1973, inspite of difficult condition, Jordan took part in Arab-Israeli wars and supported Syria inspite of Border clashes with her. In Arab-Israeli war of 1973, also Arab states of Egypt, and Syria etc, were defeated by Israel (for details see Egypt and Israel etc.) In 1974, Jordan took place in Islamic conference of Rabat and decided to give western bank of river Jordan to Palestinian guerillas, whenever it may be conquered from Israel according to decision of Islamic conference of Rabat of 1974.

In 1978, National Consultative Committee of 60 members was formed to develop and industrialize Jordan. Policy of Jordan is to make efforts for Arab Unity, to continue enmity with Israel with the support of Arab League and Arab powers. Jordan is making progress inspite of clashes, war and disturbances created by Palestinian guerillas in 1990. It supported Iraq against Saudi Arabia and U.N.O. when Iraq conquered Kuwait in 1990 and so it is facing refugee problem but it emerged successful due to shrewdness of her ruler. Later on Jordan remained neutral in U.N.O. or Iraq war but P.L.O. was given territories west of river Jordan, which became part of new Palestine state.

On July 25, 1994, Israel and Jordan signed a joint declaration in Washington ending 46 years hostility. King Hussein who ruled for 47 years, died in Feb. 99 and his son Abdullah became King in June. Jordan is making all round progress as 99% of population have access to electricity and safe water and 94% literacy. Industry accounts for 25% of G.D.P., agriculture 10% and service 65%. Tourism is its main foreign exchange earner.

26

SYRIA AND LEBANON

Syria (Syrian Arab Republic)

Syria's capital is Damascus and Area is about 1,85,180 sq. kms. Its population is 16.6 M and Language is Arabic. Religion is Islam and its Currency is Pound. US $ 1-£ Syr 8.50.

The Syrian Arab Republic in the Middle East lies in between Turkey, Iraq, Jordan, Palestine and Lebanon. The Mediterranean Sea is on its West. The Orontes and Euphrates rivers etc. pass through Syria. The chief sea port is Latakia and Tartous etc. Damascus is capital and main city. It was the capital of Umayyad Caliphs also.

Syria, the seat of an ancient civilization became a fully independent sovereign republic in 1946. In ancient days it was part of Babylonian, Assyrian and of Arabia Empire.

Agriculture and cattle-breeding comprise the major occupations of the people. The chief crops are cotton, wheat, tobacco and olives etc. The only mineral found is oil. Industries include oils, soap, textiles, leather and tobacco etc.

President : in 2001 Basher Alazad. Prime Minister : Muhammad Mustafa Mero.

Syria made great progress during Islamic empire of Ummayad Caliphs and Damascus retained for a long time capital of Islamic empire but with the emergence of Abbasid Caliphs, Damascus lost its importance and Baghdad became capital of Islamic empire.

Syria came under Turkish Empire and later on under French empire but it became independent soon with the emergence of Jewish state of Israel in 1948, its conflict is going on with Israel along with other countries. In 1990, it opposed Iraq's conquest of Kuwait. Syria has been unable to patch her differences with

Israel, so both are dagger drawn. In war of 2003, it leaned towards Iraq, no relation with U.S.A. became intolerable.

Lebanon and Its Impact

Its Capital is Beirut and Area is about 10,400 sq. kms. Its Population is about 2 million and Language is Arabic. Religion is Christianity and Islam. Its Currency is Pound U.S. $l = £ leb. 1875.

The Republic of Lebanon occupies a strip of land along the Mediterranean coast between Syria and Israel. Lebanon became independent in 1941 from French rule when Germany occupied France. Christians are 42% and Sunni Muslims are 57% so terrorists activities continue.

It is primarily agriculture country. Lebanon produces olive, oil, grain and fruits. The chief industries are oil refining, food processing and cement etc. Tourism is a valuable source of income.

Its President is Emile Lahoud. Prime Minister : Rafiq-al-Hariti.

Lebanon has become cockpit of the world because Palestinians ousted from Israel, occupied it. These troublesome Palestinians raid Israel to create terror among Jews civilians. This brings retaliation by Israelies. Syrians also fish in troubled waters and create anarchy and chaos here. Christians, Palestinians, Sunni Muslim lead by Syrian forces, Jews lead by Israeli forces and Shiates lead by Iranians fight constantly with one another. Thus Lebanon inspite of being a tiny state is torn by constant strife and now it has become probably the most troubled state of the world. Like Iraq, Syria and Israel etc., it was also formerly part of Babylonian, Assyrian, Arab and Turkish Empire. Now it is an independent country constantly torn by conflict but U.N.O. is bringing peace to this unhappy land. Inspite of all this, constant feuds continue. Israel withdrew troops in May 2000 but Syrian troops are still there, so Syria dominates Lebnan.

Arab-Egyptian Conflict with Israel in Middle East

Egypt and Mesopotamia are considered cradle of old civilization but Syria and Palestine differed greatly from Egypt, although the Egyptian influence was here recognizable there as early as 2700 B.C. Ancient cities like Babylon and Ugarit were older than Memphis and on a level with Thebes as centers of civilization. Ugarit (modern Ras Shamra, on the Syrian coast opposite the easternmost cape of Cyprus controlled probably more than 80 towns and villages lying in a territory of about 40 square miles. This old city could equip 150 sea-going ships for a trading expedition. Seven languages, from Cypriote to Sumerian, and five scripts occur in Ugaritic documents of the thirteenth century B.C. The Ugaritic language, is akin to Hebrew, and the texts written in this language illustrate a civilization closely akin to that of Canaan (Palestine) on the eve of the Hebrew settlement. The mythological tales of Ugarit narrate deeds of Baal and other gods, whom the Hebrews rejected. On the other hand, Ugaritic documents mention names and details that also appear in Biblical narratives, for instance. Abraham, or the adoption of a grandson by the grandfather, a legal act also performed by Jacob with regard to Ephraim and Manasseh according to Bible.

Thus, by contrast to Nubia, Syria remained to a considerable degree culturally independent of Egypt and rather indebted to Babylonian civilization. Even in the days of Egyptian supremacy the chieftains of Syria salaaming before the pharaoh ("Seven and seven times I fall at the feet of my lord") did so in the Babylonian language. Thus origin of Salaam of Islamic world, is due to Babylonian civilization.

During the New Kingdom, the worship of Syrian gods became popular in Egypt. The pharaoh Rames II named his favourite daughter "Daughter of Anat" after the Semitic goddess of war also began to be worshipped in Ugarit. Thus Egyptian civilization and Babylonian civilization came in contact but differed with one another.

The pharaoh Thutmose I, about 1525, announced by anticipation that his empire extended from the third cataract of the river Nile, to the "inverted water" of the river Euphrates, which unlike the Nile, runs from north to south. Afterward, he actually reached the Euphrates. Two of his successors in the fifteenth century B.C. repeated the same feat. As such in the thirteenth century, the pharaohs dreamt of the river Euphrates frontier, and in the meantime tried to control as much part of Syria as they could possibly do so.

The conquest of Syria and her wealth began in earnest, when the pharaohs mastered the instrument that made this task realizable: the horse. Dates are approximate to the nearest decade. Thus Egyptian and Babylonians seeds of conflict have ancient beginning.

The struggle for Syria continued for almost the whole third quarter of the second millennium. Between the campaigns, the courts entertained amicable relations and the rulers on the river Euphrates and in Asia Minor exchanged gifts and letters with the pharaohs of Egypt. The king of Babylon, when he fell sick, expected to receive condolences from the Egyptian pharaoh, and the statue of the goddess Isthar travelled from Nineveh to Thebes, to help an ailing pharaoh. The Asiatic kings sent their daughters with fitting retinues (for instance once with 317 girl servants) into the pharaoh's harem. But a king of Babylon was curtly rebuked for asking for an Egyptian princess in Exchange. (He then begged the pharaoh to send him any good-looking Egyptian girl with a big dowry : who would dare to say, she was not a princess?) Marriages were part of the old bartering system and also form of international trade. And international trade, like domestic trade was not above bazaar tricks and bargaining etc.

These transactions, the diplomatic correspondence, and the intermittent ware etc., created the interdependence of the lands of the Levant. It was probably the first international age for the Near East. The course from Susa to Thebes corresponded in the same Babylonian language, and from the Black Sea to Nubia chariotry dominated the military art. The use of this new weapon and horse required professional soldiers, and this new military technology changed the social structure. In Asia Minor and in Syria the chariot warriors received fiefs in return for military service. In some Syrian cities they formed a kind of nobility, membership of which was generally conferred by the ruler. One of these famous feudal lords, Ugarit possessed 200 horses. Even in Egypt, the military, enriched by the wars, came into the forefront of the society. The pharaohs now affected uniform. When the Eighteenth Dynasty became extinct three generals in succession ascended the Egyptian throne, and the last of them founded the Nineteenth Dynasty. One of these crowned generals stated that the equipped temples of Egypt with priests chosen from the army. In other words, the military appropriated the choicest morsels of the Egyptian economy.

The other phenomenon of the new Levant was the emergence of a new great power. The troops fighting the Egyptian armies in the fourteenth century were directed from a far away capital near the Black Sea, and when the peace came, it was inaugurated by the marriage between Egyptian king and a Hittite princess from Asia Minor.

The Hittite

The Hittite who ruled a vast territory capital was Hattushash, modern Bogazkoy, some 110 miles east of Ankara, the capital of modern Turkey. The civilization of the Hittites was essentially, derived from Mesopotamia *i.e.,* from Iraq, Syria and Lebanon etc.

From their capital the Hittite kings with varying success extended their supremacy over a great part of Asia Minor. They preferred indirect dominations, a conquered country or city became a vassal of the Hittites kingdom. About the middle of the fourteenth century, having destroyed the kingdom of Mitanni in northern Mesopotamia, they took over its Syrian dependencies and its role in the struggle with Egypt. About 1270 B.C., the struggle ended in stalemate. King Rameses II of Egypt made peace with the Hittites, who preserved their sphere of influence in northern Syria.

Ramese II, was the last powerful imperial ruler of Egypt. His fame reached Greek tradition and, through it in English poetry. He is the Ozymandias of Shelley. He fathered 162 children during his reign of 67 years. He raised the most colossal statue at Abu Simbel which is about 66 feet high. He covered the walls of his enormous temples with vainglorious pictures and inscription. After this "Sea peoples" began to descend on Egypt after 1230 years. For some fifty years the pharaohs had to fight off the migratory waves by sea and by land. They swept away the Hittite empire and destroyed the cities of Syria and Palestine (which received name Palestine from the Philistines, one of the "sea peoples" who settled there. Egypt survived but lost her empire in Asia. After this Babylonian and Assyrian empire were established. Assyrians used weapons of irons.

Advantage of Iron

The advantage of iron, however, was the universal distribution of iron ore, which is 500 times more common than copper in the earth. Even a small, low-grade iron deposit in the neighbourhood was sufficient to free a city or a tribe from dependence on distant sources of copper, tin and lead etc. This abundance and utility of iron replaced other metals and brought iron age in existence.

Language

The creation of the alphabet was the most important advance in the transmission of knowledge between the invention of writing and the art of printing. This creation of alphabet was the work of Sumerions of Mesopotomia. After 1500, scribes in Syria, trying to invent a script fit for their Smitic dialects, hit on the device of a consonant alphabet. Hieroglyphs reproduced words so the cuneiform script was syllabic. But the inventors of the alphabet used signs to represent the ultimate particles, the "element". In Ugarit an alphabet of 31 characters was already in use about 1400 B.C. and the scribes arranged the signs in essentially, the same ABC order as the letters of our alphabet. About the same time there also appeared, the first predecessors of the Phoenician alphabet from which, via Greece and English alphabet has descended. The knowledge of hundreds of signs was necessary for both the hieroglyphic and the cuneiform script; this limited literacy to trained professionals and scholarship to few. No great effort was needed to memorize two or three dozen alphabetic characters; now anyone could learn to read and write. The alphabet is democratic and so it played a great part in spread of Education with the development of knowledge and culture. Hebrew, Greek and Roman culture developed in ancient period which are quite different from Arabic culture which developed with Semitic culture. Thus courses of conflict began in ancient days. Egyptians and Palestinians which included Jews, Syrians, Lebanon etc. remained daggers drawn even in ancient days. Later on when Hebrews lead by Moses founded Jews religion and Arabs founded Islamic religion. This conflict took shape of religious wars. For centuries Jews suffered untold hardships but in 1948, Jews were able to form tiny state of Israel but Egyptians and all the Islamic states of Middle East are determined to destroy the state of Israel but now with the establishment of Muslim Arab state of Palestine other Arab states have accepted existence of Israel.

The fate of Syria and Lebanon under Arab rule and Turkish rule

Under the rule of first four Caliphs, Islamic rule made notable progress and Muslim empire spread far and wide. Later on Munniya and his son Yezide established Khilafat of Umayyads and made Damascus as Capital of Islamic empire.

During Umayyad Caliphs rule Syria with its capital at Damascus became center of Islamic empire and probably the most renowned and richest city of the world. But during rule of Abbassid Caliphs, center of gravity shifted to Baghdad and during rule of Caliph Haraun Ul-Rashid it reached to pinnacle of its glory.

During Mongol raids Baghdad was destroyed and Syrian cities also have to suffer terrible calamities, Mongol rule was replaced by Turkish rule. Turkish general conquered Baghdad in 1055 and Turks rule was gradually established in Syria and Lebanon also. Ottoman Turk rulers became Caliphs and Arab Caliphate became to be Ottomonized. Ottoman Turks ruled over Iraq, Syria, Lebanon, Israel and over whole Arab empire for more than eight hundred years. Situation changed with the opening of 20th century, as Ottoman power weakened, so urge for freedom came among Arabs. Turks formed privileged class and neglected Arabs, cultural and linguistic differences kept the Arabs and Turks separated but Turk rule continued over Syria and Lebanon upto 1914 but when Turkey joined Germany, Britishers and French helped Arabs to throw Turkish rule.

The Rise of Nationalism in Syria and Lebanon and Impact of 1st World War over These Countries

European contact aroused nationalism among Arabs. During the First World War to weaken the Turkish power, Britishers gave encouragement to Arab nationalism. Through the Western literature, the ideas of nationalism spread in Syria and Lebanon through French influence. It also inaugurated a literary revival in Syria and Lebanon. The arrival of jesuit fathers, the catholic missionaries of France and the American Preslyterian mission in Syria and Lebanon brought about the spread of western education. Many schools to impart western education were established in Syria and Lebanon. A teacher's training college was established in Lebanon. The Syrian Protestant college was founded in Beriut in 1866, which became famous Stigoseph's American University.

The Arabs particularly people of Syria and Lebanon were also awakened by Pan Islamism which indirectly fostered the Arab nationalism. Many cultural societies such as Syrian scientific societies were formed which prepared ground for Syrian nationalism, several secret societies were founded by the Arabs in different cities to spread the idea of separate states for Arabs.

When the war clouds were gathering in European continent, the Arab national aspirations were taking shape and on the other side British and French were making plans to establish their rule over Arab Countries.

At last First World War began in 1914 and with British and French support Arabs rose in revolt against Turkish regime.

The Condition of Syria and Lebanon during First World War and during Peace Conference

An Arab Conference was held in 1913 in Iran, to demand independence of Iraq, Syria and Lebanon etc. and another was held in 1914, in which Sheriff Hussein of Mecca and Ibn Saud etc. were present. Sheriff Hussein joined Anglo-French side in 1915 and T.E. Lawrence famous as Lawrence of Arabia was sent to help Arabs. Sheriff Hussein's sons Faisal and Abdullah helped Britishers to conquer Iraq, Lebanon, Palestine and other Arab lands. Consequently Abdullah was made king of Traps Jordan and Faisal of Iraq but Sheriff Hussein who declared himself king of Arabs was defeated by Ibn Saud.

During war Sykes-Picot agreement was entered between Anglo-French diplomats conferring Syria and Lebanon to France and remaining Arab lands to Britishers. On the other hand infamous Hussein-MacMahon correspondence gave impression of Arab independence, General Allenby and Lawrence of Arabia with the help of Arab leaders defeated Turks and conquered Arab lands.

Problem of division of spoils of war created difficulty but relations do not deteriorate, provided full and complete Arab independence was granted and recognised. It was also made clear that no modification to the proposal of full Arab independence was acceptable to the Arab leaders. The Amir and Arab leaders also presented his case before Paris Peace Conference in which they laid stress on the formation of a federation of Arab States. This demand was however, not accepted, as the Jews were not prepared to give up their claims of forming separate Jew state or to modify the demand in which way the Arab liked them to do. As such existence of separate Arab states continued.

King Commission. When Amir Faisal saw that his demands were not likely to be accepted by the Peace Conference of Paris, he demanded that a Commission be appointed to visit Syria and Lebanon to find out for himself the aspirations of the people and also to assess whether anything short of full independence will satisfy them. England straightaway rejected this proposal and made it clear that she will not serve on that commission; U.S.A. however, accepted these proposals and nominated Dr. Henry C. King and Charles R. Crame as members of this Commission. This League Commission was accordingly known as King Commission. Following example set up by England,

France also decided to boycott the commission. But inspite of this attitude of Britain and France, the commission went ahead and reached Syria on 10th June, 1919, but at this time riots broke out with the result that the League Commission could not carry on its work and scheme failed.

Syrian Congress Meet. Amir Faisal saw clearly that Britain and France were totally opposed to Arab home-land and as such, he gave his people a clear idea that unless they became aggressive and sternly adopted revolutionary attitude, they could not hope to get Arab State. This provided extremists and terrorists an opportunity to accelerate their activities. Syrian congress which claimed itself as sole representative body of Syrians met in Damascus in July 1919 and adopted several resolutions. Among other things, it declared that Syria should be declared as an independent State and there should be democratic understanding that Allied forces were fighting against German to give the people of the world, their birth right to govern themselves and liberate subjugated nations and also to give them a right to free themselves from alien yokes. Thus Iraq, Syria and Lebanon demanded independence.

T.E. Lawrence's Note. With all these assurances, the Arabs, pinned high hopes on the Britishers. They felt that as soon as the First World War was over, the Arabs will get their freedom. This point was made amply clear by T.E. Lawrence in a note, in which he said that the Arabs rebelled against the Turks during the First World War, not because they were interested in changing masters but because they wanted independence. It was stated in note that any attempt short of independence will not satisfy them. Liberation and not change of master was their ultimate aim and objective. Their hopes greatly increased when after the great war was over and whole of Arab land upto Jerusalem came under British-French control after the defeat of Turks.

Jewish Demand for Home-land. But as has been pointed out in chapter of Israel that in order to win the support of the Jews in First World War, the British Government committed itself to give a homeland to the Jews. This was also made clear in Balfour Declaration of 1917. This complicated the situation and the British and French diplomats failed to evolve a procedure whereby they could satisfy both the parties.

Amir Faisal's Attempt for Arab Homeland. Since the Arabs had actively co-operated with the allied powers during the First

World War of 1914-18, therefore. Amir Faisal approached British and French authorities to fulfil their promise of giving them a homeland. He was directed to see Dr. Weizmann, who represented the Jews and to have some settlement with him. They both reached an agreement by which it was provided that both will have close cooperation with each other and the Arabs in Palestine will have their agents who will ensure that mutual relations should be reconciled but this did not happen. For details see chapter on Israel. However Syria and Lebanon came under French mandate. Thus France began to rule over Syria and Lebanon under the mandate of League of Nations and Britain over Iraq, Jordan and Palestine.

A Detailed Description of French Rule over Syria and Lebanon and Its Impact

When Prince Faisal galloped at the head of his Arab cavalry into Syria, he was assured of fulfilment of Arab independence. Political and intellectual leaders were deeply stirred by the thought of a modern state in which Arab peoples might work and achieve the regeneration of their language, culture and society in a modern independent setting. From the sincere-sounding promises and public statements made by allied officials Arabs anticipated the creation and general recognition of an Arab national state. On the horizon, to be sure, were a few dark clouds like the Balfour Declaration of 1917, promising homeland to Jews and the Sykes-Picot agreements etc., but probably the bright sun of peace would also evaporate these war time mists.

Amir Faisal and his supporters advanced northward taking lands and pressing upon Aleppo, while the British proceeded along the coast to Alexandria in Egypt. During 1919, the Allies (British) controlled the coastal regions of Syria, and Arab's held its interior. Since the latter inhabited that area they found it rather incongruous that they were supposedly occupying enemy territory.

After war, two trips to London and Paris with respect to the peace settlement, Amir Faisal belatedly discerned his naiveté in accepting wartime commitments at face value. Learning at first hand, the unreliability of Western diplomats, he became the personal victim of slippery French diplomacy and astute British imperialism. The Arabs desired independence, and the Allied Powers would not grant it and League of Nations imposed mandate.

Arab Demands

Throughout 1919, little headway toward a satisfactory settlement developed, the Anglo-French Agreement was a crushing blow, as it cut off Palestine and provided for a French military occupation of Syria and Lebanon. By December General Gouroud and French troops replaced the British in Beirut and along the Syrian littoral. Amir Faisal's Army held the interior. The general Syrian Congress, composed of 85 members, elected from all parts of Syria, including Palestine, met in Damascus in July and after considerable free discussion passed resolutions, which clearly defined Arab aims. Inspired by the newly formed Arab Independence party, these resolutions, requested independence for Syria, Lebanon including Palestine, with Amir Faisal as king. They demanded independence for Iraq with Abdallah as king. They demanded repudiation of the Sykes-Picot Agreement and the Balfour Declaration of 1917, and rejection of mandate idea. Another resolution called for refusal of assistance from France in any form. In many ways actions of the Syria, Congress resembled and paralleled those of the Kemalist Nationalists of Turkey, who at that moment were meeting in Ankara.

Obtaining no redress, the General Syrian Congress declared on March 8, 1920, the independence of Syria, including of Palestine and of Lebanon. They declared a constitutional monarchy under Faisal. The French declined to recognize this announcement; and a meeting of the Allied Supreme Council at San Remo answered the Syrian action by acknowledging, informally yet firmly, a French mandate over Syria and Lebanon and separation of Palestine under British mandate.

French Control over Syria

Amir Faisal was caught between the superior forces of the Allies and the national patriotism of the Arabs. His wavering caused French General Gouroud to fear an Arab build-up in Damascus, where the San Remo awards completely blighted faith in British and French integrity. When he obtained Senegalese reinforcements, General Gouroud sent Amir Faisal an ultimatum on (July 14, 1920), demanding within four days unqualified acceptance of the French mandate and end of Arab conscription, reduction of the Arab army, and adoption of the new French-issued currency in Syria, control of Syrian railroads, and arrest of persons guilty of acts, hostile to the establishment of French mandate. In the face of a French army advancing from Beirut to occupy Damascus, Amir Faisal telegraphed his agreement, but the French did not foresee that their ultimatum would be accepted, so new conditions were added and the march of French army proceeded. Amir Faisal ordered the disorganization of the Arab army, but isolated groups opened fire on the French army. A bloody engagement occurred at Maysalun Pass, and with the help of aeroplane, and the rattle of machine-gun fire General Gouroud captured Damascus on July 25, so Amir Faisal left within a few days, and the French occupied the whole Syria and Lebanon in rapid order.

French Mandate. Although full legal title to the French mandate did not materialize until the Treaty of Lausanne in 1923 and although America did not recognize, the French mandate authority until 1924, the actions of 1920 confirmed French possession over Syria and Lebanon. Detailed French administration began at once, General Gouroud dividing the mandate for Syria and Lebanon into four separate districts. Aleppo, including Alexandria, Latakia, and Damascus etc. The Jebel Druza area in the south and all remaining interior regions. This plan seemed to be to divide and rule like British policy in India.

Detailed Description of French Rule over Lebanon and Its Impact

The day before the French mandate was established, General Gouroud issued, a decree which added the city of Beirut, coastal regions to the north and south including Tripoli, Sidon, and Tyre, and the Bikea valley and Baalbek to the old Sanjak of Lebanon to form a new greater Lebanon. Since 1861, the Sanjak had an autonomous political existence under an elected central administrative assembly consisting of four Maronites, three Druzes, two Orthodox Christians, and one member each for the Malkhites, Matawilahs, and Sunnis, etc.

Thus attempt was made to reconcile different interests. By extending the area, the French Christians, changed the population to proportions and also increasing Sunni Muslims, so that Christians held over all majority and intentionally reducing the preponderance of the Maronite sect. Thus in Lebanon French made an attempt to establish Christian majority.

French Mandate over Lebanon

After the high commissioner's decree of September, 1920, a provisional administrative commission for Lebanon was appointed to serve until local governmental authority for Lebanon could be created. The governor of Lebanon was a French. A Lebanese governor, it was said, would cause too much jealousy and friction among the different religions. But the usual departments of Lebanon Government were formed and staffed by Lebanese, where competent and local individuals could be found, but of course, each Government department of Lebanon had many French officers and advisers.

Above the governor of Lebanon stood the French high commissioner, like Viceroy of India who had a government of his own to assist him separated into departments such as security, education and public works etc. This administration was manned by Frenchmen and French officers, who served as the authority to which the Lebanese government looked for orders. A most important group under the French high commissioner was that of the information officers, who served in every district of Lebanon. They reported developments to the high commissioner, exercised unlimited influence over local affairs, and stood as "tutors" to prepare the country and its people for full independence.

Certain functions of government such as customs, posts, telegraph, railways, public utilities, currency, and local troops levies were not divided locally by the four administrative units. And the French high commissioner reserved for his own government full supervision of these "Common Interests". Income from the central operations paid common expenses and the balancc was apportioned among the four state units, always with bickering and dissatisfaction. Thus French mandate rule over Lebanon was introduced.

One bright point in favour of the mandate system was the allowance for two parallel governments one held and administered by the mandatory power; and one was completely local in case of Lebanese, organization to be instructed by the other. In theory and in principle, this system was probably excellent. In actual practice, it allowed for a fully determined colonialism to operate more or less unmolested behind a semblance of local self-government. Thus French kept real power in their own hands making show of autonomy to local institutions.

French Imperialism in Lebanon and Its Impact

French imperialism manifested itself in Lebanon in many ways. In number of districts in case of disturbances martial law was established, and throughout the mandate period the French were quick to decree its use. The press was muzzled effectively : and numerous papers accepted French subsidies and published accounts of all events in a version favourable to French rulers, interests, French investors largely owned and operated the railways, public utilities, companies and banks of Lebanon. The entire fiscal and economic policy was controlled and initiated by the French. New concessions and general contracts were granted by the Lebanese governments. Profit went to French concerns or to Lebanese firms with strong French connections.

Finances

In 1920, the Bankue de Syries et du Grand Liban was founded as the bank of issue. Stable Egyptian currency had been introduced with Allenby's army, but the French found it wayward to buy their monetary needs in Egypt. The new currency was tied to the French franc, one Lebanese pound being exchangeable for twenty francs. However, it had the disadvantage of fluctuation with depreciating French currency — the fall of the franc probably an important role in uprisings in Syria and Lebanon in 1925. Head-quarter of the bank were in Paris, and over eighty per cent of the capital shares were also held by Frenchmen.

French Impact

French imperialists spoke of their "civilizing mission", a phrase which expressed the view that an area, region or people would be permanently and indissolubly linked to France if French language and culture flourished in their midst. To gain this, many French cultural missions visited Beirut and other cities and important towns of Lebanon. But the chief work was accomplished through education and use of French, as a second language. French schools of primary, secondary, and lycee rank opened in many cities and these always obtained more funds and aid than school where Arabic or some other language was taught. All Government schools taught French; and text-books for history, social sciences, and of literature and of the humanities had a French collaboration on every page. French newspapers were encouraged, and French was an official language in the courts, government offices, contracts and every walk of life. French language was considered as a mark of educated and cultured person in Lebanon and Syria as English in India.

There were, however, many favourable aspects of French rule, a concrete indication of which was the higher standard of living and growth of western culture and population. Schools improved and increased In number, food and clothing became more plentiful; roads were built, motorcars and transport became available; doctors were trained; disease was controlled; and sanitation and health standards were greatly raised. As such striking changes came in the city of Beirut, but developments were widespread across the whole state. Emigration declined, as life in Lebanon grew more attractive. Populations and standards of living were of course, on the rise around the world and Lebanon also shared in this world trend; credit, however, must also be given to French administration, selfish and blind as it may often have been, one could even find an American drugstore in Beirut, where real American chocolate, milk shakes could also be bought. Thus French mandate developed modern culture and amenities in Lebanon.

Local Lebanese Government

French Government gave local self-government to Lebanon because in Lebanon as conditions of life flourished, local desire for independence and true self-government spread. In March, 1922, a representative council was also elected, which began meeting in May. Famous French General Waygand, the second high commissioner, instituted a Lebanese council of state and won Lebanese confidence and affection by his intelligent and judicious decisions. His sudden replacement in January, 1925, by General Sarrail altered the peaceful developments almost immediately. This unfortunate move resulted from the electoral victory of the anticlerical Left in France and adversely affected Lebanon.

General Sarrail's Administration over Lebanon. General Sarrail's arrogant manners, unwise tactics, anticlericalism, inopportune appointments, and brusques officialism etc. fomented quarrels with the Maronite Church, the Druzes, and also among many Lebanese leaders. He insulted the representative council abolished the old elective system, rejecting religious divisions of the people. He appointed an unpopular Frenchman as governor of Lebanon after first stating that he intended to name a Lebanese native. He offended the Christian patriarchs, and perhaps also permitted his war with the Druzes of Syria to spread into Lebanon.

When the general uprisings of 1925, which General Sarrail provoked refused to burn themselves out, the incompetent general was recalled and he was replaced in December by Henri de Jouvenel, editor of Le Matin and French representative at the League of Nation.

New Constitution

Henri de Jouvenel called upon the representative council to draft a constitution which would recognize the French mandate and French responsibility for Lebanon's foreign affairs and give the French high commissioner veto power and the right to dismiss the executive head of the state and dissolve the legislature. Beyond those restriction de Jouvenal readily surrendered to the Lebanese authority, to manage their own affairs. On May 23, 1926, the Lebanese Republic was proclaimed. Charles Dabbas, an Orthodox Christian, was chosen president by the assembly which consisted of the old representative council and a new senate of twelve members appointed by the French high commissioner in accordance with the constitution.

Although de Jouvenel resigned in July, his successor August Ponsot, carried on tactfully. No major political problem or riot arose until the acute world a economic crisis and its repercussions in trade, unemployment, and finance in Beirut caused High Commissioner Ponsot to suspend the constitution in 1932. The president remained head of the government, and a new cabinet was appointed with instructions to supervise and regularize all expenditures more closely. A new constitution for Lebanon was promulgated in 1934 a new high commissioner, Count de Martel. The power of the assembly was restricted, and the sectarian basis of election and membership in previous assemblies was also ignored. Political life in Lebanese maintained an uneasy calm, until disturbances in 1936, it forced France to reassess her position in her mandates and negotiate a treaty with Lebanon as also with Syria.

French Treaty with Lebanon and Its Impact

The sheer weight of French military and also of naval forces in Lebanon, kept political agitation under control. Moreover the French insinuated against a Muslim tidal wave required full trust in France and co-operation with French rule. However, British concessions to nationalism in Iraq and Egypt etc. incited the Syrian uprisings. These in turn enjoined France to initiate the treaty arrangements with Syria and Lebanon, in 1936, as was done by Britishers in Iraq.

Negotiations of the Syrians for a treaty with France also forced similar actions in Lebanon. The French could hardly be less generous to a more friendly Lebanon than she was to a recalcitrant Syria.

Inhabitants of Lebanon. In the Sunni Muslim parts of Lebanon, which the French decreed to Lebanon in 1920, were divided in their sentiments and wish in 1936. Many belonged to the Syrian National Party of Lebanon and agitated for union with Syria. Other preferred the more stable political life and the higher standard of living in Lebanon. The latter began only to fraternize with Christian groups : and Christian reciprocated by emphasizing their common interest, race, language, and general culture and by making much of the tacit arrangement by which the president of Lebanon was always to be a Christian and the Prime Minister to be always a Muslim. The Maronites wished to avoid the chances of greater Lebanon being dissolved; for they understood that the old mountain Lebanon was too small to be viable in the twentieth century.

Treaty

Negotiations for the treaty were opened in October 1936, in Beirut between President Emil Edde and the French High Commissioner. A twenty-five year Fanco-Lebanese Treaty of Friendship and Alliance was signed November 13, 1936 by which independence of Lebanon was recognized, and France pledged to support Lebanon's admission in to the League of Nations within three years. Lebanon also agreed to respect French interest and national outlook to maintain the established party of the two currencies. French troops were permitted in Lebanon to stay without restriction. In Beirut, the Christians and many Muslims did not feel happy, as they inherently hoped to reunite Lebanon with Syria. As such conflict resulted and casualties occurred; yet the Lebanese assembly ratified this treaty in four days and independence looked assured. In January, 1937, the Lebanese constitution of 1926 was restored, but difficulties loomed ahead, first, negotiations with Syria over economic matters and a settlement of "common interest" affairs dictated by these treaties with France hit a snag. Then Socialist coalition blum government of France fell in Paris, and the insecure international position frightened French conservatives into refusing and rectifying, the treaties, which the conservatives rightly believed would weaken France still further.

Badly disappointed, the Lebanese marked time, while World War II was brewing. Local political parties of Lebanon continued their manoeuvres the conflict centering upon local matters and more often than not upon local personalities. The Unionist party, led by Emile Edde, was pledged to separate independence for Lebanon, while the constitutionalists under Bisharar al-Khurin looked with favour upon close and friendly relations with the other Arab states and did not object to some ties to Syria. Thus Syrian groups clashed with one another and these clashes are continuing now though Lebanon became independent after treaty, as such Lebanon is still torn by strifes.

French Mandate for Syria and Its Consequences

Syria was seat of Umayyed Caliphs who made Damascus their capital. All other divisions of Syria created by the 1920 decree, had a life during this period, even more variegated than Lebanon's when the decree was issued, native governments were ordered for Latakis, Aleppo, Damascus, and the Jebel Druze etc, with Alexandria attached to Aleppo as a special province, Damascene Syrians felt that France was deliberately blocking them from the sea and never admitted the legality of Syrian fragmentation by French. In June, 1922, independence of the Jebel Druze was proclaimed; and the remaining states were grouped into federation with an Antichene Turk, Subhil Barkat, as president of the federal council. The following year, each territory acquired a representative council "appointed by an indirect election". In 1924, just before quitting Beirut, French High Commissioner General Weygand, laid the foundations for treaty settlement with the mandate similar to that which the British gave Iraq. At the same time he recognized, a separate government; the Alawis and amalgamating Aeppon into the state of Damascus, which then became Syria Alexandria, though a part of Syria, had its own administration. However this policy was not followed by his successor, General Sarrail, but every action taken by General Sarrail seemed to be wrong. He antagonized the Christians in Lebanon by pursuing the line of domestic French political anti-clericalism in a religious state that had been organized on a religious basis for centuries. In the Jebel Druze, he touched off a bloody uprising by supporting the French delegate, Captain Carbillet. The latter had been doing a splendid job in building new roads, irrigation channels and did reforms of many types; but he was ignorant of the Druze Character and was wholly tactless; as such the more

Carbillet did for them, the more they disliked him. Since the decree of 1920, called for a native governor, Druze leaders petitioned for Carbillet's removal and fulfilment of the French Government's promise, General Sarrail replied by inviting the Druze leaders to Damascus, where they were arrested. Due to this unjustified act, Revolt flared rapidly across the entire Syrian mandate. General Gamelin was given command of the French forces under General Sarrail in September, and severe fighting occurred in the Jebel Druze, In October Druze columns appeared even at Damascus, and the bombardment of that city caused damages estimated at several millions of dollars and considerable loss of life. This tragedy brought Sarrail's immediate recall. Henri de Jouvenel, his successor, called for elections in Latakia and Syria. Bubhi Barakat, resigned the presidency. The presidency was then offered to Taj al-Din Hasani, Chief Judge of Damascus; but since his eleven-point programme was unacceptable to the French, he refused the proffered post. Every succeeding Syrian request over the two decades was based on Taj al-Din's platform. He demanded that Latakia and the Jebel Druze be joined to Syria and Lebanon; and a treaty be negotiated and entered into with France. It was proposed that Syria may join the League of Nations; and French troops be evacuated and a currency reform be enacted. It was demanded that Syria be entirely independent in matters of domestic affairs. When the French high commissioner refused these demands and Damad Ahmed Nami, was appointed president of Syria. Guerilla warfare continued, and General Gamelin tried to pacify the Syrian territory. In May, 1926, Damascus was again shelled. This time fighting was even more destructive and savage than the fight of previous October. Ponsot replaced de Jouvenel. Both France and the Syrian nationalists began to realize that some compromise was necessary. As such the latter asked France to forget the past, and Ponsot announced that a constituent assembly would be elected, a constitution drafted by Syrians will be allowed and a Syrian government will be inaugurated, and a treaty of alliance with France will be concluded, in that order. Thus French and Syrians came to terms.

Local Syrian Government

French made arrangement for local self Government in Syria in a good way, Damad Ahmad Nami resigned in February, 1928 and Ponsot appointed Taj al-Din President of a Syrian council of ministers to form a provisional government and hold elections. This was done in April, the constituent assembly of seventy members meeting took place in June, Fifty-two of the members were Sunni Muslims; and in this body, the nationalist block under the leadership of Ibrahim Hanam Jamil Mardam, Hashim al-Atasi and Faris al-Khuri began to take shape. A more radical independence wing of the bloc was led by Shukral-Kuwatli, Nabih al-Azmah, Adil Arilan, and Riyadh al-Sulh etc. The constituent assembly entered into the task of drafting a constitution, which Hananu presented to the assembly in August. It established a Western-type republic with President, Prime Minister, cabinet, unicameral legislature, and High Court etc. Syria was pronounced to include Lebanon and Palestine; the official religion was to be Islam; and in this no mention was made of France as a mandatory power. Since several articles violated French international commitments and were contrary to League stipulations, so Ponsot found the constitution unacceptable. In a conciliatory speech, he urged that five articles be withdrawn and sixth be redrafted. The assembly refused to comply and the quarrels were resumed.

In 1929, the assembly of Syria was prorogued, but debate over the constitution continued. In a surprise move in May, 1930, Ponsot unilaterally promulgated new governments for Alexandria, Latkia, and the Jebel Druze etc., simultaneously, he established in Syria the new constitution, including the five censured articles and the altered sixth. Elections were not decreed, however, until the spring of 1932, and when the chamber of deputies met in June, it comprised fifty-four moderates and seventeen nationalists, Muhammad Ali-al-Abid, a middle of the road candidate, was elected President of the Syrian Republic, Hakki al-Azm a moderate, accepted the Prime Ministership and selected his cabinet equally between moderates and the nationalists. The latter soon took the lead and pressed for conclusion of a treaty of independence with France.

Disturbances

Throughout 1933, all political conversations centered about a treaty. The French insisted upon exclusion of Lebanon, Latakia and the Jebel Druze etc. The nationalists demanded the end of all foreign privileges and dismissal of French armed forces. Unfortunately in May in the midst of the bitter debate; Ponsot fell ill, and his successor, Count de Martel, did not arrive until October. When Hakki al-Azm did present the proposed treaty to the chamber in November such a opposition arose that the high commissioner suggested its withdrawal. Parliament was suspended and later on it was dissolved, with the president governing by decrees, which were recommended by his cabinet. In 1934, Taj al-Din became Prime Minister and held on as Prime Minister nearly for two years.

However, from January 11 to March 1, 1936 Damascus and most of the towns of Syria became the scene of an organized strike against the French regime. In the midst of the strike Taj al-Din due to pressure resigned as Prime Minister and was replaced by Ata al-Ayyubi, who was a moderate leaders. The French sensed the writing on the wall even if they could not see it; and de Martel came to terms with the Syrian Nationalist Party leaders, Hashim al-Atasi, Jamil Mardam and Faris al-Khuri negotiations for a treaty were resumed in Paris, on the basis of Alexandria being a part of Syria and Lebanon being recognized as a separate state. The long discussions ended only after Yvon Delbos took over for the Blum government and agreed that the Jebel Druze and Latakia be incorporated into Syria. Rejoicing, Syria, elected the Nationalists to power in November, 1936. As such Hashim al-Atasi became president of the Syrian Republic and Jamil Mardam headed the cabinet as Prime Minister. The Syrians ratified the treaty which would free them from French imperialism; but as with the similar Lebanese treaty discussed above, the French government never did ratify it.

In 1939, the Syrian cabinet and president resigned, and the French High Commissioner suspended the chamber of deputies. Syria was thrown back as she was in 1920, when the French mandate began. At the outbreak of World War II *i.e.* 1939, Syria was being governed by an appointed council of directors under the immediate and supervision of French High Commissioner Gabriel Puaux, who replaced de Martel in January, 1932 and World War II began in September 1939.

The bitterest event for the Syrians was to swallow the gift of Alexandria to Turkey. From the beginning in 1920, the French, declared a special administration for Alexandria, in view of the large Turkish population residing there. At first, it was attached to Aleppo but under separate rule. When questions over its status were raised by the Turks in 1936 and conversations initiated, Syrians objected to it. As discussions proceeded to France-Turkish responsibility, to an independent Hatay, and to outright annexation to Turkey in 1939, Syrian nationalists protested every step of the French steps. With considerable justification and legality, they declared that the terms of the League mandate forbade France form any such action.

A Critical Estimate of French Rule over Syria

For two decades-France tried to govern Syria and failed badly and ingloriously. Policies dictated by Paris were high-handed, improper unwise, and based on an almost complete misunderstanding or disregard of the Syrian situation. To cap these mistakes French administrative personnel sent to govern Syria were generally either pompous, unwise, incompetent or officials transferred from North Africa, where situation was different. French officers were unable to rule Syria and Lebanon properly. French failed to make themselves popular to the Syrians, so French mandate did not succeed but treaty gave it freedom.

The Condition of Syria and Lebanon after 1939

It has been already stated that French mandate over Syria and Lebanon ended in treaty of independence. In World War II, German forces defeated France in 1940 so undoubtedly with quite different motives, the U.S.S.R., China, and the United States of America, recongnized the unconditional independence of Syria and Lebanon in 1944. Shortly thereafter, both declared war against Germany in accordance with the Yalta programme and joined the United Nations as charter members of U.N.O. Immediately, the question of the presence of British troops antagonized only the more uncompromising, but the French symbolized the previous mandate-colonial states. Fear of the permanence of French control governed emotions in Lebanon at Beirut and in Damascus in Syria.

French President General de Gaulle understood that the French troops would have to be withdrawn, but he evidently hoped to retain a strong French influence in the Levant by means of treaties with Syria and Lebanon which would be at least as favourable as the British treaties with Iraq and Egypt etc. He particularly desired that in the schools French language may be accepted and taught there. He also desired that the French schools be entirely free from Lebanese and Syrian control. Naval, military, and air bases for the French would be held indefinitely, and assurances would be given that the Levant remain a French sphere of influence particularly in economic matters and in literary aspect.

Syria and Lebanon indicated a willingness to discuss these points and negotiate treaties, but only after departure of the French troops. The landing of additional French soldiers in Beirut was interpreted as French military pressure. Open resistance to the French was staged, and so the French shelled Damascus in May, 1945. This goaded Prime Minister Churchill of Britain into serving an ultimatum upon French President de Gaulle to cease fire and detain his troops in their barracks while British forces restored law and order. Therefore the only question remained was when and how would the French troops be withdrawn. The British and French discussed the evacuation at great length and in great detail throughout 1945 to 1946. The Syrians came to believe that British troops were there to present disorders resulting from the presence of French troops and the French troops were being kept there because the British troops would not leave. The Security Council of the United Nations, prodded by the U.S.S.R. and the United States of America recommended that foreign troops should leave Syria and Lebanon as soon as practicable. As such the last French troops departed from Syria in April, 1946 but remained in Lebanon until December, 1946. The two countries of the Levant had achieved independence before 1947.

Glimpse of Syria's History

History of Syria has already been stated but brief account may be repeated. Both England and France wanted to have maximum control over the Middle East by dividing Turkish empire. They wanted to support every effort, which could weaken Turkey. Though they proclaimed again that they were quite keen to given independence to the Arabs, yet in reality they did not wish to do so. All that they wanted was that the Arabs should change their masters and instead of Turkish supremacy, they should accept British or French mandate. The Arabs were however, not prepared for this situation and they wanted to have their own independent homeland free from Turkish, British or French control.

Position after World War I. The Arabs in order to have the homeland were prepared to help the Britain and France during their First World War of 1914-18, if both powers agreed that after the War was over, the Arabs will be given their homeland. They were sufficiently encouraged by Hussein-MacMahon correspondence which provided ambiguously for Arab homeland. On November 7, 1918 an Anglo-French Declaration made it probably clear that "The goal envisaged by France and Great Britain in prosecuting in the East, the war set in train by German ambition is the complete and final liberation of the peoples, who have for so long been oppressed by the Turks. As such the aim is of their setting of the national governments and administration that shall derive their authority from the free exercise of the initiative and choice of the native population". The same declaration also further elaborated this point by stating that. "In pursuit of these intentions, France and Great Britain agree to further assist in the setting up of indigenous government and administration in Syria and Mesopotamia". (Now Iraq). It was also stated that these governments will be recognized as soon as these are set up. Not only this, constitutional monarchy was promised under Amir Faisal in Syria. French mandate over Syria should be withdrawn. It was also demanded that the idea of creating a Jewish State in Palestine should be given up. This Conference also went to the extent of saving that no economic and military aid should be accepted from France. Thus, Syrian Congress showed anti French attitude.

Partition Scheme Again. When Syrian National Congress and Amir Faisal adopted hard attitude, Britain and French tried to follow middle course policy. It revived the old partition scheme under which Palestines was to be divided into two parts, one each for the Arabs and the Jews. Not only these proposals were made but these were soon implemented and French troops started occupying coastal land of Syria, leaving hinter-land to the care of Amir Faisal. In order to reach some settlement the French also offered partial autonomy to the Amir Faisal but all this was quite unacceptable to Syrian nationalists, who unilaterally declared independence of the country on 8th March 1920, along with that of Lebanon. Amir Faisal was declared as constitutional monarch as stated before. But this was unacceptable to Britain and France, who decided among themselves to have Palestine and Iraq on the one hand to British and Syria and Lebanon on the other hand to France.

Flight of Amir Faisal. The situation became bad to worse and France demanded from Amir Faisal that he should accept French mandate over Syria and Lebanon. It was also made clear that in case, this demand was not accepted, France will take resort to armed forces. The threat instead of solving the problem, complicated the issue and Syrian nationalists decided to face French armed intervention with full determination. There were bloody fights in several parts of the country, but the superior French forces captured Damascus and created a situation under which Amir Faisal had no other alternative but to leave this country. In this way France was in a position to establish his mandate over Lebanon and Syria again under League of Nations.

French Mandate over Syria and Lebanon

French followed the Policy of Divide and Rule like British in India. As such when France again became a mandatory power it was hoped that she will do her best to unify Syria and Lebanon and to create a situation that with the passage of time she will be in a position to become a self-governing country as stated in League mandate. But France followed just a reverse policy, so that she was in position to perpetuate its influence in Syria and Lebanon. Instead of consolidating the country, the French divided the country into several small states namely Greater Lebanon, the Alwi, Syria and Jalelud Druz etc. The French mandate created such a situation that these states always fought with each other and did not come pear to each other. An effort was also made to put Christian population against the Muslim population of Arabs and make them eight with each other. But inspite of all these tricks, the French could not create a situation according to their own desire. The result was that they had to keep strong, French armies in the country to make their presence felt. Mandatory power took very few effective steps either promote a sense of self-government or for spread of education. France also tried to give economic set back to Syria by promoting their own economic interests in this country, instead of promoting local economy, trade and commerce. In fact Syrian economic and commercial interests were always sacrificed in comparison to French interests. Even in their own country they were provided few employment opportunities. Their local culture and civilization was disregarded and every effort was made to promote French culture language and civilization and efforts were made to establish superiority and supremacy of French culture.

Uprising of 1925. For sometime Syrians watched the situation, on the hope that the situation will improve and the French government will discharge its obligations as a mandatory power of League of Nations. But as the time passed, it became amply clear that the mandatory power had no interest in introducing self-government or in promoting Syrian culture and civilization. Unemployment went on increasing, with the result that the living standard of the Syrian people went down. As a result there was resentment against France in Syria and as a protest in 1925, riots broke out in Druz which soon spread to Syrian capital of Damascus and also in other parts of the country. Practically whole of Levant area was captured by them. When the rebels captured Damascus, French forces had to leave the place, which was however, again captured by French forces after heavy fighting and French rule was re-established.

Setting up of a Syrian Constituent Assembly. But now France had realized that there was sufficient political awakening in the country and their policy of repression and suppression will not serve the purpose. As a mandatory power of League of Nations, French Government will have to discharge its obligations seriously and sincerely. Accordingly in 1926, a constitution for Lebanons Republic was proclaimed. A proposal was also made of for setting up a Constituent Assembly for Syria. France also proposed a constitution for Syria on French pattern which was rejected by Syrian people.

French Agreement to Leave. France made every effort to reconcile Syrian aspirants of autonomy to come down as near to their proposal of a French type constitution as they could amicably do but they failed. They wanted to conclude a treaty with Syria and Lebanon, but these efforts too failed. As such, they offered more concessions to the people of Syria, but again and again the French offers were rejected and in 1936, serious riots broke out in the country. France, therefore, had no other alternative but to compromise on the lines acceptable to Syrians. Accordingly in 1936, a compromise formula was reached between two countries by which France agreed to leave Syria and Lebanon within a period of 3 years. It was also agreed that Syria will be admitted to the League of Nations and that France will also give military training and other help to Syrians.

Independence of Syria. In September 1939, Second World War broke out and Nazi Germany was in position to humble France in 1940. France then recognized independence of Syria on June 1, 1944 and within two years the troops of both Britain and France withdrew from both countries. In this way both Syria and Lebanon became free from the yokes of their French masters.

Thus, there was a long drawn struggle in which immense sacrifices had to be made, there were also bloody baths and repressions and suppressions before Syria and Lebanon became independent and free from foreign yokes of French mandatory powers. After independence Syria and Lebanon indulged themselves in internecine quarrels and in Arab Israeli wars which created chaos there and Lebnon quarrels become cockpit of Middle East.

Rule of the French in Syria and Lebanon

In 1920, following the San Remo Conference, a French army moved against Syrian capital Damascus and ejected king Faisal from the throne of Syria. After this incident the French took over the mandates of Lebanon and Syria and ruled on behalf of League of Nations.

In 1925 the Druses, a proud Muslim sect living in the mountains, revolted and brought two years of civil war. An artillery bombardment of Damascus by the French forces aroused widespread resentment. The French then instituted a more conciliatory policy. In 1926 Lebanon was recognized as a republic and the same status was accorded four years later to the four administrative divisions of Syria also. In practice, however, these republics continued under effective French control and supervision. Relative tranquillity reigned until 1935 when a new wave of nationalism shook both Syria and Lebanon. As a result the liberal popular Front government in France. Syria and Lebanon entered in two treaties with the French Government. Under these treaties both Syria and Lebanon were recognized as independent republics which were to become members of the League of Nations and France was granted certain privileges by their treaties in these territories, such as the right to maintain troops and military bases. However, the French parliament kept postponing ratification to these agreements, and finally in 1939, the Syrian constitution was suspended.

Some historians say politically, French rule was a failure both in Syria and Lebanon. At the beginning a popular Arab king had been ejected, and for the next twenty years the French administration often retained and suppressed personal and political liberties. Under French mandatory rule, however, the modernization of Syria and Lebanon proceeded rapidly. New roads and public buildings were constructed, and the use of electricity and irrigation works was extended. Agriculture, trades industry, art, culture and education was developed.

Republic of Lebanon's Condition after French Withdrawal

In Lebanon, the nationalist-minded leaders, who had controlled the quasi-independent regime since 1943 remained unchanged. The confessional aspect of the state of Lebanon was upheld, as was the tradition that the president be a maronite Christian and the Prime Minister a Sunni Muslim. At that time, the Lebanese chamber of deputies included 30 Christians and

25 Muslims; and during the final departure of the French forces, Riyadh al-Sulh formed a coalition cabinet in Lebanon at the invitation of President Bishara al-Khuri.

New elections for the Syrian chamber of deputies were held in 1947. The Constitutional Party, the one in power, succeeded easily to manipulate and manage the elections and continued in office. Beirut newspapers protested; and Kamal Jumblat, a young Druze socialist, resigned from the cabinet. But the leaders were unmoved. The problem of Palestine, the economic detonations resulting from independence, the post-war relaxations, and the East-West crisis, gave Lebanese politicians ample opportunity for disagreement. Perhaps the smallness of the country and lack of the paucity of its natural resources, and the diversity of religious affiliations, the customary attribute of national distinction in the Middle East-bound together, all political leaders except the extremists. Among themselves, they quarrelled over favors, prestige, position, privilege and power, but they usually closed ranks on foreign crises. Cabinets changed frequently, but the leaders shuffled the various ministerial posts among themselves. In the years following the departure of the French troops, Prime Minister succeeded one after another as coalition Government were unstable. Between 1946 and 1958 ten different men occupied position, many of them on several occasions like French coalition Government. But most of them were in the cabinet, when holding the Prime Ministership Bishara al-Khuri was over thrown in September, 1952 by a bloodless public strike and demonstration which resembled a vote of no confidence. Since General Fuad Shihab refused to call out the army so al-Khuris only recourse was to resign. Mismanagement, corruption, and arrogance etc., were the charges against him. Kamal Shamun, leader of the progressive Socialist party of Lebanon was elected President; and was given full powers for six months. Elections in July 1952, showed little changes since membership in the chamber of deputies was to a large extent predetermined by its proportional representation according to religious ideas, so 13 Maronites, 9 Greek Catholics, 2 Armenian Orthodox, and 1 collectively to the major groups such as protestants, Jews, and Roman Catholics etc. Abdallah al-yali, a Beirut lawyer, became Prime Minister again and also held for a time the portfolios for interior, defense, and information to concentrate power in his own hands.

Minor Parties

Minor parties did not succeed in winning many seats or supporters, but they did have considerable nuisance value and kept the leaders in offices more alert to their responsibilities and work. The largest of these parties, the nationalists Bloc, at one time led by Raymond Edde believed that Lebanon's destiny, and probably independence, rested upon close relations with France, of course influence of this party declined after the French departed. Kamal Jumblat pursued a Utopian socialist doctrine, whereas Mustafa al-Aris and Khalid Bakdash professed Marxist dogmas and probably served as Soviet agents. Antun Saada denied the partition of Syria and formed his Syrian National Party, a pro-fascist group which strove incessantly and often violently for the reunion of Lebanon with Syria. Thus difference of religion and of political outlook created anarchy and chaos in Lebanon.

The fundamental political problem in Lebanon after 1945, revolved around her geographic location. A narrow populous strip along the coast, Lebanon is an Arab state of many religions tied strongly to Arab culture and Arab traditions. Yet, the wealth of the state and many of its people depended upon the sea and commerce with the outside world, mainly with the West. As a result, Lebanese political leaders attempted to pursue two different courses which created unbridgeable rift.

Trade

Beirut and the other important Lebanese towns on the sea coast, prospered greatly during the French mandate period, mainly from commerce. Beirut became westernized to a remarkable degree, and during the Second World War served as a port and base for operations in the Levant. National independence gave Beirut the opportunity to become one of the great markets in the Middle East. Her merchants proved equal to this responsibility, and Beirut evolved rapidly into a great Middle Eastern commercial and financial city. Shortly after 1948, Lebanon established a free money market, which also attracted middle Eastern moneys to her banks. Officials and favourites of Middle Eastern Potentates transferred their funds to Beirut banks or invested in appartment houses and business and enterprizes of many types. Beirut developed into a wealthy and busy port, and the airport, which welcomed large trans-continental and world airliners. Probably it was served by more airlines than any other in the world. Industry established foothold here and challenged the free traders in the halls of the chamber of deputies.

Although the Lebanese rejoiced over the departure of the French forces but they were not bitterly anti-France. The many business connections precluded a complete break. And Lebanese-Syrian currency remained tied to the French franc until 1948, when France devalued the franc by fortyfour per cent without increasing the cover for the Syrian-Lebanese pound as had been agreed in 1944. France offered to make up the balance in properties, claimed by France in Lebanon, in European currencies, in credit for purchases in France, and also in additional French francs. Lebanese leaders protested vigorously but in the end accepted French offer, fearing a breakdown in trade and commerce. Lebanon obtained a ten-year guarantee of her currency against French devaluation and a liquidation of all French government property claims in Lebanon. This financial settlement improved relations with France, and trade between the two countries was maintained at its customary level. In 1955, France extended to Lebanon a credit of 15,000,000 for the purchase of French goods. Thus French influence in Lebanon remained considerable even after departure of French forces.

Since Syria refused to accept the French offer, a new and separate Lebanese currency was established. Within a few weeks the currency break with Syria presented difficulties of payments, exchange rates, and also of trade balances. An agreement also extended the economic unity of the two countries for an additional three years and it was arranged that fortyfour per cent of the aggregate customs receipts at all frontiers would be credited to Lebanon. However, divergent economic interests of the two countries caused one storm after another and in 1950 this precipitated an economic break and the closing of the frontier for nine months. Syria exported grain and live stock and aspired for rapid industrial development. Lebanon lived mostly by foreign trade and her industry and probably had not reached the point where a protective tariff, such as Syria desired, appealed to the majority. In 1952, an economic agreement with Syria was signed at Shtoura, providing that royalties from oil lines of the Iraq Petroleum Company and the Trans-Arabian Pipe Line Company would be divided equally and that no duties between the two countries would be levied on agricultural produce or livestock, Tariffs on industrial products would also be protective for certain categories of goods in which Syria and Lebanon had manufacturing interests.

American Lebanon Relations

Relations between Lebanon and the United States of America were also most cordial during this period. Dr. Charles Malik, Lebanon's representative to the United Nations and ambassador to the United States, carried a message of goodwill and understanding to the American people. Dr. Bayard Dodge and Dr. Stephen Penrose, Jr., Presidents of the American University of Beirut, served as unofficial yet very effective ambassadors of the American people; and several official American ambassadors of Exceptional imagination and tact. This furthered the warm relations between the two nations. The very considerable emigration from Lebanon to the United States of America in the past also played an active role in maintaining interest and understanding between the two countries. Thus in Lebanon next to French influence, influence of U.S.A. prevailed while in Syria influence of Soviet Union prevailed.

Caill Problem

The Trans-Arabian Pipeline to carry oil from the Saudi Arbian fields to the Mediterranean Sea had its terminus near Sidon in Southern Lebanon. In 1947, Lebanon forced work to cease on the line because of the American position on the partition of Palestine. Construction, however, was resumed in 1949, and oil began to flow in 1959. A refinery was built in Sidon to process petroleum, and a second was also erected in 1955. On the coast north of Beirut, the Iraq Petroleum Company's pipeline touched the sea at Tripoli, and after World War Second two new parallel lines were laid to offset the disuse of the Haife line and the increased Iraqi production. The lines and refineries brought a very welcome income to Lebanon. But in 1956, a new law was passed, imposing heavy taxes retrospectively from 1952 on foreign oil companies having pipelines in Lebanon. Aimed at Iraq Petroleum Company and TAP-line, this law was sponsored by Prime Minister Abdullah al-Yafi and Minister of State Saib Salam, who was also chairman of the Ministers' oil committee. The latter was negotiating with TAP-line officials and representatives of Syria, Jordan, and Saudi Arabia etc., was suggested that the usual fifty per cent of the profits be divided equally among the above mentioned four Arab states. Lebanese Ministers, wanted fifty per cent of the profits on oil passing through pipelines in Lebanon. IPC immediately objected, dropped its plans for an additional pipeline to reach Tripoli, and discharged employees in the Tripoli area. Lebanese opposition attacked the government for its ineptitude in the retrospective tax law. As such not until 1958, an agreement was reached to provide higher royalties for Lebanon. This created tension.

Russia's Role in Lebanon and Its Impact

Although the U.S.S.R. recognized Lebanon in 1944, the Soviets union gave only passing interest to Lebanon and Communists groups there. In Beirut, the Communists were extremely active in the Trade-Union movement. They were led by Mustafa al-Aris, Street demonstrations were so frequent among the students at the American University in organizing parades and protests that governments officials closed it temporarily in 1954. Yet, in the 1953, elections, all Communists failed miserably at the polls, and their Communist sympathizers were defeated. Communists were never popular in Lebanon and even now Soviet Union has not made impact over Lebanon.

After 1954, the U.S.S.R. changed her earlier indifference. Lebanon signed an economic agreement with Russia in April; and a similar trade pact was initiated in 1955 also with East Germany. Russian technicians surveyed Lebanon in 1956, for various economic and industrial possibilities, and trade agreements were negotiated with Communist China and with Bulgaria in 1957. Rapidly expanding population, limited land resources, and unemployment offered fertile fields for Soviet Union's, activities. Lebanese officials recognized the challenge and initiated various projects, the most promising being the Litani River irrigation and hydroelectric power plan. In 1956, the International Bank also loaned 27,000,000 to finance purchases for part of the construction, which was started in 1957, So Communists influence lessened and Russians were unable to make their influence felt in Lebanon.

Lebanon's and Her Relations with Israel

By far the most pressing event for Lebanon, probably is to consider in the decade after World War II, arose from the partition of Palestine and the birth of Zionist state of Israel, Lebanon showed her Arab character by joining the Arab League at its inception and vigorously participating in its decisions and actions. She argued in the United Nations organization against partition and also revealed her hostile attitude by halting work at Sidon on the pipeline. However, Lebanon's part in the Palestine war was very small, and so she suffered only a handful of casualties. Fawzi al-Kawukji, a native of Tripoli and an old soldier, from the days of Ottoman army service, led a group of irregular soldiers; some of the Lebanese, into Palestine before the end of the British mandate to try to prevent the formation of the state of Israel. Whenever, he visited Lebanon, he was always honoured by public demonstrations, which definitely indicated Lebanese sympathy for the Palestinian Arabs and hostility to Jews. Further more, Lebanon lodged no protest when he based the operations of his National Liberation army in Lebanon. Allowing of Palestinian Liberation Army *i.e.* P.L.O. to stay in Lebanon became a thorny problem which made Lebanon cockpit of Asia. It was a blunder.

Israeli Lebanon Relations

Lebanese found no difficulty in subscribing to the various truces declared in the Arab Israeli wars and easily entered into armistice negotiations. Israeli forces withdrew from four Lebanese villages which they had occupied during War and on March 23, 1949, an armistice was signed, recognizing the previous Palestine-Lebanon frontier with demilitarized zones on each sides. Lebanon refused to recognize Israel, and also adopted the boycott practices of the Arab League. Since unemployment was widespread in Lebanon, the influx of over 100,000 Arab refugees, equal to almost ten per cent of the total population of Lebanon, injected great explosive factor of the Palestinian settlement. The Palestinian refugees were located in fifteen camps scattered from Tripoli to Tyre and were supported by United Nations grants and subsidies but their continued presence graphically illustrated to Lebanese citizens, that Israel was a disturbing factor in Middle Eastern society. Lebanon desired destruction of Israel like other Arab states and so Lebanon and Israel become daggers drawn.

Impact of Suez War

The relative peace in Lebanon was shattered in 1956 by the Suez crises. President Shamun supported Egypt in her nationalization move, and mass rallies and strikes condemning Western and Israeli pressures on Egypt were permitted in Beirut and in other Lebanese cities. When the Suez Canal war began in 1956, Lebanon declared state of emergency and Shamun invited the heads of all Arab Governments at Beirut to determine that what action should be taken against France, Israel and

Britain. Lebanese leaders spoke vigorously in the United Nations and in many forums, opposing the aggression upon Egypt and urging the speedy withdrawal of British, French and Israel forces from Gaza and the Straits of Tiran etc. Thus Lebanon sided with Egypt in Suez crisis.

Condition of Lebanon after Suez Canal War of 1956

As soon as the most irritating aspects of the Suez wars were soothed, Lebanese leaders engaged in a bitter Parliamentary election. Abdallah al-Yafi fell from office in November, 1956 and a new electoral law was replaced by sami membership of the chamber of deputies to 66 and calling for four-year terms. Campaigning soon began in earnest, and a National Union front announced its opposition to Sami al-Sulh and President Shamun etc.

Collecting around several disgruntled former Prime Ministers such as Saib Salam, Abdallah al-Yafi, and Husayn Uwayni, the front presented a five-point platform : no amendment of the constitution, allowing Shamun to succeed himself; absolute neutrality; rejection of foreign military bases and pacts like the Baghdad pact etc., refusal of any foreign aid which would compromise Lebanon's sovereignty; and a close and Impartial co-operation with other Arab states. Election clashes occurred, and on one occasion Saib Salam was beaten by the police and he was also arrested. General Shihab declared the elections would be conducted fairly; and in July, the government won 50 seats, the National Union Front 8, and the Independents 8. Significantly, Saib Salam, Abdallah al-Yafi, Kamal Jumblat, Rashid Karami, and other prominent politicians failed to win election and, in August so, Sami al-Yafi reshuffled his coalition cabinet.

Trouble in Lebanon

The disgruntled politicians who found themselves frozen out of office commenced a battle to regain power and discovered eager allies in Syria and Egypt. Arms smuggling from Syria became frequent, and Lebanese frontier police personnels were shot in attempts to halt the illicit traffic. Terrorists bombed the Lebanese parliament building, and also the government secretariat. Lebanon's public acceptance of the Eisenhower doctrine, became a prime target of the opposition. Foreign Minister Sharles Malik reiterated that Lebanon should side with Arabs' rights and aspirations. (He warned, however, that Middle Eastern conflicts could not be solved by alliances with

Communists.) When the Syrian fued arose with Turkey in 1957, an aggression against Syria was acknowledged as an attack also upon Lebanon. Nevertheless acts of terrorism persisted and it was necessary to deport numerous Syrians and Jordanians to curb-disturbances but these continued.

Syria and Egyptian Influence

The achievement of the United Arab Republic increased pressures and tensions surrounding Lebanon. Leaders announced immediately that Lebanon would not join the United Arab Republic or the Arab Federation but infiltration of arms and men from Syria and Egypt mounted. Malik confirmed a report that he had received a promise of unlimited military and economic aid from the United States to maintain the Lebanon's independence, although in the fiscal year begining in July, 1957, direct American aid was programmed at only about $ 15,000,000.

In March, 1958, the reorganized Lebanonian cabinet under Sami al-Sulh won a vote of confidence of 38 to 15 with 13 abstaining. But at the same time 82 Lebanese leaders, including the heads of several of religions communities, signed statement, warning President Shamun against amending the constitution and seeking re-election, when his term expired in September. Political agitation grew pernicious, and in May a pseudo civil war was inaugurated by outbreaks and demonstrations in Tripoli and at Beirut etc. Soon designated as rebels, politicians out of office extended independently their sway over specific areas. Mr. Saib Salam in the Basta quarter of Beirut; Kamal Jumbliat in the Druze mountain area, Rashid Karami in the sector north of Tripoli and others in two or three-isolated regions. Syrian and Egyptian nationlists commandos, and arms, with the silent connivance of Damascus and Cairo, helped the rebels in Lebanon but the fracas reached a stalemate as General Fuad Shihab refused to commit the Lebanese army to either political camp and acted only to maintain public peace and order.

American Influence

Civil strife languished after President Shamun passed out the word he would not seek re-election. After this a team of United Nations investigators came and a trip to the Middle East by U.N.O. Secretary General Dag Hammarsk found the complicity of the United Arab Republic. At this juncture, in the Iraq Revolution erupted and the possibility of sizable intervention from Syria became so real that President Shamun called upon U.S.A. President Eisenhower for an urgent relief. The immediate landing of American marines in Beirut stopped the quarrel of local Lebanese politicians to the level of the cold war between East and West. Many blustered, and Nasser of Egypt flew to Khrushchev in Moscow; but it was soon evident that no one would seriously challenge the American position. The Americans asserted that the marines of U.S.A. would be withdrawn as soon as peaceful solution of Lebanese politics could be devised. As was expected, the Presidential election resulted in the choice of General Fuad Shihab, and the rebels declared general satisfaction, if and when the American troops would leave. The expressed desire of most political leaders of Lebanon resolved itself around the widespread hope in Lebanon and in many quarters of the Middle East that genuine neutrality would descend upon Lebanon so she could become "the Switzerland of the Middle East". But all these hopes were shattered on sharp rocks of reality and strifes, petty wars and terrorism flourished and Lebanon is now cockpit of Middle East through in May 2000 Israel has withdrawn hertrooks.

The Republic of Syria after World War II

When World War II ended, Syrian political leaders who had battled for complete independence in the French mandatory period were in power and had the satisfaction of forming the first fully sovereign Syrian republic. Shukri al-Kuwati held the presidency; Saadallah al-Jabri was Prime Minister; and Jamil Mardam, Faris al-Khuri, Hashim al-Atasi, and Khalid al-Azm etc. were prominent political figures, who held other important posts. A new chamber of deputies, elected in the summer of 1947, confirmed the position of the government leaders; and Jamil Mardam, who had become Prime Minister in December, 1946 remained in office for two years more.

During this period national feeling in Syria ran high. The actions of the French had been more drastic in Damascus and the interior provinces of Syria than in Beirut. Three times in recent month, they had not only shelled Damascus, which had been the site of the Arab Kingdom in 1920. All French schools in Syria were closed in 1945; and when France devalued the franc in 1948 Syria's own separate Syrian pounds was brought immediately. In April French offers of reconciliation were refused, and any official who appeared friendly or compromising towards the French was digging his own political grave. Thus Syrians developed hatred for French Government.

The dream of United Arab State to include Lebanon, Syria Trans Jordan, Palestine, and Iraq etc. never died in Syrian imagination. As Syria emerged independent upon the close of the World War II, the value of union appeared greater than ever; many Syrian regarded it as almost a necessity. Each state separately was weak; together they would have strength. Let an arrangement to accomplish even partial federation required political unity but after the area had been divided between England and France, unification had been probably impossible.

The Condition of Syria and Lebanon during World War II and After It

France was defeated by German forces in 1940, so the fall of France in 1940, whetted Abdullah's ambitions to join Syria to Trans Jordan; but in 1947, President al-Duwatli of Syria publicly stated that Trans Jordan would be annexed by Syria. Syrian political leaders had no intention of being governed by Abdullah or his greater Syria from Amman. Indeed, they did not relish the thought of surrendering position and power in Syria to any group or person. Others within Syria, looked forward to the merger of Iraq and Trans Jordan, which were the two Hashimite kingdoms, and proposed the eventual inclusion of Syria and Lebanon. Leaders in Iraq and Syria discussed the union of their two states into a Fertile Crescent union. The Syrians believed that they possessed a more advanced population and that though slightly smaller, they would dominate Iraq. On the other hand Iraqis recognized that their country contained greater wealth, both developed and potential, and felt certain that Iraq would lead the combined state of Iraq and Syria. The drawing together of Iraq and Trans Jordan threw Egypt and Saudi Arabia into each other's arms. Egyptian leaders could not contemplate other leadership than of Egyptians in the Middle Eastern Arab states; and Ibn Saud, an enemy of the Hashimites and the Wahabi king of Saudi Arabia since the days of World War I, was apprehensive about an enlarged Hashimite state on his northern confines may endanger Saudi Arabia. Thus, Iraq and Saudi Arabia became enemies.

Syria played an active part in the formation of the Arab League, and attended all its conferences, Syria also agree to all Arab League declarations of united Arab opposition to the partition of Palestine, and promised to cooperate militarily against the formation of Zionist state of Israel. In 1947, the Palestine liberation committee, obtained over 27,000 volunteers in Syria for commando units, and Druze chiefs also notified to the government that they could furnish 10,000 men for the fight. In the spring of 1948, various high Syrian army officers, including Colonel Adib al-Shishakli, participated in operation in the Palestine wars; but in the actual fighting Syrian forces proved to be in effective against the Israel. Three small villages in the Hulah Marsh area were occupied, but there was no great enthusiasm to shed Syrian blood so that king Abdullah in Trans Jordan or king Farauk in Egypt might have more territory to rule by annexing Palestine.

Coup

On March 30, 1949, Chief of Staff Husni al-Zaim carried out a bloodless coup d'etat. Learning that President al-Kuwati was planning his dismissal, al-Zaim arrested the President, the Prime Minister, and also many leading political figures. The public approved this coup for a number of reasons; the Palestine war was a failure and the corruption was not reduced. The Syrian constitution had been amended to permit the president to succeeded himself; and al-Kuwati also opposed the Fertile Crescent unity plan. The Politicians in their governmental techniques had failed to bring to Syria the "promised Day" after ousting French and foreign influences. As new cabinet was formed : al-Zaim as Prime Minister also held the portfolios of defense and interior. Political parties in Syria were outlawed, and a new constitutions of Syria was planned. In June "The Leader" was elected president; but on August 14, General Same al-Hin Nawi arrested al-Zaim, who was immediately shot. Thus a kind of chaos prevailed in Syria. Perhaps Husni al-Zaim had started out marvellously, arranging a cease-fire agreement with Israel in April and obtaining assurances from Nuri Alsaid that Iraq would come to the assistance of Syria if attacked by Israel. Husni proposed unity with Iraq "on the basis of a full autonomous state for each country", and militancy figures journeyed between Damascus and Baghdad. Fearing Hashimite rule in Syria, Egypt and Saudi Arabia rushed diplomatic and financial support to al-Zaim. At this point al-Zaim abandoned unionist policies, and became President of a new Syrian Republic. Worst of all, he showed an inclination to restore to France some aspects of her cultural influence. French, for instance, became an official language, along with Arabic.

Upon the execution of unpopular al-Zaim, General al-Hin Nawi called upon Hashim al-Atasi, an elder statesmen to form a new government. A constituent assembly of 114 members was elected in November, and al-Atasi was chosen head of the state. (Women voted for the first time.) Meanwhile, discussions with Iraqi officials proceeded to a point of drafting the framework of a common regime. It was proposed Syria and Iraq would have a common army, a supreme cabinet including foreign affairs, defense, finance, and economy, and also a customs and monetary union. But the Republican Bloc, enemy of union, stirred the army to move. On December 19, 1949 Colonel Adib al-Shishakli arrested al-Hin Nawi, who was charged with treason and conspiracy with a foreign power (Iraq). Thus, conflicts continued in Syria and anarchy prevailed.

Rule of Col. al-Shishakli and His Successors

Colonel al-Shishakli did not at first rule directly. The constituent assembly declared Syria to be a republic and Hashim al-Atasi was elected president and Khalid al-Azm became Prime Minister. No one, however, doubted who was the real power in the Syrian government. Early in 1950, al-Shishakli visited Cairo and Riyadh. In the former, he was welcomed; and in the latter he obtained a loan of $ 6,000,000, which was to be repaid by shipments of Syrian goods over a three year period, commencing in 1955. It seemed more natural geographically and in most ways for Syria to be drawn towards Iraq; yet the diplomacy and wealth of Egypt and Saudi Arabia reportedly proved irresistible to Syrian leaders. The Prime Minister, Khalid al-Azm, voiced the opinion of many, when he declared that "he resented finding Syria like a commodity offered for sale by contending parties."

In June Nazim al-Kudsi of the People's Party, which was the largest single party in the Syrian assembly, became Prime Minister. Unity with Iraq and Trans Jordan had been defeated, since the People's Party stood for an Arab union of all Arab states and peoples a posture which in 1950 meant victory for the Egypt to-Saudi bloc over Hashimites rulers of Iraq and Trans Jordan.

New Colonel al-Shishakli desired sincerely and eagerly to return Syria to civilian government; and al-Kudsi's cabinet reflected that intention except for Colonel Fowzi Silu, al Shishakli's close friend in the ministry of defence who kept the army's interference on political affairs. A liberal constitution adopted in September which contained detailed and specific articles with respect to education, labour, land ownership, and the rights of the citizens etc.

Constitution

The new constitution of Syria did hot usher a new flourishing economic order. Syrian frustration led to a refusal of United States, point four aid and a pronouncement that Syria would "go it alone". However, Syria began to look to the Soviet bloc. Maaruf al-Dawalibi, one time minister of economy and a leader of the Islamic Socialist Front, concentrated on an anti-Western campaign. As such attacks were made upon American activities, and Syria was urged to sign a non-aggression pact with the U.S.S.R. but conditions were not stable.

Communist Influence

As such one cabinet succeeded another in 1951; and in November a prolonged cabinet crisis ended with the election of Maaruf al-Dawalibi as Prime Minister. In Berlin during World War II, he had been political secretary to the ex-Mufti and had been hunted in Paris by the Western powers and he was now a leader of the Islamic Socialist Front. The philosophy of this group, as one member described it, was "a Marxist drink in a Muslim Cup". He was opposed by other factions.

Colonel Adib al-Shishakli acted swiftly. Most of the cabinet Ministers were jailed. President Hashim al-Atasi resigned and Colon-nel Jawzi Silu became Prime Minister. Political parties were out-lawed, and plans for a new government and a new constitution were initiated. The new constitution was not presented until July, 1953, at which time al-Shishakli became President and Prime Minister. He organized an Arab Liberation party which won seventy two of the eighty two seats in the parliamentary elections in October 1953, since the other three major Syrian parties boycotted this election.

New Constitution

Colonel al-Shishakli over reached himself, but his time was running out. He arrested many leading political figures, including Al-Atasi etc. and declared martial law in Damascus and Aleppo etc. But the army revolted in the latter city, forcing al-Shishakli to flee in February, 1954 Hshim al-Atasi became President again; the 1949 constitution was reinstated; and the 1949 chamber of deputies was recalled. Elections for a new Parliament were held on October, 1954, returning eighty-one independents out of a total membership of one hundred and forty-two. Khalid Bakdash, leader of the Communist Party, became the first Arab Communist, duly elected to an Arab Parliament on a Communist ticket, Ex-President Shukri al-Kuwatli returned from five years of exile in Egypt and was elected President in August, 1955. A succession of Prime Ministers fought with the complex economic, social, and political problems of Syria after the overthrow of Shishakli but none found a constructive and useful programme largely because of virulent nationalism and the submergence of Syrian interests to those of Egypt and Saudi Arabia.

The political instability in Syria in the decade after World War II was extremely detrimental to economic planning and its progress and development. Excellent plans for the division and distribution of large tracts of land among poor and landless peasants were enacted into law, but like India were not implemented to any great extent. Intentions in that direction antagonized the large landowners and led in part to the demise of the al-Shishakli regime in 1954. After the breakdown of economic relations with Lebanon, Syria took active steps to improve the port facilities of Latakia and channels of Syria's foreign trade through that point. A port authority was established under the able direction of an American trained Syrian engineer; but Latakia did not have the geographical advantages of Tripolie, Beirut, Sidon, and other Lebanese ports, so it did not prove very beneficial.

Oil pipelines for Saudi Arabia and Iraq passed through Syria, and Syria obtained generous royalties for oil flowing through its pipes. In 1949, a concession for oil in Syria was granted to the Syrian-American Oil and Gas company, but no significant resources have been located. Other plans with Jordan for the development of electric-power stations and irrigation projects etc., on the Yarmuk River were also advanced, but political uncertainties and mutual jealousies prevented their implementation.

Syria and Israel

Frequent raids and counter raids on the border of Israel and hatred of Jews kept Syrian insistence on non-recognition of Israel alive. The greatest of their raids was committed in December, 1955, however, the Syrian political leaders turn more directly to the Soviet bloc and begin to put into effect the old Persian axiom that my enemies' enemies are my friends. As such the signing of American supported the Baghdad pact in March, 1955, galvanized Syrian policies and directed Syrian politicians into the Egypto-Saudi camp. The Syrians were already suspicious of the series of treaties of friendship among Turkey, Iraq, and Trans Jordan etc in 1946; but the Baghdad pact, especially after the ready adherence given to it by Britain, was anathema to Syrian nationalists and aid incited most of them to join the Egyptian camp. The earlier Arab League collective-security pact had been an Egyptian political move to forestall an Iraqi-Syrian union rather than to provide defence against Israel. Rejection of the Middle East defense organization, likewise, had been vigorously pleaded in order to assure that an increase of power would accrue to the Hashimite rulers of Iraq and Jordan.

Friendship of Syria with Saudi Arabia and Egypt

Syria quickly closed ranks with Egypt and Saudi Arabia, declaring that Syrian armed forces would be joined with those of her friends under a unified Egyptian command. In October, 1955 the Damascus pact in opposition to Baghdad pact was signed, pledging mutual assistance and establishing an alliance among the three states of Syria and Egypt and Saudi Arabia. In January, 1956, this pact was consummated by a £10,000,000 loan to Syria by the arrival of Soviet war material from Egypt. Syria signed trade agreements with the U.S.S.R. and with China in November, 1955, and with Rumania in January, 1956. Syria also joined in denouncing all acts of the United States of America and the pronouncements of the Syrian representative to the United Nations became more bitter and more fiery against NATO powers but Syrian friendship with Saudi Arabia and Egypt grew.

The Role of Syria in Suez Canal Crisis

Shukri al-Kuwatli, who was elected President in 1954, lived in exile in Egypt from 1949 to 1954. There he drank the waters of the river Nile and witnessed the exciting successes of Colonel Nasser. In Damascus any role other than that of a friend to Egypt was unpardonable and impossible, since the new and young army staff officers of Syria were ardent supporters of Colonel Nasser and his Egyptian revolution. Thus, when Col. Nasser nationalized the Canal, Syrian demonstrations were more open and enthusiastic probably than those of other Middle Eastern states. Syrian spokesmen swore that the oil pipelines would be sabotaged, should the West be guilty of aggression against Egypt. And in November, 1956, when the invasion occurred, they made good on their threat. After the fighting in Sinai dessert ceased, Syria did not permit the repair of the pipelines until Israeli forces withdrew from the Gaza Strip, Thus Syria whole heartedly supported Egypt in Suez Canal crisis.

Russo-Syrian Relations

In June, 1956, Sabri Al-Asali became Prime Minister again. He reshuffled his cabinet in December, 1956, and again in January, 1957, when he received a vote of confidence of 69 to 4, with 49 of the constitutional Bloc abstaining. He had organized several disordant political cliques into a loosely knit, unprincipled coalition, he was freely supported and influenced by liberal donations and pertinent broadcasts from Saudi Arabia and Egypt etc. Opposition to the Baghdad pact acted as the mortar binding them together against the Constitutional Bloc, most of whose members represented Aleppo and were receptive to the older idea of union of Syria and Iraq. Thus political parties differed in Syria.

To distract attention of the masses from political sniping, a running series of plots, accusations of treason, scandals, and political witch hunts etc. were offered in Syrian capital of Damascus. Israel, the United States, Iraqi royalty, Turkey, and Al-Shishakli etc. were the most convenient whipping boys. At one time forty-seven prominent politicians were court-martialled on charge of fomenting a revolution in support of western powers. Most were tried in absentia, but many who appeared confessed meekly to the charge. Incidents such as these abetted its drift toward the left; and trials with regard to the 1955 assassination of leftist Chief of staff Colonel Adnan Malki added fuel to the fire. These affairs, however, were not entirely effective; for serious "anticonspiracy-trials" riots occurred in Aleppo etc. where the government of Sabri-al-Asali, supported by such wily and skilful politicians as Akram Hurani, Michel Aflaq, Khalid al-Azm, and Salah al-Bitar, was unpopular.

This new regime needed arms to prevent an internal coup by the dissidents also to strengthen Syria's position vis-a-vis Israel and Iraq, etc. and also to wield important influence upon the affairs of Jordan. Further more, the army was moving rapidly into the political arena; and officers had a natural desire for more improved weapons in greater quantities. Following Col. Nasser's example, Syria applied to Moscow and received about $60,000,000 in tanks and other war meterials in 1956. President al-Kuwatli visited the U.S.S.R., and a dozen MIG-17 jet fighters also appeared in Syria. Soviet-bloc ships un-loaded their cargoes at Latakia. In 1957, Khalid al-Azm on his return from Moscow and Prague announced a loan of $150,000,000 on very favourable interest rates and repayment terms. The projects totalling $570,000,000 to be financed by the Soviet bloc were revealed along with an economic and technical distance agreement with the U.S.S.R. Many observers believed that Syria was almost irretrievably on her way behind the Iron Curtain and has became follower of Russia.

Concomitantly with these anti-Western developments, Syrian concern for Jordan was also marked by the sending of heavy arms to assure the Arab solidarity pact, agreeing to contribute about 7,000,000 to support Jordanian resistance to Iraq and the Western powers. Early in 1957, Syria signed the Arab solidarity pact, agreeing to contribute about $7,000,000 to support Jordan in her break with Great Britain. When in April this crisis arose in Jordan' Syria moved an armoured regiment into Jordan to bolster General Ali Abu Nuwar in his bid to throw Jordan into the Nasser's Egyptian camp. After Husayn personally quelled the rebellion, Syria acceded to his demands and unwillingly withdrew her army. Although Syrian leaders fulminated and plotted against Husayn's regime, they were again foiled by the airlifting of American arms into Jordan capital of Amman in September, 1957.

Each frustration drove the Syrians further to the left and strengthened Soviet bargaining, and emboldened the Pan-Arabists in Aflaq's Arab Renaissance party. It also brought to a head an acute rivalry brewing in the army for decade. Young army graduates of the Homs Staff Collage were fiery Arab nationalist who pointed to the defeats in Arab-Israel wars and the weakness of Syrian policies as positive proof of the senior officers' incompetence. Lt. Col. Adb-al-Hamid Sarraj, chief of army intelligence, emerged as the leader of the junior officers and in March, 1957, the issue was joined when the elder officers tried to isolate him by sending him to a minor post in Cairo. He refused to go; and General Afif Bizri, new chief of staff, was surrounded by Sarraj's friends.

Temporary Union of Syria with Egypt

Meanwhile the plot to unite Syria and Egypt Germinated. As early as July, 1956, the Syrian chamber approved appointment of a committee to negotiate a federal union with Egypt. President al-Kuwatli of Syria proved to be a willing tool, and the schedule for the union's consummation and the various steps towards union were outlined. The danger to the intriguers lay in the resistance expected of Aleppo from officers opposed to the youthful clique. To drown all possible opposition in a bath of emotional nationalism, conspiracies jeopardizing national integrity were unearthed and ordinary frontier incidents involving opium smugglers and cattle rustlers along the Turkish acts of aggression etc. were imputed to machinations of Western imperialists.

The resulting tension not only silenced internal opposition, but it also served as a screen for the arrival of Egyptian troops to forestall a likely Syrian coup d'etat of the 1949 variety. The shallowness of the Turkish crisis was disclosed, when king Saud offered to investigate the charges. Syria refused, and Khrushchev of Russia quickly dropped the issue. But the Egyptian regiments remained in Syria. In November, the idea of union was approved in principle; and in February, 1958 the union was officially declared in principle; by the Syrian government and Col. Nasser. The latter, however, was somewhat cool and the haste in which the union was effected, proved fickle and temporary. A few days following the announcement, Khalid Bakdash, leader of the Arab Communist party, emplaned from Damascus with his family for Moscow; and there was a very considerable flight of capital (estimated at $200,000,000) to Beirut, Col. Nasser of Egypt become president and al-Kuwatli vice president of the United Arab Republic, which was divided into two regions of Egypt and Syria. A plebiscite was held, and al-Kuwatli invited all Arab states to join. Col. Nasser appointed a combined cabinet composed of 20 Egyptians and 14 Syrians, many of the posts being occupied by two ministers, one for each region. In cabinet included were Sabri al-Asali, Akram Hurani, Salah al-Bitar, and Abd al-Hamid Sarraj etc. All political parties in Syria were dissolved by Col. Nasser's order so that no open resistance could be expected.

Union was probably not the natural expression of a long-cherished dream of most Arabs. The eventual submergence of Syrian national interests and treated per capita wealth by Egypt and lack of the political skill of Nasser and his cohorts brought dissatisfaction and the union of Egypt and Syria failed and now both are fully independent.

The Condition of Syria in 2004

After independence Syria came under the influence of Soviet Union. No Syrian Government was stable. Consequently there were plots and counters plots of mily, generals and of political leaders. There were frequent murders of Presidents and of Prime Ministers due to plots and counter plots.

In February, 1958, Syria formed United Arab Republic with Egypt and Yemen in which Col. Naseer of Egypt became President and Kuwatli of Syria became Vice-President but this union was shortened and it ended in September 1961, as Egyptian dominated this union which was resented by Syrian youths and soldiers. Relations of Syria became strained with Jordan and Saudi Arabia and border clashes took place with Jordan as has been already described and diplomatic relations of Syria were broken with Jordan and Saudi Arabia.

In 1967, Arab Israeli war took place because Arab states wanted to wipe out Israel particularly Col. Nasser of Egypt was too ambitious. For details see Israel and Egypt Chapters. In June, 1967, Syria took vigorous part in Arab-Israeli war along with Egypt and other Arab powers. Israel defeated Arabs and Israeli forces entered inside Syria and in Golan mountains Israeli forces are still in possession of lot of Syrian territory.

During 1966 to 1970 Nuruddin Atassi remained in power as President of Syria inspite of defeat of Syria in Arab Israeli war but later on crack developed in the ruling party and plots and counter plots took place and a kind of civil war ensued in Syria. In this civil war Hafiz-Assad emerged triumphant and he declared new Government of Syria on 13 November, 1970.

Hafiz Assad in order to stop frequent changes of Government centralized all power in his own hands. As in 1967, in Arab-Israeli war Syria was defeated and its lot of territory was in possession of Israeli forces. So Syrians and Egyptian forces attacked over Israel with soviet arms and with the help of other Arab powers in May, 1973.

Arab Israeli War of 1973

In Arab Israeli war of 1973, in the beginning Syrian forces gained an upper hand due to Soviet arms and Egyptians got advantage of sudden attack but soon Israeli forces fought with determination with their back to wall knowing attack of Arabs over Israel is merely an sport but for Israel it is question of life and death so in the end Israel won the war of 1973 due to valour, sacrifice and firm determination.

In spite of defeat President Hafiz Assad remained in power from 1970 to 1990 and his Government, seems as stable as government of Saddam Hussein of Iraq or of Nehru dynasty in

India or of Mrs. Thatcher in England. It seems era of unstable Governments, in Syria has ended and it has been replaced by centralized and stable power of Hafiz Assad.

Syrian forces have captured lot of territory of Lebanon in 1976, due to supply of arms and support of Soviet Union. Syria has created anarchy and chaos in Lebanon so continuous warfare is going in Lebanon due to presence of Palestinian guerillas and Syrian forces, Syrian differences are also with Iraq about Euphrat river. Hafiz Assad has followed the policy of friendship with Soviet block and co-operation with Arab powers and of occupying Lebanon. Syria supported Iraq.

The Condition of Lebanon after 1960

According to Lebanon's constitution President should be Christian and Prime Minister should be Muslim. There should be some minister of Shias and of some other minorities. As such Kamel Samun remained President from 1953 to 1958 but Prime Ministers frequently changed.

Lebanon became cockpit of Middle East because Christians and Muslims were daggers drawn. Moreover, there was enemity between Shia and Sunni Muslims. Later on Palestinian guerillas arrived here and fomented all kinds of troubles and disturbances in Lebanon. Later on Syria and Iran began to fish in troubled waters. Syrians began to support Sunni Muslims and Shia Muslims were supported by Iran and refugees of Palestinian Liberation Organization were supported by various Arab powers. Iraq and Soviet Union created disturbances and riots, raids over Israel and retaliation of Israeli forces against P.L.O. refugees who made their headquarter in Lebanon. All this created anarchy and chaos in Lebanon. P.L.O. refugees made constant raids over Israel so in retaliation, Israeli forces destroyed strong holds of P.L.O. in Lebanon but guerilla warfare continued. This guerilla warfare of P.L.O. and clashes between Christians and Shia and Sunni Muslims have become common feature of Lebanons life. Western powers such as France, U.S.A. and Britain etc. tried to bring peace to this war torn country but their efforts failed particularly because terrorists of various factions began to kidnap important persons of western powers and began to demand fabulous amount as ransom for kidnapped persons. As such Lebanon became probably most troubled and disturbed country of the world.

Progress, peace and prosperity cannot be expected in a tiny country which is constantly ravaged by faction wars but in spite of constant chaos, anarchy and guerilla warfare Lebanese Government, continued to work due to its good constitution which allows representation to all factions.

In 1964, Charles Helur became new President and ruled upto 1970. He had to face emigration of lot of Palestinian refugees who had to leave their home land because Israel occupied lot of Palestinian territory due to victory in Arab Israeli war of 1967. These Palestinian refugees continue raid in Israel and carried on guerilla warfare against Israel and against other factions in Lebanon. In 1970, Suleman Frenzie became President and remained in power upto 1976. In order to protect themselves from attacks of Muslim factions and Palestinian refugees, Christians formed Phalangist organisation and a kind of civil war ensued in Lebanon, Syria sent her forces in Lebanon and occupied lot of Lebanon's territory but Syrian forces prove useless to curb civil war and disturbances in Lebanon.

In 1976, Elias Sarkis became President of Lebanon he and his successors unsuccessfully tried to give peace to Lebanon but P.L.O. (Palestinian Liberation Organization) lead by Yasser Arafat; Shias supported by Khomeni's Iran and Sunni is supported by Syrian forces continued disturbances and faction fights. As such Lebanon has become most disturbed country of the world.

In foreign affairs Lebanon followed the policy of supporting Arabs against Israeli. Due to its sympathy with Arabs, all refugees of Palestine who ran way from Israel came to Lebanon and began to conduct guerilla warfare against Israel and against western powers by hijacking aeroplanes and kidnapping civilians of western powers and by attacking Christians of Lebanon. As such Lebanon's sympathy to Arab cause brought continuous warfare and disturbances. Christians of Lebanon are sympathetic to Christian powers such as U.S.A. and France etc. but threat of Arab countries to stop oil brought western powers to Arab countries side but U.S.A. sympathised with Israel the factions were created in Christians also. On the other hand Syrian forces intervened in 1976, supported Sunni Muslims and occupied its lot of territory and Shias supported by Ayotollah's Iran created faction wars and terror. In 1979, Egypt patched up differences with Israel and got back her territory from Israel and ousted P.L.O. refugees who came in Lebanon and began to create terror so disturbances are continuing even now in 2004 unabated.

Christian population of Lebanon has dwindled due to lack of children but population of Muslims is constantly increasing due to abundance of child births so Muslims are in favour of discarding tradition of Christian President and are desirous of grabbing both the posts of President and Prime Minister. As such Christians are in favour of separate autonomous tiny Christian state while other Arab states as Syria etc. want to grab Lebanon. Efforts are being made for equal representation to both Christians and Muslims in Lebanon but peace cannot come in Lebanon until Arab Israeli differences are minimised. At present civil wars faction fights and guerilla warfare is going on unabated and Lebanon has become one of the most troubled area of the world though in May, 2003 Israeli troops have left Lebanon but Syrian troops are still there. It is hoped that with U.N.O. efforts peace may prevail in Lebanon also. Syria and Lebanon as well as Israel fight with one another so there is no peace, Syria always opposed Israel. In 2003, when Anglo-American forces attacked govt. of Saddam Hussein in Iraq Syrian govt. showed sympathy with the govt. of Saddam Hussein, so U.S.A. became annoyed. Moreover, Syrian domination over Lebnon annoyed Israel and western powers. In spite of all this Syria succeeded in managing good relations with many countries including India. Shri Atal Bihari Vajpayee visited Syria and entered into many treaties.

Syrian domination over Lebanon is resented by Israel and U.S.A. etc., so Israel and U.S.A. and Syria are daggers drawn to one another.

27

TURKEY OR NEAR EAST

Turkey

Capital of Turkey is Ankara. Its area is about 779,452 sq. kms. and population is 70 million. Language is Turkish Arabic and Kurdish. Religion is Secularism but its main religion is Islam. Its currency is Lira which is equal to US $1-600 TL. Literacy rate is 82%. President Ahmet Necdetsezer, P.M. Bulent Ecevit.

Turkey is a republic in south eastern Europe and Asia minor. It occupies a strategic position, linking Asia and Europe at the Straits of Bosporus, between the Mediterranean Sea and the Black Sea. The major portion of Turkey lies in Asia Minor, but it is a country joining fringes of Asia and Europe.

Asiatic Turkey, that is, Anatolia, was the seat of one of the earliest civilizations known to history. Istanbul, the present capital was first known as capital of Byzantium empire and then as city of Constantinople in the name of Constantine. The Ottoman Turks conquered Constantinople from Christian-Eastern Roman emperors in 1453 and founded Turkish Ottoman Empire. In 1923 Turkey became a republic. Its Republican leader was Kamal-Ata-Turk or Mustafa Kamal Pasha who modernized Turkey.

Agriculture maintains about 64 per cent of its population. The chief products are tobacco, wheat, cotton, olive oil and sugar etc. Turkey is the world's second largest producer of Sultana raisins. Sheep and cattle abound in the plateau of Anatolia and provide mohair for which Turkey is famous. The main minerals are iron ore, copper, chromium, beuzite and coal etc. Its population contains Turkish-Muslims but Christians, Jews and Muslim Arabs also live in it.

President is Ahmet Needetsezed and P.M. is Bulent Ecevit the Old History of Turkey

History of Turkey is old and glorious. Old Troy described in Homers' Greek legends is situated in Turkey. Hitite emperor also developed and declined here. Later on Eastern Roman empire called Byzantine Empire made glorious achievements. Emperor Constantine 288-337 founded the city of Constantinople. Later on Seljuk Turks ruled over a large part of Turkey. They were replaced by Ottoman Turks, who defeated last Byzantine emperor and conquered Constantinople in 1453 and established Ottomon Turks Empire which contained Arab Egypt, Syria, Iraq Palestine etc. and other counties. Sultan of Turkey became Caliph of Islam.

In Turkey first Seljuks emperors established a powerful state and later on Osman Ali Turks or Ottoman Turks established a vast powerful empire covering Asia, Europe and Africa. Most of the lands of Muslim empire came under Ottomon Empire. So Ottoman Turk rulers became Caliph of Islam and claimed Suzerainty overall Muslim countries except Shia rulers of Persia and Moghul rulers of India. Ottoman rulers held sway over Arabia, Iraq, Syria, Palestine (now Israel) and Egypt and over Muslim lands of Africa. Not only this, they succeeded in defeating eastern Christian Roman empire called Byzantine Empire in 1453 and established their rule over whole of Eastern. Europe containing Greeks, Yugoslavia, Bulgaria, Romania and Albania and Cyprus etc. Rise of power of Russia under Peter the Great-Catherine the Great gave a death-blow to power of Ottoman Turks and Russia gradually grabbed most of the lands of Turkey and Turkey became sickman of Europe. Sensing weakness of Turkey, Austria, England and French began to covet Turkish empire and grabbed Iraq, Palestine and Syria and Lebanon but these lands gradually became free and Turkey became an republic and Khilafat was established.

A Glimpse of Ottoman Empire of Turkey

The awe which Europeans felt for the old Holy Roman Empire *i.e.,* eastern Byzantine Empire of Constantinople established by emperor Constantine was watched by the fear and dread which they entertained of the new Turkish and Muslim Ottoman Empire. In this, they were justified. For, if the Holy Roman Empire was weaker in fact than in appearance, the Ottoman Empire of Muslim Turks displayed a real vigour commensurate to its higher pretensions and great ambitions and constant aggressions.

In a sense this Turkish-Ottoman Empire was not "new". It represented, politically and geographically, a continuation of the imperial tradition of the Near East of the Greek (Byzantine) or Christian Roman Empire of the middle ages, of the Eastern Roman Empire of Byzantine emperor Justinian and Constantine etc. and of the much earlier empire of Alexander the Great. It was built directly on the ruins of the Eastern Roman Empire which was called Byzantine Empire. It embraced the same area and nearly the same populations; and it took over, with changed names, with changed religion *i.e.*, Muslims instead of Christians and Turks in place of Greeks but with the same institutions and practices and administrative set up.

Impact of Islam

What was "new" about the Ottoman Empire was the shift of south eastern Europe from Christian to Muslim control, the accompanying renewal of military energy in that quarter, and the fair promise that a large part if not all of Europe might speedily be incorporated in this vast Turkish empire which in its government and culture would be based on Islam rather than on Christianity and Greek or Roman culture founded by Prophet.

Islam was, of course, the religion of Mohammed, neatly summarized in the formula that "There is no God but Allah, and Mohammed is his prophet." *i.e.*, La-Illillah-Muhammad Rasul Illah". It had originated in Arabia in the seventh century; and within a hundred years, thanks to amazing proselyiting zeal and astounding military conquest, it had largely supplanted Christianity, "Judaism in western Asia and northern Africa and had penetrated even in south western Europe. Against south eastern Europe and Asia Minor, it had hoped in western Europe but in battle of Tours Charles Mortel gave a crushing defeat to Muslim forces and after that Islam lost hope of establishing its rule in western Europe. The Christians Roman Empire in the Eastern Europe of the Byzantine Greeks had then been too strong for Islamic forces till 1453. Thereafter, the huge Muslim Arab Empire had broken up into mutually warring fragments and the expansive force of Islam had seemingly been exhausted. During the middle ages Christians of western Europe as well as those of the Byzantine Empire took the offensive against the Muslim powers, and for a time it appeared as though the whole Near East might be wrested from Islam and may be restored to Christendom.

The crusades taken to free pious Christian lands, eventually failed, however. Indeed, they proved to be, from the Christian standpoint probably worse than a failure. They aroused and revivified the forces of Islam, while sowing new seeds of discord between Christians of the West and those of East of the Byzantine Empire. They evoked a second great wave of Muslim conquest of the Ottoman Turks which expanded Islam in eastern Europe and contracted Christendom and conquered Constantinople in 1453.

The Origin of Ottoman Turks and Their Expansion

The Turks were a tribal people whose original home was in the steppes and deserts of the Turkestan of central Asia and who had emigrated from these during the middle ages, both as nomads and as permanent settler to Mesopotamia, Syria, Egypt etc. and particularly to Asia Minor. They had adopted the Muslim religion of the populations of those places among whom they proved or settled. One of the Turkish tribes which penetrated into Asia Minor had a chieftain about the year 1300. Whose name was Osman or Othman and who assumed the title of Emir *i.e.* of (prince) of the Turks like Mahmud Ghaznavi who raided India and declared himself Amir. The Turks who were subject to Othman and his successors were henceforth called the Ottoman Turks and their empire was called as empire of Ottoman Turks.

Osman or Othman and his immediate successors were valiant warriors and gifted statesmen. They annexed other Turkish states and slowly but surely they built a powerful Turkish and Islamic military state. It was this rising power of Turkish growing state of the Ottoman Turks which was destined to become the outstanding champion of Islam and to renew with Christendom the struggle for mastery of the Near East of middle East and perhaps of all Europe.

Expansion

In the first half of the fourteenth century, the Ottoman Turks devoted their energies to the conquest of Asia Minor. They gradually extended their sway over all the Muslim peoples of this region, and to the east they reduced the Christian Armenians. Simultaneously, to the west, they pushed the boundary of the Byzantine Empire farther and farther back, capturing one Greek city as after another such as Ephesus, Brusa, Nicxa, and Nicomedia etc. By the middle of the century they had undone the work of the Christian crusaders and had wrested all Asia Minor from the Greeks. They made Brusa the capital of their empire, and the Ottoman Emir took the title of Sultan.

As the territory of the Turkish Muslim Empire of Ottoman Turks grew, that of the Eastern Roman Christian Byzantine Empire diminished. This empire can be said as the uninterrupted continuation of the ancient Roman Empire which was now steadily declining and deteriorating. Asia Minor was finally surrendered to the Ottoman Turks. Crete, the Egean islands, and most of the Greek peninsula were occupied by the Venetians of Italy. A large part of the Balkan Peninsula was in the possession of Slavic peoples such as Yugoslavia and Bulgaria who maintained independent states of their own and disputed with the Greeks and Byzantine emperors the control of south eastern Europe.

The Advancement of Ottoman Turks Towards European Continent

The Greece-Roman (Byzantine) Christian emperors in Constantinople thus found themselves, by the middle of the fourteenth century, attacked and hemmed on all sides. Their empire was actually restricted to their capital of Constantinople and to a part of Thrace, and to a narrow strip of seacoast along the Egean. They were confronted with foreign forces of Turks, Slavs, and Italians etc. They were, to be set with grave domestic problems and they were short of soldiers and money. They were also weakened by recurring revolutions and quarrels over the imperial succession.

In the second half of the fourteenth century the Ottoman Turks transferred their military activities and successes from Asia Minor to south eastern Europe. They early crossed the straits in force in 1360, and in the following year they captured Adrianople and made it their capital. In 1387, they conquered Salonica and two years later, on the fateful field of Kossove, they overwhelmed, the Yugoslavs. In 1393, they decisively defeated the Bulgarians. In the meantime they were seizing islands in the Egean and fighting the Venetians of Italy in the Greek peninsula. At the end of the 14th century, the Ottoman Turks, dominated the entire Balkan peninsula except Constantinople and a few other posts which were still held by Greeks or Italians.

End of Eastern Roman Empire

In desperation the Byzantine emperors begged aid of western Europe, and in alarm the popes preached new crusades and besought all Christians to go to the assistance of the Eastern Roman emperor. Some Christian princes did lead armies against the Turks; the kings of Poland and Hungary repeatedly tried to stem the tide of Muslim conquest; and the Venetians, with their commercial interests in the Near East clearly at stake, turned crusaders and fought manfully against the Turks, but it was in vain. The Turks still advanced inspite of stiff resistance.

In 1453, after elaborate preparations, Mohammed II, the ablest and greatest of the Ottoman Sultans, with an army of 150,000 men, laid siege to Constantinople, which was capital of Byzantine empire. The city, was defended by a pitifully small Christian army, numbering perhaps not more than 8,000, of whom half were Greek (including monks and priests) and the other half comprised detachments sent by the Pope from Rome and by the Italian city states of Venice and Genoa etc. "for the glory of God and the safety to Christendom." What the Christians lacked in numbers they made up in grim determination and reckless bravery, and for almost about two months the little Christian garrison held the Muslim host at bay. It was only when they were still further reduced by deaths and wounds and were utterly exhausted, that the Christians gave way and the Turks poured in, and even then the gallant band of Greeks and Italians fought on until they were all killed. In their midst, fighting up to the very end, perished in 1453, Constantine XI who was the last of the lincal caesars and Greeco-Roman emperors of Eastern Roman empire called Byzantine empire.

The Impact of Fall of Byzantine Empire and Conquests of Turks

The transfer of Constantinople from the rule of the Byzantine Emperor Constantine XI to that of the Ottoman Sultan Mohammed II was a sensational step in the revolution which was transforming the traditional empire of the Near East from Greek and Christian hands to that were Muslim and Turk. The events at Constantinople in 1453 depressed all states peoples of Christendom, as they hated the Turks and followers of Islam. For Constantinople was viewed by both Christians and Muslims as one of the greatest and strongest cities in the whole world, embodying most perfectly the traditions of ancient Roman rule and antique Greek culture. It was the ancient and capital city of a glorious Empire. Its possession carried great prestige. As Christians had held it from the time of the first Constantine in the fourth century to the days of the last Constantine in the fifteenth century etc. upto 1453, so the Muslim were determined to possess, it at any cost. Besides, this, it was naturally a city, comparatively easy to defend and specially accustomed to undertake distant conquests and to exercise wide domination. As it had been for more than a thousand years the center of a Christian empire called Eastern Roman Empire or Byzantine Empire of the Near East, so it would be in modern times the capital of Muslim empire of the Near East of Middle East.

The Rule and Achievements of Various Ottoman Sultans

Mohammed II (1451-1481) succeeded in doing what the preceding, Christian Byzantine emperors had failed to do. He not only ruled in Constantinople but he brought together within his empire many territories, which had been preciously lost to the Byzantine Empire. He reunited the whole of Asia Minor and the entire Balkan Peninsula. He did more : he conquered the Rumanian lands at the mouth of the river Danube and the Russian and Mongol lands north of the Black sea. Thus he extended the sway of Ottomon Muslim Turkish empire in the lands which never accepted control or domination of Byzantine Empire. For almost a century after the death of Sultan Mohammed II *i.e.* from 1481 to 1571, the Ottoman Turkish Empire grew rapidly and extensively and flourished mightily. In large part, it grew at the expenses of other Muslim states. The Sultans, as the champions of Muslim (Sun-nite) orthodoxy, waged wars against the Persians as the exponents of the principal Muslim (Shiite) heresy, and wrested from the Shahs of Persia the city of Baghdad which was capital of Caliphs and the valley of the Tigris and Euphrates *i.e.,* Iraq etc. One of the Sultans named Selim I (1512-1520) conquered Syria and Egypt, and obtained from the chief claimant to the old Arab Empire, then resident in Egypt, the title of Caliph, that is, head of all orthodox Muslims. Thenceforth the Sultans of the Ottoman Turks claimed to be successors both of the Roman emperors and of the Muslim caliphs, who claimed both spiritual temporal powers over Muslims. The Sultan likewise gained recognition of Ottoman supremacy in the holy cities of Jerusalem, Mecca, and Medina etc. and in other Arab towns. Also, by means of growing maritime power, the Sultans acquired suzerainty over all the North African Ottoman coast from Egypt to Morocco, including Tripoli, Tunis, and Algeria etc. Thus, Ottoman Sultan became Head of Muslim empire as Caliphs and extended their Ottoman empire in Near

East and in Middle East as well as in Africa. Eastern Europe under the Sultan Suleiman II (1520-1566), who was rightly and appropriately termed "the Magnificent," the Ottoman Empire comprised virtually the same territory as had constituted in the East Roman Empire called Byzantine Empire in the time of emperor, Justinian. But Suleiman the Magnificent would not stop here. Eager to expand his dominions in Europe, as they were already extended in Asia and Africa, etc., he, with the main force of the Muslim world behind him, turned a new force against the states of Christendom.

Suleiman the Magnificent

In 1521 Suleiman the magnificent captured Belgrade and crossed the river Danube. In 1526, he defeated the king of Hungary and destroyed the flower of Hungarian chivalry in the terrible battle of Mohacs, and occupied Budapest. Pushing on against the emperor of Austria, which had sought to aid Hungary, he laid siege to Vienna in 1529. Though he could not take Vienna but he compelled the Holy Roman Emperor of Austria to agree to a partition of Hungary and the smaller portion went to Austria and the larger portion passed to the Ottoman Empire and become a Turkish province. Thereafter the Holy Roman Emperor of Austria and the king of Poland too, made repeated and protacted attempts to drive the Turks out of Hungary and Rumania, but almost invariably they met defeat at the hands of Suleiman the magnificent. As the Byzantine Empire had fallen prey to the Muslim Turks' Ottoman empire in the fifteenth century, so in the sixteenth century the weakened and distracted Holy Roman Empire of Austria, Hungary appeared to the Christendom's last poor bulwark against the powerful on rushing and triumphant Muslims empire of Ottoman Turks. In the meantime Ottoman emperor Suleiman subdued the Caucasus and made the Black Sea a lake within the Ottoman Empire. Simultaneously his warships and pirate-ships wrought havoc in the Mediterranean Sea they successfully and bravely combatted Venice and Genoa and terrorized the seafaring merchants from Christian countries. Christendom, in the first halfs of the sixteenth century, seemed to be weak and exposed to Muslim assault on land and as well as on sea, at the very time when Christendom was faced internally with political rivalries of unprecedented rancour and with fundamental religious disunion due to rise of Protestants. Yet so great was the external threat that rival Christian monarchs and mutually vituperative Christian clergymen could agree with Pope and

Holy Roman Emperor of Austria and Hungary in cursing the Turk — "the infidel." But all efforts of Christian powers failed against Ottoman Empire and according to Philips Price, Turkey became the single greatest power in Europe and the Middle East rule.

Glimpse of Administrative System of Turks Ottoman Rule

The Ottoman Empire of Turks of the sixteenth century, was similar to the earlier East-Roman (Byzantine) Empire, not only in territorial extent but also in political institutions. It was not a national state, any more than the old Roman Empire had been a national state. It was a military political and administrative union, under Turkish leadership, of many diverse peoples. Only in Asia Minor did the Turks constitute a large proportion of the total population, and even there sizable minorities of Armenians, Kurds, and Greeks etc. persisted and constituted about 1/4th of population. In Mesopotamia, Syria and in Palestine, and across northern Africa, the Turks were a mere sprinkling among the mass of Arabs, Jews, Egyptians, Negroes, (Copts), Berbers, and Moors etc. In southern Europe the conquered nationalities remained — Greeks, Yugoslavs (Serbs), Bulgarians, Albanians, Rumanians, and Hungarians (Magyars) etc. and some of them, notably the Greeks, continued to furnish the Near East with its leading merchants and traders. Most of the conquered Christians, however, were reduced to a condition of serfdom and were treated as second class citizens and were obliged to support the Muslim Turks, who came to live among them as soldiers and officials and formed a privileged upper class and ruling elite class like Britishers in India, during British rule in India from 1818 to 1947. The government of the Ottoman Turkish Empire was an autocracy, not unlike that of the Byzantine Empire which it supplanted. The Sultan was Caliph and "commander of the faithful" and master of the conquered peoples. In theory he was Caliph sovereign and supreme. He made and enforced the laws; he appointed the local governors and army officers; he declared war and concluded peace. In practice, the Sultan was often influenced or controlled by his harem, army, vazir, or officials; and local agents and tax-gatherers etc. These were frequently harsher and more despotic even than the Sultan. Thus Ottoman emperor's powers in reality were exercised by his ministers, generals, harem and tax gatherers who were greedy and cruel. The Ottoman Empire was a Muslim empire, as the Byzantine Empire had been a Christian empire. Only Muslims could be full-fledged "citizens" :

Christians and Jews were "subjects" or zinmmis or II class citizens. For "citizens," there was the closest union of church and state and the Sultan was head alike of temporal and spiritual affairs being Caliph of Islam and civil law as well as religious faith and teachings traditions etc. were derived from Mohammed and the holy Koran. Moreover, the Ottomon Sultans supported the public worship of Islam. They transformed the venerable and historic Christian cathedral of Saint Sophia in Constantinople one of the architectural wonders of the world *i.e.,* into a Muslim edifice, and wherever their armies marched, they sometimes appropriated the principal Christian churches and often converted them into mosques. The Ottoman Sultans set aside a share of the spoils taken from Christians for the financial support of Muslim institutions. They taxed Christians far more heavily than Muslims like India where Zejiya was imposed on non-Muslims. Jews and Christians were excluded from most public offices. They did not allow Jews and Christians to bear arms or serve in the Ottoman army, but every year they conscripted a certain number of Christian boys, reared them as Muslims, and trained them as a special army which was so called army of the Janizaries and this army proved to be a peculiarly effective auxiliary to the main Turkish army and achieved remarkable victories. Some of them became governors and even Mumluk Sultans. Most of the Christians, among the Albanians, became Muslims, but the Armenians and the mass of the conquered peoples in the southeastern Europe clung to Christianity. As a matter of fact, Turks were not supremely intolerant and they did not force conversion by sword to Islam. Indeed, as soon as the Sultan Mohammed II had captured Constantinople, he issued a famous edict of toleration, not only according religious freedom to the Greek Christians but constituting them a special "nation" (or "millet") under their own patriach and with their own law and law-courts and traditions and customs. Other sultans created similar "millets" for the Armenian Christians, the Catholic Christians, and the Jews etc. In this way, the Ottoman Sultan was enabled to hold the patriarchs who were of Christian Church and other heads of "millets" personally responsible for the good behaviour of the subject Christians and Jews etc. At the same time the privileges accorded to the several, "millets" kept alive the spirit of nationality among the conquered Christian and Jew—people served to emphasize the confused and heterogeneous character of this vast Ottoman Empire which contained people of different races and of different faiths under their sway. Besides, beginning, with the reign of Suleiman the Magnificent, the Ottomon Sultans entered into treaties with powerful Christians states, granting to their citizens permission of pilgrimage to the Holy Land, privileges of trade and commerce in the Near East, and the right to live under their own laws and customs and to maintain their own law-courts while they were residing in the Ottoman Empire. The first of such treaties or "capitulations," as they were called—was concluded in 1535. Thus Ottoman Empire followed tolerant policy and it grew in power and prosperity in 16th century.

The Activities of Ottomon Empire after Suleiman the Magnificent

After the death of Suleiman the Magnificent in 1566, the Ottomon Turks continued to strengthen their hold upon Hungary and to fit out piratical expeditions in the Mediterranean Sea. The latter repeatedly ravaged portions of Sicily, southern Italy, and even of the Balearic islands, and in 1570 an Ottoman fleet-captured Cyprus from the Venetians. As such Malta and Crete remained as the only Christian outposts in the Mediterranean Sea. In this extremity, a Christian powers league was formed to save Italy. Its inspirer and preacher was Pope who was determined to save Italy from Muslim powers. Its inspirer and preacher was Pope Pius V, but Genoa and Venice furnished the bulk of its normal fleet, while Philip II of Spain supplied the necessary additional ships and the commander-in-chief in the person of his half-brother, famous Don John of Austria. This expedition, which comprised 208 vessels, met the Ottoman fleet of 273 ships in the gulf of Lepanto, off the coast of Greece, on 7th October, 1571, and inflicted upon Turkish fleet a crushing defeat. The Turkish warships were almost all sunk or driven ashore; it is estimated that about 8,000 Turks lost their lives. When news of this victory reached Rome, Pius V intoned the famous verse, "There was a man sent from God whose name was John." In this way, Pope praised Don John who was naval Commander of Christian fleet. As this victory was achieved due to Spanish help so it enhanced the prestige of Philip II.

The battle of Lepanto was of great political importance. It gave the naval power of the Muslims a death-blow from which it never recovered and it ended their aggressive warfare in the Mediterranean Sea. It was probably a crusade. King Philip II of Spain became champion of Roman Catholic Church and of

Pope. Hardly a noble in Spain or Italy was not represented in this battle. Volunteers came from all parts of the world. The celebrated writer Cervantes lost an arm at the battle of Lepanto in 1571. Western Europe was henceforth to be comparatively free from the Turkish peril. This battle ended the supremacy of Muslim powers in sea and later on Spain, England. Holland etc. became great naval powers and succeeded in discovering new trade routes, new lands and succeeded in establishing their colonies and empires in far off lands. According to Phiuips Price, "After this (Battle of Lepanto, 1571) Turkish naval power was confined to East Mediterranean while empire consolidated both in Europe and Asia."

Condition of Europe before Turkish Conquest

Weakness of the restored Byzantine Empire gave rise to the Ottoman Turks. The Christian disunion led to fall of Constantinople in 1453, which was capital of Byzantine Empire from many centuries.

The Byzantine Empire, which for centuries had stood as the bulwark of European civilization against the Muslim powers was shaken beyond recovery by the Latin conquest. The Greek restoration of 1261, though productive of a late flowering of scholarship and literature, was followed by not to revival of Greek power and Greek culture. The Emperors of the house of Palaeologus, re-entered upon a shrunken and divided heritage of Eastern Roman Empire but the acknowledged weakness of this empire was a perpetual invitation to insolvent attack of other powers. While the great Anatolian recruiting grounds of the old Byzantine Empire had long passed under the control of the Turcoman Sultan of the house of Seljuk Turks. The Turcoman ruled at Iconium and controlled vast lands. The major part of the Balkan peninsula was in the hands of the Bulgars. They ruled over land which is called, now Bulgaria. Greece, save for a province in the Peloponnese, was medley of Frankish fiefs. What remained to this old, Eastern Roman Empire was only a narrow strip of the Asiatic littoral, Constantinople and western Thrace, Thessalonica and the Thracian Chalcidice, the despotat of Mistra (in the Peloponnese), and a few islands in the Aegean. These, even if they were as valuable as Rhodes etc. which was taken by the Knights of St. Johan in 1310, the Eastern Christian Roman Emperor was unable to defend against any serious attack of any powerful power. This Christian Eastern Roman empire gradually became very weak.

History of Rise of Ottoman Turks

The history of the Ottoman Turks is one of a family of simple shepherds and herdsmen, gradually gathering power and influence by patience and justice, mingled with cruelty and craft, attracted the most heterogeneous elements to its service until it was in a position to make gigantic conquests, and to fashion and support a mighty Turkish Empire. Othman or Osman was the founder from whom the Ottoman Turk race derives its name. The scene of life work of Othman or Osman was the ill-defended frontier province of Bithynia, where he was engaged in warfare with the Greek Christians, first as an soldier, under the Seljiuk Turks but after 1307, he emerged as an independent prince. His religion was deep and his policy was adjusted to the counsels of the holy man of his faith. His administration of justice was remarkable in those venal and violent times for impartiality. But passionate as were his Muslim beliefs, he had the vision to discern that while the Muslim religion might be the creed of a great state, a Turkish tribe's rule could not suffice for its foundation. He must win by marriage, conversion, and by enslavement, his adherents. He chose his wife from Cilicia and seized a Christian damsel for his son, and employed as his after ego in war, Micheal of this Forked Beard, a Greek apostate from the Christian faith. Thus Othman or Osman extended his Turkish rule by all means and believed that end justifies the means.

The conquest of Bithynia which was begun by Othman was completed by Orchan, who was his eldest son. The two famous cities of Nicomedia and Nicaes etc. were conquered by Ottoman Turks. Later on Orchan conquered the fruitful Bithynian capital of Brusa. Instead of leading his Ottoman Turks against the Emirs of the Asiatic coast, or the people of the Balkan peninsula, the wise Orchan and his advisers employed themselves in building mosques and colleges, hospitals, caravansaries, and in the establishment of a coinage. They prescribed a national headdress (a plain cap of white felt) and, most important of all they organized the powerful army. It is in this period that the foundation of distinctive Islamic rule which made the Ottoman Turks for many centuries, the terror of eastern Europe was laid. The feudatory cavalry, the Ottoman Sultan's guard, and above all the famous infantry force, which won wars came into existence during this period.

Janissaries

The "Janissaries", or new soldiers, were Christian children, taken by force from their homes and brought up as Muslims, in seminaries designed to efface all trace of the pliable instruments of the Ottoman Turkish State. Some of them and those the most unfortunate were drafted off to serve as pages in the palace, others were employed in the civil service, but the main body passed into an infantry corps. Janissaries army was so brave and devoted that no Turkish army could match with Janissaries. An iron discipline effaced the army which expand the mind and the ideals which give elevation to the will. An iron discipline effaced the past and impoverished the future. He was made to forget father and mother, brothers and sisters. He could never hope for wife or children. The mily barrack was his home, fighting was his trade, the holy Koran was his religion, and he went forth to slay the enemies of the Sultan and of Allah with fanaticism of a monk or religious fanatic. The suggestion that this force should be recruited by a tribute of Christian children is said to have come from Black Habil, the proud Vizier of Orchan. It is clear that probably without such a tribute of children, a regular recruitment could not have been maintained. It followed, as a consequence, that the Ottoman Empire was made and maintained, not only, or even mainly, by men of the Ottoman Turkish race, but by Janissaries who were the slave children of Christian parents. The Janissaries, with the appointed stamp of military sub-service and the Muslim faith contributed a lot for the Ottoman empire and the most distinguished men of the Ottoman empire will be found to have passed from Christian homes through these institutions.

Rise of Serbs

While an Ottoman State was thus forming on a new mould in hither Asia, a new power, profiting by the civil wars and eruption of the Greeks, had manifested a raw vehemence in the Balkan Peninsula. It was power of the Serbs which became dominant in Balkan lands and later on formed the state of Serbia which is now Yugoslavia. Serbia was extended from the river Danube to the Aegean by the seizure of Albania, Epirus, and Thessaly etc. Triumphs which are deeply printed on the national memory of the Serbs, failed to satisfy the impatient leader of an impatient people. With an ambition which expanded with success Serbian leader Stephen assumed the imperial title, and proposed as the goal of his endeavors the subjection of the Greeks of Byzantine Empire. A year after Stephen's death, with his last dream unaccomplished Suleiman, the heir and successor of Orchan, crossed the Hellespont and founded on the Gallipoli Peninsula the first Turkish settlement of Serbia on European soil. Thus Suleiman I, laid the foundation of the Ottoman Power in Europe.

Ottoman King Murad I

With the accession of Suleiman's brother, Murad I, Europe at last discovered, what before it had not even suspected, the mighty force which had been steadily accumulating for more than a generation in the small unimportant Ottoman state beyond the Hellespont crossed to the Gallipoli Peninsula. Turkish force found itself invincible so Thessalonica and Adrianople, the two cities of the Greek Empire, passed into the hands of Turks. But as Orchan was cautious, so was Murad. He thought a pause was necessary to consolidate the European conquests and to convert Adrianople into a Moslem capital, and to set up that system of military fiefs which was necessary for the supply of the cavalry for army when these objects had been achieved, and the supremacy of the Ottoman Sultan had been established in Asia Minor, an advance might be made on Constantinople and Belgrade etc. The Christian Emperor was pliant. The spirit of the Greeks was low and submissive. It was only in the north-west, on the side of Serbia, that the Christian cause was likely to find an effective champion. Serbian leader Stephen Dushan was dead, but something of his spirit still survived in the breast of Kind Lazarus, his son, so while Ottoman Sultan was engaged in a victorious campaign against his Turkish adversaries in Asia, a great confederacy of the Christian people of south-eastern European states was organized under the leadership of the Serbian king for the destruction of the Mussulaman power of Ottomon Turks. Serbs and Bulgaria, Bosnians and Albanians, Poles, Hungarians, and even Mongols from the Dobrudja came together to oppose Ottoman Muslim powers. This improvised army, in which seven languages were spoken, proved inferior to an experienced Turkish force in which long and arduous discipline has been infused. In the battle of Kossove, which is commorated in the heroic and famous poetry of the Serbs. The Turks were victors, but in the hour of victory Sultan Murad fell by the hand of a Serbian patriot.

Twelve years of continuous success followed the Turks against the Christian Slavs. By the extension of the Ottoman

Empire's borders to the river Danubar from Euphrates and Tigris. The pitiless Bayazid, achieved victory both on the European and on the Asiatic front. As this Ottoman Sultan surveyed the scene from his voluptuous court at Brusa, he reflected upon his vast harem and vast kingdom was attacked by Taimur Lane.

Taimur Lane's Victory

Timur (or Taimurlane) the half Mongol, was an intellectual specialist in chess, theology, and conquest, and perhaps the greatest artist in destruction known in the savage annals of mankind. Bayazid was rash enough to provoke Timur. On the wide plain of Angora, the famous Ottoman army, the instrument of so many conquests, was enveloped and destroyed by an overwhelming force of Mongol cavalry of Taimur. Bayazid was made a prisoner, and as he proceeded in a closed litter upon his melancholy journey to Taimur's capital of Samarkand, the victorious army streamed westward to destroy his capital, and to ravage his country to the brink of the Hellespont and the Aegean.

The recovery of the Ottoman Empire after this overwhelming disaster is probably as remarkable as the inability of the Christian powers to turn it to its own advantage. As such what was lost in Asia was saved in Europe. Adrianople was now a Muslim city, in which where concentrated the resources of experience, courage, and memory and perseverance necessary for the restoration of the Turkish State. As such soon Ottoman Turkish State was established and Christian powers, did not try to check expansion of Ottoman power.

With the death of Sigismund in 1437, the scene was changed and when Murad the Ottoman Sultan was engaged in his wars of recovery the Hungarians discovered a great soldier in Hohn Hunyadi, reputed to be the natural son of King Sigismund by a Hungarian mother. He was placed in command of the army of Christian confederacy which was so wide so as to include not only Hungary and Poland, Serbia and Wallachia, the Duchy of Burgundy, Genoa and Venice, the Pope in Rome, and the army of Emperor in Constantinople. While a fleet of Italian and Flemish galleys was despatched to the Hellespont, Hunyadi, at the head of the vast Christian army of the league, crossed the river Danube and chased the Turks out of Serbia, and routed them both in south and north of the Haemus, and so the first time in their history, the Ottomans were compelled to sue for peace. Later on Ottoman Empire gained strength and it adopted again course of conquest and expansion.

Turkish Peril and Its Impact

Selim I and Suleiman the magnificent achieved notable victories. They captured and began expansion of Turkish Empire. For Mohammed the conqueror the fall of Constantinople, in 1453, was not an end but a beginning. This able and ambitious ruler regarded himself as commissioned to conquer the world for Islam, just as Lenin and his successors long afterwards, aspired to convert mankind to the Communist faith. Obedient people trained to every hardship but that of independent thought; a skilled professional army, and with powerful artillery gave Mohammed a commanding advantage against his divided Christian opponents. The roar of the Turkish guns was heard on the river Eupharates as well as on the river Danube, and on the Albanian coast. When this Sultan died in 1481, Asia Minor, Greece, and the main part of the Balkan Peninsula had been subjected to his rule. The army of Turks was astride to the Adriatic, holding the Ionian islands, Scutari, and Otranto etc. and menacing the security of Italy and Rome. After the brief rule of the nerveless Bayazet, the course of Turkish conquest was renewed by two of the most remarkable rulers of the Ottoman house, Sultan Selim I, who dethroned his father Bayazet in 1512, is next to Mohammed in conquests to his grand father. He was the principal architect of that vast Turkish Empire which endured the strain and stress of many centuries and was broken only by the tremendous shock of the last great war. It was Selim, who conquered Syria, Egypt, and Arabia etc. and upon the resignation of the last Caliph of the Abbassid line, brought the Kaliphate into the Ottoman house. To him were solemnly tendered the keys of the Kaaba at Mecca which was a symbol of both spiritual and temporal supremacy over the Muslim world. From the days of Selim, Istanbul the capital of Turkey became the undisputed center of Islamic power in these continents of Europe, Africa, and Asia Baghdad, which was the capital of the Abbassid Caliphs and the principal scene of Islamic civilization far beyond the reach of the Turkish mind, now sank to the insignificant city of a distant provincial city.

Conquests of Suleiman

Three great victories specially distinguish the military record of Selim's strenuous successor, Suleiman the magnificent. The capture of Belgrade from the Hungarians, the forced capitulation of the Knights of Hospitallers in Rhodes, and the bloodstained field of Mohacs (1526), which, sealed the doom of Hungary as an independent Kingdom were his great achievements. Belgrade was the gateway into Hungary, Rhodes the half-way house between city of Constantinople and Egypt, and Hungary the last effective barrier between the Turks and the Austrians who posed themselves as emperors of Holy Roman Empire.

The effect of these triumphs has the more impressive by reason of the high military reputation of the Magyar nation, and the confidence which was generally reposed in the skill, and valour of the Christian garrison of Rhodes. Under Hohn Hunyades and his son, Mathias Corvinus (1458), the frontiers of the Hungarian Kingdom had been triumphantly defended and the Turks were more than once were previously compelled to accept defeat. The reputation of the Knights, Hospitallers of Rhodes was perhaps of a different order, for while the Magyars had only recently won their way into the forefront of European history as the main defenders of the Christian land, the Knights of Rhodes had ever since the crusades been the eastern most point of defence at Christendom against Asian forces and Islam. Rhodes was a small island so, the Hospitallers in number and equipment were far inferior to their Turkish assailants. But they had survived so long that it was natural to think that they would survive for ever. That they were permitted to go down before the Turks, with passive acquiescence of Genoa and to the unconcealed satisfaction of Venice, was a sharp advertisement to the west that the Turkish navy, was mistress of the Aegean sea and that the two great Italian cities which had conveyed the Crusaders to Palestine had now turned round and had joined the formidable enemy.

The collapse of Hungary was equally spectacular and for the history of Europe probably far more momentous. It has been one of the standing misfortunes of Europe that the Poles, the Czechs, and the Magyars have never been able to devise any durable form, of political co-operation. An incompatibility of temper based upon differences of language, race, and religion has always proved stronger than the computation of political unity. From Bohemia, the richest and perhaps most civilized of these three monarchies; Poland was estranged by religion, Hungary by religion, race, and language alike. As the nobles of Poland, Bohemia, and Hungary knew how to extract a full measure of selfish indulgence from a weak and elective kingship, it followed that at the very time when the princes of the west were consolidating their power, the states in the eastern Europe were undergoing towards the opposite process of feudal dissolution.

The last act of Bohemian and Hungarian independence was marked by one of those rare opportunities which, once missed probably never return. In the spring of 1458 two remarkable men were elected to the thrones of Bohemia and Hungary. George Podiebrad who was a Czech noble and who had won the confidence of the Bohemian nation by his successful defence of the Hussite faith against a strong Catholic and Germanizing minority. His firmness, his moderation, his willingness to treat religion as a question upon which the State might tolerate different opinions, as well as his success in putting down rebellion gave him a position of national authority such as no Bohemian ruler probably had enjoyed since the days of Charles IV and perhaps no Bohemian ruler was destined to enjoy again till the days of Mazaryk. This youth who almost simultaneously mounted the Hungarian throne enjoyed a comparable advantage. Like Podiebrad, Mathis Corvinus was of national stock. He was the son of that illustrious soldier John-Hunyades, who had driven the Turks from before the walls of Belgrade. He inherited much of his father's vigour and valour and activity. To the qualities of a soldier, he added adherence to the arts of peace. This conqueror of Vienna was also the founder of Pressburg University, and the first to introduce among the backward nobles of Hungary many of the accomplishments of arts of Italy. A close alliance between two men, each in his ways so remarkable, would have been of the greatest value. The conjunction of Hungary and Bohemia under such rulers might have probably imposed a final limit upon the incursions of the Turk and averted from the two Christian monarchies of south-eastern Europe the destiny which was awaiting them of absorption in the Austrian Empire. It is strange that the two men though united by marriage, drifted into material antagonism which proved to be harmful to both kingdoms. Bohemia was attacked by Hungary, and Hungary in its turn, unfriended and alone, was allowed to go down before the Turk invaders. The cause of the sudden downfall of the kingdoms apparently on the high road to stability and power was probably religion. George of Bohemia stood by the compacts of the Council of Basal, which accorded to the Hussite Church in Bohemia the use of the cup by the laity in the sacrament. But to the Papal Curia, which had never accepted the Compacts, the policy of the Hussite chief was abohrant and intolerable. Podiebrad was ex-communicated. It was determined in Rome to depose the heretic and so king yielded to temptation and joined forces with the Catholic malcontents of Bohemia. In the terrible civil war which ensued, the Bohemian patriot was able to held his own, but in self-defence he was compelled to name as his successor a Roman Catholic prince from the Polish royal family. In 1471, on the death of Podiebrad, Vladislav Jagellon succeeded to his throne.

The advent to power of this insufficient polish alien who was in turn called to govern Bohemia and Hungary was a signal in each country for an outburst of aristocratic pretensions. Among the turbulent landowners of the eastern kingdoms the pole ruler was helpless like a French master in a class of rebellious English school boys. He had neither army nor treasury so he could do nothing and was expressly debarred from introducing any novelties into Hungary. Against the serious discipline of a Turkish army the feudal levies of such a monarchy were bound to fail.

The issue was tried upon the field of Mohacs (1526), a battle big with consequences for Europe, for after that Hungarian army had been defeated and Louis the last Jagellon king was killed, and the whole country up to the gates of Vienna had been over run by the Ottoman Turks, there was no life left in the proud Magyar aristocracy. The greater part of Hungary was seized and held by the Turks until late in the seventeenth century. The remainder part of Hungary fell to Ferdinand of Austria, the brother-in-law of Louis and the heir to his pretensions. The long subjection of Bohemia and Hungary to the Habsburg house of Austrian lasting until the Treaty of St. Germain after the World War I, was the direct result of that fatal day. Not until the Italian victory of Vittorio Veneto in 1918 had sent the Austrian Empire to disintegration were the effects of the field of Mohacs finally undone. According to Philips Price, "On the middle Danube, the Ottoman empire was clearly reaching the high tide of western advance." There was born upon the field of Mohacs a new spell of life for the Holy Roman Empire of Austria-Hungary for the Habsburg house. The defence of Christian Europe against the Turks, which might otherwise have been conducted by the Hungarian nation, now devolved as necessity upon the Archdukes of Austria as emperor of Holy Roman empire of Austria-Hungary. Their "Framshackle Empire," built up but a succession of happy marriages, received a justification in the eyes of Christian Europe by reason of the fact that though the eclipse of Hungary it had become the necessary and only valid bulwark against a great and aggressive Muslim Empire of Ottoman Turks. But as the Empire of the Habsburgs was made due to Turkish peril, so at each stage in the decline of Ottoman power it lost something of its original prestige power and authority. In the end Turks and Austrians both succumbed to the same enemy. The spirit of nationality born of the French Revolution first, set aflame the Christian nations of the Balkans and then, spreading among the Croatians, the Czechs and the Poles, involved the Austrian Empire in ruin : along with Ottoman empire in first world war of 1914-18. According to Philips Price, "In the reigns of Mohammed II, Selim the Grim, Suleiman the Magnificent, the Ottoman Empire reached its zenith in political power."

Rise of Russian Power and Its Impact over Ottoman Empire

Russian power grew under Ivan the terrible and Peter, the great in the 16th and 18th century. In the late 17th century, the Russians began a movement of expansion southwards. Under Peter the great according to Philips Price, "In the early 18th century, he accomplished what Selim the Grim and Suleiman the Magnificent had done for the Ottoman Empire in the 16th century when they opened the way to the East and the Mediterranean sea." Russia and Turkey became natural and hereditary enemies. Russia in 18th century had strong rulers while Turkey had a series of weak ones. Most important was Catherine the great about whom we will study in next section.

The Russo-Turkish Relations during Catherine's Rule

No sooner had Catherine of Russia secured the Russian crown she by her inactivity permitted Frederick the Great, to bring the Seven Years' War of 1756-63 to a successful issue. The death of Augustus III, elector of Sexony and king of Poland, gave her an opportunity to interfere in Polish affairs. She was not content with the Sazon line which was more or less under Austrian influence. With the astute aid of Frederick, of Prussia, she induced the Polish nobles to elect one of her own lovers, courtiers and favourites, Stanislaus Poniatowski as king who after election in 1764 became king Stanislaus II, and proved himself as the last king of an independent Poland. Catherine used her lover as a sacrificial goat and grabbed Poland. With the accession of Stanislaus II, the predominance of Russia was established in Poland. Russia entered into a sordid agreement with Prussia to uphold the anarchical constitution the unhappy and victimized Poland. When patriotic Poles made efforts, as they now frequently did, to reform their government, to abolish the liberum Veto, and to strengthen the Polish state, they found their attempts thwarted by the allies either by force of arms or by bribes of money or by tricks. Feuds among the Polish nobles, together with complaints of religious discrimination, afforded sufficient pretexts for the intervention of the neighbouring powers, especially Prussia and Russia etc.

A popular insurrection of Polish Catholics against the intolerable meddling of foreigners was crushed by the Russian troops of Catherine the great with the single result that the Russians, in pursuing some fleeing insurgents across the southern frontier, violated Turkish territory and in the way precipitated a war between the Ottoman Empire and Russia.

Russo-Turkish Relations during Catherine's Time

This Turkish war lasted from 1768 to 1774 and in this war Russia gained an upper hand. The Ottoman government was profoundly alarmed by the Russian foreign policy. It believed that the intrigues in Poland would end in the annexation of that state to Russia and consequent by upsetting of the balance of power in the East. Once Poland was disposed of, the turn of Turkey would come next. The Turks, moreover, were arranged by the French government, which, anxious to preserve the balance of power and to defend the liberties of Poland, was far off and financially too embarrassed to undertake a great war against Prussia and Russia.

The war between Russia and the Ottoman Empire fully confirmed the belief that the power of the Turks was rapidly waning. The Turkish troops, badly armed and badly led suffered a series of defeats. The Russians again occupied Azov, which Peter the Great had been compelled to relinquish. They overran the Rumanian principalities of Moldavia and Wallachia; and seized Bucharest. They seemed likely to cross the river Danube and enter in the Balkan peninsula. Catherine went so far as to fan a revolt among the Greek subjects of the Ottoman sultan, which as later on developed war of independence.

Treaty of Kuchuk Kainarji. At length, in 1774, the treaty of Kuchuk Kainarji was concluded between Russia and Turkey. It was a landmark both in the expansion of the Russian Empire, and in the contraction of the Ottoman Empire. By its provisions,

(1) the latter formally ceded Azov and adjacent territory to Russia and renounced sovereignty overall land north of the Black Sea; (2) The Ottoman Empire retained Wallachi, Moldavia, and Greece, etc. but promised that they would be better governed; (3) Russia obtained the right of free navigation for her merchant ships in Ottoman waters; and (4) Russia was recognized as the protector of certain churches in the city of Constantinople.

Within a few years after the signature of this treaty of Kuchuk Kainarji in 1774, Catherine the great established Russian control over the various Tartar principalities north of the Black Sea, whose sovereignty the Ottoman sultan had renounced. By a supplementary agreement in 1792, the Dniester River was made the boundary between the Russian and Ottoman empires.

The policy of Catherine the Great in respect of the Ottoman Turkish Empire bore mainly three significant results. In the first place, Russia acquired a natural boundary in southern Europe, and became the chief power on the Black Sea. Her ships might now pass freely through the Bosphorus and the Dzrdanellers straits out into the Mediterranean Sea to trade with western Europe. Russia's second "window to the west" was gained. In the second place, Russia was henceforth looked upon as the natural ally and rather friend of oppressed Christian nationalities of Eastern Europe within the realm of the Moslem Turks. Finally, the special clause conferring on Russia the protectorate of certain orthodox Greek churches in Ottoman Empire throughout afforded her a pretext for a later claim to protect orthodox Christians of Greek church throughout the Ottoman lands and consequently to interfere incessantly in Turkish affairs. After the treaty of Kuchuk Kainarji, the Ottoman Empire decayed and declined with ever-increasing rapidity, and Russia became an eager candidate for a liberal share of the spoils.

Ever while Catherine the Great was engaged in war with the Turkish Ottoman Empire, she had not lost sight of her Polish policy. Frederick the Great had undoubtedly hoped that she would, be busy in Turkish affairs. But the Wilytsarina Catherine was never so immersed in Turkish or in other matters that she may neglect, Russian ambitions in Poland. In 1772, therefore, she joined with Frederick of Prussia and with Maria Theresa of Austria in making the first partition of Poland. Prussia took major share. Prussia took West Prussia except the town of

Danzig. Austria took easily Galicia, except the city of Cracow. In all, Poland was deprived of about a fourth of her territory, a fifth of her population, and almost a half of her wealth. The Polish nationality no longer had common state or a common sovereign.

The partition of Poland of 1772, sobered many of the Polish magnates and brought them to perceive the necessity of radical political reform in Poland. Yet every effort which was made in this direction was rendered abortive by the shameful and hypocritical attitude of Catherine and the neighbouring sovereigns. For another twenty-one years Poland the wretched country struggled on became a victim of foreign tutelage. Although both Frederick and Maria Theresa died in this interval, their successors proved quite as willing to cooperate with the implacable Catherine as before. In 1793 Russia and Prussia effected a second partition of Poland, and in 1795, following a last desperate attempt of the Poles to establish a new government, Austria joined Russia and Prussia in the third and final dismemberment of this unhappy country of Poland. Desperately did the Polish patriotic leader, Kosciuszko, try to stem the tide of invasion which poured in from all sides. His few forces, inspite of great valour, and bravery were no match for the forces of veteran allies and the defence was vain. "Freedom shrieked when Kosciuszko fell." King Stanislaus resigned his crown and took himself to St. Petersberg. Poland ceased to exist as an independent State.

By the partitions of Poland of 1793 and 1795, Austria obtained the upper valley of the Vistula, and Prussia the lower valley including the city of Warsaw, while the rest of Poland, the major share — went to Russia. Ruthenia (or Ukrainia) and almost the whole of Lithuania thus passed into the hands of Catherine. Russia thenceforth bordered immediately on Prussia and Austria and Russia became geographically a vital member of the European family of nations. Thus Russia became too strong for Ottoman Empire.

Catherine the Great died in 1796. She thus survived her friend and confederate, Frederick the Great by a decade and after the final partition of Poland by a year. If it can be said of Peter that he made Russia European power. It can be affirmed with equal truth that Catherine made Russia a great power. The eighteenth century had witnessed marvelous growth of the Russian Empire in Europe, at the expense of Poland and

Turkey. It had acquired territory and strong capital. Her boundaries had been extended westward into the very center of the European Continent. It now embraced, not only Russians, but Ukrainians, Lithuanians, Estonians, Letts, and Poles and Grimea and Azov etc.

The rise of Russia was at the expense of her neighbours such as Sweden, Poland and Ottoman Empire. It gave them death-blow, Sweden had surrendered her eastern provinces and lost her control of the Baltic Sea. The Ottoman Empire had been forced to yield its monopoly of the shores and trade of the Black Sea. Poland had disappeared from the map. Probably greatest external factor for down-fall of Ottoman Empire was expansion of Russia at the cost of Muslim powers in Asia and at the cost of Ottoman Empire in Eastern Europe.

Russia tried to grab Ottoman Empire which was opposed by Britain, France and Austria, so Ottoman empire escaped from dismemberment. But ultimately Russian diplomacy succeeded in winning over France in 1894 and Britain in 1907. With the cooperation of Britain and France, Russia fought in First World War on question of Serbia. First World War brought end of the Ottoman Empire. The Muslim lands ruled by Chengiz Khan, Taimur Lane, Babar etc. were captured gradually by Russians and after World War II whole of Eastern Europe came under Russian influence. As such probably with the rise of Russian power fall of Ottoman Empire and of all Muslim lands became inevitable. Consequently British and French rule from Muslim countries such as Iraq and Palestine, Egypt and Syria and Lebanon etc. has disappeared and these countries have become independent but Russian rule over Mongolia, Turkistan, Samarkand, Bokhara and Taskend etc. remained intact and her influence over Eastern Europe remained strong but change is inevitable law of universe. Gradually power of Russia *i.e.*, of U.S.S.R. declined and gradually eastern European states became independent. With the failure of U.S.S.R. in Afghanistan, U.S.S.R. lost its integrity and U.S.S.R. became divided into many petty states though Russia remained greatest among them. Thus, U.S.S.R. which replaced Turkish empire disintegrated and now most of the Turkish states which were part of U.S.S.R. became minor independent states of Central Asia, as these are not considered states of Middle East, so need not to be described in this book dealing only with Middle East.

28

TURKEY

Turkey after 1453

After winning Constantinople Ottoman Empire became a world Power extending in three continents. But Battle of Lepanto of 1571, brought relief to Christian powers of Europe but Tunis, Algiers and Tripoli remained Ottoman's strongholds on the north shore of Africa and remained an Ottoman possession until 19th century. In 1574, Suleiman II died and period of decay and decline of Ottoman empire began just as fall of Mughal empire began after Aurangzeb. Most of the successors of Selim II were indisciplined and incompetent young men who proved unworthly to rule over such a vast empire. During 125 years of decline of Turkish Empire, a dozen Sultan ruled but all proved incompetent and worthless as ruler. The Ottoman political system which depended on personality of Sultan began to crumble. It is said the Character of Selim II and influence of Ibrahim and Rokelina began this process of downfall of Ottoman Empire. The wealth, splendour and ease of court sapped the energy of Sultans and their officials and army. Enormous size of Ottoman Empire and its administrative problems and economic difficulties contributed to its downfall. Equally damaging to its affairs was the influence and even actual formation of policy by women of the palace. The Sultans were surrounded by fanning officials and courtiers, truckling women and slaves, jugglers, wrestlers, musicians, buffons, dwarfs, eunchs soothsayers, astrologers and servile literate that they were unable to give time to manage the affairs of the state like Mughal emperors.

Selim II ruled from 1566 to 1574, Murad III 1574 to 1595, Mehmet III 1595 to 1603, Ahmed III 1603-17, Mustafa I and Osman 1618-22, Murad IV 1623-40, Ibrahim 1640-48, Muhammad IV 1648-1687, Suleiman II 1687-1691, Ahmed II

1691-95, Mustafa II 1695 to 1703 and Ahmed III 1703-30 but all proved worthless and unable to stop the disintegration and decline of Ottoman empire. Treaty of Karlomitz signed in 1699 between Ottoman Sultan and European powers indirectly acknowledged that all European powers are rightly concerned with the questions of Middle East. It recognized the interest and importance of Russian Czars with respect to the Ottoman empire and the Middle East and indicated the entrance of the Sultan's Christian subjects into the diplomatic pouches of European foreign office. Treaty of Karlomitz ended the fear of an Ottoman invasion and opened avenue for intervention to European powers in the affairs of Ottoman Empire.

The Decline of Ottoman Empire in 18th Century

The Sultans of the 18th century like Mughals were weak figures and were unable to cope with the corruption inefficiency, incompetence, harem intrigue, vested interests and indolence of court was beyond their power. Austria and Venice contested Ottomans in 17th century and in 18th century Russia gave a death blow to power of Sultans of Turkey.

Treaty of Karlomitz gave Russia Azov and about 80 miles of hinterland but Peter was not satisfied. Ahmed-III ruled from 1703 to 30 and Mahmud I from 1730 to 1754, Osman III 1754 to 1757, Mustafa III 1757 to 1774, Abdul Hamid 1774 to 1789, Selim III 1789 to 1807, Mustafa IV 1807-8 and Mahmud II 1808 to 1839. All these Ottoman Sultans proved incompetent and Viziers unfaithful. In 1711, Peter the great of Russia fell into an Ottoman trap but easy terms were granted to him due to treachery of Vizier when Turkish army was in a position to defeat Peter and crush Russian army.

Later on European powers forced many humiliating treaties on Turkish Sultans of which French treaty of 1740 allowed Frenchmen right to travel and trade in any part of Ottoman Empire, paying only 3% taxes on their goods and Frenchmen got extraterritorial rights to be tried and punished by their own officers and courts.

Similar treaties were granted to other powers. Not only this, France was given power and privilege under her flag protection to other Roman Catholic people of Europe, Catherine the Great, the most immoral queen of Russia inflicted several defeats over Turks but Turkey was saved as Austria, Prussia and Russia were more interested in division of Poland than in the affairs of Ottoman Turks. By treaty of Kuchuk Kinarji of

1774, Catherine's hold on Azov and the independence of Crimean Tartars was conformed. Navigation on river Danube was freed and the Black Sea was opened to Russian shipping Russian Ambassadors began to reside in Ottoman court and Russia got right to appoint consuls. The right of Russian pilgrimage to holy place was admitted and permission to build a Russo-Greek church was allowed. By Article XII and XIV, Sultan promised to protect Christian religion in his empire. These articles gave Russia pretext in 19th century to fish in troubled waters and to satisfy her ambitions in Balkans and straits on one pretext or the other.

Due to efforts of Peter the Great and Catherine the Great, Russian power grew and of Ottoman emperors declined, so Russians began to grab Ottoman territories. Russians also engineered revolts and supported them. So Christian subjects particularly Slav people revolted against Turkish rule and gained freedom gradually. This brought decay and disintegration of Ottoman power and intervention of other European powers in Ottoman affairs. Turkey began to be called sick man of Europe and other European powers in the beginning quarrelled among themselves but later on began to disintegrate and divide the Ottoman Empire and this brought downfall of Ottoman Empire.

The Development of Nationalism and War of Independence of Serbs and Greeks

The Serbs, with Russian backing, had revolted against the Ottoman Empire during the Napoleonic era, and for a brief time in 1812, they had maintained a government of their own at Belgrade under their redoubtable leader Kargeorge. And, though the Ottoman sultan regained Belgrade, while Russia was fighting with Napoleon Bonaparte and though Kargeorge was driven into exile and killed by a Serb rival, the restored Turkish rule was so harsh and arbitrary that it speedily invited the recurrence of rebellion in Serbia. In 1815, Milos Obrenovic, a peasant who had begun life as a cattle-driver and had served under Kargeorge, headed a new Serbian revolt, and two years later, having had Kargeorge murdered, he won from the Turks a grudging and reluctant recognition of his election as "supreme prince" of Serbia. Thenceforth, while nominally an agent of the Ottoman Sultan, Prince Milos did everything in his power to prepare the Serbian people, and to obtain Russian assistance, for a war of national liberation. Gradually Serbia became independent under the nominal suzerainty of Sultan of Turkey.

Greeks' War of Independence and Its Effect over Europe

Serbian developments did not attract much attention immediately. Austrian Prime Minister, Metternich who controlled European politics thought it insignificant, and the Tsar Alexander I perceived in it no advantage to Russia. Soon, however, there were Greek developments which troubled Alexander I and disturbed Metternich also. While these exponents of reaction and "legitimacy" were attending the international congress at Laibach in 1821, news came that the Greek governor of the Ottoman province of Moldavia the Prince Alexander Yosilanti, had just raised the standard of revolt against Sultan and was confidently expecting aid from Russia. Metternich was alarmed, he at once made appropriate representations to the Tsar Alexander I and the Tsar promptly disowned Yosilanti as such the revolt in Moldavia was easily suppressed by the Turks; and Metternich had the pleasure of confining the Greek leader in an Austrian prison for seven years. Metternich did not believe in supporting revolt anywhere.

But this was not the end of the Greek revolt as it was only a premature beginning. Earlier agitation of such Greek patriots as Rhigas and Korais was producing more and more fruit; such a nationalist secret society as Hetairia Philike was rapidly enrolling members for gaining independence. The theatrical display by a Greek prince in Moldavia was quickly succeeded by a national uprising in the Greek peninsula and in the Greek islands of the Aegean. The Turks this time were taken unprepared and were slaughtered in large numbers, so Turks had recourse to savage reprisals. The orthodox patriarch of Green church of Constantinople was murdered, and a wholesale massacre of Christians was ordered in Macedonia and Asia Minor etc. The utmost ferocity and cruelty, marked the struggle on both sides. Yet Metternich who controlled European politics was obdurate about helping the Greeks. In his opinion, they were revolutionaries and rebels against their "legitimate" sovereign, and he cynically remarked that their revolt should be allowed "to burn itself out beyond the pale of civilization" Metternich believed Peace, is indivisible and as such if Peace is allowed to be broken and it may be broken everywhere.

Nevertheless, the Greek revolt appealed to the imagination and enthusiasm of major European as nothing else did. Classicists saw in it a revival of the ancient glories of Hellas. Romanticists perceived in it a valourous struggle for national

Independence. Liberals beheld in it a popular uprising for liberty and democracy. Conservatives pictured it as the climax of the long series of crusades by civilized Christians against barbarous Muslims and against autocratic and corrupt Ottoman Empire. Youthful volunteers flocked to the Greek standard from every country of Europe. Delacroix painted sentimental pictures of Greek exploits and sufferings, and Lord Byron gave pen, fortune, and even for the cause of Greek independence. Popular sentiment, whether liberal or conservative or democratic were overwhelmingly in favour of the Greek insurgents. Not only in France and Great Britain, but, even in Russia also. Political ambition of the Tsars and a succession of wars had made Russians and Turks bitter hereditary enemies. While community of religion and culture linked the Russian and Greek peoples together. Consequently, as such it was with some difficulty that Czar Alexander I, now a most faithful henchmen of Metternich, restrained his own subjects from giving aid to Greek revolutionaries and managed until his death in 1825 to steer Russia in "legitimist" channels and did not help Greek revolutionaries.

Meanwhile the Greeks, contrary to foreign expectation and despite chronic domestic feuds proved stubborn and were more than holding their own against the Turks. But just about this time of Alexander's death in 1825, the Sultan, resolving upon a final drastic effort to subjugate his rebellious subjects, called to his assistances Ibrahim Pasha, the son of his governor Mehemet Ali of Egypt. Then for three years Ibrahim Pasha operated and fought in the Greek peninsula with energy and ferocity. He easily defeated the Greeks in the open field, and when hostile bands harassed his army, he took revenge by desolating the green country and sending thousands of the Christian inhabitants into slavery in Egypt. The resulting indignation throughout Europe decided Alexanders I's successor, the Tsar Nicholas I, to close his ear to the counsel of Austrian Prime Minister Metternich. In July, 1821, representatives of Great Britain, France, and Russian signed the treaty of London, agreeing to demand an armistic as preliminary to the settlement of the Greek question; and in October, after the Sultan of Turkey had refused to accept mediation, the combined fleets of the new allies destroyed the Turco-Egyptian squadron in the harbour of Navarino. The battle of Navarino was decisive in that it rendered useless and hopeless any further efforts of the Turks to suppress the Greek revolt, and also in that it registered a distinct setback to Metternich's policy of status quo and of preserving peace. Even the Russian Tsar was openly backing rebels against policy of "legitimacy" propounded by Metternich. Lastly Greek revolt encouraged others to revolt.

Greek's Independence and Deterioration of Turkish Empire

Russian Tsar Nicholas I proceeded to give free rein to the sympathies and patriotism of his subjects. In 1828, he formally declared war against the Ottoman Empire and in the next years, a Russian army, with some assistance from Milos Obrenovic and his Serbs, fought its way almost to Ottoman Capital of Constantinople. This obliged the Ottomon Sultan to sign the treaty of Adrianople. This treaty of Adrianople is of first-rate importance in the history of the dismemberment of the Ottoman Empire. By this settlement, the Ottoman Sultan virtually acknowledged the independence of Greece; granted practical autonomy to Syria and likewise to the Rumanian principalities of Moldavia and Wallachia etc. Ottoman, Sultan surrendered claims on Georgia and other provinces of the Caucasus to Russia; and recognized the exclusive jurisdiction of Russian consuls over Russian traders in Ottomon Empire.

An international conference in London subsequently fixed the Greek frontier at a line running from the Gulf of Volo on the east to Arta on the west, and in 1832 Prince Otto of Bavaria became the first constitutional king of Greece. This Greek independence paved the way for independence of other states of Ottoman Empire of Turkey.

The new kingdom embraced a comparatively small minority of the non Greek-speaking people, but in spite of its diminutive size and of the poverty and political feuds which long afterwards distracted it, it was a very real example of how, even despite Metternich's fulminations, nationalism and liberalism might bear fruit and get success. Greek war of Independence gave clarion call to other states to throw yoke of Turks and thus weakened Ottoman Empire as well as Metternich's quadruple and Holy alliance and policy of status quo.

Storm over the Balkans and Its Consequences

The Near Eastern Question. While Germany and Italy were achieving national unity, nationalism was also stirring among the subject peoples of the Ottoman Empire particularly in Eastern Europes. By the 1830's the Greeks, Serbs, and Montengirins were free to develop their nationhood, but the heavy hand of

Turkish weak misrule still lay upon the Bulgarians. The Rumanians languished under the "protection" of Russian. And, as nationalism sought fulfilment of hopes in the Balkans, the political scene was complicated by the rivalries of the great powers, especially the rivalry between Austria, Britain and Russia. These rivalries as they affected the Ottoman Empire formed problem what was known as the Near Eastern question.

The Near Eastern question has been defined as "the problem of filling up the vacuum created by the gradual disappearance of the Turkish Empire from Europe." Britain, which consistently opposed Russian designs on the Near East, feared that if any great power such as Russia or Germany etc. should gain control in this area, the balance of power in Europe would be altered decisively. And, if Russia were to obtain the Straits, Russian naval power in the eastern Mediterranean sea would challenge Britain's communications with India. Although most Englishmen detested the corrupt rule of the Ottoman Sultans but during the most of the nineteenth century the British government supported the preservation of Ottoman Empire.

In the nineteenth century this Near Eastern power struggle brought three Russo-Turkish wars and in two wars such as Crimean War in which France, England, and Russia fought either with or against Turkey. In addition to this numerous revolts were sponsored by subject nationalities against the Ottoman Sultan's government. The same Near Eastern question in the twentieth century led to three Balkan wars before 1914 and helped to precipitate the catastrophe of the First World War of 1914-18 which gave a death blow to Ottoman empire.

Anglo-Russian Rivalry in the Near East

Russian expansion at the expense of the Turkish Empire had begun during the reign of Catherine the Great in 18th century. After six years of war, the Turkish Sultan had been compelled to sign the Treaty of Kuchuk Kainarji in 1774, which awarded Azov and the north coast of the Black Sea to Russia, granted the Russians free navigation for their merchant ships in Ottoman waters (including the Straits), and, lastly, recognized the Russian Tsar as the protector of all eastern Orthodox Christians of Greek Church in the Ottoman Empire. On several occasions Russia was to use this final concession as an excuse to intervene in Turkish affairs and try to increase her territories and influence in Ottoman Empire.

Not long afterwards, the famous British statesman Willian Pitt the Younger denounced Russia's ambition to dismember Turkish Empire. Austria was also beginning to fear Russian expansion. Britain and Austria realized that weakness of Turkey was a danger to their national interests, not because Turkey was strong but because it was too weak. In the meantime Russia continued to take over slowly former territories of the Ottoman empire, thereby expanding westward along the north shore of the Black Sea and southeastward along its east coast, which extended into the Caucasus region. During the Greek revolt of 1821, the jealousies of the big powers finally led France, England and Russia to act cooperatively in putting an end to this fighting. The result was Greek independence without expansion of Russian influence in the Balkans. Thus Greek became free but remained out of Russian sphere of influence.

England's Policy of Protecting Turkish Empire

The Ottoman empire seemed on the very point of extinction in 1831, when the Sultan's nominal representative in Egypt, the Pasha Mohammed Ali, attacked his Ottoman master. To prevent the establishment of this new and probably stronger government at the Straits, the Tsar sent an army to protect the Ottoman capital, extracting in return the Treaty of Unkiar Skeles. In essence this treaty made Turkey a protectorate of Russia. The Straits were closed to all war vessels except those of the signatories, making the Black Sea virtually a Russian lake. Frightened by this Russian coup, British Statesmen determined to stop influence and expansion of Russia. For twenty years the leading advocate of this policy was lord Palmerston, who for a long time remained either foreign minister or Prime Minister from 1830 to 1865. Same policy was followed by Prime Minister Disraeli later on.

The Near Eastern Question and Rise of the Balkan Nations of Eastern Europe

In the nineteenth century the Turkish Empire in Europe included the whole of what is known as the Balkan Peninsula, which contained Rumania, Bulgaria, Yugoslavia, Albania, Greece and Cyprus etc. 'Balkans' is a Turkish word meaning mountains, and as a term of political geography it is applied to the mountainous country between the river Danube and the Aegean Sea. This region, from the pre-historic times, has been the meeting place of various races. Here resided Greeks, Serbs, Bulgurs and Albanians etc. Among the Balkan States it is convenient to include Rumania also, although it is situated north of the river Danube. The inhabitants of the Balkans were mostly Christians with only a sprinkling of Turkish overlords, who were Muslims. Here for centuries the Crescent had ruled over the Cross, and although the Turkish rule had not been intolerant in many ways, it was wholly incompetent and unprogressives at times of revolt etc., it could be ruthlessly cruel to rebel subjects.

Disintegration of Turkish Empire

In the eighteenth century the Ottoman power in Europe began to decline as has been briefly stated. Turkey had lost Hungary in 1699 by the Treaty of Karlomitz French gained privileges by the treaty of the 1740 and Russia had also begun to press southwards, driving back the Turks and had, by the Treaty of Bucharest in 1812, acquired Bessarabia. She thus advanced her territory to the river Pruth on the west side of the Black Sea. But the interest and passion aroused by the decadence of Turkey and the southward advance of Russia, was not generally enough to make it a matter of European diplomacy. It concerned the European Powers which were in the immediate neighbourhood viz. Austria and Russia. It was probably Napoleon who turned Europe's gaze towards the East. His attempt to seize Egypt and Syria, together with his oft-repeated insistence that Constantinople meant the empire of the world, helped to familiarise the European statesman with the importance of the Turkish question. Moreover, there was a general fear that the balance of power would be fatally upset, if, as the result of Turkey's increasing weakness, her empire was completely absorbed by the expanding and aggressive power of Russia. The Russians were next door to the Balkans and they were of the same Slav race as most of Turkey's European subjects. They were members of the same Orthodox Christian Greek Church to which most of the Christians subjects of Turkey belonged. Added to these facts was the well-known ambition of Russia, to control the Black Sea and the Straits so that she might command a passage to the Mediterranean Sea. It was this sense of Russian danger that stimulated major European powers such as Austria, Britain, France etc. to an increased attention to the affairs of the Near East. Thus one important aspect of the Eastern question was the fear of Russian aggrandisement at the expense of Turkey. In the beginning Britain and France tried to save Ottoman power from Russian aggression. With the changed attitude of the Powers there began to occur new developments in the Ottoman empire which gave rise to the Eastern Question, which confronted Europe with new aspects of the problem. The weakness of Turkey besides inviting external aggression, encouraged the subject nationalities and powerful vassals states of Europe and Egypt to make a bid for independence. The nineteenth century's awakening and ideal of nationality began to touch the Balkan Peninsula also, and the Christian nations under Turkish rule became restive under its inspiration. They sought to free themselves from Turkish yoke, with the result that wars and atrocities became almost chronic in the Balkan region during Ottoman rule. Thus the Ottoman Empire was threatened both from within and without, by aggression of external powers as well as by threat of disintegration by subject nations. By Russia, Turkey felt aggression as well as revolt, by her own Christian, subjects. This two fold aspect of the problem and the resulting conflict of interests, introduced new factors into what is known as the Eastern question. Disintegration of Ottoman Empire and rivalry of European powers gave rise to Eastern question.

Short Note on Eastern Question

In the words of Lord Morley the Eastern question may be described as a "shifting, intractable and interwoven tangle of conflicting interests, rival peoples and antagonistic faiths." Eastern question was vary complicated question. In part, it was the result of the rise of a feeling of nationality among the Balkan Christian peoples, and in part it was the problem of the declining Turkish Ottoman empire and of the divergent interests of Great Powers of European continent in the Near East. This Eastern problem, took different shapes at different times, but one of its constant factor was and is even now, the ambition of Russia at the expense of Turkey. What was to take the place of Ottoman Empire in the event of its disappearance from the world? This was central problem of the Eastern Question. Ottoman Empire extended in Iraq, Lebanon, Arab, and Syria, Palestine etc. in Asia, in Balkan Peninsula in Europe and in Egypt, Sudan, Tunisia, Algeria and Libya etc. in Africa and a Caliph of Islam, Sultan of Turkey was spiritual head of all Muslims.

"The ambition of Russia at the expense of Turkey were a constant factor in the Eastern question from the days of Peter the Great to the First World War of 1914." As stated before, that Russia was bound to the Balkan peoples by the ties of religion and race, as both belonged to Greek orthodox church and Slav race so the Czar claimed the rights of protecting them from Turkish misrule. But the Russian Czar's sympathy ran in the same direction as his ambition, and beneath his benevolent intention, there was the transparent design of securing the much-desired access to the Mediterranean sea and domination over Eastern Europe. Russian policy in the Near East had two aims in view, *viz.*, to dismember Turkey and to seize Ottoman empire as the prize, and if that would prove impossible, to dominate her by forcing upon the Sultan a number of unequal treaties which would keep Turkey and Eastern Europe in a state of vassalage under Russian overlordship. Several such treaties already existed such as those of Kachuk-Kainarji (1774) and Bucharest, which give the Czar some kind of right to intervene in the internal government of the Porte (Turkey). Being encouraged by these treaties Russia become ambitious to establish her domination over Eastern Europe. This design was checked upto Second World War but after 1945, Russia has succeeded. The lengthening shadow of the Russian bear in the Near East was very disquieting to the British Lion. Suspicion about Russian designs upon Ottoman Empire was the key-note of the British policy. British ministers, some French diplomats began to see in the Russian aggrandisement a serious menace to Anglo-French interests in the East. They feared that the establishment of Russian control over Ottoman Empire would greatly weaken British hold upon India and French hold over Indo-China. Hence they watched with keen suspicion every Russian movement which threatened to interfere with the Ottoman empire which was the gateway to Asia. Thus over the Eastern question there developed something like chronic antagonism between Great Britain, France, Austria and Russia. Throughout the nineteenth century England, France stood forth as the champion of Turkey against Russian aggression. Anglo French policy aimed at checking Russian advance by preserving the integrity of the Ottoman Empire. Lord Palmerston who remained Foreign Minister and Prime Minister was the chief exponent of this policy. He discarded and disbelieved in Turkey being a sick man and so he tried to pressure Ottoman Empire. He believed in the possible regeneration of Turkey and held that, given suitable opportunity, she might again become a respectable power. For a long time England was successful in holding Russia in check but she could not prevent the dismemberment of the Turkish Ottoman Empire due to revolt of his subjects. It is somewhat ironical that while posing as the champion of the integrity of Turkey, England and France had managed to put a valuable share of Turkish spoils into their own pockets.

Austria's interests in the Balkan region were perhaps more vital than those of Russia and Great Britain and France etc. Austrian empire faced Ottoman attacks and saved Europe from Turkish menace. She was an almost land-locked empire with only a short-coast line at the head of the Adriatic where her position was precarious. Austrian empire contained Austria, Hungary, Czechoslovakia and parts now included in other countries at that time but she was badly placed for sea-borne traffic. Hence economically it was very essential that the Austrian empire should have a secure outlet to the sea and for this she must expand in the direction of the south-east which was under Turkish empire. Secondly, in the absence of good ports, the great volume of her commerce passed along the Danube valley, and so it was her vital interest to prevent the establishment of Russian supremacy at the mouth of river Danube. Thus Russia was sure to grab-eastern Europe conquests and if her southward move towards Ottoman Empire was allowed to go on unchecked. Thus Austria was Russia's rival in the Balkans. In the first half of the nineteenth century Austria did not take any active part in the affairs of the Near East as it remained busy with French affairs but kept a vigilant watch upon Russia's movement. Austrian Prime Minister Metternich sought to counter Russia's Balkan ambitions with the doctrine of legitimate dynasties. But after the expulsion and loss of Austria of the possessions of Italy and Germany, she turned with increasing consciousness to the south-east in order to find compensation at the expense of weak Turkey. Besides, this she feared the growth of the pan-Slavic movement in the Balkans, which was encouraged by Russia and which was stirring the race consciousness of the Slavs. She felt nervous that this movement might spoil the loyalty of her own Slav subjects in her own southern dominions. Henceforth it became her policy to cripple and confine the leading Slav states in the Balkans, *viz.* Serbia, Bulgaria and Rumania etc. whose growing nationalism was a menace to the integrity of the Austrian Empire which contained various races and which was surrounded both by Ottoman empire and Russian dominions. To France, the Eastern question involved issues commercial and religious, rather than political. She was the traditionally of Turkey and of Abbasid Caliphs since the time of Charlemagno and had befriended her on many an occasion in the eighteenth century. As a consequence she had obtained special trading privilege and right to protect Roman Catholics she was mainly interested in developing them in Ottoman empire and specially in Syria and Egypt etc. She was also the traditional protector of the Roman Catholic Christians in the East. But in spite of this traditional friendship, France was never a consistent or enthusiastic champion of Turkey. To her the Eastern Question was mainly one which concerned her naval and religious and commercial position in the Mediterranean sea and in Ottoman Empire. As regards Germany, the affairs of the Near East did not appeal to her till the last quarter of the nineteenth century. Bismark held himself aloof from Balkan complications and remarked that "the whole Eastern Questions was not worth the bones of a single Pomeranian grenadier." But in 1878 at the Congress of Berlin in which he presided, he posed himself as an "honest broker" and administered a check to Russia in order to befriend Austria which created rift between Russia and Germany and lead to Franco Russian alliance later on. Thenceforth Germany began to develop greater diplomatic activities in the East, fraternising with Turkey, drilling her army and securing permission for German capitalists to build the Berlin, Baghdad Railway. Thus after Berlin conference of 1878, Ottoman Empire of Turkey and Germany came close to each other and developed friendship and both fought together and suffered defeat which ultimately brought disintegration of Turkish Empire.

The Causes of Decay of the Ottoman Empire

Main cause of disintegration of Ottoman Empire was that it depend on personality of Sultan and all Sultan after 1574, who inherited there were inefficient, luxurious weak and worthless. Perhaps one cause of the decay of the Turkish Empire was administrative inefficiency. The Turks were warriors but they never displayed any aptitude for civil government. Everywhere the administration was paralysed by inefficiency insubordination and corruption. The control of the Central Government over the provincial governors and other agents was deplorably defective. The Sultan's representatives in outlying provinces like Egypt, Algiers and Tunis etc. behaved more like tributary princes than administrative officials of Central Government. Thus, the process of dismemberment was going on Turkey like Mughal Empire due to selfishness of governors and officials and nobles even before the rise of the Christian nations of the Balkans. The same lack of administrative capacity was emphasized by her inability to weld together into a political whole the disparate dominions and provinces which vast empire of Turkey had amassed. She had subdued many races in south eastern Europe as well as in Asia and Africa but had made no attempt to assimilate them, nor to fuse them into one body-politic. Full of contempt for the conquered people the Turks cared only to exploit them, leaving them in a kind of semi-independence position as far as administration was concerned. Secondly, the Turkish Empire was built up by military power, and when this declined, the empire lacking any other cohesive force, began to fall in pieces before the onslaught of the aggressive nationalism of the Balkan peoples. There was religious difference which created enemity between ruling Muslim class and Christian subjects. In Egypt and in Arab provinces ambition of governors brought ruin of Turkish Empire.

According to S.N. Fisher "The character of Selim II or the influence of Ibrahim and Roselend has been described as a cancerous development which brought its downfall." The shift in world trade from Mediterranean to Atlantic lessened Turkish trade and income and paved the way for its downfall. Source of booty disappeared as conquests stopped and according to S.N. Fisher in the regimes of Sultan from 1566 to 1730, financies were always strained. With the reign of Murad III, the Sultans began to obtain bribes for appointment which quickly filtered down to the lowliest officials. Incompetent favourites began to be appointed on high posts which brought downfall of Turkish empire.

According to S.P. Fisher, the influence and even the actual formation of policies by women and slaves of palace proved harmful. According to S.N. Fisher presents of pretty and clever slaves was made to distract Sultan Murad's attention from state affairs. Murad fathered about one hundred children of whom 20 sons and 27 daughters survived him. As such strangling of brothers became common and Mehmed III 1595-1603 strangled 19 brothers. This practice contributed a lot to bring downfall of Turkish Empire. In such an atmosphere intrigue flourished. Personal spies, agents, forgeries, intercepted letters, perjury and personal gossip according to Fisher became acknowledged technique of Government. Apparently executions of Suleiman's sons, Mustafa and Beyzid resulted due to such machinization.

Slave system proved harmful. The degradation of Sultan, high officers of the state and the military invited insubordination and revolt in army. Debacuhery, sodomy, indolence, wine sapped the energy of ruling class and ruddy warrior in boots became pale persons in petticoats. Efforts of all reforms failed on the sharp rocks of reality. In such an atmosphere African governors such as Mehmet Ali of Egypt revolted and revolts began to occur in the whole Empire because to quote Fisher again, no person, no property was secure against seizure from Sultan Ibrahim. "The Ottoman Empire was the scene of court intrigue, mily insubordination and violence, judicial venably, local oppression and provincial revolt. All these things were enough for bringing downfall of Turkish Empire.

Above all this development of nationalism brought revolt of Christians in Eastern Europe and of Arabs in Egypt and in Fertile Crescent. Above all ambitions of Russia whose policy was to grab Turkish parts brought its downfall. Britain and France tried to preserve Turkish Empire from Russian aggression so its disintegration was delayed but when Britain and France and Russia came together and Turkey fought on the side of Germany, it fell. Egypt, Iraq and Palestine was grabbed by Britain, Syria, Lebanon and Algeria to France and Rebt to Russia but later on all became independent and rivalry is now breaking world peace.

Dismemberment of Turkish Empire

Like Poland, Turkey in her moribund and declining state might have easily provided a territorial feast to the ambitious powers like Russia. Bat the "sick man" of Europe showed unusual recuperative powers, and his political heirs had to wait long before they could succeed to the inheritance and division of spoils. There were two main factors which delayed the dismemberment of European Turkey and also of Ottoman empire First, although a declining power, the Turks retained their fighting genius and could as late as 1788 could defeat the Habsburg forces of Austrian empire. Secondly, by her geographical position Turkey was removed from the center of European politics. Europe was more interested in empire and was primarily concerned with Turkey. It was only in the nineteenth century that the Eastern Question aroused European interest and was lifted into the prominence of an international problem. To these causes may be added the conflicting interests and rivalries of the European Powers. These made the Eastern question very difficult of solution and prevented the adoption of any agreed settlement to Eastern question Turkey also was clever enough to make use of the jealousies of the Powers to prolong the longevity of her empire. Turkey first gained support of Britain and France to check Russian aggression, consequently Crimean War and Berlin conference thwarted Russian designs. Later on Turkey took support of Germany but when both Turkey and Germany were defeated in World War I so its disintegration became inevitable.

The Dismemberment of the Turkish Empire and Its Consequences

The first national rising in the Balkan Peninsula took place in Serbia in 1804. It was led by Kara George, a pig-dealer because pigs and pig-dealer were hated in Islam. For a time the Turks were harassed and driven away from Serbia but they regained it in 1815 as Europe, then was in the grip of the Nepoleonic wars and could not take any notice of this movement and so the Serbs fought on alone against mighty Turkish power. In 1817, Kargeorge, the rebel leader was murdered by a rival party headed by Milosh Obrenovitch, who now assumed the leadership of the Serbian national cause. After many years of war and negotiations Milosh Obrenovitch strongly supported by Russia, secured from Turkey some measure of autonomy for Serbia and the recognition of his own right as the "Hereditary Prince of the Serbs" under Turkish suzerainty. Serbia, though still tributary to Turkey, became autonomous with a hereditary princely house. Within a short time this little state was placed under Russian protection. Later on conflict of Serbia and Austria brought World War I as Serbia was supported by Russia and France and Austria by Germany. Serbia is now called Yugoslavia.

Relations of Turkey and Greece

It is said that "Independence of Greece gave a death blow to Ottoman Empire and its disintegration began". The second step in the dismemberment of the Ottoman Empire was taken by the Greeks. Among the subject races of the Porte *i.e.* Sultan of Turkey the Greeks had been treated with marked favour and toleration due to their ancient culture and wisdom. They had been entrusted with high administrative posts and were also allowed to control a large share of trade and commerce. In the Greek Islands and on the coasts of the Aegean seas they enjoyed practical autonomy. Their religion was fully tolerated. But towards the end of the eighteenth century the aggressive national consciousness of the Greeks was stimulated by an intellectual revival which recalled the glories of the ancient Hellas. Into the soil thus prepared, the French Revolution had flung by broadcast echoes of liberty equality and of fraternity etc. the seeds of new ideas, which awakened aspirations for national independence in Greeks. The first practical manifestation of this new spirit took the shape of a secret society founded in 1814, and known as Philke Hetaria. Its objects were to disseminate and propagate nationalist doctrines and to expel the Turks from Eastern Europe and to revive the old Greek empire of the East. This society expected Russian support because the Greeks and the Russian belonged to the same branch of Christianity, and because the downfall of Turkey would contribute to Russian aggrandisement and expansion of domination. Relying upon Russian support, and stimulated by the example of Serbia, the Hetaria began armed preparation for a revolt against Ottoman empire at the earliest opportunity Greeks also had British and French sympathy so they took courage to engineer a war of independence against weak and corrupt Turkish Government.

The War of Greek Independence

It is said that Greek war of independence was a clarion call for other states to flight for independence against Ottoman Empire because after Greek War of independence other countries which were under Turkish Empire revolted and got freedom.

The much-looked for opportunity came in 1821 when Ali Pasha, the Turkish Governor of Janina, quarrelled with the Sultan and went to fight war with him. This internal dissension of ruling elite class of Turkish gave opportunity for revolt, and insurrections broke out simultaneously in Moldavia under Prince Hypsilanti, and in the Morea in Southern Greece. The Prince Hypsilanti expected Russian help, but forgot that Czar Alexander I was the founder of the Holy Alliance and, as such, would not countenance a revolution. As such Hypsilanti was defeated by the Turks and the movement of Greek independence fizzled out due to lack of support of Russia and Metternich's policy of non-intervention and of not giving help to rebels. But in the Morea and in the islands of the Aegean sea, this rising assumed formidable proportions. The Greeks began the war with a wholesale massacre of the Turks and with other acts of revolting cruelty. The evil example thus set was too faithfully followed by the Turks to take revenge. This war thus developed into one of mutual extermination, and was conducted on both sides with the utmost ferocity and blood-curdling atrocities. For the first six years *i.e.* from (1821 to 27) the European Powers did not intervene forcefully and Greeks were mostly left to their unaided efforts. The concern of European Powers was not so much for the Greeks as for the attitude of Russia who might exploit this situation for her own aggrandisement and expansion. Metternich who controlled European politics at that time with his dread of insurrection against legitimate authority, looked upon the Greeks as rebels, who must be left to their fate. He wanted to let this revolt "burn itself out beyond the pale of civilization." The King of Prussia and the Czar of Russia Alexander I were persuaded by Metternich to share this point view. Great Britain also, with her doctrine of non-intervention and respect for the integrity of Turkey, followed the same policy of inactivity in the beginning but volunteers like Lord Byron fought for cause of Greek independence and by 1827, there came a change in the situation, which made foreign intervention inevitable. The Ottoman Sultan had called upon his vassal, Mehemet Ali who was governor of Egypt, to come to his help. Ibrahim the son of Mehemat Ali, landed in the Morea and swept everything before him. The fall of Missolonghi in 1826, followed by the capture of Athens next year, broke the backbone of Greek resistance. The Greek cause of independence was on the point of collapse. A wave of sympathy spread through out Europe for Greek people with such a rich cultural heritage Loud were the protests and agitations against the ruthless subjugation of a country which is the cradle of European civilisation. This sympathy for the Greek people was reinforced by the fear of the princes. The European Powers feared that Russia might take isolated action. The wavering Russian Czar Alexander I died in 1825 and was succeeded by his more resolute brother, Nicholas I. The new Czar of Russia had a will of his own and did not consider himself bound to the policy of the Holy Alliance or with the policy of Metternich Lord Canning, who had succeeded Lord Castlereagh to the British foreign office, was a firm friend of liberty abroad. His policy was to help the Greek cause without alienating Turkey. To prevent independent action on the part of Russia, he induced France and Czar Nicholas I to combine with England in forcing an armistice on the Porte, and compelling her to accept the joint mediation of European powers. A joint note was accordingly despatched to Turkey but the Ottoman Sultan *i.e.* Porte refused to accede to the proposals of armistice. Thereupon the allied fleets of France and England completely destroyed the Turkish fleet at Navarino after a joint encounter in 1827. This naval victory encouraged the Greeks and eventually secured their liberation and Greek became an independent country. But apart from this, all the advantages of joint intervention were reaped by Russia alone, Lord Canning was dead and his policy was reversed by Lord Wellington who now became British Prime Minister. As England was still officially at peace with Turkey, Lord Wellington hastened to apologise to the Porte, declaring Navarino as an "untoward event." He withdrew England from any further participation in the Greek question because he favoured preservation of Turkey to protect Indian and Eastern Empire and thus allowed Russia a free hand. The result was that the situation which Lord Canning had striven to avert, did come to pass and the Greek question virtually lay in the hands of Russia. On her own responsibility Russia declared war against Turkey and forced her to come to terms. By the treaty of Adrianople of 1829, Turkey recognised the independence of Greece and granted practical autonomy to the principalities of Wallachia and Moldavia. To Russia she granted an increase of territory in Asia, as well as increased commercial and political rights. By the convention of London in 1832, the new kingdom of Greece was placed under the joint guarantee of the major European Powers. Thus Greece became independent and this served as clarion call for other countries to lead a revolt against Ottoman rule. The Treaty of Adrianople was thus a signal victory for Russian policy. It gave Russia increased rights and privileges, and initiated the process of dismembering the empire of Turkey which Russia wanted. It largely added to the power and prestige of Russia, for it was she, who ushered into the world an independent Greece under her influence patronage. The policy of England, on the other hand was cloudy, wavering, hesitating and inconsistent. Her action in supporting Greece was contrary to her general policy of maintaining empire of Turkey. After Navarino, she let the matters drift and allowed Russia, whose advance she dreaded to carry off the laurels.

Importance of Greek Independence

The Greek question is highly significant. It afforded the first example of the victory of nationalism since the Congress of Vienna, and as such it struck a stout blow to Metternich's system and policy of non-intervention. Secondly, it demonstrated the common interest of the European Powers in the Near East, and the practical possibility of a resuscitation of the Christian States against weak Ottoman Empire. The help which Turkey had to seek from Mehemet Ali, as well as her defeat at the hands of Russia, exposed her weakness to the world. This led to the next development of the Eastern question and disintegration and fall of Ottoman empire.

Beginning of Reforms in Turkey

For a very long time Turkey was one of important world powers and dominated Islamic World. Russia rose as a great power during the rule of Peter the great and Catherine the great and in 1774, Turkey suffered a disastrous defeat at the hands of Catherine of Russia and had to sign the humiliating peace of Kuchul Kainarji. As such Abdul Hamid I came to conclusion that if Turkey did not reform her army and administrative system of Government end would not be far off. As such he encouraged his son Salim III to being reforms.

Conditions of Turkey during 18th Century. It was during 18th century that military power of the Ottoman Empire declined. During this period, Turkey had to come in conflict with Russia, which was following an aggressive policy under Catherine II. In 1783, as a result of aggressive policy, Russia could extend her empire upto Black Sea and annexed Crimea. This annexation was a step forward towards disintegration of the Ottoman Empire. If the Ottoman Empire was to save itself from disintegration it was unavoidable that military reforms of far reaching importance and significance should be introduced. According to M. Philips Price, "Turkish society had been democratic in a Prime Minister and tribal sense in the days of Seljuks and the early Osmanales and had only been over laid by the authoritarian rule of Sultans."

Support from France. When Russia was following aggressive policy, it was quite natural that all such countries which had clashing interests must protect themselves from hug of Russian bear. Accordingly, France became conscious, because she feared that at any time Russians might advance their claim in Levant where French were interested. On way to check Russian aggressive policy was to strengthen Turkey. Accordingly, France extended her hand of cooperation and provided competent military officers for training military officers of Turkey on latest methods of war. But due to certain peculiar circumstances Turkey got involved in war with Austria and Russia and the whole of training just got held up. According to Philips Price,

"As a result of continued defeats at the hand of Western Europe and of Russian the Turkish began to realize that medieval society was passing, if the Ottoman empire did not wake up, it would sooner or later end, so reforms began."

Military Reforms under Selim III. Sultan Selim III was quite keen that army of Turkey should be trained on modern lines and that in strength and equipment it should not in any way be inferior to any military force of a European nation. Nizami-i-Cedid was prepared which gave guidelines on which military of the country was to be prepared, type of arms equipments to be provided and sort of discipline to be introduced and enforced. A new corps of infantry was introduced in the Turkish army. The Ottoman Sultan fully realized that without adequate finances reforms could not be introduced. He, therefore, provided adequate funds for introducing military reforms. Naval schools were also opened in the country and both navy and fortification of forts was both improved as well as strengthened. In the modernisation of Turkish army and in its training France extended both co-operation as well as facilities, which went a long way in improving military standard of the country. Foundation of strong army was laid so in 1916, it was able to repulse attack of British navy.

Social Changes. Military reforms and contact of Turkish military officers with the French officers had far reaching consequences and effects. These officers came to know and understand about social problems of western society, their approach to persisting social problems and also their social, moral and cultural values and modern approaches to these problems. In many respects they appreciated their approach to life. In fact these young military officers developed new ideas and became an elite class in themselves. They became a distinct class and their approach to many problems of life was quite distinct from Orthodox people.

Contacts with the West. Turkey's military contacts still more developed when Turkey began to develop diplomatic relation with the western countries. For quite sometime Turkey did not like to maintain any diplomatic contacts with any western power. Whensoever any problem arose, she used to send special missions to that country which was involved directly or indirectly in dealing with that problem. Since she had no diplomatic contacts, the result was that she was not considered a member of family of nations by European powers.

When, however, Sultan Selim III came to power, this situation changed. He was quite keen that the country should have diplomatic relations with the western world, so that Turkey could know about what was happening in that part of the world and how friendly these were in reality towards Turkey. As these diplomatic contracts developed so much change came in Turkish way of life. Young Turkish officers on diplomatic mission came in contact with western diplomats and people and so they were greatly influenced by their manners, customs, dress and both way of living and thinking, cultural out-look.

It was the time when revolutionary ideas were quickly spreading in the west. These progressive ideas also greatly influenced Turkish young officers. Some of them were so deeply influenced that when they came back from their diplomatic missions they themselves began to spread these ideas in their own country. In this way gradually conservative outlook changed.

Contacts with France. As already stated that Turkish officers began to be trained by French officers. When however, Napoleon Bounaparte conquered Egypt, which was part of Ottoman empire, relations between the two countries got strained and traditional and old friendship got set back. But when he withdrew from Egypt, relations between the two sufficiently improved. Turkey became a friend of France and Napoleon Bounaparte was allowed to pass his armies through Turkey in his war both against Russia and England as Russia was traditional enemy of Turkey.

It was also during this period, that Turkey developed diplomatic relations with many other countries of the world also. Thus Turkey came out of her narrow shells.

Deposition of Selim III. Turkey was however, not fully ready for the reforms, though Selim III took every care to see that the pace of reforms was gradual and slow. France under Napoleon Bounaparte was spreading revolutionary ideas of liberty equality and of fraternity which the elites or the Turkish society were not prepared to accept. Philosophy of secularism also spread in many western countries but in Turkey, it was considered a serious threat to religion of the country. It was felt that to talk of reason was also to challenge well established doctrines of Muslim religion as approved by God and Prophet Muhammad. The result of all this was that both on social, political and religious, fields, the people of Turkey expressed their wrath against their Sultan and he was forced to leave the country in 1807 and reforms got a temporary set back.

Deposition and After. Deposition of Sultan Selim III put the whole society in reverse gears and work done by him was temporarily undone. His new army was disbanded and those of his Ministers, who helped him in carrying his reforms, were punished. Chief Mufti became the chief master of the show in the country he opposed all social, economic and political and cultural changes to country. Deposition of Salim II for all practical purposes meant end of reforms and modernisation of Turkey.

Rule of Mahmud II

Turkey Under Mahmud II. Deposition of Selim III gave a serious temporary set back to reforms movement in the country. But the process once started could not be easily checked. Selim III as succeeded by Mahmud II who was equally keen that his country should be modernised as quickly as possible. He, therefore wanted to end orthodox thinking and strongholds of the old system. He destroyed, Pretorian guards, who were known for their corrupt practices and were frequently opposing and interfering in governmental policies.

Another stronghold of orthodoxy were the Ulemas and Mullahas. They were reactionaries and opposed every reform movement and secularism. He did his best to waken their position and was successful to a great extent.

Provincial rulers of Turkey were his other problem. He knew that as long as they enjoyed power and influence, the Sultan of Turkey shall not be in a position to introduce any reforms. He, therefore, weakened their influence and power as well.

Tanzimat

Era of Tanzimat. Having thus weakened them, he initiated era of Tanzimat, which in Turkish history means great reforming edicts which aimed at modernising Turkish administration and society. But his task was not easy because those who were opposed to his moderate reforms, would never allow him to introduce far reaching reforms.

Another difficulty was that the methods and means through which reforms were to be introduced were inadequate. There were no competent and honest officers and administrators who could be depended upon for introducing modern reforms. In fact in the whole Ottoman Empire the number of progressive persons who were capable of introducing reforms were very inadequate and masses were indifferent.

Feudalism was deep rooted in the Ottoman Empire. Feudal lords were in no mood to introduce reforms because they felt that reformatory measures were bound to challenge their authority and supremacy and traditional out-look.

In this way struggle for modernisation and introduction of reforms continued in Ottoman empire. The task before the Sultans who were keen to introduce reforms was in no way less difficult particularly when means of transportation and communication etc. in the country were very difficult. It was very difficult to approach the people and convince them quickly about the utility and desirability of reforms because there were no T.V. or radio and newspapers etc. to propagate to popularise Government views.

Such were difficult problems and tasks before Sultan when he took upon himself the responsibility of introducing reforms in Ottoman Empire. The task which laid ahead was really difficult and problems which the Ottoman Empire faced were in no way less insignificant and solution was not easy.

Reforms of Mahmud II of Turkey

In 1789 Salim who was about 20 years old became Sultan of Turkey. He was an educated man and took his position seriously and desired to maintain power of Central Government and to reform the Turkish Government. But during his regime Nepoleon attacked Egypt which was a province of Ottoman empire. With British help Nepoleon was forced to leave territories of Ottoman Empire but this opened the way for other powers to take advantage of weakness of Ottoman empire. As such Serbian revolt took place which has been already described. Ruling elite class deposed Salim and his cousin Mustafa IV was made Sultan in May, 1807 but he remained Sultan for a short time and Mahmud II became Sultan. He carried out many reforms. According to M. Philips Price Mahmud II actually did not accomplish much but he laid the foundation of Tanzimat reforms.

Reforms of Mahmud II. By noble rescript of the Rose Chamber, it was provided that each and every person will enjoy life and honour and property rights. Special privilege to Muslims will be abolished and every body will be equal before law. A council of justice was created and traditional system of running administration through tax farmers and Pashas was abolished.

Education and New Code of Law. A council of public instruction was created and University system of education was introduced. New code of law *i.e.* Kanuns made all equal before law and commercial courts were created on the lines of French legal system Jajiya was abolished. These reforms faced great obstacles but paved the way for further reforms. He died on July 1, 1839.

In spite of the fact that Mahmud II knew that the task of introducing reforms was not easy, he decided to introduce western type of several reforms. He issued reform edicts and tried to bring modern type of administration.

Nobel Receipt of the Rose Chamber. By this it was provided that each and every person will enjoy life and honour. They were given right to property to be tried in public by fair means. It was provided that special privileges of the Muslims will be ended. A council of justice was created. The traditional system of running administration through Pashas and tax farmers was abolished and new system was introduced.

New Code of Law. New code of law was called 'Kanuns' (as in Urdu) under which all subjects of the Ottoman Empire were treated equal before law. Commercial courts were created on the lines of French legal system. University system of education was introduced and a council of public instructions was also created to develop education.

Working of Reforms. Though the reforms received opposition from the orthodox Mullahas and Ulemas. Yet efforts were made to introduce these inspite of opposition Jaziya was abolished. The reforms were introduced with French help but under Abdul Hamid II Turkey was not keen to introduce new reforms. The difficulty also arose because they were started at without popular backing. The people did not like reforms because they were economically poor. Another problem was that Turkey was faced with many international problems.

Evaluation of Reforms. The movement laid foundation stone for more and more reforms. Reforms produced new educated elite class and citadel of orthodoxy was pierced as this new educated class was eager to model Turkey on western lines.

Mahmud II was succeeded by Abul Mejid I who at once issued the imperial decree of the famous Tanzimat reforms.

These reforms laid down a commercial code and a criminal code was drawn up on the model of French code Abdul Mezid succeeded in 1861 and was deposed in 1876 and was succeeded by Murad V but he was of a very weak mind so he was succeeded by Abdul Hamid after a few months in 1876.

Early Career and Achievements of Midhat Pasha

Turkey needed reforms to develop herself and to save itself from the clutches of western powers. But orthodox and religious leaders on the one hand and weak position of some of the Ottoman Sultans on the other hand did not take the Turkish country long way on the road of reforms. When however, Midhat Pasha became Vizier and came to power, the process of reforms somewhat quickened. But unfortunately international situation was not suitable so reforms could not be rapidly introduced. Western powers were gradually grabbing Turkish territory and Turkey began to be called as sick Man of Europe. It was a time when Russo-Turkish war could break but at any time and Russia was stronger than Turkey.

But Midhat Pasha was determined to introduce reforms. These reforms came on account of international pressures as well because educated persons were not at all prepared to tolerate tyranny in Ottoman empire Midhat Pasha knew that in case for far reaching reforms internal affairs of country should be improved.

It was more or less under the pressure of western powers that Sultan Abdual Hamid was brought on the throne, in 1876 and Midhat Pasha was given the charge of Grand Vizier of the Ottoman empire.

Midhat Pasha was quite keen that reforms should be introduced in Turkey. He was however, not without his opponents. Charges were levied against him that he was a Pro-British and is danger, to Islamic state and his opponents successfully banished him. His throwing out of the country was not cherished by the Britishers who put pressure on Turkey so Midhat Pasha was called back. But on his return his opponents again became very active. He was accused of false charges and again was banished from Turkey on account of his reforms he created so many enemies that he was imprisoned and murdered in 1883. Thus reforms of Midhat Pasha did not bear fruit immediately.

Reforms of Midhat Pasha. Midhat Pasha introduced reform in Turkey with new modern approach and vision. He wanted that arbitrary and autocratic powers of Ottoman Sultan should be checked by his Ministers. There should also be a national constituent assembly to give constitution to Ottoman empire. The Assembly should be constituted without making any distinction on the basis of caste classes, creed, race or religion. He also did not like centralisation of authority but wanted considerable decentralisation of power. He was quite convinced that all this could be achieved only with the help of a popular constitution. He was thus champion of parliamentary form of government like Britain. In his ideas about reforms he was much influenced by western political thought and philosophy and administrative setup.

The Ottoman emperor who was not initially prepared to accept all these reforms, subsequently agreed when he was made to realise that unless reforms on these lines were introduced, there could be intervention by western powers at any time, which might wipe out even the existence of empire of Sultan himself. Then another reason advanced was that if Turkey gave a liberal constitution with a parliamentary form of government, then she could hope to get assistance of England and France etc. in Russo-Turkish War which was round the corner.

Keeping these factors into consideration, the Sultan promulgated—a liberal constitution conferring rights to masses.

Character of Sultan Abdul Hamid. The Ottoman Sultan realised that Turkey needed reforms but he was tyrant and believed in despotism. He was not prepared to give up his powers. If he talked of reforms or sided with the champion of reforms, it was simply because he knew that both at home and abroad any attempt to disown reforms or opposition to reforms was bound to make him unpopular and even revolt may occur by which he may have to lose his throne. Thus he kept up an appearance for reforms. In other words on the one hand were western powers and the Grand Vizier, whereas on the other was the Sultan Abdul Hamid. Whereas the former really wanted to introduce reforms, the later was opposed to these at Hezrt. It was in this unreconcilable situation that real tragedy lay in reforms.

The Constitution of 1876

Turkish Constitution of 1876. Though the Sultan promulgated the constitution, yet he was not quite keen to give effect to all its provisions. While inaugurating the

Constitution, he declared that "I have only one desire and that is the progress of our country and peace for all of our subjects. This will be proved by the logic of the facts, the fulfilment of the promise of reforms."

The Constitution of 1876 had 119 Articles and was divided into 12 parts, the main provisions of the constitution were :

(a) It was the prerogative of the Ottoman Sultan to appoint Grand Vizier and the Shiekh Ul-Islam.

(b) The country shall have bicameral system of legislature. The Upper House to be called as Senate and Lower House and Chamber of Deputies like France. Both the house were to have coequal power.

(c) Ministry was to be responsible to the Chamber of Deputies. The Chamber could never be suspended.

(d) If the Chamber expressed a lack of confidence in any minister, he should either be dismissed or House may be dissolved for immediate re-election.

(e) All the nationalities in this country were given proportional representation. Thus it was unlike Indian Constitution where representation is provided either to scheduled caste or general constituency and all others have been left.

(f) This constitution declared equality of all subjects and even provided equality of representation by means of proportional representation. In a country having people of different religions such as Muslims, Christians and Jews and nationalities like Kurds, Turks, Arabs and Armenians etc., it was probably a good solution.

Difficulty came when young Turks gave prominence only to Turks later on. Thus constitution of Turkey of 1876, gives a lesson that a country having many religions and races, proportional representation according to population brings stability and a race or religion or caste which was neglected and did not get representation engineers revolt as it happened when young Turks neglected others.

(g) Under the new constitution the people were given religious freedom, liberal education and freedom of speech and press etc.

Problems of the Constitution of 1876. As already pointed out the Sultan Abdul Hamid was not quite keen to give constitutional reforms to the country. That was one serious problem. Another serious problem was that it was rather very difficult to introduce parliamentary forms of government to reconcile it with absolute powers of the Sultan. Another difficulty was before these reforms were introduced the people of Turkey had not been fairly educated and given a clear idea as to what was significance of these reforms and how far and in what way they will be benefited by these reforms? The people did not know how to elect their representative properly and the later were also quite unaware of their responsibilities as elected members of parliament.

Still other difficulty was that there was probably no section of society which was satisfied with these reforms. The conservatives felt that the reforms were too sweeping whereas the liberals were of the view that the reforms were meaningless as the hold of the Ottoman Sultan had in no way weakened.

Ottoman Sultan Abdul Hamid thus when found that the popularity of Vizier Midhat Pasha was on the decline, he took advantage of the situation. He propagated that war with Russia was on the cards and that it was not the time for the nation to waste its energies in talk of constitution and reforms. As such taking advantage of this, constitution of 1876 remained suspended for about a decade.

The constitution did not remain in operation for long. It was also clear that the elected representatives and electorates both lacked training. Now it became clear that the people of Turkey needed reforms and will not like to remain under the thumb of tyrant rulers for a very long time. The seeds for working under parliamentary form of government were thus sown by this constitution of 1876. Importance of constitution of 1876 was that it paved the way for constitutional Government in future.

Rule of Sultan Abdul Hamid

Ottoman Sultan Abdul Hamid was a very shrewd ruler. He was opposed to the introduction of reforms in his country, but at the same time, he realised that any active opposition to reforms movement was bound to make him unpopular in the eyes of the western powers. He, therefore, always showed hypocritic sympathy to every proposal of reforms which was put before him. He even gave a liberal constitution to his country. But did not miss the first opportunity to dismiss liberal Vizier Midhat Pasha and even suspend the constitution. He managed his exile from the country and subsequently he imprisoned him and it is alleged that he got him murdered in the prison and thus got rid of him for all times to come.

Autocratic Rule of Abdul Hamid. Once liberal Vizier Midhat Pasha was murdered and the constitution was suspended, the Sultan got back all those powers which as an absolute ruler he could enjoy. It was fortunate of him that treaty of Berlin was concluded in 1878, by which European powers agreed not to interfere in the internal affairs of Turkey. This was sufficient guarantee for the Ottoman Sultan he become still more autocrat. He, therefore, used his power and authority with maximum suppression and oppression and curbed democratic institutions.

All those who championed the cause of reformation were demoralised. They were either put behind the bars or exiled form Turkey and their properties were confiscated. He established his authority by means of espionage and repression. He introduced strict censorship on all journalistic activities and ensured that nothing came out in the press which was against him or against his policy or political authority. Impartiality of justice and judicial courts was brought to an end. The judges were brought under the influence of Sultan of Turkey and made to pronounce such decisions which were liked by Sultan. In cases where there was least suspicion about the person or about his intentions towards the Sultan, he was exiled or detained without any trial. No political opposition to Sultan was tolerated in any manner. Every care was taken that subjects remain loyal to the Sultan of Turkey and his government.

Policy Towards the Arabs. The Sultan Abdul Hamid however, realised that Arabs were freedom loving people and any haste to put restrictions on their freedom was bound to invite their wrath and bitter opposition and bring revolt from them. Not only this but Sultan Abdul Hamid also found that in Arab world, there was already sufficient consolidation of activities against the Ottoman empire and any further suppression of their feelings were bound to accelerate the process of nationalism in that Arab world. In order to consolidate his position the Ottoman Sultan wanted to have their goodwill and co-operation. One of the methods he adopted was that he conferred honours on the Arab leaders and patronised institutions of Arab learning. In order to please Arab religious people, he got both Mecca and Medina repaired and sent his personal bodyguards as spies in different parts of the Ottoman Empire particularly in Arab lands.

But Sultan Abdul Hamid was a shrewd political person so he knew that inspite of all that which he was doing for the Arab, they could at any time challenge his supremacy and authority. He therefore wanted that Arab solidarity should be disturbed because as long as Arabs remained united their national movement could not be checked. He therefore sent his spies in the guise of preachers to tour the Arab world. Their main aim was to exploit local and family feuds and to widen the gaps which existed among the Arab leaders. Wherever possible, it should be aim to kill the rising leaders and rulers assassinated. The spies were also expected to keep the Ottoman Sultan informed, if any Arab chief was becoming disloyal so that they could be kept under constant supervision either at home or in Constantinople. It is believed that he kept one Arab chief named Sheriff Hussain of Mecca under informal captivity for a long period of over 15 years because his loyalty towards the Ottoman Sultan was doubted by his spies.

Ottoman Sultan of Turkey as Caliph. The Turkish Sultan fully realised that he could become very successful if along with political powers, he also enjoyed religious powers. He therefore began to rule both as Sultan as well as Caliph. In the past Caliphs used to have both political as well as religious authority. But as the time passed the Sultan becomes symbol of political authority and Caliph that of religious authority. Sultan Abdul Hamid now wanted that both religious authority of Caliph and political authority of Sultan should be merged and represented by the Sultan. He was greatly successful in it with the result that he could win active co-operations of all Muslim people, but educated people challenged it. Due to this challenge to his authority was considerably reduced.

Sultan Abdul Hamid's Foreign Policy. Sultan Abdul Hamid wanted to secure his reputation and position in the international field as well. One of the methods was that the Sultan of Turkey should become an undisputed leader of the Muslim world. By becoming Caliph, he got unqualified support of millions of Muslims living in different parts of the world. He encouraged and allowed Ulemas and other Muslim religious leaders to gather around him. He posed to the whole world that his personal life was strictly according to Muslim law and religion and that he was the custodian of Muslims of the world. He constructed a railway line to make journey to Mecca and Medina comfortable and easy. He spent money to get the mosques repaired and gave liberal financial assistance to the poor and needy Muslims. His policy of becoming leader of the Muslim world paid him rich dividends with the result that Kaisar William II of Germany accepted him as his friend and thus threat of any aggression from Germany directly or indirectly came to an end. Not only this German ruler promised help to Muslims and so Turkey and Germany became friends.

Critical Estimate of the Work of Sultan Abdul Hamid

Much controversy has surrounded about the work and achievement of Sultan Abdul Hamid. On the one hand, there are historians who are of opinion that the Sultan Abdul Hamid did a great harm to Turkey by stalling the process of modernisation and also that of stopping reforms. They are of opinion that had he not done so perhaps now the country would have been one of the most important and advanced countries of the world. According to them by creating an atmosphere of tyranny and fear, he very much harmed the nation for which the nation will never forget him.

On the other hand, there are other writers who believe that the Sultan Abdul Hamid did a real service for the country. It was a time when the nation was not prepared for parliamentary reforms and Constitutional form of government. In fact Turkey was quite unfit for that. With this absolute powers he kept the country united and saved that country during his rule from further disintegration and disunity. By combining in itself religious and political authority, he kept country united. Not only this but by becoming Caliph, he made Turkey united as one of the most respectable countries of the Muslim world. It was due to his wisdom that Turkey became leader of the Muslim world and even Kaisar William II of Germany extended his hand of cooperation and friendship for Turkey.

In this way the opinions are divided but it can be said that with his wisdom and maturity he saved Turkey from disintegration and slowed down its process of dissolution. Not only this but he won international co-operation for his country. It is probably equally true that he annoyed the supporters of reform, who considered him as stumbling block and wanted to remove him from the power as quickly as possibly could be done.

It was on account of his suppressive and repressive policies that Young Turk Movement in the county gained momentum and ultimately became responsible for his removal from the throne. Had he carried reformers with him perhaps shape of Turkey would have been altogether different.

According to Philips Price "Abdul Hamid ruled harshly but not without ability. He secured elements of the population loyal to himself, especially among the Albanians, the Arabs, the Kurds to whom he granted special privileges." Above Author remarks, "He worked on the principle of Divide and Rule. But the expensive administration and Politics system which he set up burdened the finances of the state and had to be in part financed by foreign loans and yet the Sultan was able to rely on assistance from outside by playing on the Jealousy of European powers. The Ottoman power was in decline but no one dared to give it the coup de grace.

The Crimean War and Its Consequences

Russia invaded Turkish territory in 1853 but was soon confronted with a declaration of war from France and Britain. For his part, Napoleon III saw in this war with Russia an opportunity to enhance the reputation of his dynasty, and take revenge of defeat. In 1854, French ruler, Nepoleon III to take revenge of defeat of his great uncle Napoleon Bounaparte and Sardinian troops invaded the Russian Crimea and besieged the great fortress of Sevastopol. French and British forces got an upper hand in this Crimean War and Russia had to eat an humble pie.

Contrary to Russian expectations (Russia had aided Austria in crushing the Hungarian revolution of 1848). Austria refused to ally itself with Russia and maintained an unfriendly "neutrality" in this war which forced Russia to evacuate certain Turkish territory *i.e.,* (Rumania) etc. near the Austrian borders. In September 1855 the fortress of Sevastopol finally fell. Thwarted in the attempt to carve up the "sick Man of Europe." Russia sued for peace.

The treaty of Paris in (1856) affirmed the integrity of the Ottoman empire. Specifically, it provided for the neutralization of the Black Sea (neither Russia nor Turkey was to maintain forts or naval force on its shores, Crimean war temporarily checked Russian designs and indirectly brought unification of Italy.

According to Philips, "The Crimean war in a sense was defeat for Turkey, too, and nothing was gained by the sacrifices."

After Crimean War Paris conference of 1856, held under Nepoleon III. It Close the Straits to foreign warships, and declared that no power had the right to interfere on behalf of the Ottoman Sultan's Christian subjects. To reduce Russian influence in the Balkans, the Congress of Paris of 1856, ended the Russian protectorate over Rumania which had been established in 1829. It placed the country under the protection of the great powers of Europe and permitted Turkey to maintain its suzerainty over it.

The Crimean War momentarily halted Russian advance into the Balkans. But it did little to assuage the bitter international rivalries in that area. Bitterly resentful of having Austria as an ally in the carving up of the Ottoman Empire. Russians decided that objective of dismemberment of Ottoman Empire now requires the weakening of Austria. As such in First World War Russia fought with Austria to grab Eastern Europe and succeeded in grabbing it in 1945, but lost it in 1991-92.

Pan-Slavism as Agent of Russian Expansion

The anti western Slavophile movement, which lauded Russian institutions, took on a political complexion after the Crimean War. Known as Pan-Slavism, this movement championed Russia as the protector of its "little brother Slavs", with the duty of freeing them from the barbaric rule of the Ottoman Turks. Moreover, exponents of Pan-Slavism preached that it was Russia's destiny to create and rule a great Slavic empire containing all Slav lands such as Serbia, Romania, Bulgaria, etc. In the 1860's and 1870's, Pan Slavism carried the message of Slavic solidarity to the Balkans, states encouraging revolt in Ottoman Empire. Thus Pan Slavism was useful to Russia for extending her sway and ending Ottoman rule.

Rumania and Bulgaria

Meanwhile, the Balkan people were slowly moving toward modernization. Rumania, though self-governing, was still nominally under Turkish control; but as law and order were achieved, roads were constructed, and a postal system was inaugurated. Gradually Rumania advanced towards nationhood. Despite the opposition of the great powers, Rumania which had heretofore consisted of two separate territories, became a single, united state in 1862. By 1870 it was virtually free, progressive and prosperous.

Bulgaria

The story of Bulgarian liberty became entwined with events of Balkan Peninsula in the whole Balkan area and with the growing interests of the European great powers in this troubled region. In 1875, peasants revolted in the district of Bosnia, a Turkish-governed Serbian province not included in the autonomous Serbian state. This insurrection was followed by a declaration of war by Serbia and Montenegro against Turkey.

At the same time, the Bulgarians also broke into revolt, but the Turks crushed the rebels with terrible cruelty. The "Bulgarians massacres" caused a wave of horror among enlightened people all over the world. In one incident, over one thousand people, including children, were burnt alive in a Christian Church where they had sought sanctuary. Gladstone in England cried for action but Disraeli who was Prime Minister at that time kept mum but later on this question gained prominence.

The Treaty of San Stefano and the Congress of Berlin of 1878

Balkans' problem came on forefront out again before European powers. While public opinion was being aroused in Europe against the "unspeakable Turk," the Serbs and Montenegrins had been forced to sue for peace with Turkey. Thereupon a conference of the ambassadors of the great powers at Europe met in Constantinople and demanded an end to Turkish cruelties in the Balkan lands. When the Sultan demurred, the Russians Tsar declared war against Turkey.

The Russo-Turkish war of (1877-1878) was a hard fought war. In one case a beleaguered Turkish army held off the Russians for five month before accepting surrender. Faced with an imminent Russian attack on Constantinople, however, the Sultan of Turkey finally sued for peace. The resulting Treaty of San Stefano (1878) gained complete Independence for Serbia and Rumania, while the Independence of Montenegro was also reaffirmed. A large Bulgarian state was set up, nominally still tributary to Turkey but actually under the dominance of Russia.

Reaction of Britain and Austria

Britain was alarmed over the prospect of much of the Balkans coming under the domination of Russia. And Austria was determined that Turkey as a political entity must be preserved or, at least, its territory be prevented from falling under Russian influence. The Astro-Hungarian position was explained by an Austrian statesman as given below :

Turkey possesses a utility almost providential for Austria-Hungary. For Turkey maintains the *status quo of* the small Balkan states and impedes their (nationalistic) aspirations. If it were not for Turkey, all these aspirations would fall down on our heads...if Bosnia and Herzegoviana should go to Serbia or Montenegro, or if a new state should be formed there which we cannot prevent, then we should be ruined and should ourselves assume the role of the "Sick Man."

Congress Berlin's Decisions

Fearing an increase of Russian power in the Balkans, Britain and Austria forced a reconsideration of the Treaty of San Stefano at the congress of Berlin later in 1878 presided by Bismarck. Russia was compelled to agree to a revision of Bulgaria's status, and the large Bulgarian state set up by the Treaty of San Stefano was divided into three parts. The northern most of Bulgarian part remained an independent principality paying tribute to Turkey; south of this region was made an autonomous province to be occupied by Turkish troops; the southernmost region was given back to Turkey to administer it liberally.

Among other provisions of the Berlin settlement of 1878, was one relating to Bosnia, where the revolt of 1875 had started. This province and the province of Herzegoviana were given to Austria "to occupy and administer" them. Thus Austria added to its polyglot empire two new territories, one of which was to be the scene of the incident which set off World War I of 1914-18. Thus treaty of Berlin contained germs of World War I. Russian expansion had been checkmated — but at a high price. The Turks continued to oppress and even massacre the Balkan Christians left under the rule of the Sultan. Meanwhile the Russians made a mockery of Pan-Slavism by trying to control the policies of their "brother Slaves" just freed from the Turks, particularly in Bulgaria. Russian satellites, so much discussed following the creation of Soviet puppets in eastern Europe and the Balkans after World War II are nothing new in history. About Berlin conference foreign Minister of England Lord Salisbury who later on became Prime Minister said that "We have betted on a wrong horse". Probably his words proved true. Neither the disintegration of Ottoman Empire could be checked nor peace could be maintained for a long time. Finally, after World War II not only states of Balkan Peninsula but

Hungary and Czechoslovakia states of Austrian empire and of Central Europe and East Germany also became Russian satellites.

Nor was it only Russia's expansion in the Balkans that gave Britain concern is a complex question. Russian pressure in Central Asia sparked British diplomats to control Afghanistan and make it a friendly buffer state between the Russia and India. This policy was followed by Britishers till their empire lasted in Indian *i.e.* upto 1947. Turkey, the "sick Man of Europe." Nicholas I, stern soldier and unbending autocratic czar of Russia was determined to carry on his predecessor's policy of expansion at the expense of weak Turkey. Visiting in 1844, the Tsar referred to Turkey as "a dying man" and proposed that England should join in a dissection of the Ottoman carcass, British statement refused to be party to an agreement that would result in Russia's taking over Constantinople and major part of Ottoman empire.

A quarrel over the management and protection of the holy places such as Jerusalem etc. in the affairs of the Ottoman Empire. Ostensibly motivated by religious sentiments, the Tsar reconfirmed Russia's protectorate over all Greek Christians of the Ottoman Empire. His primary interest, of course, was the traditional Russian goal–to secure control of Constantinople and to ensure an entrance from the Black Sea to the Mediterranean Sea and to gain as much territory as may be feasible.

Condition of Turkish Empire in Later Half of 18th Century

After the death of Mahmud II, condition of Ottoman empire further deteriorated and antagonism of France, Britain and Russia brought Crimean War. The outbreak of the Crimean War was an important event in Europe in the nineteenth century. It reopened the Eastern question, and what was more serious it profoundly disturbed the states system and policy of maintaining peace by co-operation of major European powers established by the Congress of Vienna got set back. Hence it has been aptly remarked that the "Crimean War was in a general sense the watershed of European History." Like a great river overflowing its banks and fertilising them, the Crimean War let loose force which secured the triumph of liberalism and constitutionalism and of nationalism in Europe and began to spread in other continents. It swept aside Metternich's policy of status quo, and inaugurated an era of progressive achievements and of construction. Its first fruit was the union of Italy. In Russia it led to far-reaching reforms and emancipation of serfs which lifted her out of her medieval stagnation, and set on foot for a movement towards liberalism and democracy. Lastly, it led to an important regrouping of major powers, which made the unification of Germany possible. The causes of the Crimean War might appear trivial. Critics may differ as to its immediate results. It has been branded as the "only perfectly useless modern war that has been waged." Again it has been maintained that but for this and the policy subsequently adopted by Lord Beaconsfield Disraeli, who was Prime Minister of England in the Balkan, states would never have achieved their independence, and Russia would have probably occupied, Constantinople or some territories of Ottoman empire. But as stated above the importance of the Crimean War is to be measured not by its immediate tangible results, but by the other most important political developments to which it was a prelude.

The Crimean War (1854-56) and Its Consequences

For ten years after the Convention of London there was repose in the Turkish Empire. But this calm was disturbed by storm *i.e.,* by the outbreak of a quarrel between the Latin monks and the Greek monks over the custody of the Holy Places in Jerusalem. Though the quarrel was apparently trivial, it led to startling developments which opened a new chapter in the history of the Eastern Question in Ottoman empire. By previously different treaties France had acquired right to protect Roman Catholics and Russia right to protect followers of orthodox Greek Church in Ottoman Empire. Turkey had, by an old treaty, conceded to France the right to protect the Latin monks and Roman Catholics in her dominions, and these monks were also given special privileges including the guardianship of the Holy Places of Jerusalem where Christ was born and brought up. But during the pre-occupation of France in the time of the Revolution, the Greek monks and followers of orthodox Greek Church had gradually encroached upon the rights of their Latin rivals. In the dispute that followed, Napoleon III revived the claim of France and demanded a full restoration of the rights of the Latin monks. Czar Nicholas I championed the cause of the Greek monks. The Porte *i.e.,* Sultan of Turkey at first conceded the demands of Napoleon III but the Czar Nicholas I insisted upon the withdrawal of the French concession. Driven between the two powers, the Porte attempted a compromise which, however failed. As a matter of fact neither France nor Russia wanted compromise. Both Napoleon III and Nicholas I had ulterior objects in view, which they wanted to attain under the cover of the struggle over the Holy Places. Napoleon III, ruler of France conscious of the weakness of his usurped position, wanted to signalise his accession to the French throne by a spirited foreign policy which would reconcile the French people to his rule. A War with Russia in support of the Latin monks would suit his purpose to a nicety. It would please the Clerical party in France, whose support he considered essential to retain his position as King. It would, be avenging the humiliation of Moscow defeat of his uncle Napoleon to gratify the French national pride. It would be an old Napoleonic gesture of victory which would go a great way towards stabilising his somewhat unsteady throne of France. Lastly, he had a personal grudge against Nicholas I who had slighted him by refusing to address him in the courteous form usual among monarchs of great nations. All these happenings ultimately brought war.

The controversy with France over the Holy Christian Places had stimulated the ambitions of Czar Nicholas I. He believed Turkey to be weak and called her "sick man of Europe" and was firmly persuaded of the impending dissolution of the weak Turkish Empire. In 1853 in the course of his conversations with the British ambassador at St. Petersburg, he declared his intention to come to an arrangement with England, which virtually amounted to a partition of the dominions of Ottoman Empire of the "sick man" before his death. He suggested that England might have Egypt and Crete, and that Russia might be allowed to control Constantinople and the Dardanelles although not in proprietary right and other parts of Ottoman Empire. England refused to admit that the dissolution of the Ottoman Empire was imminent or to be a party to any scheme of partition of Turkish Empire. She believed in the regeneration of Turkey, and her policy was to maintain the integrity of the Ottoman Empire as a check upon Russian Aggression and expansion to safeguard Indian empire and to maintain balance of power in Europe.

Nicholas I, however, was bent upon an aggressive and expansionist policy. He despatched as ambassador to the court of Constantinople, charging him not only to obtain satisfaction about the Holy Places, but to demand the recognition of Russia as the protector of all the Christians of the Greek Church in the Ottoman Sultan's dominions. This claim was made on the strength of the Treaty of Kachuk-Kainarji. This additional demand, if conceded, would have given Russia a perpetual right to interfere in the internal affairs of Turkey. It would thus amount to the transfer of allegiance of a large portion of Turkish subjects from the Ottoman Sultan to Russian Czar. The Sultan, at the advice of the British ambassador, Startford de Redcliffe, kept the two questions apart. He agreed to satisfy the Russian demands concerning the Holy Places, but refused to recognise Russian protectorate over the Orthodox Christian subjects of Turkish Empire. Thereupon a Russian force occupied the Danubian Principalities (Wallachia and Moldavia) by way of putting pressure upon Sultan of Turkey. The attitude of Russia is significant she first sought to dismember Turkey, and when that was found not feasible, she sought to control her by interfering in the internal affairs of the Ottoman Empire under lame excuse and on the pretext of protecting the Orthodox Christians in Ottoman Empire.

The Cause and Impact of Crimean War

The conduct of Russia caused a flutter in the courts of Europe and the whole question assumed a general European importance. England, France, Austria and Prussia put forward their proposal in what was called the Vienna Note which was presented both to Sultan of Turkey and Russian Czar. The Note confirmed the Treaties of Kainarnji and Adrianople and asserted the need of protecting the Christian subjects of the Prote. Russia accepted the Note and interpreted it as "protection by the Czar", while Turkey at the instigation of the British ambassador, Lord Stratford de Redcliffe, interpreted it as "protection by the Porte". The ambiguity might have been overcome but for the stiff attitude of British ambassador Lord Stratford, who wanted to force Russia to a specific undertaking and renunciation of her claims "He virtually overruled the decision of four powers including of his own Government" and caused the rejection of the Vienna Note after it had been accepted by Russia. His conduct laid England open to the charge of preventing a peaceful settlement of this complicated question.

Outbreak of the Crimean War

Turkish court succeeded in creating division which was only way to save Ottoman Empire from disintegration. Diplomacy having failed, the question could be settled only by the sword. After rejecting the Vienna Note, Turkey being encouraged by France and Britain called upon Russia to evacuate the Turkish Principalities. But Russians refused to do and so Turkey declared war upon Russia and took the offensive on the river Danube. There upon the Russian Black Sea fleet retaliated by completely destroying the Turkish fleet at Sinope. The massacre of Sinope, as this event was called, inflamed popular opinion in England and France, as noticed before, was ready to move. Hence the two Powers sent a joint ultimatum to Russia demanding the evacuation of Turkish Principalities. As Russia refused to comply with this demand, France and England signed a treaty of alliance with Turkey and declared war upon Russia in 1854. Next year the Allies were reinforced by troops from Sardinia-Piedmont whose king joined the war due to diplomacy of Prime Minister Cavour in the hope of securing the friendship of a great Power, specially France who may help the cause of unification of Italy.

The original object of this Crimean War, *viz.*, the expulsion of the Russians from the Turkish Principalities, was quickly secured. Czar Nicholas I held up by the gallant defence of Silistria by the Turks, and menaced by the war like attitude of Austria, withdrew from the Turkish principalities. But the Allies thought it necessary to check the menace and the power of Russia so that she might not again threaten Turkey. Hence it was decided to capture Sebastopol, the "very heart of Russian power in the East." The Allies after landing in the Crimea marched towards Sebastopol, defeating the Russian forces who tried to stop them in a battle on the river Alma in 1854. The Allies then besieged Sebastopol, and the rest of the war centered in this siege and in the Russian efforts to save it. The Russians attacked the British base of supplies at Balackava but were repulsed. The battle of Balackava is memorable for the magnificent but useless charge of the famous Light Brigade praised by Lord Tennyson. Another attempt to raise the siege led to the battle of Inkermann in which also the Russians-were defeated. The last attempt of the Russians to break through the besieging forces was frustrated on the river Techernaya chiefly by the gallantry of the Sardinian army. The death of Czar Nicholas I, who was the prime author of this war, led to negotiations for peace. Sebastopol fell after a year's resistance and this practically brought the Crimean War to a close in (1855). After the war Peace conference was held at Paris under the Presidentship of Napoleon III of France.

Peace of Paris

By the Peace of Paris (1856) which closed the Crimean War. Russia lost her protectorate over Moldavia which were made self-governing states under Turkish suzerainty and the collective guarantees of the European Powers. Russia also renounced her claim of the protectorate over the Orthodox Christian subjects of the Porte. The Black Sea was declared neutral and neither Russia nor any other Power was to have warships there or to maintain arsenals or army on its shores. The river Danube was internationalised and its nevigation was thrown open to all countries. The Russian frontier was withdrawn from the river Danube by the cession of Bessarabia. Turkey was admitted to the Concert of Europe and her territorial integrity was guaranteed by the European Powers. She in her turn promised reforms for her Christian subjects and liberal reforms in her empire.

Results of the Crimean War

In Turkey attempts were made for reform and a liberal constitution was formed but all proved temporary. The Peace of Paris which closed the Crimean War checked Russian design upon Turkey for a short time. Russia had to abandon all claims to a protectorate over the Orthodox Christian subjects of Ottoman Empire. She was kept back from the river Danube by the cession of Bessarabia to Moldavia, and from the Black Sea which was neutralised. Moreover, the creation of two autonomous states (Wallachia and Moldavia) placed a barrier between Russia and Turkey and thus for a time due to these buffer states Russia was prevented from pursuing a policy of aggrandisement against Turkey. Secondly, in a sense Turkey was the greatest gainer by the Crimean War. She obtained a new lease of life under the joint protection of the Powers, her territorial integrity was guaranteed and she was admitted as a member of the Concert of Europe from which she had been previously excluded. She thus got a fine chance to set her house in order and to develop herself into a respectable power. Looked at from these points of view the Peace of Paris may be regarded as offering a satisfactory solution of the Eastern question and a chance to preserve Ottoman Empire. Russia was checked and the "Sick man" was set on his legs again. But after this war there was an uneasy feeling that the results obtained were not commensurate with the heavy sacrifices involved, and whatever little was accomplished was not likely to endure long. Future events justified this premonition and confirmed the view that the Crimean War was probably the most senseless war of the nineteenth century. Just fourteen years later, Russia threw to the winds the provision concerning the neutrality of the Black Sea and in 1878 completely wiped away the Crimean humiliation by again recovering Bessarabia etc. The hopes entertained of Turkey reforming herself proved deceptive, and integrity of Turkey which was sought to be bolstered up by Paris treaty became a diplomatic fiction because Sultan Abdul Hamid proved deceptive and cunning. Thus as a solution of the Eastern question and bringing reform in Ottoman Empire. According to Philips Price Crimean War was in a sense was defeat for Turkey too, and nothing was gained by sacrifice thus Treaty of Paris was perhaps failure.

Indirect Results

On the political value of the Crimean War widely different opinions have been held by historians. But probably this war "was an important chapter in the Eastern question and the prelude to the most important political developments of the nineteenth century." In other words, the indirect consequences of the Crimean War were far-reaching "Out of the mud of the Crimea a new Italy was made and, less obviously, a new Germany." The Kingdom of Sardinia Piedmont having joined the Allies, gained French sympathy was admitted to the Paris peace conference. There Cavour, the minister of the Sardinian King, opened the Italian question before the assembled diplomats and enlisted the sympathy of the Powers, and won over Napoleon III to the cause of Italian independence. Italy was liberated and the arrangement which the Congress of Vienna had made, there was upset. Secondly, the Crimean War had far-reaching effects upon the fortunes of Austria. Her attitude of hostile neutrality irritated Russia who had saved the Austrian Empire from dissolution during the Hungarian revolt of 1848-1849. The result was that the old alliance of the three despotic powers (Russia, Austria and Prussia), which was the cornerstone of Metternich's policy which till now had saved the Austrian Empire from danger and disruption, was not broken. Furious at Austrian ingratitude Russia turned to Prussia whose friendly neutrality she appreciated. This state of things led to a new regrouping of Powers which gave rise to important developments afterwards. Bismarck took advantage of Russia, estrangement from Austria, and began to court the friendship of the Russian Czar in order to further his project of ousting Austria from Germany. The result was that Austria was completely isolated during the Austro Prussian War of 1866 that followed, Russia remaining neutral as Austria had done. Austria was defeated, and the German Empire that Prussia subsequently built up after Austria's defeat was largely based upon Russian neutrality. Austrian ingratitude was more than avenged.

A feeling grew in Turkey that the success of Tanzimat reforms should not depend only on Sultan. So young Turk movement began to take shape under Mehmet Beg Namak Kemal and Nury Beg. This war also affected Russia deeply. At home it led to a series of reforms carried out by Czar Alexander II, the most important of which was the emancipation of the serfs. Abroad, it gave a new turn to Russian expansion towards the East. That expansion, checked in Europe, was transferred to Central Asia where she began to push forward with giant strides. The British statesman realised that the Russian danger was only transferred from Europe to Asia, threatening British position in India and in the East.

The Motives of the Different Powers in Crimean War and Its Impact over Ottoman Empire

England took part in Crimean War because she feared that an aggressive Russia expanding into Mediterranean Sea and regions too near the route to India would be a serious menace to British interests in the East. It was a cardinal principle of British policy to maintain the integrity of the Turkish Empire as a safe guard to her eastern empire by creating barrier to Russia. As stated before, the French Emperor, Napoleon III, was influenced by a variety of motives to turn his arms against Russia. A war with Russia in support of the Latin monks would please the French Roman Catholics whose support, he considered valuable for his throne. It would by avenging the humiliation of Moscow, gratify the French national pride, and win for France glory and for himself popularity. This would stabilise his somewhat shaky throne and he will take revenge of defeat of his great uncle Napoleon from Russia. Sardinia Piedmont joined the allies in the hope of securing the good will and active support of an influential Powers of Europe particularly of France for realising the nationalistic ambitious of unity of Italy.

Austrian Attitude and Its Results

Lastly, although Austria did not take part in the war, her attitude was one of hostile neutrality. She was alarmed at the Russian occupation of Wallachia and Moldavia as it interfered with the freedom of the navigation of the river Danube, upon which depended the bulk of her trade and her commercial traffic. Hence she joined the allies in putting all sorts of diplomatic pressure upon Russia, demanding the evacuation of the Turkish principalities. When Russia complied with the demand, Austria herself occupied these principalities and thereby prevented Russian armies from advancing towards Constantinople. It was an Austrian ultimatum which forced the Russians, after the fall of Sebastopol, to sue for peace. Thus Austria's hostile neutrality was an important factor which probably indirectly contributed to Russian defeat. It should be noted that Czar Nicholas I had counted upon Austrian support in return for the services he had rendered to Austria in suppressing the Hungarian revolt in 1848-1849. But to his great disappointment he found that political considerations outweighed Austria's gratitude. In future Austria had to pay dear for her selfish conduct and she was defeated by Prussia in 1866 which brought unification of Germany and by France and Sardinia which brought unification of Italy. Consequently Austria lost her premier position in Europe and began to covet Ottoman territories which lead to World War I and disappearance of both Ottoman and Austrian empire.

In short the Crimean War had its origin in an apparently insignificant dispute between the Latin monks and Greek monks over the custody of the Holy Places in Palestine. France supported the Latin, and Russia the Greek monks. An attempt was made by Turkey to settle the dispute by compromise but it failed. Thereupon Russia enlarged her claims and demanded the right to protect the orthodox Christian subject of Greek church of Turkey on the strength of the old Treaty of Kachuk-Kainarji. The fact was that Czar Nicholas had already declared Turkey to be a "sickman" and proposed to England a scheme for the partition of the Ottoman Empire. As England rejected this plan, she desired about for pretexts to secure his hold upon Turkey. His opportunity came when Napoleon III raised the storm by taking up the cause of the Latin monks. Czar Nicholas took up the cause of the Greek monks and, in addition, demanded a Russian protectorate over the Christian subjects of Turkey. When the Sultan of Turkey rejected his latter proposal

Nicholas replied by occupying the Turkish principalities. Thus arose a crises which the Powers sought to avert by diplomacy. They presented the Vienna Note both to Russia and Turkey. But difficulties arose as to its interpretation, Russia and Turkey interpreting it in different ways. Turkey, at the instigation of England, refused to accept the Russian interpretation and declared war upon Russia. Thus as regards the responsibility for the out break of the war, it may be said that French started the conflict, Russian sought to take advantage of it to strengthen her hold upon Turkey, while England out of fear for Russian aggrandisement, prevented a peaceful settlement of the dispute. All diplomats of Ottoman empire realized only way to preserve Turkish empire is to divide them and when diplomats of Turkey became sure of division of European powers, they initiated and declared war on Russia. Terms of treaty of Pairs of 1856 which was concluded after Crimean War were favourable to Ottoman Empire and gave it chance for reform and for preservation but Ottoman Empire was decaying rapidly so all chance of reform or for its preservation failed and its disintegration became inevitable. Young Turk movement and reforms of Midhat Pasha etc. were also out come of Crimean war.

Eastern Question from 1856 to 1878

Emergence of Rumania

Ottoman Turkish Empire did not show any improvement and at the Treaty of Paris of 1856, European statesmenship had failed to recognise that the Turkish Empire in Europe was doomed. The European Powers, especially England sought to bolster up what was evidently on the road to destruction, and so their attempts were reduced only to a succession of barren expedients. The nineteenth century ideal of nationality had touched the Balkan states of Ottoman Empire and the Christian nations under Turkish rule became restive under its inspiration. The result was that in spite of the ostensible protection of the European concert the Ottoman Empire began to disintegrate and break up. The official Eastern policy of Europe had alternative but to recognise grudgingly a series of accomplished facts. As such during the period from 1856 to 1878 there followed a series of glaring violation of the Treaty of Paris, which the Powers had to connive at. Turkey needed reforms but orthodoxy on the one hand and weak position of some of the Sultans failed to bring reforms so revolts in eastern Europe became common. The first of these act of defiance was the union of Wallachia and Moldavia into one kingdom, viz. that of Rumania. Both these principalities were inhabited by a people who came from the same stock and spoke the same language, and who applied to themselves the single term, Rumanian. Animated by the prevailing impulse towards national unity these people wanted a union of the two provinces under one national government. By the Peace of Paris of 1856, it was declared that the two principalities were to be autonomous but were to remain separate. This arbitrary separation they challenged in 1859 by each electing the same person, Alexander Couza, as their Hopsdar or Prince. England, Austria and Turkey etc. opposed this union as it was breach of the Treaty of Paris of 1856, but Napoleon III of France showed himself sympathetic to the nationalist aspirations of the Rumanians. In 1861, the European Powers had to recognise the union as an accomplished fact and the nation of Rumania came into existence.

In Ottoman Empire, under the pressure of western powers Abdul Hamid was made Sultan and Midhat Pasha was made Grand Vizier with promise of reforms but due to policy of Abdul Hamid revolts became common. In 1867, Serbia, aided by Austria and England, secured the evacuation of her fortresses by the Turkish garrisons. Serbia thus practically became independent of Turkey. Lastly, Russia as soon as she had recovered from the blow of the Crimean War of 1854-56 began to interfere vigorously in the affairs of the Ottoman Empire. Thus in 1865, she encouraged the Cretan rebellion and 1870 helped the Bulgars to obtain ecclesiastical independence from Sultan of Turkey. Next year came a startling infraction of the Peace of Paris. In the midst of the Franco-German War 1870 in which France was defeated and Nepoleon III lost throne of France. Russia was encouraged by Bismarck to repudiate the Black Sea clauses of the Treaty of Paris as Nepoleon III, the main architect of treaty of Paris was no more in power and France was weak so Russia broke treaty and recovered the right to refortify Sebastopol and maintain a fleet on the Black Sea. England protested but in vain. Finally, in 1877 she decided to make war upon Turkey and Disraeli, the Prime Minister of England gave ultimatum to Russia and Austria showed hostility toward Russia.

The Russo-Turkish War (1877-78) took place because Russia relied on the friendship of Bismarck who was greatest and most powerful statesman of his times and Prime Minister of Germany. In 1875, the Eastern Question once more entered upon an acute phase in Ottoman Empire. Two things had become clear in the Balkan Peninsula. One was the increasing restlessness of the subject states of Turkey, due to their growing nationalist aspirations and race-consciousness. The spectacle of the Serbs, the Greeks and the Rumanians winning their partial or complete freedom inevitably aroused the other non-Turkish Christian inhabitants of the Balkans to attempt a like movement for freedom. This feeling was especially strong among the different Slav people of the Balkans, who were influenced by Pan Slavism of Russia and were sure of Russian support so they began to be conscious of their racial kinship with the Slavs of Russia, Poland and Austrian dominions. This Pan Slavic feeling was encouraged by Russia whose agents carried on an unceasing propaganda among the Balkan Slavs of the South to stir up racial consciousness and national hostility and rise against Ottoman Empire. Nationalism was thus becoming tinged with racialism. The leadership of the South Slav agitation seemed about to be assumed by Serbia who began to dream of uniting under her rule all the Serbs and their close relations, the Croats etc. into the kingdom of Serbia which is now called Yugoslavia because it has become much larger by absorbing Croats etc. Besides Pan-Salvism and the growth of national feeling, there was another factors in the Balkans which precipitated this crisis. This was the disappointment of all hopes of Turkish revival and reform. The Sultan Abdul Hamid had not carried out his promised reforms for his Christian subject. On the contrary his incompetence and extravagance had imposed upon them a burden which was almost past endurance. As a protest against the cruelty rapacity and grinding extortion of his tax-collectors the peasants of Bosnia and Herzegovina rose in revolt 1875. Their fellow-Serbs of Montenegro and Serbia sympathised with them in their distress and helped them. This movement and revolt threatened to be widespread and so to localize the conflict, the European Powers presented to the Porte what is known as the Andrassy Note (After the Austrian Chancellor Count Andrassy) protesting against Turkish misgovernment. Sultan Abdul Hamid accepted the protest and promised reforms, but the insurgents demanded more substantial guarantees than elusive promises of deceptive Sultan Abdul Hamid. Meanwhile Bulgaria caught the letter and so the European Powers to prevent a general conflagration issued another note, the Berlin Memorandum, calling upon the Porte to make concessions and threatening armed intervention in default. But as Great

Britain refused to be a party to any measure of coercion and war against Turkey, Sultan Abdul Hamid was encouraged to ignore the protest of European power. As the Bulgarian rising threatened Turkish rule nearer to Constantinople so it was put down with horrible cruelty. The atrocities committed by the Turkish irregulars thrilled all Europe with horror. In England ex. Prime Minister, Gladstone thundered against the Turks, declaring that they should be cleared out with "bag and baggage from the province they have desolated and profaned." But it was Disraeli, the Jew, and not Gladstone, the ardent Christian, who was then Prime Minister of England and Disraeli's concern was more for what Russia might do in the Balkans than for the oppressed Christians of Bulgaria. Disraeli's attitude made joint action and declared war against Turkey in 1877. She could not ignore the suffering of her co-religionists of orthodox Church and fellow-Slavs so war between Russia and Turkey began.

The Russian army crossed the Danube and invaded the Turkish territories in Europe and Asia. The Chief feature of the campaign was the famous siege of Plevna which the Turks under Osman Pasha defended with the most gallantry and heroism which excited the admiration of the world but all was in vain. The fall of Plevna broke the back of Turkish resistance and the Russian forces marched towards Constantinople. The Ottoman Sultan sought peace and agreed to the terms of the Treaty of San Stefano, which Russia forced upon her. This treaty practically decreed the dissolution of the Turkish Empire. The Ottoman Sultan was to recognise the independence of Serbia and Montenegro, etc. with increased territories. Reforms were to be introduced in Bosnia and Herzegovina. Russia was to acquire Batum and Kars in Asia and Bessarabia in Europe. Rumania was to be recognised as an independent power and was to receive Dobrudja in compensation for the loss of Bessarabia. But the most striking feature of this treaty was the creation of the "Big Bulgaria" which was to be an autonomous state nominally tributary to Turkey, and was to extend from the river Danube to the Aegean sea and from the Black Sea to Albania. This Treaty of San Stefano was a great triumph for Russia. It wiped out the humiliation of the Crimean War and promised her once again the predominance in Ottoman Empire specially in the Balkans. In especial, she expected to control Bulgaria which was her creation. The extension of Russian influence over Ottoman Empire and in the Balkan States was prejudicial to England's interests and so she demanded a revision of this

Treaty of San Stefano by a Congress of European Powers. Austria-Hungary also cherished ideas of expansion in the Balkans and so did not like either the creation of strong Balkan states like Bulgaria or the extension of Russian influence in the Balkan peninsula. Hence she joined hands with England in asking Russia to submit the Eastern Question to the collective decision of the European Powers, as this question affected them all. The war-like attitude of England and hostility of Austria at last compelled Russia to agree to refer the settlement of the Turkish question to a Congress of European Powers. Bismarck of Germany promised to act as honest broker so under his Presidentship conference took place.

Berlin Congress

The Congress met in Berlin in 1878 under Bismarck's presidency. It drew up the Treaty of Berlin by which the following arrangements were made : (1) Montenegro, Serbia and Rumania were declared independent of Turkey. (2) The "Big Bulgaria" of the Treaty of San Stefano was divided into two parts; one part was made a self-governing principality, subject to the payment of an annual tribute to the Ottoman Sultan, while the other part (southern part) was constituted as the province of East Roumelia with an independent administration under a Christian governor but under the nominal Turkish suzerainty. A considerable portion of the Macedonian territories, which was formerly included in the Big Bulgaria, was again restored to Turkey. (3) Austria was allowed to "occupy" and administer Bosnia and Herzegovina, which nominally remained under the suzerainty of Turkey. (4) Russia received Bessarabia and also a number of territories in Asia Minor. (5) England, by a separate treaty with Turkey, secured the control of Cyprus.

Critical Estimate of Treaty of Berlin

This treaty of Berlin has been greatly criticised by historians. By the Treaty of Paris of 1856, the Powers had guaranteed the territorial integrity of the Ottoman Empire. But by the Treaty of Berlin on the other hand dismemberment of Ottoman Empire was decreed. Three of the Balkan states — Serbia, Rumania and Montenegro etc. were declared entirely independent of Turkey, while a new state, Bulgaria, was called into existence and was made only nominally subject to the Porte. Besides, two of the guarantors of the Turkish integrity, Great Britain and Austria, helped themselves to grab large portions of the Turkish spoils. The Treaty of Berlin of 1878, was thus an ironical commentary on the good faith of the Powers who affected so much solicitude for Turkish integrity. It is perhaps difficult to resist the conclusion that the diplomats of Berlin revised the Treaty of San Stefano not in the interest of justice and equity or in the interest of Ottoman empire but in the interest of Austria and Great Britain. They made a settlement of Berlin which ignored the interests and sentiments of the Balkan peoples. They simply sought to harmonise the conflicting interests of England, Austria and tried to appease Russia by a policy of balance and compromise. Thus, as a set off to Russian acquisitions, Austria was allowed to occupy Bosnia and Herzegovina, and England Cyprus. But this arrangement, based as it was upon selfish principles of major European powers completely ignored the national sentiments of the Balkan peoples. Thus Roumania was offended by the Russian acquisition of Bessarabia, a territory peopled by Roumanians and not by Russians. The same disregard of national sentiment was shown when the Slavs of Bosnia and Herzegovina, who desired union with their fellow Slavs of Serbia, were handed over to Austrian rule against their wishes. This act later on brought World War I in 1914.

This alarmed as well as irritated Serbia. The division of the "Big Bulgaria" of the Treaty of San Stefan was a cruel blow to the national aspiration of the Bulgars and it was made only to please Austria-Hungary, was feared that a Big Bulgaria, friendly to Russia, might block the path of the future Austrian expansion towards the Aegean Sea. Lastly, the Christians of Macedonia were left in the hands of the Ottoman Sultan even after the Bulgarian atrocities had shown what kind of treatment they might expect. This undesirable arrangement was made in order to bolster up Ottoman Turkey although her empire had been mutilated beyond revival. It simply prolonged the process and multiplied the pains of extinction, and the Macedonian question was to be a constant source of unrest and revolt and of friction in the future settlement, which took little heed of the Balkan peoples and much less of Turkey, as such it could not be a satisfactory solution of the Eastern question. The subsequent history of the Balkan states and of Ottoman Turkey is no credit to the statesmanship of those who designed the Treaty of Berlin. Probably treaty of Berlin contained the germs of Balkan wars and even of World War I of 1914 and of disintegration of Ottoman Empire, Disraeli returned from Berlin claiming to have brought "peace with honour." For the time being there was temporary peace no doubt but it was a calm before storm and as to honour opinions differed. He had, indeed, negatived the right of individual intervention claimed by Russia and compelled her to acknowledge the collective authority of the European Powers in the affairs of Ottoman Empire. A check had been administered to Russia in the interest of England and Austria, and Turkey was allowed to recover a portion of the territory which she had lost at treaty of San Stefano. But on closer inspection it will be found that the triumph was only apparent. Russia, though checked, had practically recovered all the losses of the Crimean War. Bessarabia was hers and the Black Sea was no longer closed to her war vessels. Besides this if the shadow of the Russian bear was shortened in the west *i.e.,* in Balkans, it began to lengthen in Central Asia until it touched the mountains guarding the north-west frontier of India. Thus the Russian menace to British interests was transferred from Europe to Asia, but was not removed. Thus the treaty of Berlin had not the intended effects of weakening Russia and strengthening Ottoman Turkish Empire. Besides, to look upon this treaty as honourable, to England, as claimed by Disraeli, one must revise one's idea of honour. An arrangement which took advantage of Turkey's extremity to tear away from the Cyprus, Bosnia and Herzegovina etc. looked very like robbery, specially when it was made by those who professed the principle of the integrity and presentation of the Ottoman Empire. Preservers of honour emerged as rapists. This lead Ottoman Empire to disintegration and decay and decline.

Lastly, the diplomats of Berlin were not far sighted enough to see that the Treaty of Berlin of 1878 contained within itself seed of perilous developments in future. In holding back one great Power *i.e.,* (Russia) from the Balkans they let loose another viz., Austria. Austria was allowed to commit herself to the policy of acquiring territory in the Balkans in direct opposition to Russian and Serbian national feeling and opposition of Ottoman Empire. Her occupation of Bosnia and Herzegovina embittered her relations with Serbia and Russia and this in the long run gave rise to complications which directly led to the First World War of 1914. Again, Bismarck although he posed himself as "honest broker," was obliged to take sides between Austria and Russia in this crises. He chose Austria and thereby alienated Russia. As a consequence the latter was thrown into the arms of France. Here was the remote origin of the estrangement between Russia and Germany, which before long divided Europe into two armed rival camps *i.e.,* to the Dual Alliance between

Russia and France and Bismarck's Triple Alliance. Thus, the political situation in Europe began to take that formidable shape which produced the Great War of 1914. Lastly, the Macedonian problem led to the Balkan wars of 1912 and 1913, which broke peace of Ottoman Empire and of Europe. Thus instead of bringing about the pacification of the Balkans, the Treaty of Berlin contributed to increase the unrest and friction among the Balkan peoples and unrest in Ottoman empire, which produced in the future local conflicts and world-wide conflagration. This treaty of Berlin proved harmful to Ottoman Empire and ultimately lead to its fall and dismemberment. Problems created by disappearance of Ottoman empire gave rise to conflict in Near East and Middle East which still baffle solution, and are a threat to world peace.

The Condition of Ottoman Empire from 1878 to 1908 and Balkan Wars

Sultan Abdul Hamid of Ottoman and Turkish empire inspite of loss of territory in Berlin conference continued to pass time in intrigues without caring for the fate of his empire. As noticed before the Treaty of Berlin disappointed the hopes it had raised and so its terms generally were honoured more in their breach than in their observance. As a matter of fact the subsequent history of the Balkans is a tale of the successive violations of the Berlin settlement of 1878 and of the international complications of Balkan states which resulted therefrom. The Balkan nations snapped their fingers at this Treaty. Nor were the European Powers very keen upon its observance, while one of them (Austria) openly flouted it. The major European Powers had their own rival ambitions in the Balkans and Ottoman empire as a whole so that they could not follow any agreed policy in grappling with the Eastern Question. Hence the Balkan region and Ottoman Empire continued to be storm center of Europe, and the buffetings of these storms which began to blow from all points of the compass brought European Turkey almost to the point of extinction. Gradually Egypt was grabbled by Britain, Algeria by France and Libya by Italy thus European powers were grabbing territories of Ottoman Empire. After the Treaty of Berlin and the Eastern Question began to reveal new developments. First, the freed Balkan nations instead of being content and satisfied with their freedom, wished to add to their realms those people of their nationality who still remained under Turkish rule. As their claims often overlapped, the Balkan region provided a spectacle of increasing unrest, frequent wars and of growing ambitions. Secondly, Turkey was touched by the prevailing national spirit and made a serious attempt of reforms of revival. But this movement never had a chance through constitution was launched in 1876. For the Balkan Sates and other Powers took advantage of the opportunity provided by the "Young Turk" revolution to grab Ottoman territories and aggrandise themselves at the expense of Turkey and to embroil her in international complications. Thirdly, the intrusion of Austria into the Balkans brought in new complications. Backed by Germany she began to pursue a course of action which antagonised Serbia and Russia which precipitated the Great War of 1914. Lastly, there was a newcomer to the Near Eastern politics, *viz.*, Germany. She sought expansion of her influence there, for reasons both political and economic. Under Kaiser William II, she became the friend of the Sultan of Turkey, in the nineties, training his army, posing as the protector of the Mohammedans throughout the world and planning the Berlin-Baghdad Railway under German auspices. All these acts annoyed Britain, France and Russia, so they came together against Ottoman empire, Germany and Austria. They even began to think of dividing Ottoman Empire by secret treaties as previously propounded by Czar. The following are some of the important developments of the Ottoman Empire and of the Eastern Question after the Treaty of Berlin of 1878. During the reign of Sultan Abdul Hamid, Grand Vizier Midhat Pasha tried for reforms but got little success. As such Union of Eastern Roumelia with Bulgaria took place and Turkey was able to do nothing. In fact after 1878, Turkey became helpless in Balkan affairs. As such Bulgaria was the first state to challenge the Berlin settlement of 1878. The separation between Bulgaria and Eastern Roumilia as effected at the Congress of Berlin. It was an arbitrary and artificial act as it corresponded to no racial divisions. It was done because the European Powers feared that a big Bulgaria, brought into existence by Russia, would be a mere tool in the hands of the Russian Czar. But racial kinship is stronger than the treaties, and the people of Eastern Roumelia effected in 1885, a bloodless revolution had proclaimed their political union with their kinsmen of Bulgaria. The Bulgarian king, Prince Alexander of Battenburg, responded to their call and declared himself as Prince and ruler of the United Bulgaria. The Ottoman Sultan Abdul Hamid protested against this violation of the Treaty of Berlin, and the Czar of Russia in anger recalled his officers from the Bulgarian army, but the British Government headed by Gladstone approved this union of Bulgaria which was then accepted as an accomplished fact by the other Powers. The only state actively to oppose this union was Serbia who out of anger, sentiment and jealousy declared that the Bulgarian aggrandisement threatened the balance of power in the state of Balkans, and went to war with Bulgaria. In this Balkan war that ensured Serbia was badly beaten by the Bulgarians who were, however, stopped in the midst of their victorious career by Austria who forced a treaty on the combatants on the basis of maintaining status quo, in Balkan Peninsula, Ottomon empire ruled by Abdul Hamid remained a silent spectator and could do nothing. With regard to the attitude of the other Powers towards Bulgaria, a curious inversion of position should be noted. At the Congress of Berlin, England lead by Disraeli was loudest in denouncing the Big Bulgaria which was the creation of Russia at San Stefano. It was largely owing to her insistence that the division of Bulgaria was effected. Now Government of England lead by Gladstone condoned the violation of the Treaty of Berlin and approved the union of Bulgaria with Eastern Roumelia, while Russia opposed this union and denounced a Big Bulgaria which she had created at San Stefano. This change of attitude was due to the fact that Bulgaria instead of being the cat's paw of Russia as anticipated in Berlin, showed herself very independent attitude towards her blustering patron (Russia). England realised that an independent and strong Bulgaria hostile to Russia would be a surer bulwark against Russian aggrandisement than two weak Bulgarias, still under the influence of decadent Ottoman Turkey. Though England displayed a change of attitude, she still adhered to the main object of checkmating Russian in Balkans as well as in Afghanistan.

After Bulgaria in the Ottoman Turkish Empire and the Armenian question had baffled solution. The Ottoman Turkish Empire contained people of diverse, races, religion and culture but nationalist feeling soon grew. The Armenian subjects of the Turks were exposed to periodical outrages throughout the nineteenth century. Armenia was England's protege and in the Treaty of Berlin, as well as in the Cyprus Convention between Turkey and England, the later had extracted from the Ottoman Sultan, promises of better treatment of the Armenians. The Porte, however, proved incorrigible because Sultan Abdul Hamid, was a man of dubious nature. The Turks feared that England like Russia, would set up another independent state in Armenia and so Turks were resolved upon exterminating the Armenians. Throughout 1894 and 1895 the merciless massacre of the Armenians continued and scenes of carnage was transferred to Constantinople itself, where about 6000 Armenians were done to death in a single day. There is no doubt that all these massacres were inspired or at least connived at by the Turkish Government of Sultan Abdul Hamid and inspired by religious and social feelings as Armenians were mostly Christians. What were the Powers doing whose slogan and goal was of collective responsibility in the Eastern Question? Russia would not stir because she did not like to set up another ungrateful Bulgaria in Armenia and because she wanted to have her revenge on England who had thwarted her in designs in Bulgaria. England's Prime Minister Disraeli had cared little for the Bulgarian atrocities and so Russia now cared less for the Armenian massacres. Germany was now anxious for Turkey's friendship and so instead of putting pressure on the Ottoman Sultan, ostentatiously displayed her good intentions towards him. Austria who was friend of Germany followed suit. England, left alone, protested and threatened in vain. She realised her mistake in having hitherto supported Ottoman Turkey and in making herself responsible for the good conduct of the deceptive Sultan Abdul Hamid who inherited throne after Abdul Aziz and Murdad V in 1876. Hence Lord Salisbury remarked that in trying to uphold the integrity of the Ottoman Empire, England had hitherto "put her money on the wrong horse." According to S.N. Fisher about one lakh people lost their lives in Armenian massacre and non Turkish subjects began to call Abdul Hamid II as the "Red Sultan" or Abdul, Turks began to be called "Terrible Turkus" and they lost sympathy of other people and as such the damned and Greaco Turkish war (1897) took place which brought another set back to Turkish Empire.

Greece had high hopes of obtaining a rectification of her frontier at the Congress of Berlin of 1878. But as nothing was done in that direction so the Greeks threatened war with Turkey. The European Powers, however, held her in check as they were not inclined to tolerate another Balkan war just then. But in 1881, the Sultan Abdul Hamid was persuaded by the British Government to cede Thessaly and a portion of Epirus to Greece. But Greeks greed increased which ultimately lead to Greaco-Turkish War of 1897.

The acquisition of the island of Crete next engaged that attention of the Greeks. This strategic island was inhabited mostly by the people of the Greek race, who wanted to throw off Turkish sovereignty and desired to unite themselves with Greece. Agitation for union grew stronger and insurrections against Turkish rule became chronic and common in this Island. But nothing came of these petty revolts except empty promises of reform from Sultan Abdul Hamid. In 1896 the flame of Greek rebellion flared up worse than ever and the revolutionaries in the Crete headed by Venizelos, proclaimed their union with Greece. This time Greece yielding to the popular enthusiasm sent an expedition to help the Cretan insurgents. Thereupon Ottoman Turkey declared war upon Greece, easily defeated her, and compelled her to abandon the project of annexing Crete and also to cede a portion of Thessaly to Turkey. After long negotiations among European Powers, it was decided that Crete should be an autonomous state under Turkish suzerainty. The Island of Crete was placed under an international commission of four Powers with Prince George, a son of the king of Greece was appointed as a governor there. This arrangement did not satisfy the Cretans who made several attempts at union with Greece but were held in check by the European Powers. It was not until after the Balkan War of 1912 in which Turkey was smitten hip and thigh that they finally recognized the union of Crete with Greece in 1913, through Turkish minority gradually emigrated and according to S.N. Fisher, "by 1908, union was finally achieved less than 10% of population was Muslim". In this way Ottoman Empire was deprived of Crete also.

The Young Turk Movement and Its Consequences

The Young Turk movement according to S.N. Fisher was a natural reaction to oppression, absolution, and corruption in the regime of Abdul Hamid II. The Eastern Question entered upon a new and startling phase in 1908. It grew from the organisation of secret society in 1889 at Istambul Imperial Medical College. A reforming party had grown up in Ottoman Empire, consisting of Turks mostly educated in the West. They wanted to change and modernise Turkey and to free her from the tutelage of foreign Powers and to pursue a strictly national policy. These Young Turks effected army mutinies and later on a bloodless revolution which forced the Sultan Abdul Hamid II, to grant a constitution.

A Turkish parliament was summoned and many liberal reforms were promulgated.

But Abdul Hamid II who had ruled Turkey from 1876 to 1909, attempted a counter-revolution for which he was deposed and his brother, Mohammad V, was proclaimed Sultan in (1909) as Young Turks after capturing Constantinople with the aid of army got a resolution passed in the Turkish parliament for dethroning Abdul Hamid II and installing Mohammad V.

The prospect of Turkey, rejuvenated and reformed under aggressive Turks made the European states uneasy and so there followed a series of startling infractions of the Treaty of Berlin. Bulgaria declared its complete independence of Turkey. Austria definitely annexed Bosnia and Herzegovina, the provinces which under the Treaty of Berlin, she was authorised only to 'occupy' and administer. By this step Austria pushed her frontiers several miles nearer the Aegean Sea towards which she had been turning her eyes for a maritime outlet ever since her expulsion from Italy and Germany. Russia strongly protested and Serbian people rose against Austria's conduct, but as Russia was weakened by her war with Japan in 1904-1905 she was not prepared for a fresh war. Thus Treaty of Berlin was openly flouted, and England, France and Russia had to swallow their humiliation for the sake of peace. But the state most aggrieved by this occurrence was Serbia. Bosnia and Herzegovina were mostly inhabited by the people of the Serbian race and the Serbians had long entertained the ambition of annexing them dreamt of forming Yugoslavia *i.e.* big Serbia. The annexation of those provinces by Austria not only dashed their hopes to the ground but also prevented their expansion to the sea. So the action of Austria made the Serbians highly indignant — a situation auguring ill for the future peace of the world.

Italy had long been looking for expansion to the northern shore of Africa and had marked out Libya *i.e.* Tripoli as her share of the Turkish spoils. She saw her chances threatened by the nationalist revival by Young Turk movement in Turkey and so suddenly declared war against the Ottoman Sultan and compelled him to cede Tripoli in 1911. On October 1912, Treaty of Orchy was signed. Under the terms of this treaty Turkey withdrew from Libya but Italy agreed to assume a share of Turkey's debts and authority of Caliph was recognised in Libya. Thus Libya went to Italy.

The policy of the Young Turks was to establish their own

dictatorship under the constitutional rule of Mohammad V who was a mild gentleman. He was the constitutional Monarch for Young Turks. Though professing constitutional principles the Young Turks disappointed popular expectations. Executive committee of Young Turks called society of Union and Progress ruled. Their policy was one of "Turkification", in other words, they sought to maintain the uncontrolled domination of the Turks over various people of their composite empire containing people of diverse races people of the subject races were harassed and different religion and colour cruelly prosecuted. Especially cruel was their treatment of Macedonia and Albania etc. The result of this unwise and senseless policy of prosecution was to produce widespread disaffection in Ottoman Empire and even among Arabs who were orthodox Muslims which soon brought Turkey to decay, decline and lead to the point of extinction. Policy of Turkification brought revolts in Asia minor, in Yemen and Asir and in Albania and in Macedonia etc. and finally lead to Balkan wars. Young Turks lost Libya, Bulgaria, Bosnia, Herzegovina and Turkish Empire lost 80% territory and about 2/3 population due to mismanagement.

The First Balkan War, of 1912 and Its Consequences

Being aware of weakness of Turkey and annoyed by policy of Turkification Bulgarias, Greece, Serbia and Montenegro decided to fight with Turkey and to share spoils of wars. As such the next crisis in the Balkans arose out of the unsatisfactory state of affairs in Macedonia. The condition of Macedonian Christians under Turkish rule of Young Turks was miserable and the European Powers had very often interfered to secure redress of their grievances. The Young Turks saw that this last remnant of the Turkish Empire was gradually passing under the foreign control and so they pursued a vigorous policy of Turkification in Macedonia. This attempt to impose the Turkish rule more firmly on the Christians intensified their distress, and as a consequence provoked the resentment of their Balkan kinsmen and co-religionists. Hence they wanted to liberate Macedonia from Turkish rule and to divide this territory among themselves. As this would be very difficult under a revived and rejuvenated Turkey ruled by young Turks, they chose the moment when Turkey was still being harassed and weakened by her disastrous war with Italy. Four of the Balkan states-Serbia, Bulgaria, Greece and Montenegro, forgetting their differences formed a league to take joint action against the

Ottoman Empire. They pressed for the execution of reforms in Macedonia and when Turkey which was ruled by Young Turks refused to concede their demands, they declared war against her. In their Turkification intense nationalism the Young Turks had sown the wind and now they had to reap the whirlwing. The European Powers warned the Balkan states declaring that they would not allow any modification of the territorial integrity of Turkey, but in vain. The four allied Balkan states launched attacks upon Turkey on four sides and within a short time the Ottoman Empire was reduced to Constantinople and to nearby territory and to Arab Muslim states of Asia. Overwhelmed by disasters on all sides Turkey appealed to the European Powers who imposed an armistice and called a peace conference in London in 1912. But the peace negotiations failed as there were disputes concerning the cession of certain territories which Turkey was called upon to make by Balkan states. The proposed surrender of Adrianople infuriated the Young Turks who lead by Enver by violently overthrew the Turkish Government of grand Vizier Kamal Pasha of liberal unionist at Constantinople lest it should agree to it. War broke out again, in 1913 and again Turkey was defeated. The Serbs and the Bulgars captured Adrianople, and the Montenegrins and Scutari etc. The fall of Scutarial most precipitated a great European war. Austria and Italy would not allow it to be included in Montenegro. Albania was proposed to be made a separate autonomous state. They also further forced Serbia to withdraw from the coveted Adriatic port of Durazzo. Russia in the interest of Pan slavism supported the claims of Montenegro and Serbia. War seemed imminent between Austria and Russia but it was averted due to goodwill of other powers.

Treaty of London. In April, 1913, a second armistice was arranged and peace was signed between Turkey and Balkan states. The Balkan victories again forced Turkey to come to terms and the Balkan war was brought to a close in 1913 by the Treaty of London. By it Turkey lost everything except Constantinople and nearby territories with just enough territory in Thrace to hold it safe and sound. She also ceded Crete to Greece. Another important feature of this treaty was the creation of Albania as an autonomous state. This was done mainly at the demand of Austria who was determined to prevent Serbia from gaining access to the Adriatic sea. The result was that the Austro-Serbian rivalry was immensely intensified. Crete was taken from Turkey and annexed with Greece. Territories of

Macedonia were taken away from Turkey. Demarcation was made between Media and port of Aegian Island.

The Balkan league soon broke up over the division of the spoils of war. The question of partitioning Macedonia among the victors proved a very thorny question. Serbia, pushed back from Albania and cut off from her ambitions in the Adriatic sea, demanded compensation in Macedonia. This was opposed by Bulgaria. Elated with pride the Bulgarians suddenly attacked Serbia. This action roused the other Balkan states, and Greece and Rumania made common cause with Serbia against Bulgaria. Turkey joined the allies in the hope of recovering some of the territories recently lost by the Treaty of London. As such attacked on all sides by many powers, Bulgaria was hopelessly beaten and was compelled to sue for peace. By the Treaty of Bucharest (1913) Bulgaria was forced to make concessions on all sides, to Serbia and Greece she abandoned considerable sections of Macedonia which she had claimed, Rumania received a strip of Bulgarian territory while Turkey recovered Adrianople and part of Thrace etc. Montenegro and Serbia got additional lands, Greece got Salomica and even Bulgaria got remaining part of Macedonia.

Results of the Balkan Wars

These Balkan wars broke the peace of Europe and intensified rivalry of major European powers which ultimately led to great war of 1914.

"Territorially the final results of the two Balkan wars were the practical extinction of the Turkish Empire in Europe and the enlargement of the Christian kingdoms in the Balkan peninsula." The greatest gainers were Serbia and Greece. While probably Bulgaria came off worst. Turkey lost four fifths of her former European territory and was reduced to the south-eastern corner of the Balkan peninsula. Turkish empire in Europe was reduced in 1913 to l/5th of what it was in 1908 and only 2 million population out of former 6 million population remained. Constant defeats encouraged other nationalities and races such as Arabs and Jews etc. to revolt. But the wars cannot be said to have solved any of the Balkan problems. The second Balkan war was perhaps a fratricidal one and it intensified the national rivalries among the Balkan states. Bulgaria nursed a great and a deep resentment which led her to join the Central Powers in the Great War of 1914 which broke out next year. "Russia appeared again in the role of protector of the Balkan states, no longer against Ottoman Turkey, but against, Hapseburg Austria." The victory of Serbia and Greece, and their gain of Macedonia and Salonika blocked the way of Austrian penetration to the Agean sea. The phenomenal increase of Serbian power and prestige produced an outbrust of Pan-Serb and Yogo Salv enthusiasm which was very disquieting to Austria. The Slavs of Bosania and of Herzegovina under Austrian rule looked forward to the day when their free kinsmen in Serbia would liberate them from the unpopular Austrian yoke. Austria was greatly perturbed by the widespread Slav movements and looked upon Serbia as the promoter of subversive propaganda among Slav subjects of Austrian empire. So she began to look for an opportunity to crush Serbia. Serbia in her turn, was annoyed and highly exasperated by the persistent efforts of Austria to block her expansion in the Balkans. She sought to take revenge by intensifying anti-Austria propaganda and by intriguing with the Slav subjects of Austria. It was this strained relation between Austria and Serbia that before long precipitated the Great War of 1914-18. Due to these Balkan wars Ottoman Empire had to suffer a serious loss from the point of loss of territories population and to prestige and power.

Question how the results of the Balkan wars produced fierce international rivalries. Turkey and Bulgaria had been weakened, but they drifted towards central powers and became the proteges of Germany and Austria. Serbia, the recent protege of Russia, become the most powerful state in the Balkans. Hence the relation between Russia on the one hand and Germany and Austria on other hand became highly strained over the Balkan affairs. The situation become so very explosive that before long it burst forth into the catastrophic war of 1914, when rival powers came in conflict.

The Condition of Ottoman Empire till World War I

In the closing decades of the nineteenth century, the decaying Ottoman Empire was a disreputable, vicious oriental despotism though Mahmud II attempted reforms. After him Abdul Mejid succeeded and later on Abdul-Hamid II and during his rule in 1876 a liberal constitution had been issued and a new Sultan, Abdul Hamid II, had come to the throne with the support of a liberal faction but only a short time elapsed before the new ruler made himself absolute Sultan. The constitution of 1876, was abrogated in 1878, and Abdul-Hamid II began to rule without parliament, aided by about forty thousand spies.

The strict censorship was applied, and opponents of this tyranny mysteriously disappeared or were forced in exile.

At the same time, Abdul Hamid was fighting a losing battle to hold together the remainder of his Ottoman empire. In North Africa, France, which had seized Algeria in 1830, annexed Tunis in 1881; Britain occupied Egypt in 1882 and by 1900 Italy had a covetous eye on the Tripoli and whole of Libya. But there remained under Turkish rule the Arab world of the Near East, inhabited by peoples who were proud of their traditions and who were Muslim in religion and bound to Sultan of Turkey as he was Caliph but not Turkish in nationality. The same nationalist spirit which had bestirred nineteenth-century Europeans now began to arouse Arab leaders also against Turkish rule.

Young Turks and Young Arabs. Meanwhile, opposition to Ottoman Sultan's tyranny mounted among his Turkish subjects. The nucleus for this opposition was the organization known as the Young Turks, composed of reformers who had been educated in western European universities. Many converts to this reform group were officers in the Turkish army, which provided the necessary military power for successful rebellion. In 1908, the Young Turks rebelled, Abdul Hamid II restored the liberal 1876's constitution. But after gaining what they desired for themselves, the Young Turks refused to share their victory with the non-Turkish peoples. The result was a counter revolution encouraged by the Ottoman Sultan, who sought to regain power. When Abdul Hamid II turned against the young Turks, however, he was overthrown and replaced by his weak and innocuous brother.

Arabs in Syria, Lebanon, and the vast peninsula of Arabia groaned under the Young Turk's programme of Turkish supremacy and their policy of centralization, which left no opportunity for Arab home rule.

As such afterwards, when fighting against Turkey during World War I Britain found it relatively easy to turn the Arab tribes against their overlord, the sultan of Turkey who was also Caliph of Islam.

Meanwhile the disintegration of the Ottoman Empire proceeded apace. In the years between 1908 and 1913 Austria-Hungary annexed Bosnia and Herzegovina which were two Turkish provinces on the Adriatic coast that had been occupied and administered by the Dual Monarchy of Austria since 1878; Greece annexed Crete; and Italy, in the course of a short war, seized Tripoli and Cyrenaica, in Libya. Finally, the Balkan nations fought two wars with the Ottoman Empire in 1912 and 1913 and partitioned Turkish Macedonia also. These annexations and Balkan wars brought about dispute among the great powers, and in particular they created an explosive situation in the Balkans that touched of World War I, Balkan state of Serbia's two parts Bosania and Herzegovina were annexed by Austria so patriots of Serbia murdered a prince of Austria. Being annoyed Austria gave ultimatum and declared war against Serbia Russia following her traditional policy supported Serbia and Germany supported Austria. France and later on Britain supported Russia and Serbia and Turkey supported Germany and Austria which were defeated in 1918. This defeat brought complete end of Ottoman Empire. Iraq and Palestine etc. were grabbed by Britain and Syria and Lebanon by French and Arabian Peninsula became free from Turkish yoke. Thus Ottoman Empire disappeared and in its place progressive republican rule was established under Mustafa Kemal Pasha.

The Causes of Disintegration of Ottoman Empire

The reasons for the decline of the Ottoman Empire are to be sought, probably less in the inherent strength of its neighbours than in its own internal weakness and dissensions and revolts which have been already described probably domestic, as well as foreign, difficulties prepared the way for its subsequent shrinkage.

It should be kept in mind that the Muslim Turks never constituted a majority of the population of their European possessions. They were essentially a body of conquerors. In frenzies of religious or martial enthusiasm, inspired with the sword or had taken clever advantage of their enemies quarrels to plant over wide areas the crescent in place of the cross. In the European conquered regions, the native Christian peoples were reduced to serfdom, and the Turkish conquerors became great landholders and the official ruling elite class. To extend, even to maintain, such an artificial order of things, the Turks would be obliged to keep their military organization always at the highest pitch of excellence and to preserve their government from weakness and corruption inefficiency and luxury and debauchery etc. But in neither of these respects did the Turks ultimately succeed, so fall of Ottoman Empire became inevitable.

The Ottoman Sultans of the eighteenth century were not of the stuff of which a Mohammed II or a Suleiman the magnificent had been made. To the grim risks of battle they preferred the cushioned ease of the palace, and all their powers of administration and government were quite consumed in the debauchery, management of the household and the heremoslaves etc. Actual authority was gradually transferred to viziers the divan, or board of ministers, whose appointments of dismissals were the results of palace intrigues, sometimes peaceful but more often bloody. Corruption ate its way through the entire office-holding element of the Ottoman Empire from Sultan to lowest officer.

Positions were brought and sold from the divan down to the headship of obsecure village and Government office seemed to exist primarily for financial profit and secondarily as a means of opposing and exploiting the subject people.

The army, on which so much in the Ottoman empire depended, naturally reflected the demoralized condition of the Ottoman Government. While Russian Czar Peter the great, was organizing a powerful army in Russia, and Frederick the Great was perfecting the Prussian military machine in Prussia the Ottoman army steadily declined. It failed to keep peace with the scientific development and of military tactics and of new fire arms used in western Europe, and fell behind the times. The all-prevalent corruption ruined its morale and discipline, and its best organized portion-called the "Janisaries" became organisation of the masters rather than of the servants of the Ottoman sultans and of the whole Turkish government. They often revolted and exercised great influence over the policy of Ottoman Government.

It was the fortune of the Russian tsarina-Catherine the Great to know and appreciate the real weakness of both of Ottoman empire and of the kingdom of Poland, and to turn her neighbours' distress to the advantage of her own country.

Important Causes which led Turkey to Join Central Powers during World War I

The shot at Sarjevo, which killed Prince Ferdinand of Austria ultimately brought World War I in 1914 because European diplomats failed to bring compromise or reconciliation. The great majority of influential men of Ottoman Empire desired neutrality but a hard core of army leaders, dominant in the committee for union. Progress which ruled Turkey had come, under the spell of German diplomats and military generals. Sultan of Turkey posed himself as Caliph of Muslim world and

Kausir William II, the emperor of Germany extended hand of friendship to him posing himself as friend of Islamic countries. Commercial relations, plan of Berlin Baghdad railway and traditional enmity of Ottoman empire with Russia and above all ruling triumuire of Golz Pasha and of Anwar Pasha who was minister of war and of German ambassador Baron Von Waggenheim lead ruling Turkish elite class to enter in secret alliance with Germany on August 2, 1914 and this goaded Turkey to join Germany in World War I.

In this First World War Turkey achieved in the beginning success and gallopoli campaign of allies failed but revolts of Arabs, Armenians and of non-Turks shattered the power of Ottoman empire and it suffered defeat alongwith Germany and Austria etc. In treaty of Serves concluded on August 10, 1920, Ottoman empire was deprived of whole Arabia, Egypt, Syria Lebanon, Palestine and Iraq, etc. Thus Ottoman Empire became a shadow of her glorious past.

Impact. Word War of 1914 brought terrible hardship to the people of Ottoman empire so-much so that Lord Asquith the Prime Minister of England declared "the sick man had really died this time" and in 1921, Greek forces made a big attack upon Turkey but failed to take Ankara. Mustafa Kemal Pasha emerged as a leader of new Turkey, who defeated Greek forces. With this victory, Allies desired to pacify Turkey and helped it to get back the Eastern part of Thrace, Adrianpole, Amyrina, all the places of Anatolia and to preserve her hold on Kurdistan. In this way, due to efforts of Mustafa Kamal Pasha Turkey re-gained some places and prestiges but Ottoman Empire was replaced by republican national Turkish state under the leadership of Mustafa Kemal Pasha.

Mustafa Kamal's Rise to Power in Turkey

Reform measures had been initiated by the Young Turks in Ottoman empire just before World War I. Defeat in the World War I, the revolt of the Arabs, and the impotence of the Ottoman Sultan's government convinced some patriots of Turkey that only the most drastic measures could save the Turkish nation as they were embittered by the harsh terms of the Treaty of Sevres in (1920). It was bad enough to lose their empire, peopled by Arabs, but it was much worse to see their homeland, mainly Anatolia and the city of Smyrna, etc. partitioned by this treaty of Sevres and to be invaded by the Greeks and Italians inspite of loss of empire.

Imbued with a new spirit of nationalism, the patriots of Turkey rallied around the military hero Mustafa Kamal Pasha (1880-1938), who had a brilliant record against the British at Gallipoli in World War I of 1914-18. An important figure in the Young Turks movement, Kamal was a born leader, thoroughly western in education and outlook. After the defeat of Turkey, he had been sent by the Sultan Muhammad VI to demobilize the Turkish troops in Asia Minor, but disregarding his instructions, he had reorganized the troops and successfully defied the Allies. A new government of Turkey was set up in Ankara, and Kamal Pasha was selected as president and its commander in chief. Turkish patriotism was galvanized by the National Pact, a declaration of principles which upheld the rule of self determination and also proclaimed the abolition of the special rights here before enjoyed by foreigners in Turkey which was a mark of Turkish inequality in the family of nations.

Greek-Turkish War

In 1921 the Greeks advanced toward Ankara. The fighting was desperate, but the armies of Kemal Pasha were finally victorious. The Greeks fled in confusion towards the sea, and their last toe hold at Smyrna, was destroyed by fire. In 1922, the Turkish sultanate was abolished, and the following year a republic was established. The Allies had no alternative but to agree to a revision of treaty of Sevres. The Treaty of Lausanne which was signed in 1923, returned to Turkey some Aegean Islands and the territory adjoining Constantinople and other places. The heartland of Turkey-Anatolia remained intact and no reparations were demanded from the republic of Turkey. The special privileges of foreigners were abolished. Although Turkey had lost the whole Arabic speaking part of its possessions, Kamal Pasha had at least saved a large, cohesively Turkish portion of the former Ottoman Empire. He founded a secular and progressive republic of Turkey.

Kamal's Reforms. The new constitution of Turkey was democratic in form, but in reality Kemal was a dictator who brooked no interference with his plans. His dictatorship does not belong in the same category as those fashioned in Nazi Germany, or Fascist Italy, or in Communist Russia. In the new Turkey there was little of the cult of the superior race; the brutal efficiency of the purge and the concentration camp etc. were practically unknown. Dictatorship was regarded as the rough but essential highway for reforms and to parliamentary government. Kemal envisioned a dictatorship as a necessary stage in raising his people to that level of education and social and economic well-being which a system of democratic government requires.

Under his rule the old institutions and customs of a backward Oriental Islamic state were transformed or replaced within a few short years. In modern times such a wholesale adoption of new culture traits is duplicated perhaps nowhere except perhaps in Japan. The caliphate, the Ottoman Sultan's spiritual leadership of the Islamic world, was abolished. New law codes on western system were promulgated, and school attendance was required to the age of sixteen. Use of the fez cap by men and the purdah by women was forbidden. Polygamy was prohibited. In addition, the western Gregorian calendar and European numerals were introduced, and the Latin alphabet replaced the Arabic and even Turki language began to be written in Latin Alphabets.

Thus, Turkey was rejuvenated by its indefatigueable leader Kemal Pasha. More progress was made in the two decades after the end of the First World War than had been registered during the entire nineteenth century. Understandably, Mustafa Kemal was called Ataturk, Meaning "the father of the Turks" and architect of modern Turkey. During regime of George VI three credits were given to Turkey by England and in May, 1939, after the death of Kemal declaration of mutual guarantee was made by Turkey and England and Turkey remained neutral during World War II yet more committed and probably more friendly to Britain and France. In this way Mustafa Kemal Pasha modernized Turkey and he is considered maker of modern Turks and ranks with Sun-Yat San of China, Riza Shah Pahelvi of Iran etc. He made Turkey modern state with liberal democratic and secular state. In this way Turkey whose Sultan was Caliph of Islam became a progressive state. Abolition of Caliphate was opposed even in India and a movement opposing Caliphat was launched in 1921-22 along with non-co-operation movement of congress but this movement failed as Kemal Pasha abolished Caliphat and replaced Caliph Sultans rule with democratic rule.

29

THE NEAR AND MIDDLE-EAST

The Growth of Nationalism in Ottoman Empire and Its Results

Due to growth of nationalism Arabs rose in revolt against Ottoman Turkish Empire and gained many territories. The peace settlement that followed the First World War of 1914-18 gave a tremendous impetus to the principle of nationalism all the world over. The catchwords of self-determination and nationalism spread like wild fire to the Near and Middle East and stimulated the people there to throw of all alien rule and influences. Nationalism was extolled as a philosophy of life. As a consequence the twentieth century witnessed the remarkable phenomenon of nation-making all over Europe Asia, in the Near, Middle and Far East and even in Africa. In all these regions imperialism had to face a very difficult situation and had to yield by gradual steps to the forces of a new order. On the ruin of Turkish Ottoman empire, new states of Algeria, Libya, Tunisia, Iraq, Egypt, Palestine, Jordan, Syria, Lebanon, Saudi Arabia and many other states emerged and in Turkey itself new national state came in existence. In Turkey Mustafa Kamal Pasha gave slogan of Turkey for the Turks and established a Nationalist republican Turkish state.

Turkey touched the nadir of her humiliation when she was made to sign the Treaty of Severes in 1920. This treaty had stripped her of almost all her possessions so that her empire was reduced to the mountainous region of Anatolia and only to a small corner of Europe. This unusually harsh terms of the treaty shocked the Turks who lead them into immediate action. Their leader was Mustafa Kamal Pasha who smashed the elaborate structure built by the victorious allied Powers at Sevres. He after defeating Greek forces, forced victor powers to hand over many territories by which Turkey regained prestige.

The Achievements of Kamal Pasha, as Architect of Modern Turkey?

Life of Kamal Pasha. Born at Salonika in 1880, of Albanian parents Mustafa Kamal Pasha at an early age took up a soldier's life at the military staff school of Turkey at Constantinople. Here he obtained the name of Kamal, which means "perfection" for his proficiency in mathematics. He developed into a first-rate soldier and at the same time evinced a keen interest in the study of revolutionary literature. He came to detest the Ottoman Sultan's autocratic government and for a time joined the party of the Young Turks. But he disliked their muddled politics and intrigues and so in 1919, he went to France to study army manoeuvres. On coming back, he proved his military abilities by taking a prominent part in his country's wars against Italy and in the Balkan wars of 1912 and 1913. But what definitely established his reputation as an able military commander was his successful repulse of the British naval attack on Galipoli in 1915 during the First World War. When the World War I was over and the Allies imposed upon Turkey the humiliating terms in the Treaty of Sevres, Kamal Pasha felt extremely annoyed and humiliated. He sought to persuade Sultan Muhammad VI to resist the Allies and himself offered to lead the army against the Greeks. But the Turkish authorities were too timid to take any risk. So Kamal Pasha in anger resigned his command in Palestine and hastened to come to Constantinople. But the Sultan Muhammad VI's government sought to get him out of the way by transferring him to Anatolia as Inspector General in charge of the demobilization operation.

Mustafa Kamal Pasha was not the man to be baffled in this way. He went to Anatolia but instead of disbanding the army, he organized it. Then he set up a nationalist party called the People's Party with the motto "Turks for the Turks". This nationalist party of Turkey, met in two congresses and drew up a National Pact containing provisions which practically amounted to a refusal to accept the Severes Treaty. This pact was endorsed by Turkish parliament which had a nationalistic majority. But the Allies completely ignored this Pact and a British army marched into Constantinople. Government of Sultan of Turkey, proclaimed martial law and deported about forty nationalist deputies. Thereupon in 1920, Kamal Pasha summoned a Grand National Assembly at Ankara (Angora) and proclaimed it to be the sole representative of the Turkish national. The Assembly elected Kamal Pasha to be its president on October 23, 1923, and made him the commander-in-chief of the national army. Thus was set up a parallel Turkish government with Ankara as its headquarters. Kamal Pasha was to give a lead to the Turkish nation, which the Sultan Muhammad VI had failed to do. Muhammad VI who was Sultan of Turkey, left Istanbul for Malta in 1922, so grand national Assembly declared caliphate vacant and later on abolished it. This abolition brought Khilafat movement.

Kamal's first act was to clear the country of foreign troops. He compelled the Italian troops to quit Southern Anatolia and also expelled the French troops from Cilicia. By a friendly arrangement with Soviet Russia Kamal Pasha secured the surrender of Kars and communist Government of Russia which was eager to win friends. Ardahan from Communist Government of Russia which was eager to win friends. He then overthrew the recently established Armenian republic and established a new constitution in Turkey.

Kamal and the Greeks came in conflict which has been already briefly stated but main points may be stated again. The Greeks had secured valuable gains by the Treaty of Severes and so were keenly interested in enforcing its terms. They had expelled the Turks from Thrace and had occupied Smyrana. They looked with concern at the possibility of the revival of Turkish power under Kamal Pasha's leadership and so were eager to smash the nationalist Turks in their stronghold in Anatolia. In this project, they were encouraged probably by the British Government which perhaps offered them half heartedly moral and financial support. In 1921, they began their great offensive and pushed on towards Ankara. But they were checked by the stony and waterless plateau around Ankara and were repulsed with great loss by Mustafa Kamal Pasha's troops. It was a complete and colossal disaster for Greeks. Kamal then captured Smyrana and gave it up to the flames. He expelled not only the Greek soldiers but every Greek inhabitant from Asia Minor. Thus Asia Minor became purely land of Turks.

Flushed with success Kamal Pasha wanted to cross the straits in order to expel the Greeks from Thrace. But British warships guarded these straits and British Prime Minister Lloyd George threatened war if the Kamalists would attempt to cross into Europe. An Anglo-Turkish conflict seemed imminent. But it was averted and Kamal Pasha was persuaded to conclude an armistice in 1922. The Grand National Assembly of Turkey then decreed the abolition of the Sultanate and Muhammad VI fled to Malta on the board of a British ship. Next year on October 22, 1923, Turkey was declared a republic and the Assembly unanimously elected Kamal Pasha as its first President A new Republican constitution of Turkey established a nationalist, republican, secular state under the Presidentship of Kamal Pasha.

Treaty of Lausanne

Kamal's resounding victory over the Greeks compelled the Allied Powers to revise the Treaty of Sevres and they met at Lausanne in 1923 to make a new treaty to suit the altered conditions in the Eastern Europe. By the Treaty of Lausanne, Turkey regained Eastern Thrace including the city of Adrianople. Constantinople was also restored to her. Capitulations were abolished, foreign control of customs was lifted and no restrictions were placed on Turkey's military, naval and air forces. Turkey consented to the demilitarization of the Straits and gave up all claims to her Asiatic and African possessions. This treaty was probably a great triumph for Mustafa Kamal Pasha and probably great humiliation for the Great Powers of Europe. In everything except demilitarizing of the Straits, Kamal Pasha was strong enough to secure what he wanted. His firmness enabled Turkey to escape hated foreign control which had been imposed on all other ex-enemy powers but Turkey was deprived of all her possessions, in Asia, Africa and in Balkan Peninsula and Caliphhood of Islam which made her theoretical head of Islam.

The new Turkey was in form of republican and apparently democratic and secular. There was a written constitution vesting the supreme authority in a National Council called Grand Assembly to be elected every four years by universal adult male suffrage. Women got voting rights in 1934. This Assembly was to elect the president every fourth year. But in practice the government of Turkey as conducted by Kamal Pasha was a national dictatorship of one party guided by one man. There was only one well-organised political party, *viz.*, the People's Party, and Kamal was its leader. As such he controlled the Assembly and ensured his election to the Presidentship. As Commander-in-Chief he controlled the army and ensured obedience to all the organs and authorities of his government. Thus Kamal Pasha wielded dictatorial powers but he used them for the good of his country.

Reforms of Mustafa Kamal Pasha touched every aspect of life and society in Turkey. Main pillars were republicanism, secularism, populism, nationalism, statism and reformism. Kemal was a man of courage and determination and he used his authority in introducing wide-sweeping reforms which touched every aspect of the life of the Turkish people. He tore off his country from its ancient moorings and placed it in a new setting modelled on European systems. He had to face very strong local opposition from Ulemas and the conservative section of the people but he brushed it aside and went on with his plan of modernising Turkey. The two most revolutionary changes which he effected were the abandonment of Constantinople which was (renamed Istambul) as capital and the establishment of Turkey as a secular state. As the old capital Ottoman Empire was vulnerable, he removed it to the impregnable hill fastness of Ankara. The Caliphate had traditional associations with Islam and with monarchy and so Kamal Pasha looked upon it as an incongruity in the new set-up and abolished it in 1924. Further state of Turkish people was secularised by the disestablishment of Islam as a state religion. Henceforth Islam became a private and not a public or state concern. The secular character of this Turkish state was emphasised by the abolition of the old legal system based on the Sheriat or Holy Islamic Law and was replaced by the introduction of new legal codes based on western systems. Kamal Pasha created state enterprises managed by the Government. He enhanced the rights of women and encouraged them to become lawyers, Doctors, Bankers and Public Officials equally sweeping were the changes which Kamal Pasha, introduced in the social life of the people. These included the abolition of polygamy, civil marriage, emancipation of women and the introduction of European dress etc. Kamal encouraged education both primary and secondary and set up Government controlled public school in every sizable town. Adult education was promoted and all Turks under forty years of age were made to take lessons in reading and writing. An important change in the educational system was the introduction of the Latin alphabet to learn Turki and to read and write Turki.

Kamal Pasha did also much to develop the economic resources of Turkey. His government subsidized agriculture by the free grants of cattle and ploughs etc. to deserving families. Agricultural colleges were set up and agricultural banks were started to lend money to farmers. Model farms were set up where the latest agricultural machinery and techniques were exhibited. Kamal Pasha had his own model farm on which he himself worked, driving his own tractor. Steps were also taken to rapidly industrialise the country. In 1929, the Government of Kamal Pasha launched a twelve-year public works plan providing for railway extension, construction of ports and harbours, irrigation projects and reclamation of lands etc. In 1934, a Five-Year Plan on Russian model was adopted for promoting large-scale industrialisation. It provided for the establishment of factories both private and state-owned, for the development of hydro-electric power and industrialization and for the working of mines. Foreign capital and expert advice were utilised but the Turkish authorities saw to it that all industrial undertakings were national state concerns. Care was taken to safeguard Turkey's political and economic independence. He followed mixed economy and rapid industrialization as India has followed after 1947 under Nehru Government and under successive governments.

Foreign Relations

According to S.N. Fisher, "The remarkable national progress of Turkey were paralleled by success in foreign field." At first Kamal Pasha was suspicious of the Western Powers because of the harsh treatment meted out to Turkey after the First World War and at Paris Peace Conference. Hence he was drawn into friendly relations with the Soviet Union. In 1925, he concluded a treaty of mutual guarantee, and of neutrality with Russia. But he disliked the propaganda of the Russian Communists and their subversive activities and so gradually veered round to the Western powers and joined the League of Nations in 1932. Next he cemented diplomatic friendships with most of the neighbours of Turkey. In 1934, he made Turkey a party to the Balkan Pact with Greece, Rumania and Yugoslavia etc. This was followed by an Eastern Pact in 1937 called Saudabad Pact by which Turkey, Iraq, and Afghanistan promised to abstain from interference in one another's internal affairs and also to consult one another on matters of international concern. Turkey's pacific attitude won the sympathy of the Western Powers and they acceded to her request to refortify the Straits which were demilitarised by the Treaty of Lausanne. Thus was removed the last vestige of foreign influence Turkey also succeed in annexing Hatay in June, 1939 in spite of French protests.

Achievements

Mustafa Kamal Pasha assumed the surname of "Ataturk" or "Father of the Turks" which was suggested to him by the Grand Assembly of Turkey. He fully deserved this title. His achievements form a brilliant record. Alone and unaided he had defied the Great Powers of Europe, and tore up the hated Treaty of Sevres, and imposed upon them the Treaty of Lausanne. By getting rid of the so-called 'capitulations' he freed Turkey from foreign tutelage. His social and economic reforms revitalised Turkey and made her a modern, progressive and powerful nation. Turkey is no longer the "sick man of Europe" but a proud self-reliant state courted by all the great Powers. Kamal Pasha died on Nov. 10, 1938 and all Turkey went in mourning for the Ataturk. Kamal Pasha is considered as architect of modern republican Turkey like Sun Yat Sen of China by people of Turkey. Kamal Pasha is considered as a great leader in World history.

The Condition of Turkey after Kamal Pasha and Emergence of Democratic Party

Ismat Pasha better known as Inonnu, succeeded Mustafa Kamal Pasha on 10th November, 1938, and was re-elected for a full term of four years in 1939. During his period Second World War took place but Turkey did not participate in it actively like First World War though sympathy of Turkey was with England, France and U.S.A. After war in 1945, Mustafa Kamal Pasha's republican party whose leader was Ismat Pasha or Inonnu, led this party successfully.

In 1945, conservatives broke away from Republican Party and founded a democratic party. In the 1946 elections, the Democrats secured 62 seats in the Assembly and in 1950, Democratic Party defeated Republican People's Party and so Ismat Pasha or Inonnu was forced to resign and became leader of opposition.

Democratic party in 1954 gained landslide victory and leaders of this party became corrupt. They introduced a reactionary policy and a marked change was introduced in the governmental system of Turkey which brought far reaching changes.

The Impact of Second World War over Turkey

Mustafa Kamal Pasha died in 1938, and Ismat Pasha favoured neutrality. In 1939 when Second World War broke out Turkey wanted to maintain absolute neutrality. But both Britain and France wanted to have Turkey as friend. Germany also wanted to have her friendship of her old friend who fought Second World War as her supporter. But Turkey felt that participation in War will ruin her economy.

Problem of Hatay. In Hatay election, Turkey got majority in Hatay Assembly and it was declared a republic. France accepted Turkish demand and accepted Hatay's annexation with Turkey.

Turkey and French Relations. Both the countries agreed to sign a Non-Aggression Pact and Turkey received arms from France and so Turkey maintained friendship with her.

Turkey and Germany. During First World War Turkey joined war on German side. During this period famous German ambassador Papen went to Ankara to seek Turkish co-operation, but both the countries could not come closer to each other.

Turkey and Britain also signed no aggression pact with one another. In 1939, mutual guarantee pact was also signed between the two countries.

Russia and Germany also signed treaty of friendship in 1939 for dividing Poland and this created fear in Turkish mind. Moscow wanted Turkey to close straits to England for which she was not prepared and thus went nearer to England and signed a no aggression pact with that country to avoid Russian or German attack.

Stopping of Chrome Ore to Germany. Both U.S.A. and Britain assured Turkey all help. Turkey, therefore, decided to stop the supply of chrome ores to Germany. Thus Turkey showed sympathy to Britain and U.S.A. in Second World War.

In this way when war was at its highest pitch Turkey remained neutral, but at the end of war she set on the table with victors due to her sympathy with allies. As such Turkey's economy and prestige both increased.

Internal and External Policies and Affairs of Turkey after Second World War

Mustafa Kamal Pasha died in 1938 and Ismat Pasha became supreme. Turkish leadership did a good job for the country during World War II of 1939-45 because it remained neutral and this saved it from destruction on the one hand and due to her sympathy with allies, Turkey also sat at the conference table with the victors. Both her economy as well as prestige and political image went up. But after the Second World War Turkey remained faction ridden and lot of disturbances took place, so it became weak.

Turkish Internal Affairs after War. In 1938 Mustafa Kamal Pasha died and was replaced by Ismat Pasha, who very ably guided the country during difficult War days. It cannot be denied that on account of his ability and statesmanship, Turkey got international honour and prestige. He remained in power for about 12 years *i.e.* from 1938 to 1950. It was however, in 1945 that there was split in his Republican party with the result that his position weakened. Some of his conservative followers broke away from the Republican Party and founded Democratic Party, which won landslide victory and Inonnu had to sit in the opposition. Thus two party system came in existence in Turkey in 1950.

Democratic Party Rule. Democratic Party followed reactionary policy and misused power. There was press censorship and fraud in elections and character assassination of national leaders. The Democratic Party however, could not manage the affairs of the country with the result that there were frequent troubles and political riots. Many other political parties were also founded in the country. There was chaos and a sort of civil war in the country. This provided an opportunity to military leaders to stage a coup on 27th May, 1960 in which many political leaders were arrested and either put behind the bars or slain. Corrupt civil and military officials were severally punished. Coup leaders gave new constitution to the country and under the provision of this new constitution elections were held in the country. As a result of these elections Ismat Pasha or Inonnu again came to power by the coalition of Republican People's Party and Justice Party. But there was no stability in the country. Several political parties were formed and there were always coalition governments, which resulted in no stable government in the country. This sort of political instability remained characteristic feature of Turkey upto 2004 as Kurdish revolts and fanatic Islamic followers created disturbances.

Turkey's External Affairs. After the Second World War Russia demanded from Turkey the return of Kars and Ardahan and also share in Straits administration which Turkey forcefully rejected. Russia then made another demand that there should be joint Turkish-Russian defence of Straits. This demand too was rejected. As time passed Turkey began to get more and more economic assistance from the U.S.A. When Russian became aware that Turkey was under complete influence of the U.S.A., Russia demanded revision of the Montreaux Convention, but that was also opposed both by the U.S.A. and Turkey. Turkey thereafter became a member of N.A.T.O. on 18th February, 1952, to strengthen her position. Thereafter Turkey began to actively contribute in international affairs and help U.N.O. by supplying military contingent against North Korea. Turkey also concluded a mutual defence pact with Pakistan and Baghdad pact was also signed between Iran and Turkey. She also became a member of C.E.N.T.O., but later on due to revolt in Iraq, Baghdad pact was shattered. During Egyptian-Israeli war of 1956 Turkey remained neutral. In Turkey also fanatic Islamic parties are creating disturbances.

In this way Turkey changed rapidly after the World War II. Today she is an important entity in World politics, Turkey came alone to Western powers. The Balkan entente which disappeared was remained on 28th February, 1953 and a tripartic treaty of friendship was signed by Turkey, Yugoslavia and Greece which became known as Ankara but later on Turkey joined N.A.T.O.

The Condition of Turkey after 1954

In 1954 Turkey concluded a treaty of mutual defence with Pakistan as Democratic Party became supreme. Democratic Party manipulated elections so people lost faith in elections and Party. As already stated military coup took place on May, 1960. Military coup leaders formed National Unity Committee and assumed charge of Government. They executed democratic Prime Minister Andan Mendres anarchy began to prevail. As such in 1951, influence of Democratic Party declined. His cabinet colleagues etc. were executed like Pakistan where military leader Zia-ul-Haque got President Bhuttoo executed.

Military coup leaders formed National Unity Party and drafted a new constitution for Turkey. In July, 1961, new constitution was approved by the popular vote and came in force in October, 1961 but Ismat Pasha or Inonnu formed a coalition party of Republican People's Party and Justice Party which emerged victorious. As such Ismat Inonnu became Prime Minister of Turkey in 1961.

Rule of Ismat Inonnu 1961-65. Ismat Pasha known as Inonnu was most experienced political leader who had succeeded Mustafa Kamal Pasha in 1938 and he had support of army but his Government was coalition Government and had to face many difficulties. On 22nd February, 1962 and on 21st May, 1963 there were very serious riots otherwise petty riots were common as in India and Pakistan. In spite of all this Ismat Inonnu tried for economic development and in external affairs tried to follow independent policy. He had to face Cyprus problem. On 21st February, 1964, attempt was made to assassinate him but he escaped. At last on 14th February, 1965, his Government was defeated in National Assembly and Ismat Inonnu had to resign. After Ismat Inonnu, Suyat Hathari Urgu Pulu became Prime Minister with the support of Justice Party leader Suleman Demeriel. On 10th October, 1965 new elections were held and Justice Party won 240 seats out of 450 seats of National Assembly and so Suleman Demeriel formed Justice Party's Government on 27th October, 1965.

Suleman Demeriel's Justice Power Government remained in power from 1965 to 1971. This Government adopted aggressive attitude against Cyprus but it failed to win support of Arab nations. During the rule of this Government, labour and students agitation took pace. Government officers became corrupt and indisciplined and in international market price of Turkish currency fell. At last on 18th December, 1970, military intervened Demeriel had to resign 12th March, 1971. He was succeeded by Nihal Eram as Prime Minister who formed coalition Government.

Unstable Cabinets of Turkey. In April 1972, Nihal Eram's Ministry fell and Ferit Melen became Prime Minister. In 1973, he was succeeded by Naim Talu. After new elections of 1973, Republican Justice Party both became divided and became split in many groups so there were many Governments of short tenure and anarchy began to prevail. As such army intervened on 12th September, 1980 and Bluent Ulasid became Prime Minister. Later on like Pakistan, military gave power to elected Civilian Government and now Ahmed Necedetsezer is President and Bulentecent is the Prime Minister. Turkey is member of N.A.T.O, but is facing problem in Cyprus and has strained relations with Greece. In spite of all this, Turkey is free from problems and is making all round progress and prosperity. Turkey sided with American led multinational forces against Iraq. Kurdish revolt and terrorism of fanatic parties are creating disturbances.

Foreign Policy of Turkey after World War II

Turkey formed policy of peace after World War I of 1914-1918. Mustafa Kamal Pasha was confronted with internal problems so he followed cautious policy which was characterized neither by isolation nor by aggression. Dispute with Iraq was settled and through League of Nations, Brusles Line was recognized boundary between Turkey and Iraq. Mosule went to Iraq but some compensation was given to Turkey. Friendly relations were maintained with France, Britain and Italy etc. Hatay of Syria was acquired under mandate of France.

By Saudabad treaty of 8th July, 1937, Turkey created friendship with other countries and also with Russia by another treaty thus Turkey followed policy of national interests and kept Turkey aloof from IInd World War. After World War II, Turkey got help of U.S.A. against Russian supported communist guerillas and massive aid to improve her economy so Turkey became member of N.A.T.O. on 28th February, 1952. On 14th December, 1951, Turkey entered into a treaty of friendship with India but it did not prove beneficial so Turkey entered into treaty with Pakistan on 2nd April, 1954 and with Iran on 24th February, 1955. On 28th February, 1953, a Balkan treaty was signed with Greece and Yugoslavia and Turkey also remained member of Baghdad Pact and C.E.N.T.O. etc. but all these treaty organisations disappeared but Turkey remained in N.A.T.O.

In 1963, Turkey became a co-opted member of European Common market but also tried to have good relations with Soviet Union. In Asia Turkey tried to establish good relations with Iran and Pakistan and sided with American lead multinational forces against Iraq in 1991. Turkey intervened in Cyprus Turkish dominated Cyprus.

Turkey did not involve herself in Israeli-Arab Egyptian war of Suez Canal of 1956. Turkey mostly kept herself aloof from all the wars of Arabs and Israel and disputes of Arab League. Turkey recognized Israel, so its relations with Arab states became strained. She did not show any interests in Arab-Israel wars. The Turkish policy could not reconcile with Pan-Arabism or Pan-Islamism of Middle East. Turkey did not support P.L.O. though India supported P.L.O. against Israel. Turkey also followed neutral policy in Iraq-Iran war and kept mum when Russian forces occupied Afghanistan but showed its opposition to Russian aggression in U.N.O. and in Islamic conference. In short, amidst troubles and tribulations, Turkey developed stable international relations keeping in mind the internal progress and economic development inspite of the fact that Turkey is member of both N.A.T.O. and the organisation of Muslim States.

Turkey entered in treaty with Bulgaria on 22nd March, 1968 and with Greece on 31st March, 1968 to solve minority problem as Turks are in these states and some Bulgars and Greeks are in Turkey. Only in case of Cyprus, Turkey had to face very difficult problem but Turkey emerged far more successful than India while Indian Peace Keeping Force failed to achieve anything in Ceylon for Tamilians but Turkey achieved Turkish Cyprus having 40% territory for 18% Turks which is described in detail in next section. Thus in short inspite of short lived Coalition Government Turkey achieved notable success in foreign affairs and is supporting U.N.O. against Iraq. Turkey had to face internal disturbances caused by Kurd and fanatic parties.

Cyprus and Its Relations with Turkey

Cyprus is a very tiny country near Greece and Turkey. It is situated on such a strategic place that it connects three continents of Asia, Europe and Africa.

It has area of 9251 sq. kms. having population of about eight lakhs in which 82% are Greeks and about 18% Turks. As such its religion is both Christianity and Islam and language is Greek as well as Turkey. Its capital is Nicosia. At present, it is divided in Cyprus and Turkish Cyprus having 60% and 40% area respectively.

In recorded history Cyprus came in prominence by the millennium B.C. It remained part of Greek and later on of Eastern Roman empire and of Ottoman Empire. After that it was given to Britain by Berlin conference of 1878 and so Cyprus remained under British control upto 1960 and a republican Government was established here. In 1974, it was invaded by Turkish forces to support Turkish population which came in conflict with Greek Christian population and occupied about 40% of its territory. So it became divided in Cyprus and Turkish. Cyprus as 40% of its territory is under Turkish influence.

Cause of conflict in Cyprus was that Greek population of Cyprus desired its unity with Greece. But the minority Turks revolted to safeguard their interest. As such when on 16th August, 1960, Cyprus became free, a treaty of guarantee between Cyprus republic and Britain-Turkey and Greece was signed. It was incorporated into the new constitution. It forbades union or partition. It is also a guarantee which cannot be amended, by way of addition or repeal "Despite the fact Greece and Turkey were members of the Ankara pact and of N.A.T.O., the Cyprus issue disturbed their relations. As such Turkish controlled area of northern Cyprus containing about 40% area of Cyprus declared its separate independence in 1983 and named themselves as Turkish Republic of Northern Cyprus. A coalition Government headed by Dervis Eroglu was installed in 1985. His party *i.e.,* National Unity Party is allied with the communal liberal party having 32 seats in 50 member parliament of Turkish Cyprus against pro-Russian parties. Prof. Dernish is President of Turkish Cyprus.

Feud between Cyprus and Turkish Cyprus is bone of contention between Cyprus and Turkish Cyprus.

Cyprus is mainly an agricultural island. Its main exports are potatoes, wine, citrus, carrots and fresh vegetables etc. Industrial exports are readymade clothes, footwear, cement, water-pumps, furniture and minerals etc. Cyprus proper is the member of U.N.O. as well as of non-aligned countries but both U.N.O. and non-aligned countries failed to save it from partition or from its becoming bone of contention between Greece and Turkey. Problem of Cyprus is like problem of Tamils of Sri Lanka but while Indian Peace Keeping Force *i.e.,* I.P.K.F. failed to solve Tamilian problem of Sri Lankans but Turkey has solved it by taking about 40% territory of Cyprus for 18% Turks, so Turkish Cyprus is separate entity. President of Cyprus is Spyros Kapriano but this tiny Island stands divided as Cyprus and Turkish Cyprus. Now in spite of division Cyprus has made a great progress and friendly relations have developed between India and Cyprus.

Turkish Cyprus has an area of 3355 sq. kms., population of 140000, language — Turkish. Majority of people of Turkish origin follow Muslim religion. The Turkish controlled area of Northern Cyprus unilaterally declared independence in 1983 and formed separate Turkish state with the sympathy and supports of Turkey. It has been named Turkish republic of northern Cyprus having 50 member assembly. Prime Minister's Dervis Eroclo.

Turkey became a secularized modern state due to efforts of Kamal Ata Turk *i.e.,* due to Mustafa Kamal Pusha but now fanatic Islamic parties are making efforts to make it again a Muslim state. As such Religion and ethnic tensions and disturbances caused by Kurds, who are 12 millions are causing disturbances. Recently they accepted peace.

In 1993, Turkey had the first women Prime Minister Tansu-ciller. A rail link completing the "Silk Route" between China and Turkey started operation through central Asia in 1996. In 1997, Turkey succeeded in separating Turkish Cyprus from Cyprus due to her efforts. In 1999, terrible Earthquake took about 1200 lives causing tremendous loss. Turkey is second largest producer of Sutana raisins and is rich in minerals. Deprived of empire, Turkey is still an important state with glorious Past. The constitutional court banned the Islamist opposition party in 2003 on the ground that it had flouted country's secular order.

During Anglo-American war with Iraq, Turkey remained neutral. Recently in 2003, India's Prime Minister Shri Atal Bihari Vajpayee visited Turkey and succeeded in maintaining satisfactory relations with Turkey. Now Turkey is making progress as it has curbed Kurdish, revolts and disturbances caused by fanatic muslim militants. Turkey has recovered from loss caused by earthquakes but in 2003 fanatic Muslim organisations attacked British banks, Consulate and Jews but Turkish govt. succeeded in maintaining peace.

30

PERSIA OR IRAN

Islamic Republic of Iran (Jomhori-e-Islami-e-Iran)

Introduction of Iran and Its Brief History

Iran's capital is Teheran. Its area is 1,648,000 sq. kms., population is about 7 crores. Its language is Persian (Farsi), Currency : Rial. US $ 97.21 Rial. Its religion is Islam of Shiate ideology. So Iran is champion of Islamic Shia religion. Iran is a country of old civilization like India. Literacy : 79%, Language : Persian (Farsi), Arabic, Turki, Kurdish.

Iran (Persia) is a country of great antiquity. It is celebrated alike for its culture and military valour and now-a-days for its religious zeal though recently it has subsided.

The last ruler of the Pahalavi dynasty, King Mohammed Reza Shah Pahalavi was forced to flee Iran in face of nation-wide revolt against him. In February 1979, Ayatollah Khomeni, a high priest of Islam and great Shia spiritual leader returned to Iran to guide its destiny. He brought an orthodox Islamic Shia state in Iran with definite aim of establishing and propagating orthodox Islamic Shia religion.

Agriculture is the major occupation of the Iranian people. The chief agricultural products are wheat, barley, rice, fruits, wool and sugar beets etc. Fish (from which caviar is obtained) in Caspian Sea provide an important source of income. Iran is one of the biggest oil producing regions in the Middle East. Emeralds and other gems are found in Khorasan and Kerman. Persian carpets, made on handlooms are famous all over the world. Iran got new religious zeal under Khomeni but Iraq-Iranian war began in 1980 and ended in 1989. After which Ayatollah Khomeni died in 1989 and new elections took place.

President Mohammad Khatmi. Now Iran is most orthodox Islamic republic of Shia faith challenging western countries like U.S.A. and Britain etc. but it has good relations with India.

Mission in India. Embassy of the Islamic Republic of Iran, 5, Barakhamba Road, New Delhi–110 001, Tel : 385491.

The Rise of Persia or Iran and Its Ancient History

Iran is a very ancient country having Aryan population. Persian imperialism grew when Assyrian empire decayed. During the long reign of Nebuchadnezzar, the powerful Chaldean empire flourished; but after his death (562 B.C.) Chaldean power soon crumbled. Meanwhile the Persians suddenly rose to prominence and soon eclipsed all the great states of the ancient world. Within twenty years Cyrus the Great, the vigorous Persian leader, created a great Persian Empire. In 550 B.C., he threw off the Median yoke and after defeating King Croesus four years later, he also gained control of the Lydian Kingdom and of those Greek cities in Asia Minor which were under the nominal control of Lybia. Then he turned towards east, succeeded in establishing his power as far as the frontier of India. Babylon was next to his list; with little resistance this famous ancient city capitulated to the Persians in 539 B.C. Following the death of Cyrus his son Cambyses conquered even Egypt. At the beginning of the fifth century B.C. the next ruler, Darius I, began a series of campaign against the Green mainland. The struggle between the Greeks and the Persians ended above 150 years later with the resounding defeat of the Persians by the youthful Alexander the Great of Macedonia. Persians established a great empire but battles of Marathon and Thermophyle with Greeks brought downfall and finally Alexander the Great brought end of Persian Empire.

Persian Government. The Governmental structure of Persia was built upon the Assyrian model but was far more efficient than its predecessor. The imperial system, first designed by emperor Cyrus the Great, to administer his extensive dominions, was carried to completion by Darius. For capitals Susa, Ecbatana, Babylon, and Persepolis were established in various parts of the Persian Empire; and the total Persian empire was divided into twenty-one provinces or satraps, each governed by a provincial governor called a satrap. To check the satraps, a secretary and a military official representing the central government of king were installed in every province. Also, special inspectors, "the Eyes and Ears of the King", travelled throughout the realm and informed King about the condition and administration of Persian provinces.

Realizing the need for good communications, the Persians built great imperial post roads, which in the throughness of their construction on rivaled the later Roman roads. The main highways connected the important cities of the Persian Empire. Along the Royal Road between Sardis and Susa there was a post station after every fourteen miles, where the king's messengers could obtain fresh horses. By means of this ancient pony express, royal messengers could cover a distance of the 1500 miles in a little more than seven days; ordinary travellers took three months. Roads and communications and efficient administration kept Persian Empire intact, efficient and stable.

The Persian Empire was the first to attempt governing many different racial groups on the principle of equal responsibilities and rights for all people of Persian realm. In the Persians' treatment of people there was a humaneness and consideration that had been absent completely previously in traditions of the Assyrian government. For example, the Persians respected the gods and traditions of all conquered peoples. The king of Persia concerned himself with the prosperity of every section of his empire, so that all provinces would be able to pay the tribute levied against them but the tax burden, however, was not excessive. The introduction of a uniform system of coinage did much to weld the Persian Empire together and facilitated trade and commerce.

Persian Religion. The humaneness of the Persians may have stemmed from the ethical religion founded by the prophet Zoroaster, who lived in the early sixth century B.C. and was a contemporary of Buddha and Confucius of China. Zoroaster sought to replace "the lie" — ritualistic, idol-worshipping cults and their Magipriests — with a religion centered on the soul minded "good thoughts of the mind, good deeds of the hand, and good words of the tongue" from those who would attain paradise (a Persian world). This new religion made little progress until Darius adopted it. The Magi soon followed; they revived many old gods as lesser deities, added much ritual, and replaced monotheism with dualism by transforming what Zoroaster had called the principle or spirit of evil into the powerful god Ahriman, rival of Ahura-Mazda. This complicated evolution of Zoroastraianism as is shown by its holy writ, the Avesta ("The Law"), assembled in its present form between the fourth and the sixth centuries A.D. Zoroastrainism influenced Judaism and Christianity, and its followers (Parsees) still exist in India and are richest and most influential community of India. Zoroastrainism is extinct in Persia but is flourishing in India.

After the conquest of Persia by Alexander the great, it began to be ruled by Greek generals and governors but soon powerful empire was again established for a short duration.

In 7th century Persian rule weakened and so in the decisive four day battle at Kadiayah in 635, Persians who were lead by famous general Rushtom were defeated by Islamic forces of Arabs. Islamic forces of Arabs were helped by many Arab tribes of Syrian desert and so the Arab forces were able to conquer whole Persia and Mesopotamia etc. Calips wiped out old religion and imposed Shia Islam over Iran.

Persia came under Arab forces of Islam and whole of Persia embraced Islam but a few persons migrated to India and these are Parsees who are richest and most influential community of India.

The Condition of Iran under Abbasid Caliphs

Persians made their impact felt over Arabic forces of Islam and during Abbasid Caliphs rule Persian culture dominated Islam and even Sultans and Mughal rulers of India followed Persian administrative system and Persian remained official language of India during Mughal rule and was replaced by Urdu with Persian style during British period which is still followed by Pakistan but in India it has been replaced by Hindi after Independence, so it can be said that not only in Arabic world but Persian culture dominated and influenced Sultanate and Mughal period in India.

The civil war of the Umayyads with Hussian and Iran Al-zaliyar and murder of Ali's family members and successors divided Islam in two faction of Shia and Sunnies. Supporters of Ali's claim began to be called Shias who resented Sunni rule of Umayyad Caliphs. Shias asserted that Umayyads had opposed Muhammad and Munurja's father had driven Muhammad and Muslims from Mecca, the same family should inherit caliphs, mantle was more than the Prophet's followers could stomach so Abbasid family related to prophet rose in revolt and imposed Abbasid Caliphs' rule and made Baghdad as capital. During Abbasid Caliphs' rule Persia gained power and influence.

The Condition of Iran in 20th Century

Abbasid Caliphs' rule was destroyed by Mongols. Later on Safavi rule come and after the fall of Safavi Empire Nadir Shah conquered Iran, Khurasan, Turkistan, Afghanistan and part of Hindustan but after his murder, Persia in the beginning of the twentieth century was a distracted country. It was a prey to internal dissensions and foreign exploitation. There was division of Iranian empire and Ahmad Shah Abdali became ruler of Afghanistan but there was chronic warfare among ambitious chieftains. Persia became the cockpit of rival faction and this situation was greatly complicated by the rivalry of Russia and Great Britain for the control of the country's resources and government. If Russia supported one faction Great Britain supported an opposing faction. By the Anglo-Russian Convention of 1907, Great Britain and Russia came to an agreement regarding their respective spheres of influence in Persia. This, however, seriously impaired the sovereignty of Persia and outraged the feelings of many Persians who were developing awakening and sense of nationalism. These nationalists sought to galvanise the old and conservative country into new life. Already they had forced the Shah to grant a constitution in 1906. In 1907, Anglo-Russian treaty took place dividing Iran into respective spheres of influence. Next followed in 1908, a revolution which dethroned him. Russia took advantage of these disturbances and she invaded and occupied northern Persia under the pretext of preserving law and order and frustrated all plans of reform by forcing the Persian government to remove an American adviser whom it had employed for reforming the national finances of Iran.

19th Century Iran and Impact of Westernization over it

The advent of 19th century became a starting era in the country's progress towards westernization. Europe, born on the wave of insurgent imperialism found herself deeply involved in the affairs of Persia and other eastern countries.

In the 13th and 14th centuries, diplomatic missions had passed between the powers of Europe and Mongol rulers. Commercial relations were maintained by European merchants during the Timurid and Safavi times. Shah Abbas I granted facilities to European merchants and appointed Sir Robert Shirley an Englishman to organize Persian army. Persia was drawn into the orbit of Anglo-French rivalry and her relations with Europe assumed a significant aspect. After French revolution attack on India through Persian territory was feared so missions were dispatched to court of Persian Shah under the leadership of Malcolm but after the defeat of Napoleon, French influence ended and Russian influence gained prominence.

Since the time of Peter the great and Catherine the great Russian policy of expansion at the expense of neighbours using weapons of diplomacy, political pressure and outright mily aggression was pursued. The Iranian army was defeated in a series of campaign from 1800 to 1813. By treaty of Gulistan signed on Oct. 12, 1813, Russia acquired a considerable portion of Persia and exclusive naval rights over Caspian sea. 1816-1828 war Russia again defeated Persia and acquired more territory and forced her to grant extra-territorial rights by the treaty of Turkamchai. After the treaty of Turkamchai, Persia became a mere power in the game of world politics of Britain and Russia. Under the rule Nasiruddin Shah, the fourth Qajar King who ruled from 1848-1876, Persia came under western influence. As such many Persians went to Europe and there came into existence a small intelligentia which demanded changes.

Towards the latter part of the 19th century Russians and Britishers began to demand exclusive rights in mines and extraction of oil etc. Grant of concessions was opposed by religious leaders and in 1896, King Nasiruddin Shah was assassinated by a fanatic.

The rule of Muzaffaruddin Shah weakened state authority. He took loans from Russia and so Russian influence became supreme in Iran but Russia due to her defeat in Russo-Japanese war in 1905 was unable to profit by it. In 1906, Iran parliament called Majlis was established. In 1907, Russia and Britain divided Persia in their sphere of influence.

In First World War of 1914-1919 Iran remained neutral. Revolution of 1917 of Soviet Union produced repercussions in Persia but in 1921, Persia and Russia concluded a treaty of mutual friendship. On the other hand Anglo-Persian agreement of 1919, allowed privileges to Britishers.

Situation in Persia became anarchical. Taking advantage of chaotic conditions Riza Khan who was commander of Cosack regiment with the help of Siyed Ziauddin Tubatabai deposed King Ahmad Shah in 1925 and declared himself King of Iran in the name of Reza Shah Pahelvi.

The Rise and Rule of Reza Shah Pahelvi and His Reforms

During the First World War of 1914-1918 national resentment of Iran was aroused in Persia because Russians, Britishers and Turks had fought some of their battles on her neutral soil. Besides, nationalist opinion was greatly stirred when the Iranian government consented to an Anglo-Persian treaty in 1919, which was calculated to make Persia a British protectorate. Reza Khan Pahelvi, an able soldier who had risen to the Chief Command in northern Persia, made up his mind to overthrow the government which had consent to the unpopular and hated treaty. In 1921, he suddenly appeared at Teheran the Persian capital, at the head of his disciplined troops and set-up a Nationalist government with himself as minister of war. In 1923, he became premier and in 1925 induced the Persian parliament (Majliss) to depose the youthful and capricious Shah and elect him to the throne of Iran. The dynastic name chosen by him was Reza Shah Pahelvi. He proved to be a very progressive ruler and strained every nerve for modernization of Iran. Reza Shah Pahelvi proved himself to be a very able ruler and may be regarded as the Persian counterpart of Mustafa Kamal. Under him Persia made rapid social, political and economic progress. He abolished the rights which foreigners enjoyed and dismissed all foreign military and police officers. The alien checks on national sovereignty were also removed. The autonomous desert tribes were brought under central authority and the country was to a large extent unified. Reza Shah Pahelvi undertook useful public works. He began the construction of railroads and created a small navy. The fiscal difficulties of the country were straightened out with the help of foreign financial advisers. Attempts were made to modernize and improve Persia. Laws were aimed for improving the position of women and reducing the influence and privileged status of the Muslim religion. Conditions of health and education were improved and special care was also taken to intensify national patriotism by all the technical devices of propaganda. Reza Shah Pahelvi forced the Anglo-Persian Oil Company to accept a revised lease-concession in 1933. In this new agreement, he secured for Persia far better financial terms. This was a great triumph for the Persian state which only a few years before was looked upon as a legitimate field for foreign exploitation. In 1935 the un-national name of Persia was changed and the official designation of the country became Iran. Thus like Turkey, Iran made considerable progress under the rule of Reza Shah Pahelvi and Persia *i.e.*, Iran became a modernized state.

Persia became a place of strategic importance to the Allied Powers during the Second World War of 1939-45. It was through this country that the British and American supplies were sent to the Soviet Union during Second World War against Hitler. Hence when after invading Russia, the German forces were approaching the rich oil field of Caucasus, it became essential for Great Britain to keep open feeder lines to the Russians, *viz.*, Persian Gulf and Iran etc. But the transit of supplies was threatened by Reza Shah Pahelvi who began to form and display a pro-German attitude. He permitted the influx of several thousand Nazi technicians and so called tourists whose presence was a serious menace to the transport of supplies to Russia. Hence the British and the Soviet governments requested Shah of Iran the expulsion of the German agents. But as Reza Shah Pahelvi evaded the request so British and Russian soldiers entered Iran (in 1941) and occupied Iran without stiff resistance, the chief oil centers and the one strategic railway line. Thereupon the Reza Shah Pahelvi agreed to expel the Nazis and to permit the transport of supplies through Iran. But he adopted dilatory tactics to evade his promise and hence more allied soldiers were sent to the country. At this many Iranians, particularly certain turbulent tribes, threatened attack of Anglo-Soviet forces and revolted. Thereupon Reza Shah Pahelvi was abdicated in 1941.

Reza Shah Pahelvi's Rule over Iran

Also at stake in the period between World Wars I and II was the fate of Persia (or Iran as it came to be called in the 1920's), a land which was Muslim of Shia sect in religion but not Arabic in culture. During the First World War of 1914-18, Iran was a battle ground for Turkish, Russian, and British interests. With the temporary elimination of Russia in 1919 as a serious contender in this region, the British Foreign Office sought to bring Iran closely under its control and influence.

The proposed Anglo-Persian agreement aroused nationalism to a high pitch. Before the Majlis (the parliament of Iran) could approve this treaty, the nationalists had seized power. Their agent was a brilliant military officer named, Reza Shah Pahelvi (1877-1944), who marched on Teheran, the capital, in 1921. Four years later the previous Shah was forced to resign, and Reza Shah Pahelvi took his place as Shah of Iran founding the rule of Pahelvi dynasty. Reza Shah Pahelvi is considered as maker of modern Persia like Mustafa Kamal of Turkey or Col. Nasser of Egypt or Ibn Saud of Saudi Arabia. The new ruler Reza Shah Pahelvi was a strongly nationalistic reformer who wished to emulate Mustafa Kamal Pasha of Turkey in modernizing his country. Special privileges enjoyed by foreigners were abolished, and stiffer terms in royalties were demanded from the Anglo-Iranian Oil Company, which was tapping the country's rich petroleum reserves. The restless Persian tribes were brought under the control of the Government, the army was modernized, trade and industry were encouraged, transport was developed and brought under government control, and education was extended and improved. Between 1928 and 1936 the Trans-Iranian Rail-road was built, connecting the Persian Gulf and the Caspian Sea. But in spite of his impressive record of progress, Reza Shah had a serious weakness. Impatient with delay or inefficiency, he steadily developed the behaviour of a tyrant. The government of Persia grew more authoritarian, the Majlis came to be a mere puppet body, and corruption in Persia was again on the increase. The decaying rule of Reza Shah was destined to collapse during World War II. Russian and British forces attacked Iran when Reza Shah Pahelvi showed his inclination to axis forces. He was forced to resign throne in favour of his son, Muhammad Reza Pahelvi who carried out the promise evaded by his father. Thus during Second World War Iran did whatever Anglo-Soviet forces desired.

Persia had all along looked upon Russia with great suspicion, and this suspicion was greatly increased by the attitude of the Soviet Government after the conclusion of the Second World War in 1945. During the war British and Russian troops had occupied a considerable portion of Persia for strategic reasons under a promise to leave Persia within six months of the end of hostilities with Germany and Japan. In 1945, British troops were withdrawn but Russia refused to honour her promise. Persia protested vigorously through the United Nations Assembly and it was only after heavy diplomatic pressure from the latter that Russia agreed to withdraw her troops. U.N.O did commendable work and forced Russia to leave Iran inspite of all this Iran showed anti-British attitude.

Nationalization of the Oil Industry of Iran and Its Impact

In respect of the oil industry in the Middle East, Persia was the pioneer and by the middle of the twentieth century she became the greatest oil-producing country in that Middle Eastern region. But as the Persians lacked the technical knowledge necessary to extract and refine oil, the whole management of the oil industry was by agreement entrusted to the Anglo-Iranian Oil Company. This company after paying the Persian Government the stipulated royalty on each ton of oil appropriated the huge profits derived from the industry. With the rising spirit of nationalism in Persia, there developed a keen sense of discontent at a financial agreement which enriched a foreign company at the cost of the people of the country. The terms of royalty had indeed been revised on several occasions in favour of the Iranian Government, and in 1949 by Supplementary Oil Agreement, the royalty payments had been nearly doubled. This arrangement was, however, disliked by a section of hardliners who were the members of the Majlis led by Dr. Moussadeq, an ardent and unbalanced nationalist. The members referred this Agreement to a parliamentary committee presided over by Moussadeq. This Committee unanimously voted for a proposal to nationalize the oil industry of Iran. There ensued a great commotion. Premier Razmara who was in favour of the recent Supplementary Iran Agreement, was shot dead in a mosque at Tehrean and the assassin of Prime Minister became a popular hero. Now Moussadeq became Prime Minister of Iran and in 1951 carried through the Majlis two Nationalization Acts declaring the oil industry in Persia to be nationalized. The outcome of this misguided nationalism was probably disastrous. Persia had not the technical skill to carry on the work of exploration of oil. As a consequence the Iranian oil industry slumped and deteriorated calamitously. Production of oil declined to miserably low figure and its exports became almost negligible. As such nationalization of oil did not bring economic gain to Iran.

Prime Minister Moussadeq pushed on anti-British agitation with great virulence and in 1952 broke off diplomatic relations with Britain. For a time, he assumed in Iran almost dictatorial powers. He dissolved the Majlis and tried to whittle away the authority of the Iranian Shah. All these created round him a host of opponents and enemies. Moussadeq's popularity declined and he sought to rally the nation round himself by means of a referendum. His quarrels with Britain forced him towards closer relations with Russia, the hereditary enemy of Persia. Everything was in chaos and turmoil and situation in Iran drifted from bad to worse. The Shah fled away. But the crisis was averted by the prompt action of General Zahedi who staged a successful revolt against Prime Minister Moussadeq was arrested for treason. He was tried and disgraced. The Shah returned and Zahedi became Prime Minister. Internal order was restored and diplomatic relations with Britain was resumed. Thus, Iran came under monarchial rule and mini revolution of

Mussadeq failed. Mussadeq was given three years jail but got freedom in 1956 but he soon died.

In 1954, an international oil consortium was formed and its representatives negotiated a twenty-five year agreement with the Persian Government, regarding the management of the oil industry in Iran. The terms agreed upon proved satisfactory to both sides and Persian oil was again set flowing. Now Oil began to be extracted by International companies in which share of Iran was 50 per cent. The Communist Party in Persia (the Tudeh party) was banned and the stage was set for the adherence of Persia to the Baghdad Pact. Iran became a very rich country due to oil production and people drifted towards luxury and corruption.

Baghdad Pact and its Impact

After the Second World War Persia was determined for expansion and Anglo-American block was determined to check it. After the Second World War the ideological conflict between the Communist and non-communist nations became a source of perennial tension in international relationships. In 1951, Britain, France, America and Turkey sought to set-up a Middle-East Command after the N.A.T.O. pattern to combat the threat of Communist aggression and expansion. This project as well as another, *viz.*, the Middle East Defence Organization on the basis of a military alliance between Turkey and the Arab and Muslim states like Iran, Iraq, however, took up the idea and suggested for formation of a powerful bloc among Asian nations for purposes of mutual protection. Nuri-es-Said, the Prime Minister of Iraq, held discussions on the subject with President Nasser of Egypt and the Turkish Government. He received no encouragement from President Nasser of Egypt but found Turkey sympathetic and agreeable. In the result a Pact of mutual co-operation between Turkey and Iraq was signed at Baghdad in 1955. The Pact was to continue for five years and was declared open to other states. It was subsequently joined by Iran, Britain, Pakistan etc. The Baghdad Pact became the rallying point of the Western Powers and received encouragement and financial help from the United States of America. This Baghdad Pact was aimed to check Russian expansion like N.A.T.O. pact.

In Egypt, however, this Pact was regarded with undisguised scorn. President Nasser looked upon it as an affront to the Arab League and a challenge to Egypt's leadership in Arab Affairs. Iraq's alignment with foreign powers had the effect of strengthening the neutralist attitude of Egypt, Syria and Saudi Arabia and bringing them closer to the Soviet Union. This Baghdad Pact ended when revolt took place in Iraq in 1958 under the leadership of Kassim. From 1958 to 1963 Kassim remained in power through his military dictatorship but in 1963 Kassim was killed and new Government was established in Iraq. Iran became a rich country due to petro-dollar economy but prices began to increase rapidly due to inflation and wrong economic policy.

Shah of Iran began to spend money on corruption and luxury and in purchasing weapons from U.S.A. and other western countries. From 1970 to 1978, Iran purchased arms of more than 10 billions dollars. Moreover Shah of Iran and his officials squandered away money in wine and women and in other luxury goods. On one side there was plenty and on the other side there was poverty. Poor people and middle class was suffering due to poverty and inflation and unemployment, while Royal family and officials were sunk in slumber and debauchery and in luxurious pastimes without caring for the fate of general public consequently situation became explosive. Students, labourers and Muslim orthodox, religious leaders rose against Shah of Iran but Shah tried to crush the revolt ruthlessly but failed to curb it.

The Khomeni Revolution of Iran and Its Consequences

In 1978, people's discontent took shape of revolution. In August 1978, situation became explosive and riots took place in the city of Isphan and spread far and wide. All the attempts of Shah of Iran to curb the revolt with the help of military power failed and leadership of revolution reached to religious Shia leaders. Religious revolutionary leaders accused Shah of Iran and his family of amassing lot of fortune in foreign companies and institutions. People became against Shah and so he was forced to leave the country on January 16, 1979 and later on died in exile.

After the exit of Shah, power passed to religious leaders and they gave supreme power to their supreme Shia religious leader Ayoatollah Khomeni who was living in exile in France. Ayoatollah Khomeni established Orthodox Islamic Shia Republic in Iran and crushed his opponents most cruelly and ruthlessly. He declared Jihad *i.e.,* holy war on U.S.A. and about 60 diplomats of U.S.A. were made prisoner who were released when U.S.A. paid 9.5 billion dollars *i.e.,* 15200 crore rupees as compensation to Iranian Government of Khomeni and American 52 prisoners were released on 20th January, 1981 after 444 days imprisonment. This was most heinous act but it increased the prestige of Khomeni Government and Iran began to champion the cause of Shia Muslims all over the world so Khomeni Government of Iran came in conflict with Iraq where Shia are in majority but government was in the hands of Sunni Muslims under President Saddam Hussain.

Iran after Second World War

(i) Iran (Persia) came in for attention from the U.S.S.R. which in 1945 tried to set up a Communist government in northern Iran and demanded an oil concession for Russia. The western-educated Shah Reza Pahelvi resisted and signed a defence treaty in 1950, by which the U.S.A. provided economic and military aid including tanks and jets etc, to Iran. Matters were complicated due to anti-British feeling on account of the British controlling production of oil through Anglo-Iranian Oil Company and its refinery at Abadan. It was widely felt that the Britishers were taking too much of the oil profits and in 1951 premier Moussadieq nationalized the Anglo-Iranian oil company. However, most of the world boycotted Iranian oil exports, bringing Prime Minister Moussadieq to come down, in 1954, a compromise was reached in which British Petroleum was allowed 40 per cent of the shares. Iran now took 50 per cent of the profits which the Shah of Iran was able to use for a cautious modernization and also for land reform programme. This was not enough for the left and for radical parties who resented the Shah's close ties with the U.S.A. Left parties accused that the large slice of the national wealth of Iran found its way into his private fortune. In January 1979, he was forced to leave Iran and an Islamic republic was set-up under a Shia religious leader, the Ayatollah Khomeni, who proclaimed himself as champion of Islam and brought Iran's war with Iraq.

(ii) Britain and France tried to maintain their influence in the Middle East area against that of the U.S.S.R. and to this end Britain joined the Baghdad Pact (1955) which also included Iraq, Iran, Turkey and Pakistan. Egyptian hostility to this pact contributed towards the 1956 Suez Crisis. The Pro-British policy of King Faisal, and Premier Nuri-e-Said of Iraq caused a revolution in which they were both murdered in 1958. The new government of Iraq was sympathetic towards Egypt and withdrew from the Baghdad Pact which was replaced by the

Central Treaty Organization (C.E.N.T.O.), now defunct, sponsored by the U.S.A. as a buffer against the spread of communism in Middle Eastern lands and communism did not succeed.

(iii) The Russians seized the chance to intervene during the Suez Crisis with strong support for Egypt, friendship with the Arab world would provide a useful link for the Russians with Africa and might enable them to spread communism and threaten the west's oil supplies. This prompted the U.S.A. to issue the Eisenhower Doctrine (1957) offering aid to any Arab state which wanted to resist 'communist aggression' of Russia. All these efforts have now became useless as U.S.S.R., herself has disintegrated in 16 states and communism has lost its former influence.

The Iraqi/Iranian War of 1980 and Its Consequences

Iranian Policies Annoyed Sunni Arab States Particularly Iraq. The Middle East and the Arab world were thrown into fresh confusion in September 1980, when war erupted between Iraq and Iran over the disputed Iranian province of Khuzestan, peopled largely by Arabs who followed Sunni religion and over control of the Shatt-el-Arab waterway, which formed part of the frontier between the two states. Since Iraq was being supplied with arms by the U.S.S.R. there was consternation in the West which feared the growth of Russian expansion and influence in the oil-rich Persian Gulf. This Iraq-Iran war produced a dangerous split to the Muslim Arab world. The more conservative Arab states such as Jordan and Saudi Arabia etc. gave cautious support to Iraq, but Syria, Libya, Algeria, South Yemen and the PLO etc. were critical of Iraq, believing that the Arab states should concentrate on the destruction of Israel instead of squandering resources in mutual warfare. Moreover the PLO was on good terms with Khomeni government in Iran, on the other hand the Saudi Arabia was suspicious of Khomeni's extreme Shia brand of Islam, Arab states wanted to see Iran's ability to dominate the Persian Gulf controlled. Most of the Muslim states were follower of Sunni religion of Islam while Iran was follower of orthodox Shia religion.

In the midst of the confusion an Arab summit conference in Amman in the Jordanian capital (November 1980), to draw up new plans for dealing with Israel, never got off the ground, since the anti-Iraqi states led by Syria refused to attend it. The Syrians were afraid that Jordan would co-operate with the new

American president, Reagan, in a deal to set-up a small Palestinian state based on the West Bank, thus leaving Syria alone to face Israel and apprehensions have come true.

As the war dragged on through 1981, the prospects of healing the rift in the Arab ranks seemed uncertain. The problem of the continued existence of Israel too seemed likely to exist.

New constitution Islamic Republic of Iranian was formed and came into existence on 25th January, 1980 and Hasan Banu was elected its first President but supreme power remained with Ayatollah Khomeni who converted Iran as an orthodox Muslim land of Shias and began to champion the cause of Islam all over the world.

On the other hand Iraqi-Iran war dragged on from 1980 to 1989. Lakhs of persons were killed, billions of dollars were spent, fertile lands became barren and oil production was ended but war dragged on due to whims of Ayatollah Khomeni and Saddam Hussain who is President of Iraq.

During this period an Indian born British Muslim citizen Rushdie wrote a novel containing some unsuitable remarks on Muhammad and Islam. This annoyed Khomeni and he in order to pose himself as champion of Islam gave Fatwah to kill Suleiman Rushdie in England. Britain considering it an attack on free expression of British citizen gave protection to Rushdie. Khomeni and his followers failed to kill Rushdie and his book brought him record sale and earning of many crore pounds.

U.N.O. tried to bring reconciliation between Iraq and Iran but all efforts of U.N.O. failed due to uncompromising nature of Ayatollah Khomeni and unyielding nature of Iraqi President Saddam Hussain. At last both contestants became tired after a long war of 9 years and it ended in 1989. This lowered the prestige of Ayatollah Khomeni and he died in May, 1989. After the death of Ayatollah Khomeni, new elections took place and new Government of Iran is showing signs of compromising and progressive attack and Iran is eager to cultivate friendship with India and Pakistan.

Iraq-Iran issue and U.N.O. The Iran-Iraq war continued for about ten years but in the end U.N.O. succeeded in bringing stop in this war in 1989. U.N.O. forces were sent there to supervise the cease-fire. Thus, due to efforts of U.N.O. Iran-Iraq war ended in 1989.

After the cessation of this war, fanatic Shia leader Ayatollah Khomeni died and in new elections Rafasgani was elected

President who in a mild course and at present there is somewhat peace between Iraq and Iran. Recently Iran has warned to Iraq to return back her territory. Iran's foreign minister has also visited India and Pakistan to cultivate friendship.

Inspite of all this impression about Iran is that of a fanatic Shia Muslim state which is determined to create image of terrorism. As soon as Ayatollah Khomeni came to power, he began to punish former supporters of Shah's Government. Thousands of supporters of Shah were sentenced to death. Strict Islamic law was enforced as drug addicts and persons who violated law began to be hanged. All this tarnished liberal image of Iran.

Foreign Policy. Not only this, students prompted by Iranian Government attacked American embassy and captured lot of persons and freed them after heavy ransom. This created bitterness between Iranian and American relations and diplomatic relations were broken, but later on these were restored.

An Indian born writer who acquired British citizenship Suleiman Rushdie wrote a novel having some undignified remarks about Prophet Muhammad. Author has neither read the book nor came across with extracts of remarks in newspaper, however it is acknowledged Indian tradition that prophets of all religions should be respected as such remarks of Suleiman Rushidie would have been condemned by Iran and Muslim countries by world-opinion but Ayatollah Khomeni gave Fatwa that Suleiman Rushidie must be killed. Main question is whether ruler of a fanatic country possess the right to order his murder for expressing an opinion residing in another country? However this created sensation and Britain and other western countries threatened to sever their diplomatic relations with Iran but Ayatollah Khomeni's Iranian Government cared a fig for world opinion. As such relations of Iran deteriorated with western countries because Iran supported Muslim fanatism.

Ayatollah Khomeni championed the cause of Islam to make himself undisputed leader of Islamic world but quarrelled with Islamic country of Iraq where Shia population is more than Sunni population as such in raids Shias of both Iran and Iraq are bound to suffer but without caring for this fact, Iraq-Iran war began in 1980. Muslim countries, non-Aligned Nations and U.N.O. tried to bring reconciliation between Iraq and Iran but all their efforts failed and war continued from 1980 to 1989. In this war millions of persons suffered and billions were lost and at last when both became tired and exhausted, war ended due to efforts of U.N.O. but settlement and reconcilement is yet to be achieved.

In Afghanistan Iranian Government of Ayatollah Khomeni took steps to oppose pro-Russian Government of Najibullah but after the end of Iran-Iraq war, Iran began to cultivate good relations with Soviet Union. As such now Iranian Government is striving to have friendship with Russia but it matters little because now U.S.A. and U.S.S.R. are not so bitter enemies as were before and U.S.S.R has disintegrated.

Ayatollah Khomeni died shortly after the end of Iraqi-Iranian war and new elections took place. By new elections Rajaszani was elected President. He is an experienced person with liberal opinions and it is expected that new Government of Iran will cultivate friendship, good relations with other nations as is shown by new Government's keenness to establish friendly relations with India and Pakistan and its indication to bring compromise in Afghan relations. Iranian Government is busy in restoring shattered war torn economy of Iran and it is expected Iran may follow the path of peace and prosperity in future.

Cyprus Agreement. It is also a guarantee which cannot be amended, by way of addition or repeal. Despite the fact Greece and Turkey were members of the Ankara pact and NATO, the Cyprus issue disturbed their relations. As such Turkish controlled area of northern Cyprus containing about 40% area of Cyprus declared its separate independence in 1983 and named themselves as Turkish Republic of Northern Cyprus. A coalition Government headed by Dervis Eroglu was installed in 1985. His party *i.e.* National Unity Party is allied with the communal liberal party having 32 seats in 50 member Parliament of Turkish Cyprus against Pro-Russian parties. Rouf Dervish is President of Turkish Cyprus.

Feud between Cyprus and Turkish Cyprus is bone of contention between Cyprus and Turkish Cyprus.

Cyprus is mainly an agricultural island. Its main export are potatoes, wine, citrus, carrot and fresh vegetables etc. Industrial exports are readymade clothes, footwear, cement, water pumps, furniture and minerals etc. Cyprus proper is member of U.N.O. as well as of non-aligned countries but both U.N.O. and non-aligned countries failed to save it from partition or from its becoming bone of contention between Greece and Turkey.

Problem of Cyprus is like problem of Tamils of Sri Lanka but while Indian Peace Keeping Force *i.e.,* I.P.K.F. failed to solve Tamilian problem of Shri Lankans Turkey has solved it by taking about 40% territory of Cyprus for 18% Turks and so Turkish Cyprus is separate entity. President of Cyprus is Spyros Kaprianous but this tiny island stand divided Cyprus and Turkish Cyprus.

Contemporary Iran upto 2003

After termination of war with Iraq in 1989, Iran tried to develop military power and launched a missile of range of 1300-1450 kms. A major earthquake took place in 1990 killing 45000 and injuring about one lakh and making 4 lakhs homeless, but with its own resources and help of other countries, Iran recovered. But in July 1999, students agitated for greater democracy.

In 1997, Mohammad Khatani, a moderate became President and a female Musomah Eletekar was made vice-president. Iran owns 1.5% of total oil reserves and 15% of global gas deposits. Emeralds and gems are found in Khorasan but agriculture supports 75% of people. Iran is champion and supporter of Shia Muslims and is taking secret part in Afghanistanis civil war to protect Shia Muslims. Iran supports Shia Muslims all over the world. It has given women equal rights for divorce. Now Iran has good relations with India as India's Prime Minister Shri Atal Bihari Vajpayee visited Iran and gave aid to Iran. India is eager to get gas supply from Iran.

Recently after conquering Iraq, U.S.A. and western powers have accused Iran for making destructive weapons. U.N.O. is investigating this matter. Iran has promised not to make destructive weapons and to follow U.N.O.'s directions and not to support terrorism. At present Iran is following policy of peaceful development as well as making it a powerful state as Champion of Shia sect of Islam.

31

AFGHANISTAN

Introduction of Afghanistan (Islamic-Emirate of Afghanistan)

Afghanistan's capital is Kabul. Its area is about 647,497 sq. kms., population is about 22.5 million and language is Pakhto (Pushtu), Dari, Persian; Religion is Islam. Currency is Afghani, A.F.S. 50 = US $1. Geographically historically Afghanistan has been part of Indian subcontinent. Afghanistan, a land-locked republic known originally as Ariana, then as Khorasan (the land of the Rising Sun) part and parcel of Indian subcontinent from ancient days upto 1739 but Afghanistan was formed as a separate state by Ahmed Shah Durrani or Abdali in A.D. 1747. Pro-Soviet Government came to power in December, 1979 when Soviet troops occupied this country. Later on Russian Government withdrew but war continued between Pro-Soviet Government of Najibullah. Agriculture remains the mainstay of the economy. Sheep-rearing is another main occupation and the chief exports are livestock, fruits, wool and skins. The chief minerals are coal, salt, natural gas, petroleum, iron and copper etc. Now king Zahir Shah became head and Hamid Karzai P.M. after the defeat of Taliban due to support of U.S.A. and NATO. Now new govt. under Hamid Karzai is working with the consent of U.N.O.

The Ancient History of Afghanistan

From time immemorial Afghanistan has been part and parcel of India but still modern Western and Communist writers consider it as part of Middle East though it is not correct to include Afghanistan in Middle East.

From time immemorial Afghanistan has been part and parcel of India probably Indus valley civilization also extended to some part of Afghanistan. In Vedic literature there is mention of some places of Afghanistan and also of rivers. In Mahabharat, there is clear mention of Gandhar *i.e.,* modern Kandhar etc.

Afghanistan was a part of Moryan Emipre and pillars and monuments of Ashoka's period are found there in abundance and Taxila was a great educational center during those days. Kanishka's empire's center place was Afghanistan and his capital was Purushpur modern Peshawar. Indian rulers from Punjab continued to rule over Afghanistan till the rise of kingdom of Mahmud Ghaznavi and of Muhammad Ghori.

Babar, the Mughal ruler came, from Afghanistan and made Delhi and Agra center and capital of his empire and ruled from here over Afghanistan. During Akbar's rule Man Singh acted as Mughal Governor of Afghanistan even Aurangzeb transferred Raja Jaswant Singh from Deccan to Afghanistan. Thus during Mughal rule Afghanistan remained part and parcel of India and used to be ruled as a province of Mughal Empire. Aurangzeb's eldest surviving son Bahadul Shah was Governor of Punjab and Afghanistan while Azimus Shah, second son was of Bengal and Bihar and third son Kam Bux of Deccan. After Aurangzeb the power of Mughal Empire declined but Afghanistan remained part and parcel of India till 1739.

During the regime of luxurious Mughal king, Muhammad Shah Rangila, Nadir Shah of Persia conquered Afghanistan in 1739 and India lost Afghanistan. After murder of Nadir Shah, Afghanistan came under the control of his general, Ahmad Shah Abdali, who emerged successful in the third battle of Panipat in 1761 and so attempt of Indian powers to regain control of Afghanistan was nipped in the bud and descendant of Ahmad Shah Abdali, who cut all connections from India, began to rule over Afghanistan.

Sikh ruler Ranjit Singh defeated Afghan forces and forced Afghan ruler to cede lot of territory to him. He also forced ex-ruler of Afghanistan *i.e.*, Shah Shuja to give Koh-i-Noor diamond to him.

Rise of Russian power and its development during the rule of Peter the great and Catherine the great gave a death-blow not only to greatest Muslim Turkish power of Ottoman Empire but also to all lands of central Asia where descendants of Taimur Lane and of other rulers held their sway. Famous historical places such as Samarkand, Bokhara, Taskhend etc. came under expanding Russian empire.

On the other hand Britishers succeeded in establishing their rule over Indian subcontinent after ending the rule of Mughals and Sikhs etc. Now both Britain and Russian interest began to clash over Afghanistan, Iran and over Ottoman Turkish Empire. Upto 1947, British rulers always got an upper hand over Russia and Afghanistan existed like protectorate state of British India. British rulers used to smell a rat when they used to hear any rumour about Russian move towards Afghanistan and did not allow Russians to move a step towards Afghanistan. To preserve British influence over Afghanistan, Britishers fought many wars and inspite of many debacles, Britishers preserved their influence over Afghanistan till their empire collapsed in India. Thus Afghanistan remained independent but British influences was very great.

After disappearance of British rule, Afghan kings continued to rely on Indian Government for help and guidance. Indian Government after independence continued to cultivate good relations with the Government of Afghanistan and lot of Educationist including some author's colleagues and technicians etc. went to Afghanistan. King Zahir Shah of Afghanistan kept good cordial and amicable relations with India but with the conclusion of Russo-Indian treaty of 1971, scene changed and in 1979, Soviet Union succeeded in installing pro-Soviet puppet Government in Afghanistan and Indian Government called back all his educationists and technicians from Afghanistan. According to some persons who were there in Afghanistan at the time of arrival of Russian forces in Afghanistan did not support or praise this act of Indian Government of destroying or giving up all Indian influence there which has been cultivated from time immemorial.

After the arrival of Russian forces, Muslim powers like Pakistan and Saudi Arabia etc. came on forefront to oppose Russian domination over Afghanistan. In February 1980, a conference of Muslim states was called at Islamabad of 43 states in which Soviet Union's domination over Afghanistan was opposed. As such there was no smooth sailing for Russian forces and Afghanistan proved a hard nut to crack.

This act of naked aggression of Soviet Union of grabbing Afghanistan was condemned by U.N.O. and world wide even by Communist country. China condemned and vehemently opposed Russian aggression over Afghanistan. Russian forces had to face stiff opposition and so Russian forces had to be withdrawn but puppet Government of Soviet Union of Najibullah remained in power so civil war continued. As they were supported by Soviet Russia and others were supported by

U.S.A., Pakistan and Muslim powers became so ferocious that civil war took place. Later on fanatic Taliban gained upper hand, who were later on defeated by U.S.A. supported force and new govt. under Hamid Karzai gained power.

As after Russian domination present Indian Government has given up traditional and historical policy and according to contemporary opinion India has nothing to do about Afghanistan. As such historian George Lenszowkin has stated, "The middle East encompasses all those countries of Asia situated south of Soviet Union and West of Pakistan and Egypt on African continent". Sir Percy Corrain and E. Jukat and Fisher etc. have also included Afghanistan in middle east so author inspite of having personal opinion that Afghanistan is geographically and historically part of Indian subcontinent is describing Afghanistan in Middle East. But in the opinion of present writer geographically, historically and traditionally Afghanistan does not form part of Middle East and is probably akin to Indian subcontinent than to Middle East, but as Afghanistan fell under influence of fanatic Taliban, who were later on defeated. At present new liberal govt. with American and British support is ruling. The Head of new govt. is Hamid Karzai. It has good relations with U.S.A. and India and with NATO.

Afghanistan's Condition

Afghanistan. To the east of Iran was the remote and almost inaccessible kingdom of Afghanistan. In 1919 the Afghan Amir, believing that nationalist unrest in India rendered that country a likely prize made the mistake of invading the subcontinent and was defeated with severe losses. Later the course to Turkish reform attracted to Amir's attention; but though he promulgated a new constitution, the reforms were mainly on paper. In 1928 a destructive civil war brought the Amir's brother to the throne, but no reform in government was forthcoming. Between World Wars I and II, Afghanistan remained politically unstable, its natural resources neglected and its people illiterate, so Russians occupied it and pro-Russian rule remained there for a short time but Russians were forced to leave this country and Taliban gained power, who were later on defeated by U.S.A. supported force.

History of Modern Afghanistan and Its Condition

Modern Afghanistan is a landlocked country forming the north-eastern portion of the Indian sub-continent and of Great Iranian plateau in the heart of Asia. Name of Afghanistan is recent which originated as it is the "Land of the Afghans." It is composed of the most rugged terrain in the world. Formerly it was called Ariana or Khorasan and as Subah of Kabul during Mughal days. Of this, four-fifths is given over to treacherous but startingly beautiful mountains up to 25,000 feet high, in the Hindukush range which is part of Hindustan as the name indicates. It is spread to the dry arid plains of Helmand Valley. It covers an area of about 270,000 square miles and population of 20 millions.

In geographical term Afghanistan is not the original name of the country as it was formerly called Ariana and Khorasan, the land of rising sun. This term Afghanistan was applied for the first time during the reign of Ahmad Shah Durrani (A.D. 1747-1773). Previously it had been known as Aryana, Khurasan, Pukhtunkhwa, etc. Most of the classical writers call it by the name of Aryana which signified the racial strain which inhabited this region. Khurasan, or the Land of the Rising Sun, was the next title used by early Muslim writers referring to this country which was lying east of Persia. At the same time as "Afghanistan" came into use, Ahmad Shah Abdali in his poems referred this country as Pukhtunkhwa, that is, the Land of the Pukhtuns, now Afghanistan from Afghans.

Afghanistan's unique and strategic geographic position is the key to her importance. In the remote past she has not only been the cradle and a cross-road for some of the great ancient civilizations of the world, but she has also served as the highway for travellers and the land-bridge between Arab, Europe, Persia and to the riches of China and India etc. The famous "Silk Road" passed through Afghanistan and cities of this country provided convenient trade centers and market places for Chinese and Mediterranean goods. Because of its important geographical position, bringing about as it did the mingling of men and ideas of the East and West, Afghanistan became the next of religious philosophies as well. It became the stronghold of Zoroastrianism and Buddhism and it was from here that these religions were carried to China and the Far East and to other countries such as Mongolia etc.

This Afghan land has been visited by famous travellers such as the seventh century Chinese traveller and Scholar Huan Tsang, and the thirteenth century Venetian, Marco Polo. She was overrun by the iron phalanges of Alexander the great of Macedon, the barbarian Scythians, the free-booting Turanian Knights and the Mongol hordes of Genghis Khan, the troops of Turk conqueror Timur Lane and by the Arab armies advancing the faith of Islam, and by the many others. In fact "everybody who was any body came this way," and passed through the land of the Afghans to reach the fabulous wealth of the Indian sub-continent leaving behind death and destruction. Thus Afghanistan served as gateway to India and to South-East Asia.

The Afghans on their part have had to resist strongly the incursion on their independence and territorial integrity. As a result of bloody wars, Afghan cities have been burnt, their riches were looted, and their cultural institutions were held in check or destroyed. Sir Fraser-Tytler in his book, *Afghanistan*, states "...before the last day of the Abbasids, the Valleys in the extreme north and south west were green and beautiful properly irrigated and fertile. There were many prosperous cities, some of high culture and civilization. Mongol raids in the 13th and 14th centuries destroyed the irrigation works and decimated the inhabitants. The green valleys became arid and desolate. Thus Afghanistan had to suffer a lot because it is situated in midway to South-East Asia and Middle East.

On the other hand, waves of popular migrations swept across Afghanistan from West to East and from North to South and Afghanistan became the "cross road of Asia" and a "mixing bowl" for a great variety of Central Asian Indians, Middle Eastern, South Asian, and European invaders and settlers. But despite the medley of races and languages, Afghanistan remained a nation with distinct features, qualities and culture of its own. The forces that created this unity later on were: "Islam, a tribal tradition of leadership and love of liberty, a turbulent but stirring history, the rivalry between great neighbouring empires, and also a glorious past" in medieval period.

Well-known American writer, James A. Michner, sums up the character of the Afghan as given below :

"It is great to be an Afghan man. You are tall, stout, and tough. You wear a beard and carry a gun...and you are one of the most hospitable men on the earth. The minute a stranger crosses your threshold you order a sheep to be killed for celebration, and between fights you sing and dance, and travel the high mountain passes. It is here free life." Thus, Afghans are hospitable to guests but enemies to aggressor.

Modern Afghanistan was founded as an independent state in 1747, by Ahmad Shah Durrani or Abdali who was general of

Nadir Shah and who may be called the creator of modern Afghanistan and the Father of the Afghan nation because separate state of previously Afghanistan was merely a subah of Mughal Empire. Upon the assassination of Nadir Shah in 1747, the Afghan soldiers, under the leadership of Ahmad Khan Durrani also called Abdali returned to their homes around Kandahar. Ahmad Khan Durrani proclaimed the independence of Afghanistan. The chief question at that time was who should be elected king. The Afghan chiefs according to their well established tradition, assembled to decide upon the formation of regular government for an independent Afghanistan. After eight agitated meetings the chiefs chose Ahmad Khan Durrani as their ruler. Ahmad Khan was crowned with a wheat and that is why there was a circle of wheat on the Afghan flag. By this ceremony, signifying the democratic inclination of the Afghans Ahmad Khan assumed the royal title of Ahmad Shah Durrani or Abdali.

At this time Afghanistan was a dismembered country. Some parts of the Afghan lands were also ruled by foreigners, and the other by the tyrannical chieftains. The people were divided into clans and tribal groups. The local tribal chief was respected and obeyed. He settled disputes and looked after the welfare of his people. In return the members of his tribe helped him to meet and carry out his obligation and bear arms with him in common defence. Whenever the tribal chief was faced with major decision, he confered with other members of his tribe. In the Jirga which was a tribal council, every man had a chance to be heard. On the whole this tribal community was democratic, but the chiefs, who were frequently at war with one-another, were generally proud, independent, courageous and fearless. However the relationship of the protector and the protected was generally carefully observed.

Rule of Ahmad Shah Abdali over Afghanistan

The first act of Ahmad Shah was to organize a force and his first great achievement was to consolidate various chieftainships, petty principalities and provinces into one country of Afghanistan. After which he began to build his empire. Ahmad Shah's reputation for liberality, his high ascent and warlike qualities firmly established his rule. The historians of his time unanimously considered him as one of the greatest military generals and political administrator of Asia. He defeated

Marathas in 1761 at the third battle of Panipat and shattered their dream of establishing their empire.

Ahmad Shah's system of government was pure and simple feudalism. He appointed a council of powerful influential chiefs whom he consulted on all matters of importance, and centralized power, but for the solution of important local problems each tribal chief ruled his own tribe, provided contingents and received payment of money in respect of such services. The tribal chiefs looked upon taxation by Central Government, as interference to be resisted by force. As such country depended on a primitive agricultural economy as the principal means of livelihood. There were no schools at all, the village Mullah or priest or learned man taught the boys reading, writing and religious teachings through the Koran, the Holy Book of Muslims. Ahmad Shah Abdali during his 26 years of reign could hardly devote his time to the economic and social welfare of his subjects as he remained busy in wars.

The Rule of Ahmad Shah Abdali's Successors

Ahmad Shah died in 1773 and was succeeded by his son Timur Shah. Although Timur Shah Durrani organized his government well and transferred his capital from Kandahar to Kabul but there were fericious civil wars in Afghanistan. Timur Shah lacked the energy of his father. The result was chaos and anarchy again in Afghanistan. The better part of Timur Shah twenty year's reign was spent in quelling these uprisings and he did not find time or opportunity for the propagation of knowledge or the pursuit of fine arts, or for building monuments or to care for India.

Timur Shah's son, Zaman Shah (1789-1801), considering consultation with the council of tribal chiefs to be the negation of his power and prestige neglected the council of chiefs, which was founded by his shrewd grandfather, Ahmad Shah Abdali. His policy was to keep the chiefs at his court but did not consult them in important matters relating to the state. This resulted in revolts and wars between Timur Shah's sons and later on between the Abdalis and the Barakzais became common. These wars ravaged the country for a quarter of a century, reducing Afghanistan from a vast empire to a small kingdom. It was also in this period that Sikh ruler Ranjit Singh conquered a large part of Afghanistan and Afghanistan was treated as a pawn in the international game played by Russia and Great Britain and France in Central Asia. As such

Anglo-Afghan war took place and Britishers tried to appoint Shah Shuja as king of Afghanistan but he was murdered. While claimants to Durrani succession had been poisoning and blinding and killing one-another in Afghanistan, Dost Mohammad Barakzai emerged triumphant established himself as a leader of the Afghans. Dost Mohammad was a man of some ability. He was urged to declare himself king, but being a realist he refused to do so. In the end the chieftains of Kabul proclaimed him Amir-ul-Muninin or "Commander of the Faithful." (1826-1863) but practically he ruled Afghanistan except during Afghans wars of 1839-42 when Shah Shuja with British help remained in power. Amir Dost Mohammad had no "office" for his government. His court was the Great Mosque of Kabul. But his justice and acts and administration etc. were highly praised by his subject. Dost Mohammad had great desire for the advancement of his country, but as soon as he had reunited all the provinces of Afghanistan, he was dead. Upon his death there again was chaos and war for throne which lasted about a decade. First and Second Afghan wars shattered dream of establishing British hegemony over Afghanistan but these wars created anarchy in Afghanistan also. Amir Dost Mohammad's son Amir Sher Ali (1863-1879), at last emerged triumphant and he after getting throne succeeded in consolidating kingdom. He threw himself with much zeal into reforms. He established a council composed of thirteen members to advise the Amir *i.e.* Afghan King on all administrative questions. He decided to collect land revenue wholly in cash, while before him it was collected half in kind and half in cash. King Sher Ali, for the first time, organized the Afghan army on modern line. In order to secure the regular payment for his 50,000 troops, he gave orders that the money should be earmarked from the principal provinces of Afghanistan. The soldiers were paid in cash instead of revenue on villages. Uniforms were also gradually supplied to soldiers and military schools were opened to train them. English books on military tactics and wars were translated into Pukhtu and manuals of instruction were prepared for the Afghan army. Arms and guns ammunition were manufactured at Kabul. A postal system was established and stamps were printed. A monthly paper, Shmus-ul-Nahar, came into circulation in Afghanistan for the first time. The construction of a new city in Kabul and the improvement and construction of new roads was started. But unfortunately that enlightened King Sher Ali was not able to continue his programme of reforms, mainly because of the second British invasion of Afghanistan in 1878.

Indo-Afghan Wars of British Period and Indo-Afghan Relations during British Period

First Afghan war of 1839-42 took place because British officials favoured Shah Shuja to prevent the Russian influence in Afghanistan. In military engagement English defeated King Dost Mohammad and temporarily succeeded in giving throne to Shah Shuja who was murdered and after a mily disaster had to accept Dost Mohammad again as a ruler in 1843 and he ruled there upto 1863 and was succeeded by Sher Ali which has been already described.

During the regime of Sher Ali, Russian and British interest clashed over Afghanistan. As such when Sher Ali leaned towards Russia, British Viceroy Lord Lytton following Disraeli's policy of checking Russian attacked over Afghanistan in 1878. The Afghan ruler Sher Ali took to fight and in May 1879, his son Yakub concluded the treaty of Gandmak allowing many rights to British Indian diplomats over Afghanistan, but a revolt occurred. Rebels killed British Ambassador Cavagnari therefore British force lead by General Roberts attacked over Afghanistan and captured Kabul.

During this civil war ensued in which Abdul Rahman emerged successful who also accepted some privileges of Treaty of Gandmak so Lord Rippon called back Indian forces but kept British influence. Thus English influence was maintained over Afghanistan and Russian influence was prevented.

The Rule of Abdur Rahman and His Successors

Anglo-Afghan war, which took place in 1878 due to Anglo-Russian rivalry placed Amir Abdur Rahman on the throne of Afghanistan in 1880. Amir Abdur Rahman suspected and mistrusted the outer world and foreign powers and deliberately isolated his country. He hated the Western civilization. He had noticed that how British rule had been introduced in the Indian sub-continent. He saw the form of political intrigues followed by wars and then invasion of his father-land of Afghanistan in a fashion which was utterly unacceptable to the Afghan mind and tribal set-up. He remarked about the stretching out of the British Railway in the Khojak Pass as coming closer to the Afghan frontiers as a knife being pushed through his vitals as such Afghan people were engaged in the blocking of all the roads and paths leading to the Indian subcontinent by putting rocks to put hindrance. One of the Afghan writers referred it as an "honourable suicide committed in self-defense of honour and freedom." Thus path of British intrusion in Afghanistan was blocked and Afghanistan did not come under British influence and Russians were checked by British arms. Amir Abdur Rahman besides his pre-occupation with the diplomatic war against his powerful neighbours such Russia and Britain gradually reunited all the provinces of Afghanistan. He broke the feudal power of the local tribal chiefs and the fanatical leadership of the religious Mullahs among whom every one considered himself as an independent ruler. Consequently he welded the scattered nation which was heap of turbulent tribes into a strong united nation and ruled "the iron people with a rod of iron." He ordered the tribes to pay taxes and abolished the pensions paid to the religious leaders. He improved the public revenue not by increasing the burden of taxation but by ensuring the proper collection of all duly assessed taxes. He organized a standing army well trained and well armed which was regularly paid. Army owned allegiance to none but to King. He introducted a semi-compulsory service and recruited his army under a system termed "Hasht Mafair" or one man out of eight should be in Army. In this way Amir Abdur Rahman was able to establish an efficient Government and centralized administration retaining all important powers in his own hands. Abdur Rahman's justice was very cruel and grim but it was the only way to curb the widespread anarchy and unrest prevailing in Afghanistan and to secure peace and order. Abdur Rahman set-up factories for making guns and rifles and gunpowder etc. He also imported machines of various types for making shoes, soaps, candles and cloth etc. About 100,000 men were employed in road-making and building construction and in other industries and occupations. A printing press was established and the first hospital on modern lines came into being during his regime. Mines were successfully opened and trade was encouraged by providing loans to traders without any interest.

To create boundary between India and Afghanistan British Viceroy Lord Lansdowne sent Sir Mortimer Durand to Kabul in 1892. Abdur Rahman obtained certain districts having agreed not to interfere in Surat, Bajour and Chitral areas. The claims to then Chaman Railway Station were given up by him. British Government of India increased subsidy to Afghanistan from 12 to 18 lakhs. Durand convention was agreed which made

Durand line international boundary between Afghanistan and India. Lord Curzon followed an imperialist foreign policy towards Afghanistan.

Amir Abdur Rahman kept relations tolerable and died in 1901 and was succeeded by his son Habibullah after civil war. He was accepted by the army and the nation as the lawful king of Afghanistan. Amir Habibullah though that he was as suspicious as his father but he was easily affected by western influence. He founded a High School in Kabul and named it as the Habibia College which worked on European lines and a military academy was also founded. He introducted Western medical and surgical methods on a larger scale. He established a council of state for tribal affairs and also appointed provincial governors for the adjudication of tribal cases. He also introduced in Afghanistan motor-cars, telephones, newspapers, hydro-electric schemes, tap water and Europeans fashion, thought and games etc. Finally roads were constructed to link the different parts of the country with one-another and to facilitate trade and travel with foreign countries. Amir Habibullah ruled from 1901 to 1919 was assassinated on 20th February, 1919 as he was considered pro-British. He was succeeded by his son Amanullah.

Rule of Amanullah and Nadir Shah over Afghanistan

King Amanullah gave voice to the long suppressed desire of his people for the independence of their land. The people's demand for full freedom resulted from British control. This war of independence was also known as the third Anglo-Afghan war of 1919. British aero-planes bombed Afghan cities and forced Amanullah to conclude a peace treaty on 22nd November, 1921. In this period which almost coincides with the so called period of "awakening of Asia after centuries of indolence. Afghanistan got freedom from English control of their foreign policy." Afghanistan was among the first countries in Asia to undergo a process of adoption of the Western culture and way of life probably in a revolutionary manner. Amir Amanullah accepted Durand Line as boundary between Afghanistan and India (now Pakistan in 1921). King Amanullah introduced a number of reforms in the fields of education, administration, finance, in national economy and codification of laws etc. During the rule of Amanullah Russian influence increased. He concluded a treaty with Russia on February 28, 1921 to exchange diplomatic agents. Soviet Union agreed to give arms and subsidy to Afghan ruler. In 1926, a non-aggression treaty was concluded with Russia.

Probably policy of Amanullah laid the seed of Russian dominance over Afghanistan.

Reforms of Amanullah. After King Amanullah's seven-month tour of Europe, the pace of reform accelerated. In a series of public speeches he outlined his programme of reform making frequent reference to secular education and a new status for woman like Kamal Pasha of Turkey or Raza Shah of Persia. A Loie Jirga, or the Grand National Assembly, under the instruction of Amanullah, decreed the establishment of the First Afghan Parliament to be elected by the votes of all literate Afghans. It constituted a legislative assembly of 150 members, selected from the Loie Jirga to sit at Kabul like Parliament for eight months every year. The length of compulsory service in the army was also increased from two to three years and all exemptions were abolished. Polygamy was considered as the chief cause of civil corruption and so it was decided that any civil servant who took second wife would have to tender his resignation. King Amanullah, in spite of fierce opposition from the clergy and the conservative circles, started to send Afghan girls abroad for higher education. He opened schools for girls and abolished the veil like Turkey. Several high schools and many primary schools were opened and established in different parts of the country. The teaching of French and German, besides English, was also included into the school curriculum. A large number of students of both sexes were also sent abroad for higher education. Moreover, the inhabitants of Kabul and Afghans visiting the capital were ordered to wear European dress and hats etc.

King Amanullah's reforms, especially in the educational field encountered considerable opposition from the conservative elements and resulted in many fierce civil wars as a result of which many modern buildings were burnt, schools were closed and European hats were found everywhere in heaps and street etc. except on people's heads.

The fierce civil wars which broke out in Afghanistan resulted in the abdication of King Amanullah and his exile in 1929, to Italy. The evil were caused not only by the conservative Afghans but also perhaps due to political intrigues of foreign powers and foreign elements.

After this uprising, a ruthless highway man called Habibullah, Ghazi or Bacha-i-Saqaw (water-carrier's son), came to power for nine months in (January, 1929) Bacha-i-Saqaw began to impose a reign of terror, so most of Afghanistan's political leaders were killed. He issued a proclamation cancelling all Amanullah's reforms and tried to impose his dictatorship. But he was soon removed by Mohammad Nadir Khan who obtained help from India so he collected Pathan tribes and killed Habibullah Ghazi. Mohammad Nadir Khan's impact by his selfless service to the Afghan nation was so great and his achievements so exalted him in the eyes of the Afghan people that he was elected King in October, 1929 after 9 months rule of Habibullah Ghazi *i.e.*, Bachha Sakka.

King Mohammad Nadir Shah published a declaration of his policy in ten points. This declaration included the foundation of the government upon principles of the teachings of Islam so he won over Mullahs to his side. He proclaimed the prohibition of alcoholic beverages; the establishment of a military school and of an arsenal for the manufacture of modern weapons. He maintained diplomatic relations with foreign powers amicably. The repair of telegraphs and telephones and the collection of arrears of public was carried. The advancement of public instruction was extended the reconstruction of the old council of State was carried and carried the appointment of a Prime Minister who would form a cabinet, subject to the royal approval.

As soon as King Mohammad Nadir Shah set to work, he tried to modernize Afghanistan. Schools were established. A military college was founded. A literary academy and a stock company also came into being. A medical college was started and a modern hospital was also built. Some students were sent abroad for higher education. About six dams were constructed to store water for drinking and irrigation. A few small industrial establishments were also opened. A great road was constructed to connect the capital of Kabul with the northern provinces: One of his most important works was the drafting, of a new constitution for Afghanistan, which he accomplished with the help of an elected parliament. Nadir Shah was a statesman who possessed of foreign countries as he remained previously Ambassador to France. He was thoroughly realistic. Within four years he did an impressive job of consolidation and reconstruction of Afghanistan but unfortunately his good rule was cut short by his assassination by a fanatic on November 8, 1933. The policy of modernization, education and economic development etc. which he embarked later on were carried on by his only son, Mohammad Zahir Shah who inherited throne in 1933 and ruled upto 1973. After this revolts and civil wars took place. Now in 2002 king Zahir Shah has again become the head of state of Afghanistan.

The Rule of Zahir Shah and Its Impact

Zahir Shah belonged to Abdali tribe of Ahmad Shah Durrani. Being only son of Nadir Shah, he became King at the age of 19 without a war of succession. He continued the policy of his father and tried to modernize Afghanistan. During second world war of 1939, he remained neutral. Subhash Chandra Bose reached Germany through Afghanistan crossing Indian Border as Pathan. Afghanistan remained cordial with all powers during World War II but Pakistan was created in 1947, Afghan-Pak relations became bitter. The Afghan people demanded creation of Pukhtoonistan *i.e.,* an independent Pathan state and in 1955, Afghanistan protested against the inclusion of areas inhabited by Pathans in North-West Frontier Province into West Pakistan.

In 1955, the top Russian leaders *i.e.,* Khruschev and Prime Minister Bulganin visited Afghanistan and Russo-Afghan friendship was developed. Russia agreed to give economic aid, help in construction of roads, in construction of hydroelectric stations, irrigation and to help in airfields. Russia also agreed to supply machinery, necessary equipments and know how for the development of Afghanistan. Thus during the reign of Nadir Shah, Russian influence was finally established. In 1964, Zahir Shah introduced the new constitution based on separation of powers and universal suffrage with a democratic character. In 1965, democratic elections were held in Afghanistan Dr. Usuf later on Muhammad Maiywandwal became Prime Minister who resigned in 1967. Later on Abdullah Yakat Ali and Noor Ahmed remained Prime Minister from 1967 to 1981 and later on after victory of conservative party Abdul Zahir remained Prime Minister from 1971 to 1973 but in 1973 a revolution took place under the leadership of Daud Khan who belonged to Royal family of Afghanistan. On account of the revolution of 1973, King Zahir Shah went into exile to Italy and came back in 2002 when Taliban were defeated.

Administration of Zahir Shah

Afghanistan was a constitutional monarchy during the regime of Zahir Shah *i.e.* from 1933 to 1973. The King of Afghanistan was the head of the state of Afghanistan and, like other constitutional monarchs possesses certain prerogative as defined by law. The country's parliament consisted two chambers; the National Assembly is elected for a three-year term by secret ballot of all citizens over the age of twenty. The Senate, consisting of 46 members used to be appointed by the King. These have to be men of vision and "experienced and far sighted person...".

The immunity of individuals from unwarranted interference by state officials was assured by the constitution of Zahir Shah's days. The right to participate in the Government was extended to all subjects without discrimination. No type of class discrimination was tolerated. All persons residing in Afghanistan as citizens of the country were recognized as Afghan subject without any differentiation as to race, creed, and equally enjoyed all rights conferred by the constitution and laws of the country.

The National Assembly had powers to check the activities of various Ministers, to approve or disapprove the Government's budget, and to ratify all bills presented to it with or without amendments. All bills must be passed by both the Houses in order to become law.

Besides the Senate and the National Assembly, there was another body known as the "Lora Jirga", which literally meant the Great National Assembly. This body was unique feature of Afghanistan and used to be convened on certain extraordinary occasions such as, the declaration of war or acceptance of peace terms etc. It used to be composed of representative of all the people in all walks of life and its number was not fixed. During World War II this assembly was gathered for the declaration of neutrality. It was last convened in November, 1955 and five hundred members passed three resolutions concerning the position of Afghanistan about the cold-war between U.S.A. and U.S.S.R. and on the issue of Pakhtunistan, it demanded an independent state of Pathans.

In Afghanistan, judicial power rested with three Islamic courts the Primary Court, Court of Appeals and finally the Supreme Court. Cases used to be tried openly in the Court of Justice with the exception of those, which the Muslim Hanifi legal school directs to be heard in camera. To protect his or her rights, every person may plead in the Court. Courts were popular as they provided quick and cheap justice. No one may set a special tribunal to settle particular cases out of court; further, all courts are free from state interference.

The administration of Afghanistan was conducted by the Prime Minister and his cabinet. The following Ministries were entrusted with particular government duties : National Defence,

Foreign Affairs, Interior, Justice, Finance, Education, Health, Communications, Commerce, Public Works, Agriculture, Mines and Industries, Press and Information, Tribal Affairs, and Planning etc. like France. The country was administratively divided into seventeen provinces, each headed by an official appointed by the Prime Minister and approved by the King himself.

It was only in the reign of Zahir Shah that the people of Afghanistan had a chance to think to how best to meet their needs and to bring about better economic, social and political conditions. In 1953-1958 the number of companies and corporations, both private and public rose to 149. The growth of education had somewhat the same trend as the economic growth. In 1936, there were only 16 newspapers and magazines in Afghanistan, in 1958 there were more than 50. From 1936 to 1953 there were only 378 educational institutions, but during 1953-58 the number of schools rose to 658. The number, of students was 121,090 in 1953; but in 1958, it went up to 155,014. The Kabul University, which was established in 1946, had only one faculty, namely the college of medicine. It had nine faculties in 1958, offering higher academic opportunities to more than 1295 students from all parts of the country. The Kabul University had a staff of 168 professors during Zahir Shah's rule of which 48 had been engaged from abroad. Since its establishment more than 1,595 students have graduated. The students of the Kabul University were generally proficient in at least one of the modern European languages like English, French or Russia or Latin.

Five Year Plans the first of their kind in Afghanistan, were launched in September, 1956. Various activities undertaken in these plans covering the areas of agriculture, transportation and roads, air and river ports, communication, education, health and community development, and development of mines and industries etc.

The 5 year plans for the economic development laid emphasis on agriculture based on the principle that equipment, knowledge, and financial assistance should be made available to the farmers. The establishment of Agricultural Banks, research station, more farming schools, high schools and colleges for agriculture, agricultural mechanization, and increase of land under plough etc. were the main features of 5 year plans. New irrigation projects in on Helmand and the Kabul rivers in Sarobi, were planned. On the rivers Kunduz, Kokcha, Sardeh (Ghazni),

Palto Katawaz, Kharwar (Kabul), Mahalghu and on the Kabul River near Jalabad which would have increased the arable land by about 62,500 acres were launched. The next important item of the plan was transportation. About 1000 kilometres of main roads were improved. Industrialization was encouraged. A number of textile mills, cement works, glass plants, etc. grew. Cottage industries were also encouraged, financed, assisted by the State, so lot of organised workers improved and the communists took advantage.

The Community Development programmes to cover thousands of villages were taken.

Condition of Afghanistan after the Exit of Zahir Shah in 1973 to 2002

In spite of effort of Zahir Shah to develop Afghanistan, he was not popular with ruling Afghan elite class and so a revolution took place on August 24, 1973 which, forced Zahir Shah to abdicate and go on exile to Italy.

Daud Khan, the leader of revolutionaries in the beginning gained power. He discarded constitution of 1964 and formed a commission to draft a new constitution of Afghanistan. Daud Khan grabbed all powers as President of Republic of Afghanistan like Zia-ul-Haq and Mushraf of Pakistan.

On 14th February, 1977 a new constitution of Afghanistan was proclaimed and attempts were made for economic, social and democratic reforms but Daud Khan was a man of Royal family, so he failed to create confidence among masses.

In Afghanistan Communist influence developed. Among leftist party, Parcham and Khalak parties were very prominent. On April 17, 1978 a popular communist leader Akliar Khaiber was killed and this created sensation in Afghanistan. On 27th April, 1977 a revolution took place which made Nur Muhammad Taraki the President of Afghanistan.

Rule of Nur Muhammad Taraki from April 1978 to September 1979. Nur Muhammad Taraki was a communist leader so he followed Communist policy of economic reform and took cruel steps against landlords, private entrepreneurs, Mullahs and big farmers. He entered into ten years treaty of friendship with Russia on 10th September, 1978 but he was unable to consolidate Communist rule and riots became common. As such on 16th September, 1979, he was killed by another Communist leader Hafizullah Amin.

Hafizullah Amin ruled only from September, 1979 to December, 1979. After gaining powers Hafizullah Amin acted in independent manner and did not dance to the tune of Russian rulers so on 27th December, 1979, Russia sent her forces in Afghanistan taking lame excuse of treaty of 1978. Russian forces captured Kabul and established their control over Afghanistan and made Barbak Kamal as President of Afghanistan. Thus Afghanistan came under Soviet control but this act was resented by world opinion in general and Muslim powers in particular. This act of naked aggression by a super power like Russia in total defiance of U.N.O. and world opinion created a sensation all over the world.

In February, 1980, a conference of Muslim powers was held at Islamabad. In conference of 43 Muslim countries, naked aggression of Russia over Afghanistan was condemned. It was pleaded if a super power carries naked aggression then no weak and small power will remain safe from the aggression of a mighty power. Agha Shahi, the foreign secretary of Pakistan stated Russian aggression on Pakistan concerns all Muslim countries so all Muslim countries should oppose this attack and occupation of Afghanistan by Russian forces but only Pakistan, Saudi Arabia and Iran took substantial steps to oppose Russian aggression, so Russian attempt to win Afghanistan failed.

This Russian occupation of Afghanistan was vehemently opposed by U.S.A., China and Western powers. On the other hand Russians established his puppet government of Najibullah setting aside Government of Barbak Kamal. Russian domination over Afghanistan gave rise to revolts and forced people of Afghanistan to leave the country. Consequently millions of Afghans migrated to Pakistan, Iran and other countries. This gave rise to civil war and refugee problem of Afghans. Later on Taliban govt. gained on upper hand but were later on defeated and new govt. came with U.S.A. support under Hamid Karzai.

At last Russians had to bow to world public opinion and new liberal Russian leader Gorbachov withdrew Russian forces from Afghanistan but continued to support Government of Najibullah. As such civil war continued on between Russian supported Government of Najibullah and U.S.A. and Pakistan supported Mujahadeen but later on Taliban succeeded who have been now replaced U.S.A. supported govt. of Hamid Karzai.

In April 1992, Mujahadeen council captured power under the leadership of President Buruanuddin Rabbani and Prime

Minister of Gulabuddin Hikmatyar, but both quarrelled and this govt. was overthrown by Taliban. They imposed fanatic Islamic rule and executed Najibullah, Rabbani and other ousted leaders.

Taliban established orthodox Islamic rule with no freedom to women to attend school or work, Taliban were supported by Islamic guerillas of other countries. Taliban blasted to pieces two Buddha statues of Bamiyan and supported fanatic Islamic terrorists. One terrorist Osama Bin Laden's followers made terrorists attacks on the twin world trade center towers in New York and took shelter in Afghanistan. This created horror all over the world and U.N.O. through U.S.A. took action. Taliban govt. was overthrown but main leader Mullah Omar and Osma Bin Laden escaped and have not been captured.

A new govt. was installed in Afghanistan under the exiled ex King Zahir Shah and P.M. Hamid Karzai containing many parties. Due to these conflicts, Afghanistan is one of the least developed countries of the world, but now it is making progress. Women have been given liberty and high posts. Lot of development has taken place. New government has established good relations with India and western powers and is striving for peace and prosperity.

Afghanistan Problem and U.N.O. Forces of Russia entered Afghanistan on 27th December, 1979 and Barbak Kamal was made President who got Hafizullah Amin and Afghanistan came under the control of Russians but Russian attempts to control Afghanistan ultimately failed and Taliban were also defeated and new govt. with U.S.A. support is ruling Afghanistan under the leadership of Hamid Karzai.

U.N.O. General Assembly passed a resolution with overwhelming majority on 14th January, 1980, calling for immediate, unconditional and total withdrawal of Soviet troops from Afghanistan to enable Afghan people to decide their own future without any outside intervention. But Soviet Union vetoed this resolution in Security Council and Russia continued to keep her forces till February, 1989 inspite of condemnation by U.N.O. and Islamic conference and missions of non-aligned countries failed.

At last world opinion forced Soviet Russia to withdraw her forces and in March, 1989, Russian forces left Afghanistan firmly establishing Soviet supported puppet Government of Najibullah. U.S.A., Pakistan and Muslim states desired to solve Afghan problem but Najibullah refused to quit and this brought a civil war in Afghanistan. Soviet supported Najibullah Government and Pakistan, and U.S.A. supported Taliban's fight with one-another is going on and no solution of Afghan problem is in sight. As in this fight of control over Afghanistan, Russia and Middle East Muslim powers are chief contestants so in contemporary politics Afghanistan falls in Middle East, Pakistan and Iran, and to a much lesser extent India are involved in Afghan conflict. The United Nations is only agency that can bring political settlement in Afghanistan. The U.N. Secretary General has a mandate to initiate peace process in Afghanistan but he is unable to achieve anything and Soviet Union openly and India secretly was helping Najibullah Government and U.S.A. is helping Mujahadeen.

India has urged for an early solution of Afghan problem and urged that public of Afghanistan should be allowed to decide its own future without any outside interference. As such all the peace loving nations are anxious to find out the solution of Afghan problem but all efforts have failed and war is going on unabated. Demand of Pakistan, U.S.A. and Britain is that peace may prevail while Soviet Union was determined to preserve it inspire of strong opposition.

Afghan problem is very complicated. Pro-Soviet Government of Najibullah was in power but Pakistan, Saudi Arabia and other Muslim countries replaced it by Islamic Government. Iran desired that in new Government, Shia sect of Muslims should also have representation in it while U.S.A. and Britain and other Western countries desire pro-West Government in Afghanistan but solution of Afghan problem lies in that the people of Afghanistan should have free choice to choose their own Government without any outside interference. As such it is expected that Afghan people will be given freedom to choose their own Government soon. After civil war Taliban came in front. Taliban govt. has been overthrown and King Zahir Shah has been recalled from his exile from Italy and new govt. under Hamid Karzai having persons of all groups is in power and this govt. has succeeded in gaining U.N.O. support and is trying to bring peace and prosperity in war torn Afghanistan.

Summary

Landlocked and mountainous, Afghanistan has suffered from such chronic instability and conflict during its modern history that its economy and infrastructure are in ruins, and lot of people are refugees.

It has also been afflicted by natural calamities such as earthquakes and drought etc.

Its strategic position sandwiched between the Middle East, Central Asia and the Indian subcontinent along the ancient "Silk Route" etc. means that Afghanistan has long been fought over despite its rugged and forbidding terrain.

It was at the centre so in the 19th century when Imperial Russia and the British Empire in India vied for influence.

And it became a key Cold War battleground after thousands of Soviet troops intervened in 1979 to prop up a pro-communist regime leading to a major confrontation that drew in the US and Pakistan and Afghanistan's neighbours.

But the outside world lost interest after the withdrawal of Soviet forces, while the country's protracted civil war dragged on.

The emergence of the Taleban — originally a group of Islamic scholars — brought at least a measure of stability after nearly two decades of conflict.

But their extreme version of Islam and Cruel Acts attracted widespread criticism and resentment.

The Taleban — drawn from the Pashtun majority — were opposed by an alliance of factions drawn mainly from Afghanistan's minority communities based in the north.

In control of about 90% of Afghanistan until late 2001, the Taleban were recognised as the legitimate government by only three countries.

They were at loggerheads with the international community over the presence on their soil of Osama bin Laden, accused by the USA of masterminding the bombing of their embassies in Africa in 1998 and the attacks on the USA on 11 September 2001 on its World Trade Center (WTO).

After the Taleban's refusal to hand over Osama bin Laden, the USA initiated aerial attacks in October, paving the way for opposition groups to drive them from power. Consequently, Taliban were defeated and a new liberal Govt. was established. NATO maintains security.

Infighting between local commanders over power and territory has become a striking feature of the post-Taleban period. The authorities in Kabul have so far been unable to contain the fighting in the southern and eastern regions. In spite of all this new government is trying to maintain peace and is making progress. This new govt. under Hamid Karzai has succeeded in getting support of U.S.A. and NATO and has established good relations with western powers and India.

Afghanistan Facts

Population	: 24 million
Capital	: Kabul
Major language	: Pashto, Dari (Persian)
Major religion	: Islam
Life expectancy	: 43 years (men), 43 years (women)
Monetary unit	: 1 Afghani
Main exports	: Fruit and nuts, carpets, wool, opium etc.
Interim govt. leader	: Hamid Karzai
President	: Hamid Karzai

Afghanistan has an interim administration which was chosen at a Loya Jerga — or traditional assembly of tribal representatives — in June 2002, who are acting as interim administration. It is to govern until 2004, and has the tasks of drafting a new constitution, overseeing the formation of a national army and of preparing for elections at the end of its term.

Hamid Karzai, who headed the provisional administration set up when the Taleban were driven from power, was chosen at the Loya Jerga as interim head of state.

Deputies

Mohammad Fahim

Karim Khalili

Hedayat Amin Arsala

Nematollah Shahrani

Members include:

Foreign Minister	: Foreign Minister Abdullah Abdullah
Interior Minister	: Ali Ahmad Jalali
Defence Minister	: Mohammad Qaseem Fahim
Education Minister	: Yunus Qanuni

New govt. is maintaining good relations with India, Arab and western powers.

The Near East and Its Importance and Impact

History of Middle East in the eighteenth century probably marks one of the lowest points in the long and old history of the Middle East. Various causes, from the twelfth century onward, had contributed to this decline. The crusades, the Mongol invasions, the breakdown of some of the major irrigation systems and the salination of the soil, the infiltration of nomadic tribes and the diversion of trade routes etc. contributed to its decline. In the fifteenth to sixteenth centuries the Turkish Ottoman Empire, and in the sixteenth to seventeenth century Iran under the great Safavid rulers had enjoyed a temporary revival which was marked by strong government, economic recovery, and a high level of artistic creation without, however, any accompanying scientific, technological or intellectual progress. But from 1514 until the eighteenth century these two empires were engaged in almost uninterrupted and inconclusive wars, which exhausted their strength and economy and devastated the borderlands, especially of Iraq and Azerbaijan. From the end of the seventeenth century, in both states, the central government's hold on the provinces gradually weakened. Revolts and tribal raids proliferated, order broke down, communications crumbled, and economic activity declined greatly. In the course of the eighteenth century European commerce with Iran, Syria and Egypt etc. dwindled and cultural contacts greatly diminished, increasing still further the already great isolation of this region. However, in Constantinople and in the Balkans, both trade and cultural exchanges increased rapidly, setting in motion economic, social and political forces that were to transform that region and make it prosperous and powerful and important.

The Middle East was pulled out of its isolation by international, political and economic rivalries of great powers. At first the main clash was between Britain and France, then between Britain and Russia, and finally, toward the end of the nineteenth century, between Britain and Germany and in 20th century between U.S.A. and U.S.S.R. Rivalry of U.S.A. and U.S.S.R. has brought wars between Israel and Arabs, between Iran and Iraq and war in Afghanistan. From the time of Peter the Great Russia had been encroaching on both the Turkish Ottoman Empire and Iran, while Britain's expanding empire in India made it increasingly anxious to secure the strategic land and sea routes leading to the subcontinent of India. But it was Napoleon's conquest of Egypt in 1798, and his dispatch of a military mission to Iran in 1807, that drew attention to the strategic and political importance of the Middle East and made it a center of Great Power struggle and since then Middle East is still cockpit of world, though now peace has came due to efforts of U.N.O. to a great extent. Though Israel and Palestine are still daggers drawn.

Between 1804 and 1827 Russia defeated Iran in three wars, annexing Georgia and Azerbaijan etc. But no significant Russian conquests were achieved at the expense of Turkey because the British, and sometimes the French, resisted Russian expansion. Their opposition expressed itself most dramatically in the Crimean War of 1854-56. Russia's efforts did help to liberate the Balkan's slav people, but did not lead to the domination of the area that the Russian rulers desired.

After the expulsion of Napoleon's troops from Egypt owing to Lord Nelson's naval victories, France lost all direct power in Middle East but every French attempt to regain control of this area was frustrated by the other Great Powers. But inspite of this France retained much influence in this region, thanks to its investments in the Suez Canal and in various railways, its trade, its numerous cultural and religious contacts, and its acknowledged position as protector of Roman Catholics in the Turkish Ottoman Empire. Britain became the dominant power in the Middle East after 1815 but old friendship of French Government with Muslim governments contributed a lot to continue French influence. Later on by its steady support of the Turkish Ottoman government it exerted much influence until the end of the century. Britain's naval supremacy was unchallenged, and its economic strength far exceeded that of its rivals. Except for the brief war with Turkey in 1807 and the expedition of 1840 against Sultan Muhammad Ali was undertaken at the request of the Port the short Persian War of 1856 was Britain's only direct clash with a major Middle Eastern power. In 1820-1853 treaties suppressing piracy and the slave trade ensured its predominance in the Persian Gulf. In 1839 it annexed Aden due to strategic importance and for use as a coaling station and to guard the entrance to the Red Sea. In 1878 Cyprus and in 1882 it occupied Egypt; and in 1890-1898 an Anglo-Egyptian force conquered the Sudan. Thus, Britain conquered Egypt,

Cyprus and Aden etc. in 19th century for security of British Empire.

The rise of German power, and the increasing economic and military cooperation between Turkey and Germany, which culminated in the alliance of 1914, forced a realignment of the rival forces. Britain settled claims with France in Africa in 1904 relinquishing Morocco in return for Egypt. In 1907, Britain came to an understanding with Russia about Iran, dividing the country into spheres of influence. Starting in 1915, British, France, Russia, Italy, and Greece began task of partitioning the Turkish Ottoman Empire. The Bolshevik Revolution of 1917 and Turkey's victorious struggle against the Allied forces in 1918-1922 rendered many of the provisions of these treaties inoperative, but France emerged with control over Syria and Lebanon under mandate of League of Nations thus fulfilling an ancient dream, Britain was granted mandates over Iraq, Palestine, and Transjordan etc. Thereafter, with France as a junior partner, Britain dominated the Middle East until 1945 and even after the Second World-War upto 1956.

The Turkish Policy in Near East in 20th Century

Repeated defeats by Austrian and Russian and the successful Balkan national uprisings persuaded the Turkish Ottoman rulers to take radical steps in hopes of saving their Turkish Empire. Selim III (1789-1807) and Mahmud II (1808-1839) broke the power of the Janissary army which once was considered the finest and most disciplined infantry in the world, but by now an unruly, destructive mob—and cleared the way for the Tanzimat reforms. The army and the bureaucracy were reorganized; control of the central Ottoman government over the provinces was greatly strengthened. In 1908 the Young Turk movement destroyed the absolutism of Sultan Abdul Hamid II, ushering in a brief constitutional period that lasted until 1914 *i.e.,* Turkey's entry into World War I. Underlying those political changes was steady, if very slow, modernization of the legal and judicial systems and some progress was made in economic, social, and intellectual activity and in administration.

Until shortly before the First World War of 1914-18 the official ideology continued to be "Ottomanism." All subjects of the Ottoman Sultan were encouraged to think of themselves as equal. In 1839, even Christians and Jews etc. were granted formal equality with Muslims. But the successful encroachments of the Balkan states, which by 1912 had absorbed practically the whole of European Turkey, along with Armenian national aspirations etc. were ruthlessly repressed. The rising tide of Arab nationalism, brought about a sharp change in the policy of Ottoman Turk rulers. Recognizing that the strength of the empire lay in its Turkish component, the government tried to "Turkify" the other peoples of Ottoman empire. This only exacerbated national feelings still further and led to the Arab Revolt of 1916. In 1918, the Ottoman Empire was shorn of many of its Asian provinces and these of other states also were occupied by Greek, British, French, and by the troops of the Kamal Pasha's War of liberation revivified Turkish nationalism. It was led by Mustafa Kamal Ataturk, a general who had won fame and popularity by his brilliant and successful defense of Gallipoli in 1915 against British and French forces and his dogged resistance to the British advance in Syria in 1918. The ramshackle, multinational, archaic Turkish Empire emerged as a compact, homogeneous republic, which in the course of the 1920's and 1930's was rapidly modernized by Kamal Pasha. Its economic, social, and cultural institutions were modernized. The power of the Muslim clerical establishment and of Ulemas was broken. The Arabic script was replaced by one based on Latin, the veil and polygamy etc. were abolished, and education was expanded and a great progress was made in Turkey under Kamal Pasha. Now Turkey is member of European Confederation and follows secular policies and remained neutral during U.S.A.-Iraq wars.

The History of Egypt and Its Impact

In the Arab provinces four separate forces eroded Ottoman Turks' rule. In Egypt Muhammad Ali, a tobacco merchant of Turkish origin, born in Albania in 1769 probably, with no education but endowed with ability amounting to genius, became as a soldier of fortune in the Ottoman Turkish army. By 1805, he had become a very important person *i.e.*, Pasha, or governor of Egypt. He soon secured virtual Independence and founded a dynasty that ruled Egypt until 1952. With the help of French and other foreign advisers, he established a modern army and navy and the most efficient government in that part of Ottoman region, which came under his control. He started a process of rapid economic and social development. In Arabia a puritanical religious revival, Whahhabism, enabled the house of Saud, after many vicissitudes, to extend its rule over the greater part of the Arabian Peninsula under the leadership of Adul-Aziz ibn-Saud (1880-1953), who is considered as the founder of modern Saudi Arabia. National movements in Lebanon, Syria, and Iraq took to the form of secret societies, which inspired the Arabian Revolt during 1914-18 *i.e.*, during the First World War, under the leadership of the Hussein the Sherif of Mecca. Lastly, Britain, France, and Italy occupied various countries in the Middle East and North Africa. Italy conquered Libya, France, Syria and Lebanon and Britain, Iraq, Palestine, Jordan and Cyprus etc.

The postwar settlement caused great disappointment to Arabs. Egypt, after much agitation, secured a limited measure of independence in 1922, which broadened in 1936 but still fell short of nationalist demands of independence. The Fertile Crescent containing Iraq, Syria and Palestine was placed under British and French mandates. In 1917, Palestine was declared a national Jewish home, to which more than 300,000 Jewish immigrants came by 1939. The interwar years witnessed continual agitation and revolts against the British and French mandates except in Iraq, which became independent in 1932. The results achieved by mandatory powers were slight. And the nationalist struggle led to the frequent, disruption of the constitutional processes introduced in these near Eastern countries in the 1920's, but now conditions have improved.

Note on Iran of 20th Century

In Iran, which was less exposed to Western influences than the Ottoman Empire of Turks, the absolute rule of the Qajar dynasty in Iran (1794-1925) was not seriously challenged until the Constitutionalist Revolution of 1905-1909. After an initial success constitutionalism was, however, crushed with the help of Russian troops and by the Russian-led Cossack Brigade. During 1914-18 *i.e.*, during the First World War period Iran, notwithstanding its official neutrality, became a battle ground for Turkish, Russian and British troops. The collapse of the Ottoman Empire and Czarist rule in Russia left Britain as the predominant power of this region but a nationalist uprising and diplomatic pressures forced British withdrawal. One of the leaders of the uprising was Reza Pahelvi, an army officer of humble birth and little education but of great desire and ability. He proclaimed himself Shah in 1925, and started rapidly to modernize Iran after establishing his dynastic rule. Now Iran is a Shia dominated orthodox Islamic country. Iran has been accused of making dangerous weapons but Iran has denied this charge.

The Western Impact and Recent Progress of Near East

Western interest in both raw materials and swift connections with India, Indonesia and Indo-China etc. led to the establishment, as early as the 1830's, of regular steamship services between Europe and the eastern Mediterranean Sea and between India and the Suez Canal. The opening of the Suez Canal, in 1869, channeled a huge amount of traffic through the Middle East Western European countries to South East Asia. Ports and internal transport were developed and trade increased. The first Egyptian railway was opened in 1854, and others soon followed in Anatolia, *i.e.,* in Turkey. In Lebanon, Syria, Sudan, and Iraq etc. railway made great progress. Steamboats cruised the Nile, the Tigris, Eupharates, and the Karun rivers. After the First World War road building was greatly accelerated and motor transport gained popularity.

All this, together with the inflow of European capital (nearly $2 billion by 1914) which is now 100 times more and the development of banking and other financial services, made it possible to integrate the Middle East also in the international economy. Cash crops were grown for export and cash crops such as cotton and tobacco, began to dominate the economy of these countries. The area under cultivation was greatly extended and large irrigation works were built and finally in Egypt, Aswan dam was constructed.

The value of the foreign trade of the Middle Eastern countries multiplied many fold between 1815-1914 although population was growing everywhere in the world. Thanks mainly to improved hygiene, total output of grains and goods seems to have increased faster with a consequent rise in the level of living. However, transport also opened the way for trade in European factory products, which soon overpowered the Middle Eastern handmade goods, causing great hardships to the ancient artisans and handicraft centers and to maintain segments of the population such as weavers etc.

In the 1920's and still more in the 1930's exports of these countries suffered greatly, because of the sharp decline in world agricultural prices. This brought home to Middle Eastern countries the need for industrial development. From 1939 a start was made in Turkey, Egypt, Iran, and Palestine etc. for industrial development. Foreign oil companies began drilling in this region before World War I, in Iran and Egypt etc. By the beginning of World War II *i.e.,* by 1939 the Middle Eastern countries accounted for about 6 per cent of world, soil output. By increased trade and the reorientation of trade and communications the Middle Eastern countries hoped to spark an intellectual renaissance. Missionary schools were established in Lebanon in the eighteenth century and in the other Middle Eastern countries in the nineteenth. All the main Christian sects participated in this movement, but the most active countries were Britain, France and the United States of America etc. In addition to elementary and secondary schools, foreign missions provided the Middle East with its first liberal arts colleges, notably the American University in Beirut was established in 1886 and Robert College was established in Turkish capital in Istanbul, and military schools, with technical branches, were founded in Istanbul, Cairo, and Teheran etc. But full-fledged national universities did not come into being until 1914. The Egyptian, Ottoman, and Iranian governments began to send students, mainly prospective technicians, to European centers early in the nineteenth century, and the number of students has expanded steadily manifold at the present time. Soon Western books were being translated into Turkish, Arabic, Urdu and Persian languages and these books were brought out in large numbers, by the newly established printing presses. For although a printing press had been set-up in Ottoman capital Istanbul in the eighteenth century and there had even earlier ones among the Christian sects of Lebanon and Syria etc. but it was not until the nineteenth century that printing profession attained significance. Almost simultaneously newspapers began to appear in Egypt, Lebanon, Turkey, and Iran etc. spreading new Western ideas among a broad circle of readers. This was accompanied by a literary revival, marked by greater simplicity and clarity of style and enrichment of vocabulary to cope with modern needs and social set-up and the introduction of hitherto unknown forms such as novels and plays etc. Though upto 1939 the Middle East had made no significant technical, scientific, intellectual, or artistic contribution but it had out after-reaching and irreversible internal transformation. Writers of distinction, some of whose works were translated into various foreign languages, had appeared. Peyami Safa and Zia Gok Alp in Turkey, Taha Husain and Tawfiq-al-Hakim in Egypt, Muhammad Ali Jamal-Zadeh and Sadiq Hedayat in Iran etc, were famous and prominent among them. For the first time, women began participating in intellectual and political activity, notably the Turkish novelist Halide Edip and the Lebanese Mayy

Ziadeh became famous. Some sculptors and painters began to gain international reputation. Scientists were grappling with local problems. Altogether, the intellectual and artistic horizons of the Middle East were being immeasurably broadened. Recently Near and Middle East has made great progress in all walks of life and due to its abundance in oil, it had become richest region of the world but this has attracted super powers. Due to super power rivalry *i.e.,* due to rivalry of U.S.A. and U.S.S.R. constant wars are going on between Israel and Arabian powers, between Iran and Iraq etc. but open rivalry is found in Afghanistan where Russia is supporting the puppet Government of Najibullah and Mujahadeen are being supported by U.S.A. and Pakistan etc. In this world creation and destruction goes on together so inspite of rivalries, conflicts and wars, Middle East is making considerable progress in all walks of life. It is hoped that in future peace and prosperity may reign supreme and may assure further progress.

Review of Middle Eastern Countries since 1939 *i.e.,* from the World War II

During the Second World War, major campaigns were fought along the borders of the Middle East — in the Caucasus, Greece and Crete etc. The wars were fought in Western desert of Egypt, and in Ethiopia but the region itself escaped unscathed. However, a cataclysm of such magnitude could not but have deep repercussions, and in fact the war shattered the social and political order which had been established in Middle Eastern countries through European influence. In addition to the revolutionary ideas let loose in this region, there was the presence of several hundred thousand allied troops, whose upkeep added hundreds of millions of dollars to the foreign exchange reserves of the various countries of Middle East. It also created shortages and raised prices sharply, exacerbating political and social tensions. The allied powers — especially the British — understandably subordinated local considerations to overall strategy, Britishers made the Middle Eastern governments take unpopular measures and, where proper and necessary, as in Iraq and Iran in 1941, and in Egypt in 1942, coerced or overthrew such governments. But the war interrupted or reversed the process of imperial disengagement in the region. The result was to intensify the already great political ferment and to increase nationalist resentment of the occupying powers and to create aggressive national feelings and in some states fanatic religious feelings.

The end of the World War II was, therefore, the signal for repeated attempts to end foreign control. These were generally successful, since the local forces could usually enlist the support of the United States of America and sometimes that of Britain and the Soviet Union as well. Thus France, which had formally granted independence to Lebanon and Syria in 1943, was forced by Britain and the United States of America to withdraw its troops from those countries by 1946. In Iran withdrawal of American, British, and under strong American pressure, Soviet forces early in 1946, was followed by the emergence of a Soviet-sponsored separatist government in Azerbaijan. Anglo-Egyptian negotiations were fruitless until 1954 when, thanks to United States of America efforts on agreement was reluctantly reached. Two years later, British troops were withdrawn from the Suez Canal zone, paving the way for granting the independence to the Anglo-Egyptian Sudan. In Iraq, repeated attempts to amend the 1930 treaty with Great Britain were unsuccessful, but British forces were finally withdrawn following the conclusion to the Baghdad Pact in 1955. As regards the smaller countries, Jordan received independence in 1946, Cyprus in 1960 (after prolonged Guerilla fighting) Kuwait in 1961, and Southern Yemen in 1968. Thus whole Middle East became fragmented and independent, but devoid of peace.

Palestine's History in Brief

In Palestine reconciliation of Arab and Zonist aspirations seemed impossible. A United Nations Organisation's resolution in 1947, partitioning the Palestine into Arab and Zews zone was followed by the withdrawal of British troops and fighting first between Zionists and Palestine Arabs and then, after the proclamation of the State of Israel in 1948, between it and the neighbouring Arab countries. Hostilities erupted repeatedly many wars took place and in the "Six-Day War" of 1967, an overwhelming Israeli triumph that resulted in the occupation of important parts of Egypt, Jordan, and Syria etc. made Israel greater and powerful country. Diplomatic and commercial relations remain broken; no solution has been found for repatriating about 750,000 Arab refugees, who fled from Palestine now a tiny P.L.O. state has been created.

The unity imposed on the greater part of the Middle East by the Turkish Ottoman Empire broke down after the First World War of 1914-18 and that provided by Britains predominance disappeared after the Second World War. Since then various attempts both internal and external, to unite the Middle Eastern countries or to have reconciliation have met with little success. As such region has been the scene of conflict of vested interests between the great powers. American and British efforts to bring Middle Eastern countries into a defence pact or an alliance have also failed. A Middle East Defence Pact proposal of 1951 failed due to Egyptian opposition. The Baghdad pact, concluded in 1955, linked Iran, Pakistan, and Turkey with Britain, but the only Arab country to join this pact was Iraq, which withdrew in 1959 and so it ended and Saddam Hussein of Iraq did not favour attachment to any block but his annexation of Kuwait forced U.N.O. to attach it and impose sanctions.

The main internal attempt at integration was that of the Arab League, founded in 1945 to promote political and economic cooperation among its dynastic and national ambitions and divergent interests. The various fertile crescent schemes, aiming for uniting Syria, Lebanon, Palestine and Jordan, and Iraq etc. under the Hashimi royal house, one of whose branches ruled Iraq and another in Jordan—were opposed and thwarted by Egypt and Jordan so all schemes soon broke down. With Israel there have been tensions between the Turkey and Syria, Iran and Iraq, Iran and the United Arab Republic and Egypt and Iraq and Kuwait etc. but U.N.O. was able to patch up differences and to bring uneasy calm.

Local quarrels have been both incited and aggravated by super power's intervention. A series of crises centered on Syria in 1955-1957 which led to an American and Soviet Unions's confrontation. Egypt's nationalization of the Suez Canal in 1956 and the subsequent attack on that country by Britain, France, and Israel, led to United Nations organization take action and due to American and Soviet pressures, withdrawal of the invading forces was carried under U.N.O. supervisions. The civil war in Lebanon in 1958 and the support given to the rebels by the United Arab Republic of Syria and Egypt proved a landing of U.S. Marines and Soviet Union's counter-protests. In the civil war which broke out in Yemen in 1962, Egypt backed the republican forces, and Saudi Arabia and Jordan supported the royalists regime. Egypt in turn received Soviet arms and aid, and similar support reached to the royalists from the British ruled territories of South Arabia. In addition to this the United States of America anxious to preserve *status quo* and to prevent the fighting from extending beyond the borders of Yemen following the 1967 war, the Arabs have received Soviet backing and the Israelis have received support of American Government. Thus due to conflict of interests of super powers Middle East became a cockpit of world, but with the disintegration of U.S.S.R. cold war has ended but these states are still quarrelling with one another.

In short, though established international relations in the Middle East are being determined by the countries of this regions but to a far greater degree than before on the influence of the great powers which is still considerable and probably in some circumstances decisive. This power of interference is exercised not so much through direct fight but as through diplomatic pressure and the supply of financial aid and arms etc., to the Middle Eastern governments. As such constant conflicts and wars are going on and these have increased as even countries like India are supporting P.L.O. against Israel. Now an autonomous Palestinian state has been established to satisfy muslim Arab states.

In most of these regimes established after the First World War of 1914-18 under British and French influence, power was exercised mainly by the landlords, aristocrats and upper middleclass. These regimes broke down after the Second World War which ended in 1945. At present in these main types of government are based on military dictatorships with a strong nationalist and socialist orientation. Traditional monarchies are also engaged in modernizing their countries and efforts are made to establish liberal parliamentary democracies. Syria's military revolt of 1949 was the first of many in the course of which the ruling officer groups drawn mainly from the lower middle class came to apply increasingly radical policies to win public support. In Egypt in the 1952, military group overthrew the rule of King Farouk whose scandalous behaviour had discredited the monarchy and the country was ruled by officers led by Gamal Abdel Nasser a burly military officer of lower middle class origin whose experience of the disastrous campaign against Israel in 1948-49 had led him to start the secret free officers movements. This regime has reoriented foreign policy, drastically reduced Western influence through the use of society countervailing power. In this process Nasser secured vast amounts of aid from both Western and Communist sides and sought to establish Egyptian leadership in the whole Arab world. In the name of Arab Socialism, he tried to transform Egypt's internal structure extending economic and educational opportunities to the masses breaking the economic and political power of the former ruling classes and curtailing intellectual and political liberty previously prevailing there. In Iraq, the army coup war lead by Kassim who overthrew the monarchy in 1958 but he was killed in 1963 and the country failed to produce any leader of stature, and it has been torn by armed conflicts between Arabs and Kurds but later on Saddam Hussein came to power. In Yemen Takiniti emerged as a powerful leader and successfully managed the affairs of the state. The officers who led the revolt of 1962 failed to get control over the whole country, and the war between them and royalist tribes continued and Yemen became divided in North and South Yemen, but later on the problem was solved and both Yemen became united and maintained peace.

The surviving monarchies in Iran, Jordan, Kuwait, and Saudi Arabia etc. have so far succeeded due to Muslim tradition and thanks to the loyalty of their armies, in the two fold task of checking internal attempt of coups and onslaughts, often supported by more radical neighbours such as Egypt etc. and rapidly modernizing the economic and social structure of their countries. This has necessitated some far-reaching changes, such as the Iranian land reform of 1963 which greatly reduced the power of the landlords and the political and administrative reorganization in conservative of Saudi Arabia. Their task has been facilitated by oil revenues in Iran, Kuwait, and Saudi Arabin and due to American and British aid in Jordan. As such these countries have emerged as richest countries of the world.

Turkey. In Turkey the one-party rule established by Mustafa Kamal Ataturk continued under his successor and faithful lieutenant Ismet Inonu, who in spite of his advanced age retained much intellectual vigour. It was realized that Turkey was ripe for a multi-party system, and commanded the widespread respect required to make the transition possible. The 1945 elections were contested by the Democrat party, which in 1950 took office. In the following decade Turkey saw much economic and social progress, but this was accompanied by rising prices, imbalances, repressions, and growing tensions which exploded in the army coup of 1960. In contrast with other Middle Eastern countries, however, the more radical army officers failed to gain control of the movement in Turkey and power was gradually handed back to civilians. Turkey became member of N.A.T.O. and is making progress under constitutional and republican regime. Turkey avoided active involvement in wars and quarrels of other countries except Cyprus. Turkey remained neutral during wars of U.S.A. and Iraq and of Arabs and Israel.

Lebanon. Lebanon's constitutional system has also endured, surviving a bloodless revolution in 1952 and a short but devastating civil war in 1958. Here the main tensions have been between Christians and Muslims both Shia and Sunni and they are aggravated by struggles between rival ideologies and power groups in the other Arab states such as Iran and Syria and P.L.O. etc. Similarly, Israel's broad-based democracy has not been threatened by fairly frequent changes in party alignment. Thanks to the high educational and social level of its people and to a considerable extent due to lavish, foreign aid of western power's so this country has overcome the difficulties posed by isolation and attacks from its Arab neighbours. The task of absorbing well over a million immigrants including Jews from India who were forced to leave due to anti-Jew policy of Indian Government. Most of these oriental Jews with cultural values different from those of the predominant Western-born or native Israelis. Inspite of all this Israel has successfully thwarted attempt of Muslim states supported by India and Soviet Union to destroy it and made peace with Egypt and established autonomous state of Palestine now to bring peace.

After 1945, Middle Eastern oil resources — which at present amount to 60 per cent of the whole world reserves — were rapidly developed and the oil producing countries bordering the Persian Gulf now account for more then 25 per cent of world oil output and more than 50 per cent of its exports. Oil revenues, which are running at over $3 billion a year, play a dominant part in their budgets and serve to finance a large part of the region's expenditure on Defence development. Not only this due to oil resources these Middle Eastern countries except Jordan and Israel have become richest countries of the world. Israel inspite of conflicts progressed end is a prosperous state.

Industrialization. Industrialization is also proceeding at an accelerating pace and in several countries manufacturing and mining new mines form a fifth or more of the gross national income. Transport and communications have developed rapidly; railways and ports have been built, roads have been vastly extended and improved and a network of airlines covers this region. However as in other underdeveloped regions, agricultural output has generally lagged behind the rapid population growth which is more than 3 per cent per annum in several countries.

In the Middle East which was formerly a net exporter of grain has become increasingly dependent on imports of grain mainly form the United States of America, the Soviet Union, Western Germany, Britain, India and on other countries. Thanks to oil and foreign aid the rate of economic growth in most of these Middle Eastern countries has been distinctly far ahead than that of other underdeveloped regions and the level of living is higher than ever before.

The progress achieved as in the main has taken place within the framework of private enterprises. But in all these countries the government has played a leading part contributing heavily to investment, extending social services and seeking to secure greater social justice through taxation and in several countries land reform has been done. In Egypt since 1961 and later in Syria and Iraq the bulk of industry finance and transport has been nationalized and a socialist system is well under way. In the whole region socialist ideas drawn from west European countries and Russian and Chinese sources are capturing the allegiance of the intelligents along with nationalism. Generally the two beliefs amalgamate to form the same kind of socialist nationalism which is widespread in other underdeveloped regions and countries such as Egypt and India etc. but now liberal democratic ideas have become popular.

Influence of Intelligentsia. The size of the Western educated intelligentia is growing very rapidly, because of the expansion of education and the increase of the urban population. For the first time in history more than half the boys and nearly half the girls in the Middle East are attending schools and colleges and hundreds of thousands of students of both sexes are receiving higher university education. Particularly noteworthy has been the expansion of the technical and scientific education and research etc. Middle Eastern scientists are making a very appreciable contribution to the progress of their countries, and a few of them are doing work which has wider significance. Similarly, the literature being produced in this region has reached a high standard and works written in Arabic, Hebrew, Persian, and Turkish languages have been translated into various Western languages. Among them distinguished are the novelists Samuel Agnon, the Nobel Prize winner, and Haim Hazzaz in Israel, the novelists and short story writers Nagib Mahfuz and Yusif Idris in Egypt, Mahmut Makal and Kemal Yashar in Turkey, and Sadiq Chubak and Jalal Ali Ahmad in Iran and many others.

Except in Israel and Lebanon illiteracy is generally widespread but it may be expected to fall sharply in the next decade or very soon. In the meantime other media such as Radio, T.V. and Cinema etc. are reaching the masses: transistor and radios have opened the remotest villages to the outside world, and movies and television are now available in the Middle East even in towns. Rural electrification and the spread of social services and education etc. are transforming still further the outlook of the peasants and workers who still constitute the bulk of the population. Thus the Middle East, so long left behind in scientific advancement, by history, torn by tensions, perplexed difficulties, but with renewed vitality and hope, is making tremendous progress in the modern world. Inspite of all this it may be stated conflicts are still going on and tensions are prevailing between Iraq and Iran even after the war of 1980-89. Arab powers determination to destroy Israel with the help of India and Soviet Union, constant conflicts in Lebanon and civil war of Afghanistan and terrorism is causing concern to whole world but after with drawal of Russians and end of Civil war Taliban got control of Afghanistan, but Taliban has been defeated and new liberal govt. is in power in 2003-04 but terrorism is causing apprehension everywhere.

Arab League

The Arab League is comprehensive non-western regional arrangement of Arab Muslim powers. It was formed in March 1945, when in Egypt, Iraq, Jordan, Lebanon, Saudi Arabia, Syria and Yemen signed a pact for its creation. Later on Algeria, Kuwait, Libya, Morocco, Sudan and Tunisia etc. also joined it.

Objective. The primary object is to strengthen relations between the member states, coordination of their policies in order to achieve cooperation among member countries and to safeguard their independence and sovereignty.

Organizational Structure. The chief organ of the League is the Council or Majlis. All members are equally represented on it. It meets twice a year. Its special meeting can be called at the request of at least two members. Its council supervises the execution of the multilateral agreements of the member states. It tries to settle disputes among its members peacefully. Political committee and other committees assist the council in performing different tasks. Its only unanimous decisions are bindings.

Miscellaneous. Its headquarter was Cairo but when Egypt concluded agreement with Israel, then League expelled Egypt and in 1986 opposed U.S.A. threat to Libya but in 1981, Egypt has been again made member of Arab League. It supports P.L.O. against Israel and Muslim powers against all others. The League maintains a permanent observer at U.N.O. and maintains social, economic and cultural relations among its members as well as an entity with others. It casts co-operation and common action of its members.

The Arab League and Its Impact

Immediately after the Balfour Declaration of 1917 thousand of Jews poured into Palestine and established on a firm footing within a short time. The influence of the Jews served to arouse Arab nations which hitherto had scarcely existed. The Arab nations began to feel their way towards some sort of unity to prevent the development of a Jewish state in Palestine. Their nationalism received a further impetus during the Second World War of 1939-45 when a considerable portion of the Middle East came under temporary control of the allied Western powers, who utilised it as a barrier against Hitler's Nazi and the Fascist designs of Italy in the East. This state of things, though unavoidable, offended the pride and prestige of the Arabs. Hence as soon as foreign danger was over the Arab States drew together for purposes of unity, defence and security etc. In 1944 they held a meeting at Alexandria and decided to form some kind of association for mutual co-operation. This decision materialised in the establishment of the Arab League at Cairo in March, 1945 it was composed of seven independent Arab States, namely, Egypt, Saudi Arabia, Iraq. Trans-Jordan, Yemen, Syria, and Lebanon though lot of Christians live in Lebanon. It was to have a council, a permanent secretariat and a Secretary-General. Bit-by-bit this Arab League set to work to bring about agreements for pacific settlement of disputes between the League members, for collective defence and security and general co-operation in economic and cultural and social affairs of Arab states.

The Arab League, however, is a loose organization and is too divided by political and personal rivalries to be a positive force for war or peace and stability in the Middle East. Before long Egypt and Iraq became rival for its leadership. The real bond which holds the Arab League together is the common enmity of its members to the new State of Israel aim to wipe

Israel out of existence. It has, however, some achievements to its credits. It made its influence felt in finding the solution of the Anglo-Egyptian dispute of 1954. In the settlement of Anglo-Yemeni conflict it also took a very active part. As such Britain had to abandon her proposal for the federation of the different Sheikdoms and the Protectorates of Arabian Peninsula. It, however, failed to prevent the establishment of the state of Israel which was its most cherished object. Outside the Middle East the political activity of the Arab League was directed towards putting pressure upon France to liberate her North African colonies *i.e.* (Algeria and Tunis etc.) and bringing this question unitedly before the U.N. Council. Arab League expelled Egypt when compromise with Israel was concluded but made it member of League again in 1988. This Arab League is trying to support P.L.O. in getting land from Israel winning over world opinion to PLO's came due to its influence on account of oil and money, but now autonomous state of Palestine has been established. This is a great achievement of Arab League.

Contemporary Middle East

Middle East countries are very important due to oil resources and strategic situation. Middle East is ancient land but after World War II, the world at large became greatly concerned with the Middle East. The advent of the state of Israel and the enormous flow of oil focused attention upon this ancient area and emphasised its importance in matters of politics, transportation, communication, religion, culture, markets, military strategy, imperialism and nationalism, etc. ships flying the flags of more than fifty different nations used to pass through the Suez Canal every year. As such no important nation or people could ignore the problems of the Middle East and its conflicts.

Middle East is ancient land and cradle of an old civilization but from the departure of Napoleon from Egypt in 1799, until the autumn of 1956 the British enjoyed the dominant imperial role in the Middle East. Throughout the nineteenth centuries Russia, France, Austria, Italy and German etc. and now of U.S.A. and interests in the Middle East and from time to time possessed temporary or limited hegemony in all or various parts of this area. But Great Britain held sway more consistently and her ambassadors, merchants and navy exerted a profound influence wherever they went. Power of Turkey declined after World War I and Britain after World War II. In developments of Middle

East, British and French made their influence felt. These powers left their impact over Middle Eastern countries. Developments of nationalism and of Parliamentary Government, modern legal system and administration and scientific advancement are gifts of British and French rule.

British involvements in the Middle East were various and comprehensive. Paramount solitude however revolved around the fact that the Middle East lay astride the route to Eastern British Empire India which Britishers regarded as the jewel in the crown of the British Empire. This route must be protected and kept open, at also at any cost. After the constitution of the Suez Canal this interest became stronger than ever.

Thus, imperialist powers such as Britain, Russia and France tried to dominate Middle East taking advantage of disappearance of Turkish, and Safavic Empire of Iran and Mughal Empire of India. But now influence of U.S.A. is dominating Middle East.

The British-Russians and French used every device to maintain their imperial position in the Middle East. Officials and colonial agents both in London, Moscow and Paris and the Middle East regarded the inhabitants "native" in the kipling sense and believed that the best way was to preserve peaceful and proper relations and co-operate with the native rulers but Russia followed policy of annexation. Support was given to strengthen them with their people. Wherever possible, a constitution with a house of representatives and a house of notable was introduced. Such a government created the image of the British and French governments and expected to function in friendly and peaceful atmosphere within the British family of nations. But Russia followed policy of annexation like Changez Khan and Taimur came and incorporated empire of both the conquerors, but with the disintegration of U.S.S.R., Russia has lost empires and now influence of U.S.A. is very great.

In any case the British and French by economic, financial, military and ideological means fully intended to retain their control in the Middle East. However Germany also desired to obtain control in Middle East and the World War weakened and Britain and France losses in World War II found the retention of the Middle East beyond their means in the face of rising nationalist feeling and grouping, economic strength and determination among Turks, Arabs Israelis and Iranians etc. Only Russian Empire survived due to its victory in World War II. Withdrawal of the British and French led to a realignment of the power and position of foreign states and internal faction created fragmentation and anarchy. Readjustment of these forces gave rise to uncertainty and feelings of insecurity in Middle East evidences of which were particularly notable in the countries in surrounding the issues of Jews and of the Suez Canal etc. and the various pacts and unions and federations among the Arab states.

The French Aims and Influence in Middle East

French interests in the Middle East go back as far as the crusades. French merchants prospered in the Levant in early modern times and Bourbon monarchs of France frequently sent their most skillful ambassador to the ports. In the nineteenth and early twentieth centuries French ambitions for Middle Eastern empire were avidly pursued by Napoleon III and later on republican foreign ministers, of Democratic France but without much success. Russia got success and so her empire was greatest in the world *i.e.,* more than twice of U.S.A. and China and seven times of modern India, but now it has disintegrated, so its influence has lessened.

Never able to match the power of England and plagued by miserable governments in Paris, French empire-builders, except for their brief success in Syria and Lebanon between World Wars I and II, devoted their energies to spreading language, legal system and establishing French culture among the elite of the local peoples. Cabinets and governments might come and go in the Middle East, as they did in France; but if the people were immuned with French culture and spirit and thus wedded to French civilization, a lasting sympathy for France may be generated. Such an understanding may be translated into trade, concessions, successful diplomacy, and also as allies in international conflict and wars. There were probably the true sinews of empire in Middle East. However, the utter defeat of France in World War II and the weakness of her economy and military, dispelled most of the prestige held by France in the Middle East. Admiration for French culture, manufacturers and French ways largely vanished in the post-war period, even though the French language and legal system remained popular as a means of communication in cultured circles a fact which over a longer period of time might probably substantiate the French claim to the permanence of their civilization in the Middle East though with the emergence of fanatic states like Iran, Saudi Arabia and Israel etc., it is doubtful. Now French influence is negligible. It has been replaced by influence of U.S.A.

U.S.A. Interests in Middle East

American merchants and missionaries since early in the nineteenth century were very actively engaged in the Middle East as in Far East. The United States government, however, evinced little direct concern in their affairs due to dominance of British and French Governments, so it hardly raised a finger over the Middle East until at the Paris Peace Conference President Wilson had a feeling for effecting an American settlement for this area. Since the American people in general were indifferent towards the Middle East, only a division of Mosul oil aroused Americans to any form of imperialism in that region at the end of World War I. Some oil companies of U.S.A. began to take a keen interest in oil producing countries of Middle East but Government of U.S.A. had to remain silent spectator as League mandate was conferred to Britain and France over Iraq, Palestine and on Syria and Lebanon and most Middle Eastern state were sympathetic to Britain and France.

In case of establishment of Jewish homeland, U.S.A. showed keen interest even between the two World Wars and succeeded in establishing Palestine.

American Interest in Middle East during and after World War. In the midst of World War II President Roosevelt of U.S.A. would have given to the British perhaps complete political and economic responsibility for the Middle East, not only in war time, but also in the post-war period, had not Secretary of state Cordell Hull would have objected to it. As the World War II came to an end American involvement, in Middle East affairs became more apparent and as British and French power wanted more obligatory. The American public was unprepared for its new duties, as was best indicated by President Truman's conduct and relations with the British regarding the immigration into Palestine and towards the peace of the mandate.

The American people and the American government grabbed imperial ambitions of Britain and France in the Middle East. American oil investments in this area are very extensive, so the United States exerted much pressure to maintain their interest. But the welfare and security of Israel had evoked greater concern in the United States of America than probably any other Middle Eastern Issue, although American political and financial devotion to Israel noticeably began to ebb in 1952 and suffered further decline after the United Nations vote of censure in 1955 and the aggression of Britain, France and Israel in Sinai against Egypt in 1956.

Americans in and out of government desire for exercising influence in the Middle East, through profession friendship with its people, and co-operation with its governments. The great majority of Americans believe that this goal can be attained by giving aid, by educating the people, improving their health, and by raising their standards of living. To this end grants-in-aid, point four programmes, scholarships, exchange professorships, and a variety of similar projects have been initiated by the American government. Now British and French influence in Middle East has been replaced by American influence. U.S.A. played major role in Iran and in bringing agreement between Israel and Egypt and American played notable part in Lebanon's conflicts and Iraqi-Iranian war Intervention of U.S.A. in Middle East has brought rivalry in Middle East and Middle East has become cockpit of world. U.N.O. is trying for peace with little success. Now governments of Iraq and Afghanistan are under U.S. control and Israel etc. are under its influence.

Soviet Union in Middle East and Its Impact on Contemporary Event

Soviet Russia's aim has been to secure the friendship and annexation and sympathy of Middle Eastern peoples for the way of life of the Soviet bloc people and to win the cooperation Russian domination over their governments. Attainment of these objectives has been sought by a clever mixture of pressure and inducement and even by sending mily as in Afghanistan and upon political figures to pursue Russian policies and by the steady exploitation of every incident and disturbance to keep society and governments in a constant ferment of unrest and uncertainty. Skillfully, Soviet envoys and agents have played upon the fears and aspirations, defeats and disappointments, and the emerging nationalism and on mutual differences of the Middle East in order to turn the people especially the leaders, away from the West and make them lean towards the Soviet bloc. Recently Russian occupied Afghanistan and even Soviet Union is fighting to preserve pro-Soviet Afghan government and U.S.A. opposed it, so war continued and Taliban came to power who were also defeated and new govt. is in power.

The Middle East has sometimes been referred to as "the course of the continents." Standing at the juncture of Asia, Africa, and Europe, the area links three continents by narrow land routes and by narrow waterways. The Turkish Straits, Suez Canal, the Red Sea, the Bab al-Mandeb, the Straits of Qrmuz, and the Persian Gulf etc. have through the ages served man in his communications, travels, and trade etc. Although air travel may seem to have lessened the importance of these old arteries of the world but the commotion aroused in foreign offices of world powers by the stoppage of the Suez Canal in 1956 amply illustrated tax that Middle Eastern waterways had not lost their age-old usefulness and value. Due to its strategic importance, oil and fragmentation and mutual rivalries, Middle East has become hunting ground for both super powers. As such both, U.S.A. and Soviet Union are keeping conflicts alive in Middle East but with the disintegration of U.S.S.R., Russian influence has subsided and influence of U.S.A. has increased.

Until the advent of mechanized means of transportation caravan routes across the deserts of the Middle East played a very important and vital part in the life of this area. Since World War II, fewer caravans have used the old trails, but new pipelines transporting oil across the barren wastes have brought added importance to the states of Middle East and peoples along these routes.

Importance of Middle East. Since the end of World War I the relationship of the Middle East to air routes between Europe, Asia, and South Africa has not been overlooked. By the middle of the 20th century, the great international airports had been developed at Istanbul, Beirut, Cairo, Khaitoum Jerusalem and Dhehran and Tehran etc. and almost every international airline had scheduled flights to or through the Middle East. Thus even in the twentieth century transportation of Middle East is in a position of commanding and rich as ever before.

The unprecedented expansion of the oil industry in the Middle East since the close of World War II has drawn the attention of every part of the world to the Middle East. In 1938, the Middle-East accounted for about 5.7 per cent of world oil production; in Saudi Arabia, Kuwait, Iraq and Iran, with a rapidly growing development in Qatar, the output for 1955, was about 20.9 per cent. Concentrated in Saudi Arabia, Kuwait, Iraq and Iran, with a rapidly growing development in Qatar the output for 1955 topped with more than 160,000,000 metric tons of crude petroleum and about 66,000,000 of which passed through the Suez Canal. The security and welfare of the West depends upon the flow of oil of Middle East. The great bulk is delivered to Western Europe, and without the power and heat derived from that oil the free countries of Europe would suffer incalculable losses. Recognition of the role played by Middle East oil in British and Western European countries life was contained in a speech of Prime Minister. Even in the House of Commons in March, 1956, when he said that the British were obliged to remain in Cyprus to protect the flow of oil to Treat Britain. As such when during Arab-Israel conflicts, oil producing countries threatened Western European countries with the stoppage of oil, these countries stopped support to Israel and began to support Arabs but U.S.A. supported Israel won war.

If in the past, oil production in the Middle East and the acceleration of its yields had a bearing upon Western economy, the oil reserves of the area are also staggering in their relationship to the future. Each year exploration has increased the estimates. In 1920 the potential reserves set at about 5.8 billion barrels; in 1945, at 18 million; in 1949, at about 32 billion in 1951, at 48 billion and in 1954, at more than 83 billion and new discoveries continue to be announced and in 1990 oil production has become double to 1954 production. In relation to the rest of the world the Middle East was estimated in 1949 to hold about forty-one per cent of total-world reserves. In 1954 it was about fifty-six percent; and in 1958 probably not less than sixty-five per cent. In the face of these facts no Western nation and its leader can afford to ignore the Middle East and its destiny.

To transport any appreciable tonnage of Middle East oil to the Soviet bloc requires the laying of an entirely new series of pipelines of the acquisition of a sizable fleet of tankers by the oil producing states concerned. Under normal circumstances neither of these would be feasible, and several years would be required for the accomplishment of either of these tasks. In any struggle, therefore between East and West the object of the former probably would be to deny the latter access to Middle East oil. The Soviet desire to frustrate ready and easy utilisation of the oil by the Western powers could be seen in the speeches by Russian Foreign Minister Shepilov on his visits to the Middle East in 1956.

Considering the important lines of communication through the Middle East, its graphic position at the juncture of three continents, its great oil production, and its almost unbelievable petroleum reserves, the military significance and strategic position of the Middle East becomes approaching immediately. Some strategists have likened Asia Minor to a huge anchored aircraft carrier invaluable in any military operation approaching central and eastern Europe from the south or attacking Arabia, Africa, and India from the north. Perhaps control of the north coast of Africa near East continues to be a strategic key to the Mediterranean sea and Southern Europe. One of the historic military roads to India passed through Iran and from time immemorial through Afghanistan so it is most important to Russia, America and China. Finally, there is the manpower of the Middle East. Properly trained, equipped, and officered, the Middle Eastern person would undoubtedly become a good soldier. The West usually regards the Middle East as an avenue leading to the Indian sub-continent and to East; the East regards it as a window opening out upon the West. Whichever way, it is arch military prize. Due to this Soviet Union is determined to keep pro-Soviet puppet Government in power and U.S.A. and China are opposing this.

The Middle East contains the holy places for the three great Western religions and one minor religion of Zoorists: Judaism, Christianity, and Islam etc. These religions have wide spread far and count their devotees in the millions all over the world. As such subjects of the great powers have deep and powerful emotions with regard to these holy places and to the Middle East as the birth place of their faiths. As such main cause of chaos in Lebanon is Christian Muslim conflict, of Arab-Israeli conflict is Jew-Muslim conflict and of Iran-Iraq war is Shia-Sunni conflict. In the Middle East itself religion has played a commanding role in political, economic and social aspects of life for many centuries from ancient times and in all probability it will continue to be important for a considerable time in the future as is shown by Iran-Iraq conflict and emergence of fanatic religious states. A vibrant nationalism, however, has held the center of the stage since World War I. Nationalism has grown aggressive, and has so seized the bodies of the adolescent states of the Middle East that even their leaders find it difficult in distinguishing between truth and error, fact and fancy, knowledge and poetry, achievement and wish. Nationalism in this form has often confused the real issues in question and has won hoisterious support for glib demagogues, of local leaders, diplomats and of foreign minister and of even President and Prime Ministers who promise more than they know can be delivered. In such a situation, the honest statesman is left at the starting gate. Aggressive Nationalist like Nasseer, Saddam Hussein and fanatics like Ayatollah Khomeni etc. dominate the political scene in Middle East. Power, position and prestige have been held in very high esteem in the Middle East for many ages. In the rivalry for the area each little coup, special favour, or small success or petty bureaucratic post is accompanied by much privileges, facilities and comforts etc. As such trumpeting, and "face saving" has been elevated to fine art. The means and manner of accomplishment assume and importance frequently above the end itself: and often obvious logical and beneficial course of action cannot be taken because rivals and opponents have already suggested or pursued these roads. In the land of prophets, scholars have lost their respect and respect goes to a person who grabs power by force or fraud, but this has encouraged terrorism and U.N.O. supported by U.S.A. is trying to control it.

From one end of the Middle East to the other end no word probably stands lower in the political and national vocabulary or is more hated than imperialism. Since World War I, the chief aim is to aggressive nationalism and it has been the desire of all nations to contain full and complete independence from the great imperialist powers. School books, literature newspapers, radio, political speeches, conversations T.V. and acts of every kind have constantly and continuously carried the important message. Foreign soldiers and officials economic servitude and colonialism must end. Foreign culture in national agreements of every political figure is closely scrutinized almost all over the world and even a vague allusion to some thing which might be considered submissive to outside domination or influence is abohorred but economic aid and loans and arms are welcomed.

Nevertheless the process of Westernization has marched relentlessly in the Middle East. The super powers now held the Middle East in their empires and control the governments and the economy of the Middle East. Consequently the progress of Westernization had to be denied or lamented by nationalists and politicians. Modernization was and is a more palatable term.

The exact nature of Westernization defies definition. At best it might be considered as the infiltration of scientific knowledge and its proper application into as many aspects of life as possible. As such it is difficult to assess Western influence over Islamic states who are fighting constantly on religious ground.

Machines and mechanization and destructive arms certainly will come to the Middle East in significant magnitude within a decade or two. But there is no certitude that the people will be Westernized. Leaders of some states may cast their lot and those of their people with the West as in Turkey and Israel. Some may decide that their interests lie with the Soviet bloc. Others may try to follow fanatic religious or a neutralist course. Whichever it may military administrator and colonial or official bureaucratic ruler, all testify that advances of civilization have made it virtually impossible to rule people against their own wishes. To maintain and operate the Suez Canal against the will of the people of Egypt and Afghanistan practically is out of the question now. To keep oil flowing through pipelines from Arabia to the Mediterranean sea in the face of determined Arab resistance could perhaps be hardly done. As such Shah of Iran and Russians failed to rule over Afghanistan due to lack of public support and fanatic Talibans gained power in Afghanistan, who were defeated and new Hamid Karzsi govt. is now ruling Afghanistan.

To win the Middle East therefore requires the winning of the Middle Eastern people. Like a rich girl the people of the Middle East do not want to be wooded for wealthy oil possessions or sickness or valuable real state but they wish to be courted for themselves. Their culture, skills and civilization must be understood and appreciated and their desires should be respected. The age of being "natives" has passed. Until 1980, the future Westernization of the Middle East could hardly be doubted. By 1968 the future of the Middle East had become less certain due to emergence of fanatic religious Shia state of Iran, determination of Arabs to destroy Israel and determination of P.L.O. to humble Israel and due to rivalry of U.S.A. and U.S.S.R. to impose their will over Afghanistan and Lebanon etc. consequently fanatics have gained popularity and power in Middle East. These fanatics are now committing acts of terrorism.

Suggestion for Middle East

At present super power rivalry of U.S.A. and U.S.S.R. in Middle East has created chaos, anarchy, constant disturbances and not only civil wars but wars between Middle Eastern countries and so Middle East has become pouder keg of the world. Middle Eastern state can be divided in four parts *i.e.*, states of ancient days which were cradle of civilization such as Egypt, Mesopotamia and Israel etc. The states which gained prominence due to emergence of Islam such as states of Arabian Peninsula and Turkey and Syria etc. and the states which came into existence due to bifurcation such as Lebanon which came into existence due to its separation from Syria, Jordan which was part of Palestine and Afghanistan, which was part of India, till 1739. But now states are to be grouped according to their outlook and status. As such states of Middle East can be grouped as states where modern outlook prevails such as Turkey. In second group are fanatic states such as Iran and Afghanistan and other religious fanatic states of Middle East, where religious fanatism prevails such as fanatic Muslim Shia state of Iran, Jew state of Israel and all the states of Arabian peninsula such as Saudi Arabia, Iraq, Egypt, Syria and Jordan etc. who are member of Arab League and Lebanon where Christian, Shia-Sunni conflicts are constant feature. Now even in Egypt, Turkey and Morocco etc. fanatic muslims are tying to gain power and have committed terrorist acts in Turkey and Saudi Arabia.

Historian deals with past and not with future so it is very difficult to say something about future. From time immemorial in Middle East, there were conflicts between Egyptians and Jews. It is said Moses freed Jews from Egyptian bondage. There were conflicts between Christians and Jews in Palestine. Later on conflicts of Shias and Sunnies dominated Islamic empire. Christian-Turk conflict gave rise to crusades. Later on Imperialist power curbed these conflicts but with the emergence of new independent national states some old conflicts on same lands and over same ideas have come to the fore and Middle East has become most troubled spot of the world in recent times in contemporary world.

With the emergence of Israel, Middle East has become arena of Arab-Israeli conflict. These Arab-Israeli conflicts involved not only Middle East but most of the leading powers of the world. Soviet union supported Arabs and U.S.A. supported Israel. Now due to efforts of U.S.A. matters between Egypt and Israel have been patched up and Egypt got back her lost territory but now PLO is demanding territory from tiny state of Israel and not from other Arab states the territory which was given to it by U.N.O. and has been grabbed by Jordan and other powers.

As such peace between Arab and Israel seems to be a mirage particularly because U.N.O. has failed to maintain peace or bring reconciliation. Simple solution is that Israel has right to exist and PLO has right for homeland over Palestinian land which has been grabbed by Arab powers. Now PLO has been given state so problem has been solved partially.

Long Iraq-Iran war has closed but dispute remains unsolved and recently Iran has warned that war may be resumed if Iran does not get back all her lands. Seeds of conflict lie in old Shia-Sunni dispute so it is difficult to be wiped out if religious fanatism continues unabated. Similarly tiny state of Lebanon has become scene of constant wars due to antagonism between Christians and Muslims, Shias and Sunnies and Israel's resentment over Syrian military presence and over presence of Palestinian terrorists and Guerillas who carry raids and commit act of terrorism in Israeli territory. Thus end of anarchy in Lebanon is not in sight. Only solution may be incorporation of Sunni dominated area with Syria, Shia dominated area with Iran and separate autonomous state of Christians or a federation with three autonomous states having only common defence, currency, transport and foreign affairs with the Central Government.

Afghanistan has been part and parcel of India from time immemorial and even upto 1947, influence of British India over Afghanistan was paramount but now it has become an apple of discord between U.S.A. and U.S.S.R., China, Pakistan, Iran and Saudi Arabia etc. have also shown keen interest over Afghanistan. Soviet Union was determined to have pro-Soviet puppet Government while Pakistan and Saudi Arabia desire pro-Islamic Sunni Government and Iran desires pro-Islamic Shia Government. U.S.A. and Western powers desire pro-Western Government but probably solution of Afghanistan problem lies in giving Afghan people right to choose their own Government. Similarly Iraq deserves to be ruled by the govt. of their own choice.

Conclusion. In short Middle East is very strategic, resourceful and rich area of the world but it is most disturbed area of the world due to faction fighting and due to mutual wars between Middle Eastern countries and above all due to rivalries of Western and Communist powers. Efforts of U.N.O. have succeeded in ending Iran-Iraq conflict and in withdrawal of Russian forces from Afghanistan and it is hoped PLO has succeed in getting some territory for their homeland and conflict in Lebanon may be resolved. Let us hope for the best and so it is expected that day is not far off when conflict of Middle East will be resolved and peace and prosperity will prevail in Middle Eastern countries and Middle Eastern countries will be ruled by the governments of their own choice.

CONTEMPORARY MIDDLE EAST

Gulf Crises of 1990-91, Iraqi Problem and Its Solution by U.N.O.

Iraq is an ancient land situated on the banks of rivers Tigris and Empharates, so earlier it was called Mesopotamia *i.e.,* land of two rivers. Jews prophet Moses and Suleiman and Hammuraliv and Nebuchadazar ruled here. Later on its capital Baghdad became capital of Abbasid Caliphs and Caliph Harun-Al-Russhid of Arabian knights fame, ruled here. It remained under Turkish rule and under British mandate, but got freedom like India with the liquidation of British empires. Anglo-American block wanted to make it center of C.E.N.T.O. and of Baghdad Pact but Col. Kassim usurped power and gave a death-blow to all the pacts but he met a tragic end and later on Saddam Hussein after many feeble presidents became its President.

Rise of Iraq under Saddam Hussein. Iraq, whose population is only 2 crores and 35 lakhs and area is 434913 sq. kms., containing 77% Arab and 19% Kurdish population and 55% Shia and 42% Sunni Muslim population and 3% Kurdis came in prominence during the rule of Saddam Hussian.

Life. Iraqi President Saddam Hussein passed his early days in misery as he lost his father in infancy. He tried for coup but failed and had to pass his days in exile in Egypt. He again tried for a coup but was captured and imprisoned but he escaped and took leading part in political activities and became President and later on President and virtually ruler of Iraq.

Iraq-Iran War. In Iran due to Shia Muslim revolution, Ayatollah Khomeni came in power and he was unable to see Saddam Hussein, a Sunni as ruler of majority Shia state of Iraq and on the other hand Saddam Hussein, also did not like powerful Shia state under orthodox fanatic Shia leader Ayattollah Khomeni as it may prove dangerous to Arab states. Another reason was, water dispute and territorial dispute between Iraq and Iran. Thus both came in conflict.

Iraq-Iranian War. The minor skirmishes between Iraqi-Iranian forces on border took shape of war on 22th September, 1980. This Iraqi-Iranian war, continued for 8 years. In this war, Iraq was financially helped by Kuwait and all Arab countries who feared Shia domination over Arabs if Iran won. U.S.S.R. also helped Iraq. Later on U.S.A., Britain, France and Germany also helped Iraq and supplied best equipments. Due to superiority of arms and chemical weapons, Iraq got an upper hand over Iran, so Iran had to eat a humble pie and had to accept cease-fire in July, 1988, due to mediation of U.N.O.

After humiliation of defeat, Ayatollah Khomeni of Iran died on 4th June, 1989, and Saddam Hussein became undisputed and powerful ruler of Middle East.

Attack over Kuwait. Flushed with victory, Mr. Saddam Hussein, attacked over Kuwait on 2nd August, 1990, and annexed it on 8th August, 1990 declaring it as province and integral part of Iraq. Conquest of a weak and small country of Kuwait by a powerful Arab country of Iraq brought U.N.O. to fore and a new chapter in world history due to Iraqi-occupation of Kuwait began.

The Gulf Crises and the Iraqi Occupation of Kuwait and Its Consequences

Gulf crisis was created when Iraqi President Saddam Hussein attacked a fellow Arab tiny country of Kuwait on August 2, 1990 and annexed it on August 8, 1990. It is ironic that Iraq that had become an Arab military shield against Shia Iran over the years, turned against a fellow Arab country, Kuwait, whose area is only 20150 kms and population is only 21 lakhs or nearly two millions. Iraq annexed Kuwait and declared it as 19th province of Iraq, but U.N.O. opposed this annexation.

Causes of Friction. The crisis began when Iraq accused Kuwait of sabotaging its economy by over-producing oil and thus depressing prices and reducing Iraqi's earnings. Iraq also desired cancellation of 10 billion dollar, interest-free loan, which Kuwait had given to Iraq. Iraq also demanded Rumalia oil fields and strategic Buluyan Island to improve Iraq's access to the Gulf. Main cause was that Iraq desired to annex Kuwait because it was a weak country but possessed 20% of the world known oil resources. Iraqians claimed Kuwait historically as a part of their ancient empire but U.N.O. refused to accept that plea.

U.N.O.'s Action. Conquest of a weak country by an armed and powerful country was against U.N.O. objectives. It was direct defiance of U.N.O. by Iraq. As such U.N.O. Security Council on August 9, 1990, declared Iraq's annexation of Kuwait unanimously null and void but Iraq cared a fig for it and Gulf crisis began.

The Relations of Iraq and U.N.O. over Kuwait

Iraq's occupation of Kuwait was direct defiance of U.N.O., so U.N.O. Security Council on August 9, 1990, unanimously declared annexation of Kuwait 'null and void' but Iraq refused U.N.O.'s mandate, but U.S.A. sent forces to defend Saudi Arabia. As such on August 25, 1990 U.N.O. called for use of the necessary naval forces to ensure compliance with mandatory economic sanctions imposed on Iraq for its invasion of Kuwait. It is probably first time that the Security Council has authorised military action to enforce its own sanctions. The U.S. sponsored resolution was adopted by Security Council by 13-0 with Yemen and Cuba abstaining. The resolution called on foreign navals in the Gulf "to use such measures commensurate to the specific circumstances as may be necessary", to stop ships, inspect their cargo as and determine their destinations to ensure compliance with U.N. trade embargo against Iraq. The embargo was meant to force Iraq to leave Kuwait. Only India was permitted to send medicine and grain on humanitarian basis but its ships 'Tippu' and 'Vishwajit' etc. were searched by U.S.A., Dutch and British navies but India was allowed to evacuate about 1.5 lakh persons from Kuwait.

Iraq and U.N.O. U.N. Security Council of 15 members passed 12 resolutions on Gulf crisis on between Iraq's invasion of Kuwait on August 2, 1990 to January 16, 1991, the date of expiry of withdrawal.

First resolution which came only hours after the invasion, demanded Iraqis withdrawal from Kuwait.

Four days later stringent economic sanctions was imposed. To enforce these, the Security Council on August 25, 1990, empowered states to set up a naval blockade in the Gulf and imposed an air embargo.

Lastly on November 29, 1990, the Security Council in resolution No. 678 authorised states "to use all necessary means" against Iraq unless it withdrew from Kuwait on or before 15th January 1991. Then vote was 12 to 2 as Cuba and Yemen opposed it and China abstained.

Efforts were made by all peace loving countries and by U.N.O. Secretary General, Parez-de-Cullear, himself, but all efforts of peace failed on sharp rocks of reality as Mr. Saddam Hussein refused to evacuate Kuwait. He not only defied U.N.O. but imposed many conditions which were not connected with this Gulf crisis, so there was no alternative except war. Due to occupation of Kuwait U.S.A. lead multinational forces declared was against Iraq and blame for Gulf crisis lies on Saddam Hussein because there was no alternative before U.N.O. except allowing use of force against Iraq for evacuation of Kuwait as Saddam Hussein did not care for U.N.O.

Saddam Hussein and U.S.A. and Use of Force Against Iraq for Evacuation of Kuwait

League of Nations and U.N.O.'s main purpose and objective is to maintain world peace and to achieve this, only way is to safeguard weak nation against a powerful nation. League of Nations showed weakness and allowed Japan to grab Manchuria, Italy to grab Ethiopia or Abvssinia and to Germany, Austria and Czechoslovakia, so League of Nations failed.

U.N.O. was unable to take action due to cold war between U.S.A. and U.S.S.R. but situation changed when U.S.A. and U.S.S.R. minimised their differences and U.N.O became powerful.

Defiance of U.N.O. Defiance of U.N.O. became common feature of newly emerged powerful nations. Arab powers constantly attacked Israel and tried to wipe out this tiny state created by U.N.O but aggressors did not succeed because Israel proved a hard nut to crack but Vietnam successfully defied U.N.O. and Vietnam's forces occupied Cambodia, Cuba intervened in many African states but these interventions and defiance got set back when Russian forces were forced to leave Afghanistan. Now U.S.A. and U.S.S.R. came near and so U.N.O. got strengthened but Iran defying all norms of diplomacy and tradition caught U.S.A. Embassay's people and left them after great compensation and tried to curb freedom of speech by threatening British citizen Suleman Rushidie.

In spite of all efforts of U.N.O., Iraqi-Iranian war continued for 8 years and U.N.O. was able to achieve success when both combatants became tired.

Kuwait Episode. Mr. Saddam Hussein, President of Iraq in direct defiance of U.N.O., conquered Kuwait by force, and contemptuously disregarded all peace efforts and cared a fig for world opinion and U.N.O. resolutions. In defiance of U.N.O. probably Mr. Saddam Hussein exceeded with Mussolini's defiance of League of Nations and probably even more than Hitler. Under these circumstances, there were only two alternatives before U.N.O. *i.e.*, show weakness like League of Nations, who showed weakness before Mussolini and Hitler and meet its doom or to show courage and face aggressor. U.N.O.'s Security Council unanimously choose to face aggressor and not to bow down to aggressor.

All the peace efforts failed as Mr. Saddam Hussein was determined to defy and fight with U.N.O. As such for the very existence of U.N.O., it became necessary for U.N.O. to face challenge of Mr. Saddam Hussein. Previous robbery by any robber did not confer right to another robber to commit robbery with defiance, so no argument of Mr. Saddam Hussein can be sustained against U.N.O. As such for the preservation of world-peace, there was no alternative before U.N.O. except to authorise states "to use all necessary means" against the aggressor to deprive him from fruits of spoliation.

The War between Iraq and Multinational Forces led by U.S.A.

Due to obstinacy of President Saddam Hussein, all peace efforts failed and ultimatum's deadline of 15th January, 1991, passed. Under these circumstances multinational forces of 28 countries, lead by U.S.A., came in conflict with Iraqian forces and war began. It continued with all ferocity from both sides. Iraq attacked civilian and non-combatant Israeli people with scud missiles and committed all kinds of cruelties on foreign citizens and prisoners of war. Mr. Saddam Hussein's forces made scud missile attacks on Saudi Arabia but these were mostly destroyed by patriot missiles of U.S.A. and were unable to create harms or horror but air force of multinational forces bombarded Iraq successfully and were able to break concrete bunker. Now Iraq demanded cease-fire and imposed many undesirable conditions for its withdrawal from Kuwait. These conditions for withdrawal were rejected by U.S.A. and Britain and Saudi Arabia and other Arab countries but India and Russia made efforts to bring peace in the Middle East, but war took place in which Iraq was defeated and forced to quit Kuwait.

The Effect of Gulf Crisis of 1990-91 on Middle East, U.N.O. and World.

By meeting the challenge of aggressor, U.N.O. has strengthened itself. Now aggressors have realised that to break world-peace and defiance of U.N.O. is not an easy task. Five permanent members of U.N.O., *i.e.,* U.S.A., U.S.S.R., Britain, France and China showed unusual unanimity in preserving world peace and honour of U.N.O., so U.N.O. has now become an effective, competent and powerful world body.

Effect on Middle East. Now middle East which has become cockpit of the world, may get some respite from constant wars and it is hoped in near future Middle East may get peace and prosperity and stability and respite from wars.

Effect over World. With Gulf crisis and successful action of U.N.O., small nations have got confidence that if these weak and small nations are attacked by a powerful nation, U.N.O. will come to their rescue. In this way U.N.O. has gained confidence of peace loving citizens of the world and hope for preservation of world peace through U.N.O. has increased.

With the preservation of peace and order in war torn Middle East, a new era of Peace and prosperity may emerge in Middle East in particular and world in general. With peace, new horizon for progress of mankind may come.

Afghanistan, Israel and Iraq are the countries which are facing uneasy peace. In Afghanistan fanatic Taliban govt. has been overthrown and it is expected that new govt. may bring peace, progress and prosperity to this country.

With the establishment of autonomous state of Palestine and peace treaties between Israel, Egypt and Jordan, major war may be avoided though local conflicts may continue.

According to U.S.A., Iraq under Saddam Hussein is preparing destructive weapons so action should be taken against Iraq and rule of Saddam Hussein may be ended but this proposal has not found favour in U.N.O. As such it was expected that conciliation may take place and major war may be avoided. Greatest menance to Middle East and whole world is terrorism but it is expected that it may also be controlled with the co-operation of major world powers and peace loving countries and peace, progress and prosperity may prevail all over the world as rule of Taliban has ended in Afghanistan and of Saddam Hussein in Iraq, so there is hope for peace.

Recent Events and Suggestions for Middle East

With the disintegration of U.S.S.R., super power rivalry in Middle East has lessened. Now fanatic terrorists claiming themselves followers of orthodox Islam are creating terror all over the world.

Super power rivalry as well as rivalry among Middle East countries have lessened. Israel gave back conquered territories to Egypt and established Palestinian state with autonomous powers to manage local affairs to pacify P.L.O. and Muslim Arab countries therefore conflict between Jew state of Israel and Arab countries may become lesser. With peace treaties between Egypt, Jordan and Israel, this conflict may be localized and in future conflict between Israel and Palestine may continue without active participation of other powers and countries. Thus Israel and Arab states may not enter in major war though local terrorist attacks may continue. In Afghanistan fanatic orthodox govt. who gave shelter and support to terrorists and its leader Osama Bin Laden has been overthrown, but Mullah Omar and Osma Bin Laden have escaped, it means nothing because persons without power lose Calibre and capacity to bring major war. As such it is expected that after the eclipse of Taliban govt. in Afghanistan, the new govt. may bring peace and prosperity to this war torn country. Iraq under Saddam Hussein according to U.S.A. was preparing deadly weapons so America and Britain attacked Iraq and ended the rule of Sadam Hussein and it is hoped that U.N.O. will make efforts to maintain peace by establishing governments of their own choice.

Greatest new danger, not only confined to Middle East but to the whole world, is the emergence of fanatic terrorism all over the world. Terrorism is a great menace to world peace, so to curb it, co-operation of major world powers is necessary which is lacking. But it is expected that the terrorism may be controlled and curbed soon and peace and prosperity may prevail in 21st century, not only in Middle East but in whole world because peace is indivisible. Let us hope for peace, progress and for happiness and prosperity all over the world.

32

CONTEMPORARY MIDDLE EAST

Israel is a land, where Moses and Christ preached and David and Solomon ruled in ancient age. This land of jews after seeing the Roman, Arab and Turkish rule again came into existence in 1948 because of the intervention of U.N.O. Palestinian Arabs backed by the Arab Muslim powers opposed its existence but Israel's tiny forces defeated the huge Arab-countries forces in 1948, 1967 and in 1973 and exiled the Palestinian Arabs and occupied large part of territory of Arab states.

U.N.O. and U.S.A. intervened and Israel had to give back all territories of Arab states but Palestinian Arabs remained in exile. They formed their Palestinian Arab Organization and committed to terrorism. At last in 1993, they were given territory by Israel to establish their own autonomous state with limited powers to live and maintain peace and order and to conduct their own affairs. Palestinian Arabs were given 5879 sq. kms. for population of about 16 lakhs and 363 sq. kms. of Gaza strip where now population is almost one million. Palestinian Arabs established their own government under Aseer Arafat with a council of 82 members and 15 thousand police to maintain peace, law and order. But in spite of promise of peace, Palestinian Arabs are constantly committing terrible terrorists attacks and to check their attacks, forces of Israel had to attack in retaliation. In this way the muslim Arabs conflict is still prevalent and neither the U.N.O. nor U.S.A. has been able to check it. Due to Palestinian terrorists attacks, according to two Israeli tourists, nowadays neither their lives nor property nor honour is safe. These terrorists attacks cannot be checked as Palestinian Arab terrorists are backed by the other terrorists. As such the jew-muslim Arab conflict is continuous and there is apprehension that it may prove a menace to the world peace as muslim Arab terrorists are backed by some other muslim Arab states and jews of Israel by jews residing in other countries. It can be curbed by a humanitarian outlook with a spirit of tolerance and ideal of live and let others live.

Afghanistan

Afghanistan was a part of India from time immemorial. It was made a separate state by Nadir Shah's General Ahmad Shah Abdali, whose dynasty established his monarchial rule. In 1973, the last King Zahir Shah was removed and in 1978, Marxist Govt. supported by Russia was established. Mujakdeen (holy-warriors) defeated the Russian forces and succeeded in establishing their own rule. Mujakdeen were defeated by Taliban, who established their own government under Mullah Omar. In Sept. 2002, muslim Arab terrorists made terrorists attacks in U.S.A. under Osama Bin Laden; U.S.A. and its allies retaliated, — defeated Taliban and established pro U.S.A. government under the President Hamid Karzai. This Karzai government of Afghanistan has proved to be stable and is straining every nerve to maintain peace, law and order in Afghanistan. But in spite of all efforts neither Mullah Omar nor Osama-bin Laden has been captured nor peace could be maintained as Taliban extremists are consistently committing terrorists acts killing ladies and children and old people. In this way chaos and anarchy is prevailing in Afghanistan though the government of Hamid Karzai and multi-national forces are trying to control terrorism and to bring peace and order. Now India is actively helping Karzai government along with other nations to bring peace and prosperity in Afghanistan. As such it may be hoped that Afghanistan would regain peace, prosperity and stability soon.

Iraq

Iraq under Saddam Hussein became very powerful and was able to defeat Iran in Nine Year's war. Iraq overran Kuwait in August 1990. A U.S. led coalition beat Iraq in February 1991. In this war, there were 85,000 casualties. Kuwait was freed from Iraq's yoke but Saddam Hussein was allowed to rule over Iraq.

U.S.A. suspected that after the defeat Saddam Hussein is stockpiling chemical weapons and biological and nuclear weapons of mass destruction. After the attack on U.S. World Trade Center in September 2001, Osama Bin Laden is held to be supported by Saddam Hussein and is hiding in Iraq although Osama Bin Laden has hidden himself in Afghanistan and is untraceable.

Some diplomatists believe that U.S.A. desired friendly regime in Iraq to utilize its oil resource. The reports of secret agencies of U.S.A. and of Britain created exaggerated picture of Iraq's power and preparation of destructive weapons by Saddam Hussein and predicted danger from Iraq's growing power. Thus, the second Gulf War of 2003 was not to defend enemy that attacked America or its interests but to pre-empt that remote possibility that one day it might do so. As such the U.N.O. and world opinion did not approve this war but U.S.A. with the support of Britain and other allies invaded Iran without the approval of U.N.O.

This war against Iraq for American President Bush was part of the global campaign against terrorism after the 11 multiple terrorist attacks in New York and Washington. War against terrorism began with the invasion on Afghanistan as it was suspected that the terrorist leader Osama Bin Laden got support of Mullah Omar. So Afghanistan was invaded and pro U.S. Govt. was established at Kabul. For U.S. hawks, continuous defiance of Iraq of U.N. resolutions was good enough reason for the U.S. to invade Iraq and to oust Saddam Hussein from power. U.S. Secretary of State, Colin Powel strained every nerve to gain support and approval of U.N.O. to invade Iraq, but failed to gain support of U.N.O. Though U.S.A. failed to get support or approval of U.N.O. to launch war against Iraq but succeeded in getting support of Britain and connivance of 30 nations including Italy, Poland, Spain, Portugal and Australia.

The war was launched without U.N. sanction, and was code named "Co-operation Iraq Freedom." It was launched on March 20, 2003 with active support of British forces and additional support of Italy, Spain, Poland and other powers. Forces of Saddam Hussein were defeated. On May 1, 2003 Bush declared the end of war as the forces of U.S.A. and its allies had conquered major part of Iraq.

Thus U.S.A. won wars of Afghanistan in 2002 and of Iraq in 2003 and succeeded in establishing a pro U.S. Govt. at Kabul and Baghdad. It is said U.S. and its allies have won the war but have lost the peace in Iraq as well as in Afghanistan. The major question is whether these wars have succeeded in rooting out terrorism. The answer is negative. Terroris acts have increased all over the world in general and in Afghanistan, Iraq and in Israel in particular.

Terrorists are committing acts of terrorism in Iraq. On September 14, 2004, insurgents blowed up an oil junction. Saboteurs blew up a junction where multiple pipelines cross the Tigris river and left the entire country without power. A bomb blast by terrorists in Baghdad killed 47 people and wounded 114 persons which included mostly ladies and children. As such there is no peace in Iraq. In retaliation U.S. forces are bombing cities and are committing cruel acts. U.N.O. Secretary General, Kofi Annan has declared U.S. and its allies' invasion of Iraq as illegal, as it has been launched without the approval of U.N.O. To quote Kofi Annan:

"Those who seek to bestow legitimacy must themselves embody it and those who invoke international law must themselves submit to it." He further said, in Iraq we see civilians massacred in cold blood and prisoners disgracefully abused. President Bush defended his decision to invade Iraq in his speech in U.N.O. and urged the world community to turn its attention to the fighting of war on terrorism and humanitarian concerns. He further said that the overthrow of Saddam has freed the Iraqi people from an obstinate dictator.

Now in Iraq, an interim government has been established with a promise to hold fair and impartial elections. Saddam Hussein has been captured and is in jail asking for mercy but neither terrorism has has been eradicated nor debate on Iraq has ended because the world opinion is divided. India and many other countries have refused to send troops in Iraq to maintain peace.

Tony Blair, the Labour Prime Minister of Britain, has said that the participation in Iraq war was a wrong decision but ousting of Saddam Hussein from power is a right decision. In U.S.A. Presidential debate the democratic candidate Kery has condemned attack on Iraq but Bush has defended it saying that it was right to act pre-emptively in order to subdue the potential threat to United States. Thus, attack of U.S.A., Britain and its allies is a controversial question because the world opinion is divided on its necessity and validity. Thus, in spite of establishment of interim government in Iraq with a promise of impartial and fair elections, peace has not been established in Iraq and its future remains shrouded in mystery as terrorists attacks and retaliation is breaking its peace but it is hoped that in future peace and prosperity may prevail as most of the nations are willing to help Iraq for its uplift.

Iran

Iran is a country of Islamic Shia religion. Although the Nine years war between Iraq and Iran had shattered its economy yet it has been able to regain its prosperity and power within a few years. Now it is powerful country and it is alleged that it is making nuclear weapons with the help of other countries. As such U.S.A., Israel and some countries are considering it as a potential threat to peace but it is hoped that peace may prevail with the help of U.N.O. as the world opinion is in favour of maintaining peace.

Appendix

THE RISE AND FALL OF SADDAM HUSSEIN

28	April	1937	—	Born in Al-Awja village outside Tikrit.
	October	1956	—	Joined an uprising against the royalist rulers and then became a militant of Baath Party.
	October	1958	—	Spent six months in Jail for slaying communist brother-in-law.
	October	1959	—	Took part in an attempt to kill Prime Minister Abdul Karim Kasim. Fled abroad.
	February	1963	—	Returned to Baghdad when the Baath Party seized power in a military coup, but nine months later Baathists were toppled. Caught and jailed.
	July	1968	—	Helped plot the coup that put the Baath back in power, deposing President Abdul-Rahman Aref.
	July	1972	—	Visited Moscow, marking the beginning of 15-year co-operation, specially in Arms trade, between Soviet Union and Iraq.
16	July	1979	—	Took power after President Ahmed Hassan al-Bakr stepped aside.
22	September	1980	—	Launched war on Iran that lasted for eight years, *i.e.* upto 1988 in which he won.

2	August	1990	—	Invaded against Kuwait, prompting UN to impose sanctions on Iraq.
17	January	1991	—	US-led forces began Gulf War with air attacks on Iraq and occupied Kuwait.
28	February	1991	—	Hostilities ended with eviction of Iraqi forces from Kuwait.
2	February	2003	—	In his first interview after more than a decade, Saddam denied that Baghdad has banned weapons or any links to Al-Qaida.
17	March	2003	—	US President Bush asked Saddam to leave Iraq within 48 hours or be ousted by military forces.
18	March	2003	—	Saddam defied Bush's ultimatum.
20	March	2003	—	US launched war against Iraq with strikes on Baghdad targeting "very senior" leadership.
22	July	2003	—	US military confirmed that Saddam's two sons, Uday and Qusay, were killed in gun battle in Mosul.
14	December	2003	—	Captured in Tikrit by American forces. He was found in a "spider hole".